D1452460

Standing into Danger

Also by Cassie Brown

DEATH ON THE ICE
A WINTER'S TALE

Standing into Danger

A dramatic story of shipwreck and rescue

By Cassie Brown

DOUBLEDAY & COMPANY, INC.
GARDEN CITY, NEW YORK

DOUBLEDAY CANADA LIMITED
TORONTO, CANADA

1979

ISBN: 0-385-13681-1
Library of Congress Catalog Card Number 78–1236
Copyright © 1979 by Cassie Brown
All Rights Reserved
Printed in the United States
First Edition

Diagrams and line drawings conceived by Cassie Brown
Artwork executed by Robert Burgess Garbutt

To the men of the USS *Pollux* and the USS *Truxtun* who were all heroes, and to the people of St. Lawrence and Lawn, Newfoundland, for the honor and glory they brought to our people.

CONTENTS

FOREWORD

This is the true story of one of the worst disasters in United States naval history. On February 18, 1942, two American destroyers, USS *Wilkes,* USS *Truxtun,* and the supply ship USS *Pollux* ran aground in a storm, less than a couple of miles apart, under sheer cliffs on a lonely stretch of land on the south coast of Newfoundland. The USS *Wilkes,* the flagship, was refloated within three hours, but the *Pollux* and the *Truxtun* were hard aground and were subsequently battered to pieces. Two hundred and three young American sailors died in the heroic struggle for survival. One hundred and eighty-five survived. In large part they owe their lives to eight men of Lawn and almost the entire community of St. Lawrence, Newfoundland, who worked desperately to effect the rescue.

A United States Naval Court of Inquiry was held at the Argentia Naval Base in Placentia Bay, Newfoundland, from February 20, 1942, to March 9, 1942, after which two courts-martial were conducted in Boston: from June 23 to July 3, 1942, and from July 13 to August 3, 1942.

The captain and the navigator of the USS *Truxtun* and all of the ship's records were lost in the disaster; therefore, navigation data of the *Truxtun* were not available to the inquiry. Also lost were the records of the USS *Pollux.*

The captain and the navigator of the USS *Pollux* survived, but they were named defendants, and became ineligible to testify. Only the USS *Wilkes* had complete information pertaining to the hours preceding the groundings. As the flagship, the *Wilkes* bore the brunt of the blame.

Because of the exigencies of wartime operational requirements and the necessity of returning personnel to wartime duties, the court of inquiry was abruptly terminated on the eighteenth day, although the president of the court had planned to call more witnesses.

Six officers were recommended for general court-martial. After five months only the division commander, Walter W. Webb, and the commanding officer of the *Wilkes,* John D. Kelsey, were court-martialed, and it was decided by higher authority (Admiral Ernest J. King) that "radical administrative action short of court-martial proceedings would permit the best over-all war effort." The court was directed to enter *nolle prosequi* in the cases of Commander Hugh W. Turney, (*Pollux*), Lieutenant Arthur J. Barrett, (*Wilkes*), Lieutenant William A. Smyth, (*Wilkes*), and Lieutenant (jg) William C. Grindley (*Pollux*). Therefore the suits against them were dropped.

The radical administrative action ruined the naval career of Lieutenant Smyth and forced the resignation of Lieutenant Grindley from the U. S. Navy. Over the years both men tried unsuccessfully to clear their names. Their in-depth stories are told here for the first time.

My initial interest in this disaster was in the courageous actions of the American sailors as they fought desperately to save themselves and their shipmates from certain death, and in the exciting drama of the rescue efforts made by the people of Newfoundland. But, as letters and cassettes arrived from the *Pollux* survivors, it became apparent that the full story of the disaster had not emerged from the court of inquiry or the courts-martial.

In a taped conversation with Henry Strauss I was told, "The true story is a wild one."

Said Alfred Dupuy: "It was rumored that Lieutenant Grindley, that night, pleaded with Captain Turney to change course; that the course was wrong that the SOPA [Senior Officer Present Afloat] set." In Arthur Appel's story there is also mention of the navigator wanting to change course. Thomas Turner spoke of dissension between the *Pollux* and the *Wilkes:* "Our navigation department was trying to convince them that there was trouble brewing, and they wanted a definite change of course to the right, until daybreak, but the division commander would not agree to this."

Within the confines of a formal court of inquiry, the facts emerge
from specific answers given to specific questions; but more often
than not, the human factors attendant on such a tragedy are never
revealed. Grindley, as a defendant, was silenced. The *nolle prosequi*
wrote *finis* to his hopes of clearing his name in a court-martial.

Basically, this is a book of contradictions; of facts not brought to
light during the court of inquiry or the courts-martial, all cut short
by the pressing demands of war. The story is told through the eyes
and memories of the survivors as well as through the court records.
Dialogue has been reproduced from those records, and from the
recorded and written recollections of the people I interviewed. Signalman Parkerson's story is told by the Newfoundland men involved
in the rescue of the *Truxtun* personnel.

My research began in September 1974, with time-consuming
efforts to trace survivors of the shipwrecks. My thanks go to the
women of St. Lawrence who have kept in touch with the men they
took into their homes that grim day. From these survivors, who re-
side from the East Coast to the West Coast of the United States,
came other names and addresses. Ultimately, twenty-six of them
gave me their stories through letters, cassettes, and personal interviews.

I wish to express my deepest appreciation to the following men:
From the USS *Truxtun:* Ensign James O. Seamans, Ensign William
J. Maddocks, Boatswain's Mate First Class Harry M. Egner,
and Seaman First Class R. Jim Brown. From the USS *Pollux*: Lieu-
tenant Commander Samuel C. Bostic, Lieutenant (jg) William C.
Grindley, Lieutenant (jg) George C. Bradley, Lieutenant (jg)
Jack R. Garnaus, Ensign Alfred I. Pollack, Signalman Third Class
Warren A. Greenfield, Storekeeper Third Class Alfred M. Dupuy,
Fireman First Class Lawrence J. Calemmo, Storekeeper Second Class
Laurence A. Weaver, Jr., Boatswain's Mate Second Class George L.
Coleman, Quartermaster Third Class Isaac Henry Strauss, Machin-
ist's Mate First Class Walter C. Bulanowski, Fireman Second Class
James M. Ross, Quartermaster Third Class Thomas R. Turner, Sea-
man First Class Arthur W. Appel, Fireman Second Class Ernest L.
Califano, Boatswain's Mate Second Class Jack J. Janocha, Store-
keeper Third Class Samuel L. Nicosia, Seaman First Class Thomas
J. McCarron, Shipfitter First Class William L. Stanford, and Ap-

prentice Seaman Wayne Brewer. From the USS *Wilkes:* Commander John D. Kelsey and Lieutenant William A. Smyth. From the USS *Prairie,* flagship of the U. S. Naval base in Argentia: Lieutenant Charles R. Longenecker.

I also wish to thank the following people of Newfoundland who provided details of the rescue in taped interviews: Ena [Farrell] Edwards, Lillian Loder, Isabel Farrell, Clara Tarrant, Patrick Tarrant, Adam Mullins, Henry Lambert, Theo Etchegary, Gus Etchegary, Gregory Handrigan of St.. Lawrence; Joseph Manning of Lawn.

Thanks are also due Mrs. Harry Hummell of Schuylkill Haven, Pennsylvania, sister of Lieutenant George W. Bollinger; Captain Alex J. Provan, Captain Dennis Drown, and Captain Wilfred Blackmore of the College of Fisheries, Navigation, Marine Engineering, and Electronics, St. John's, Newfoundland; Mr. Joseph J. Peck, president, Veteran's Association, 1st Battalion, 3rd Division, New York, New York; the Department of the Navy, Office of the Advocate General, Naval Historical Center, Bureau of Naval Personnel, National Archives and Records Center, Washington, D.C.

Special grateful thanks go to my sister Vera McDonald.

CASSIE BROWN
St. John's, Newfoundland
November 1978

The storm raged over the clifftops of the bleak, uninhabited stretch of coast from Lawn Head to Chambers Cove, on the south coast of Newfoundland.

In the black winter night the wind, blending with the roar of the sea smashing on the rocks below, sang its threnody of perpetual mourning.

The brooding granite scarp rose abruptly from the depths of the Atlantic. Waves, ending their long journey of more than a thousand miles, expended their force in a tremendous rush up the face of the rocky height. Spray and a sleety rain knifing from the southeast crusted the face of the land. There was no haven for sailors here.

Presently, upon the tempestuous seas, three phantom shapes, with muffled beat, loomed out of the night, steaming straight into the snarling waters at the base of the cliffs.

A cry . . . "My God! Look ahead!"

Minutes apart, the three ships grounded beneath the sheer precipice and, in a spectacular fight for survival, 203 young American sailors would die.

PART ONE

Standing into Danger

1

The weather had steadily worsened, and the USS *Wilkes,* Flagship Destroyer Division 26, along with the USS *Pollux* and the USS *Truxtun,* was navigating by dead reckoning.[1] On course 047° true, toward Argentia, Placentia Bay, Newfoundland, from Portland, Maine, the *Wilkes* pitched and rolled so wickedly that many of the enlisted kids, just out of boot camp, clung gray-faced to whatever came to hand. Not that they were scared particularly, but after two days on the North Atlantic they still had not gotten their sea legs, and suffered acutely from seasickness. Buckets, strategically anchored in niches around the ship, were very much in use.

It had been too rough for a hot dinner, and those who could face the prospect of food without wanting to die had to make do with sandwiches. Those who tried to sleep had followed the example of the experienced crew members and tied themselves, fully clothed, to their bunks to keep from being flung to the deck. The crew always slept fully clothed in order to be ready for immediate action in the event of attack.

It was a rotten night, and the older hands had told the young ones that it was going to get worse before it got better—a fact they were miserably aware of as the ship hung on a wavetop, then fell into a trough with breathtaking suddenness, and the raw southeast wind howled around the superstructure, making strange sounds in the ventilators. There was no respite when the *Wilkes* had to depart from

[1] A method of estimating a ship's position without astronomical observation.

her base course for the zigzag the convoy had been ordered to make
from the time they had met off Casco Bay, Maine, two days earlier.
At the beginning of each watch, the three ships would leave the base
course and start the first leg of the zigzag, which carried the vessels
to the left for a mile and a half, executing three 40° changes every
ten minutes, which brought the ships back to the base course for five
minutes, then off to the right of the base course for another 40°
change for the same distance, and an 80° change each for ten minutes, and another five minutes on base course to complete the first
hour of zigzag Plan 26. The second hour of the zigzag was a repeat
in reverse, beginning on the right side of the base course and ending
on the left. To the left and to the right they steamed, and the frequent shifts added variety to the number of ways the ship could pitch
and roll. With glazed eyes the youthful sailors hung over the buckets.
The older men, remembering their own early days in the North Atlantic, bore the inconvenience with a surprising degree of sympathy
for the youngsters.

What a way to fight a war!

Europe had been embroiled in World War II since September
1939, and the United States had finally been officially drawn into it
by the Japanese attack on Pearl Harbor on December 7, 1941, less
than three months earlier.

America had not been totally unprepared. As an ally of Great
Britain, the States had taken fifty old four-stackers out of mothballs
and traded them to that desperate country for a ninety-nine-year
lend-lease on certain outposts in Canada and on the island of Newfoundland, a colony of Great Britain,[2] strategically situated on the
east coast of North America. On October 13, 1940, American engineers had arrived to survey Argentia; on January 18, 1941, con-
struction on the bases had begun; on January 25, the Marines had
arrived. They had lived under canvas for months, but by the time
Japan had bombed Pearl Harbor, three major American bases were
in full operation in Newfoundland.

In fact, long before Pearl Harbor, the *Wilkes* had been escorting
Allied ships up to the general area of Iceland, where she turned them
over to the British; later, she had taken convoys all the way across
the Atlantic, and enjoyed the honor of being the first American war-

---

[2] Newfoundland became the tenth province of Canada in 1949.

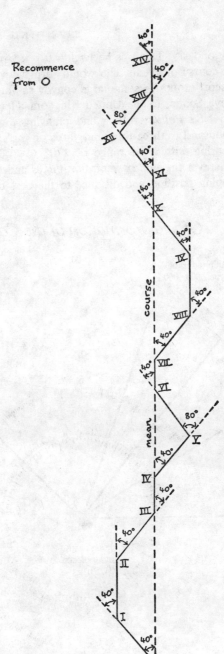

Recommence from O

Zigzag Plan 26

ship at Londonderry. This was her eighth trip to Argentia, where, in the normal course of events, she would form with other destroyers an ocean escort group for some large convoy sailing from Halifax or Sydney, Nova Scotia, to the United Kingdom. Her convoy was the supply ship USS *Pollux,* rolling and plunging through the stormy seas two thousand to three thousand yards on the *Wilkes'* port quarter at a bearing within the range of 270° to 300° true from the *Wilkes.* Wherever the *Pollux* went, the *Wilkes* and the *Truxtun* must follow, keeping position and distance to the best of their ability as

Official Formation of the Convoy

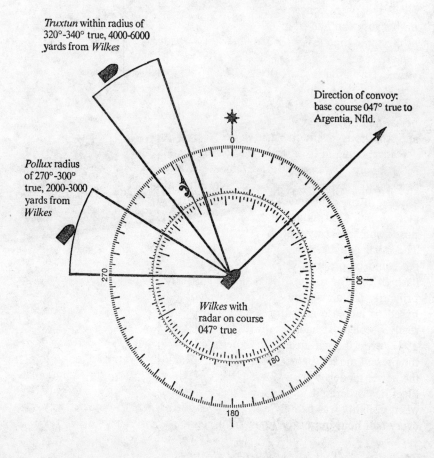

Truxtun within radius of
320°-340° true, 4000-6000
yards from *Wilkes*

Direction of convoy:
base course 047° true to
Argentia, Nfld.

Pollux radius
of 270°-300°
true, 2000-3000
yards from
Wilkes

Wilkes with
radar on course
047° true

specified by higher authority; therefore, strict adherence to the base course was imperative. The USS *Truxtun,* an ancient four-stacker destroyer, also did escort duty on the *Pollux.* The *Truxtun*'s position was on the port bow of the *Pollux,* roughly the same distance from her as was the *Wilkes* on her starboard bow; her bearing from the *Wilkes* was within a range of 320° to 340°.

Ordinarily the *Wilkes* and the *Truxtun* patrolled vigorously, alert for submarines, but because of low visibility, patrolling had been discontinued after dark. All ships were under darkened conditions and under the necessity of sending as few signals as possible.

The fact that they were escorting one only cargo ship did not give that ship any undue importance in the eyes of the *Wilkes*' officers. As far as they were concerned they were escorting the *Pollux* to Argentia because she had been the only other ship scheduled to sail there at the same time as the *Wilkes* and the *Truxtun.*

Neither ship had worked together on convoy duty before, and the journey over the stormy Atlantic had had its suspenseful moments. The *Pollux,* according to the *Wilkes*' radar, had a tendency to wander, and the *Wilkes*' crew were on tenterhooks as they kept track of her at night by radar. The *Wilkes,* the only ship with radar—a secret and wondrous invention—had to be the eyes for all three vessels.

Radar, being in its infancy, was still an unknown quantity to most sea captains. It remained pretty much of a secret and only the top officers, the communications officer, and a few chosen ordinary seamen in the communications department understood how it operated. A Sail Cast model, it was an early bedspring type with an exposed antenna array, and a set of slip rings at the foot of the array. The radar antenna made a slow revolution through 360°, and a target could be observed for a few seconds during the revolution as a flash of light or a "pip" on the radarscope. Designed and installed primarily for air search, not for navigational purposes, it was supposed to increase antisubmarine warfare capabilities but it was already obsolete. It had been installed in the *Wilkes* on December 31, 1941, even though electronic experts felt that there were defects in the present model. Better radar was being built all the time and, until the newer models were available, the Commander Destroyer Atlantic Fleet had ordered it to be used only as a military necessity, and only when visibility was bad or at night. Even then it was to be used only every half hour out of the hour to keep track of the ships.

Great care was required to keep radar in top working order. After every ten hours of use, particles collected on the grids, giving a fuzzy picture and causing the images to jump excessively. Then it was necessary to heat the grid to a white heat in order to throw off the particles and decontaminate it. This had been done at 1600 hours.

An official U. S. Fleet bulletin, not received aboard the Wilkes as yet, warned that ice, being a relatively poor reflector of radio waves, could affect the reception of bearings on radar, diminishing the range in which the indications of land could be picked up. Other information about the SC type of radar, not known to the crew of the Wilkes at this time, was that the exposed antenna array and the slip rings had been recognized by the experts as a source of trouble under conditions of ice and bad weather.

Whether radar had defects or not, this particular model had a range of nearly thirty miles, and the *Wilkes'* crew were more than thankful for it. They expected radar to indicate landfall at about twenty miles at least.

In all her experience as an escort, the *Wilkes* had never lost a ship on convoy. She had often chased the enemy, and her crew were very sure they were responsible for sinking an Italian-manned U-boat off the British Isles. The *Wilkes* was a well-trained ship, her crew thoroughly and frequently exercised in both routine and emergency procedures. Her commanding officer, Commander John D. Kelsey, had also instigated a familiarization course to expose the crew to all parts of the ship.

When she had gone to the Navy Yard in December for a general overhaul and to be outfitted with radar, most of her trained personnel had been transferred to the new ships being put into commission. As replacements she had received green troops: new young officers, Ensign Henry B. Quekemeyer, USN, Ensign J. R. Whiting III, USNR, and a bunch of kids. Only a small core of experienced professionals, both command and enlisted, remained to try to whip them into shape while carrying the brunt of the burden of keeping the ship operating at peak efficiency. On board were ten officers and approximately 180 enlisted men. Five of her crew, on leave, had missed the ship at sailing.

She still had Lieutenant William A. Smyth, chief engineer, a U. S. Naval Academy graduate of the Class of 1934. Smyth had been the first officer aboard, having been ordered from the USS *Preston,* in

Hawaii, to Boston to place the *Wilkes* in commission. He was twenty-nine years of age, slightly under medium height, with deep blue eyes, extraordinarily keen eyesight, and an engaging smile. He was knowledgeable, not only on the sea but also in the air, having qualified as a naval aviator in 1937–38. He had been assigned to VF-3 fighter aircraft aboard the USS *Saratoga,* but had returned to duty aboard the *Preston* at his own request in 1939 for additional experience as a mariner. He was a "gung ho" Navy man who believed that if one did a good job in various fields of endeavor, it would all come out favorably in the end.

The assignment to the *Wilkes* as engineer officer was definitely a "feather in the cap" for Smyth and, in effect, put him seven years ahead of his classmates; all other engineering officers of newly constructed division destroyers at Boston Navy Yard were postgraduate engineers of the Class of 1927 or thereabouts. He felt, with pardonable pride, that he was on his way up in the naval establishment without benefit of wealth or higher-up connections in the Navy Department, Washington, D.C. Little did he know that his promising career was about to grind to a halt.

At the outbreak of war between Japan and the United States, Smyth, after weighing his relative worth to the surface and air arms of the U. S. Navy, felt that the outcome of the war would be decided by who controlled the air. The United States had ships coming off the ways, and naval reserve officers who could be trained in ninety days to man those vessels, but it took about one year to train a proficient naval aviator. He was already trained. He had, therefore, requested a transfer back to the Naval Air Force. So far, nothing had happened.

Aboard the *Wilkes,* Smyth was also damage-control officer, deck court officer, welfare officer, and senior watch officer—the best watch-stander aboard. Understandably, he was a busy man. Smyth was so dog-tired most of the time, he could fall asleep at the drop of a hat, and once had done so, draped across a turbine in the engine room. He had a loyal, devoted, experienced engineering gang, and the engineering plant functioned extremely well. Even though the engineer and damage-control officer would not normally stand deck watches when the ship was under way, he had enthusiastically agreed to stand officer-of-the-deck watch on the *Wilkes* until such time as the less-experienced officers could be qualified. Consequently, to provide as strong a watch as possible, Commander Kelsey assigned the least experienced officer, Ensign Henry Quekemeyer, to stand watch with Smyth.

Lieutenant Frederick Wolsieffer, thirty-three, gunnery officer, had been aboard since the *Wilkes'* commissioning and did not stand deck watches. He was a handsome and dashing bachelor, and his adventures ashore were notable . . . but aboard ship he was all Navy.

Ensign Overton D. Hughlett, twenty-six, was communications officer, assistant gunnery officer, and officer of the deck. Boyish-looking with dark curly hair, blue-gray eyes, and cherubic features, he had also been aboard the *Wilkes* since her commissioning. Prior to this trip he had been standing junior officer-of-the-deck watches; this time, under the supervision of the navigator, he had been standing watch as OOD. As the communications officer, Hughlett, along with Chief Radioman George Koegler, had received two hours of instruction on the use of radar when it had been installed. Hughlett, Koegler, and Lieutenant Barrett, the navigator, had instructed Seamen Stark, Connolly,* and McPherson in the operation of it. To the rest of the crew radar was very much of a secret. It was a magic word.

Ensign Warren Winslow, USNR, the first lieutenant and assistant damage control officer, had been standing junior officer-of-the-deck watch since August, and for the first time was standing officer-of-the-deck watch under the supervision of the navigator.

Lieutenant Arthur Barrett, Jr., navigator and executive officer of the *Wilkes,* was thirty-five. Dogged, persistent, and conscientious, he was a big, burly bear of a man; a football player in his Academy days; a good shipmate, affectionately nicknamed "Toughie." It was a familiar sight to see Toughie with his leg curled around the alidade,[3] elbows braced on the sloping wing of the bridge, trying to steady himself against the ship's heavy rolling as he shot the star sights or sun sights. Often in the North Atlantic, they could get no celestial fixes, but his navigational prowess had brought them through.

It could be said that as a flagship[4] the *Wilkes* had two command-

* The Christian name and rank of Seaman Connolly was not established by the court of inquiry or the list from Washington, D.C.

[3] A sighting apparatus used in angular measurements.

[4] The ship that carries a commander of a fleet or squadron and flies his flag.

ing officers: Commodore[5] Walter W. Webb, the division commander, and Commander Kelsey, skipper of the *Wilkes*. Webb, at forty-seven, was square-jawed and sturdily built. With his full, bushy mustache, he looked more Prussian than American. He carried himself well and did his morning setting-up exercises before shaving. Webb was not pompous or overbearing toward subordinates, and the crew decided he was a pretty nice fellow. A veteran of World War I, he had served tours of duty around the world, and was the recipient of three medals and one decoration. He had been returned to sea duty when the *Wilkes* was commissioned, and had demonstrated that he was a good all-around naval officer.

Commander Kelsey, at forty, was tall, craggily handsome, gentlemanly, and kind, and, in his early years, had been the best watchstander on board the ships on which he had served. He had been on active duty on land and sea continuously since graduating from the Naval Academy in 1923; his assignments had been mainly as chief engineer on four combat ships. The *Wilkes* was his first command.

Although Kelsey, like all COs, preferred not to have the division commander aboard, he and Webb got along well. The relationship between them was well understood. Kelsey, as the ship's commanding officer, was responsible for the proper operation and safety of the *Wilkes*. Webb, as Task Unit Commander, was responsible for the proper operation and safety of the Task Unit.

The *Wilkes* was considered a taut ship. Her experienced petty officers and green crew were well disciplined and enjoyed good relations with the ten officers aboard, six of whom were graduates of the U. S. Naval Academy at Annapolis.

Academy men, trained in the highest ideals of duty, honor, and loyalty to their country, were a breed apart. They *were* the U. S. Navy; they commanded all ships in the Navy, and this would not change until the war took a heavy toll of top U. S. Naval Academy men.

The threat of a storm had been present from the day they had sailed, February 15, but another threat had presented itself on February 16. News had come over the Washington Broadcast schedule to ships at sea, from Commander-in-Chief, U. S. Fleet,[6] that German

---

[5] A complimentary title. His rank was that of commander.
[6] Admiral Ernest J. King.

U-boats were operating in the Cape Race–Cape Sable area, through which the convoy had to sail. The U-boat was a deadly and daring enemy: New publications issued by the Navy stated that submarines even attacked on the surface in heavy weather at speeds up to 18 knots, and they did not require visual contact for tracking or attacking. In a series of lectures Commander Kelsey had told his crew to report anything and everything. "It is better to make too many reports than too few," he stressed.

But thus far no U-boat had presented itself as the *Wilkes,* the *Pollux,* and the *Truxtun* plunged into the deepening troughs, and by noon the next day they would arrive at Base Roger in Argentia.

Darkness had come early this night, bringing with it increasing wind, heavy snow flurries, and roughening seas. The young lookouts on the wings of the bridge, miserably bone-achingly cold, squinted off into the darkness. Whitecaps, racing atop the steep waves, cast a sheen that loomed uncomfortably close when the *Wilkes* rolled heavily, and the sailors found themselves staring at a white-veined wall of black water that looked ready to engulf them. Miraculously, it never did. Not a glimmer of light showed anywhere. Darkened ship conditions gave them a feeling of total aloneness; they were cut off from the rest of the world, encircled by cold, darkness, and a menacing ocean.

The Navy was one thing, the North Atlantic was something else. Stormy seas and gray skies seemed to be the norm, and their world was one of continual adjustment as careening decks sent them reeling about their duties. As the icy spray flew over them, many wished they had joined the infantry; at least they would have had solid ground beneath them. But more immediately, they wished for the warmth and comfort of their bunks.

2

USS *Pollux*
February 17, 1942—2200 hours

If the *Wilkes* was uneasy about the *Pollux,* the *Pollux* was no less uneasy about the *Wilkes,* but for a different reason. Earlier in the day, after they had come around Cape Sable (Nova Scotia), a stream of messages about their speed and position had been directed at them from the *Wilkes.* It had been irksome, and the deck officer of the *Pollux* decided it was probably some ambitious junior OOD trying his wings during the daylight watch. It had not set well with the crew, and particularly with Commander Hugh W. Turney. A merchant Navy captain might growl, "Go to hell!" and ignore the messages, but Commander Turney was a Naval Academy man himself and since a reprimand to the ship was actually a reprimand to the commanding officer, those messages could be construed as a reprimand from his peers. The *Pollux,* as the formation guide, had to maintain the position that had been established by the Task Unit commander and, as the guide, must carry out the course and speed as directed by the commodore. They were doing that.

It is doubtful that her crew felt that their ship was causing any undue concern. In their estimation, the *Truxtun* kept looming up too close for comfort, and the watch kept a sharp lookout for any unexpected converging of that ship. It set a mood of unease; and those bothersome messages would have far-reaching effects as the convoy neared land.

In comparison to the *Wilkes'* green crew, the *Pollux* had the same crew that put her in commission in the Brooklyn Navy Yard on May

8, 1941. Not only had they trained together, but also most had come from New York and surrounding towns. They were hard workers, tremendous fighters, and they stuck together like flies on honey. They were New York's own. Her normal complement was 143 enlisted men and 16 officers. This trip there were 233 aboard, for she carried 16 passengers for the USS *Prairie*[1] in Argentia as well as 58 raw young recruits who were being transported to Argentia for training and assignment to vessels in the North Atlantic theater of operations. There was speculation that one of the passengers, Ensign Robert B. Whitney, USNR, because of his polished, refined manner, was a member of one of the famous Whitney families; perhaps the internationally known Jock Whitney or John Hay Whitney. It was pure supposition and nothing else; certainly none of the officers of the *Pollux* confirmed it, yet the identity of the young ensign created a minor interest below decks.

As a supply ship, the *Pollux* belonged to the working Navy, not the fighting Navy. Normally she supplied nuts, bolts, paint, light bulbs, cigarettes, toilet paper, and all other necessary items needed to keep the Navy going, servicing ships scattered from as far south as Port of Spain, Trinidad, to Argentia, Newfoundland. Her crew worked willingly, loading and unloading cargo on schedule, and because they performed well, regulations were kept at a minimum. Their trips alternated south and north, and in the Caribbean there was the odd beach party and sleeping on the deck under the stars. She had been an independent, happy ship. Morale was high.

The *Pollux* was also a floating national bank, and at times carried up to two-hundred thousand dollars in her safe. The disbursing officer was twenty-five-year-old Ensign Alfred Pollack, married only a month. He was a cheerful, enthusiastic young man and he enjoyed life immensely.

Commander Hugh Turney, age forty-two, was proud of his crew; he made them feel that they were a great and wonderful team. In turn, they felt that he was a great skipper. Although stern and aloof, he did make the effort, in a gentle, pleasant way, to break down the barrier a little between himself and the crew. Once or twice he had briefly attended their "beer bust" parties in the Caribbean. When at sea, he put them through different major drills every day: fire drill,

---

[1] The flagship for Base Roger.

general quarters, and abandon ship, and if some of the crew griped a little about the repetition and monotony of it, others felt that, if the real thing happened, it would pay off. Standing orders were that if anything unusual occurred while Turney was sleeping, the ship's personnel were not to hesitate to wake him.

There were rumors that he was scheduled to put the battleship USS *Massachusetts* in commission and this was his last trip with them, so on his forty-second birthday, February 13, two days before leaving port, they had made him an ice-cream birthday cake and sung "Happy Birthday" to him. What the hell! They loved the guy.

The *Pollux* was not comfortable with the escort. She had already made three uneventful trips to Argentia on her own. If, prior to this, the crew had felt a little unappreciated as their ship slipped unnoticed in and out of ports up and down the Atlantic seaboard or as they watched the destroyers herding the merchant ships together for convoying across the Atlantic, they hadn't complained. The Navy, they knew, couldn't operate without the likes of the *Pollux,* and the ship had done very well without an escort; besides, Navy singles were not normally escorted.

Now she had the honor of being escorted by not one but *two* destroyers, big guns gleaming, riding herd on her, smartly patrolling the seas, steaming forward and astern at high speed, alert for sight or sound of an enemy submarine when the *Pollux* turned on the zigzag, and falling into position on her port and starboard bows when she came back on the base course.

In the minds of the *Pollux*'s crew members, two warships escorting a lone cargo ship was, without doubt, unusual, and the ship seethed with reports that besides her official cargo of aerial bombs, radio and gun equipment, aircraft engines, a few refrigerators as well as nuts, bolts, and toilet tissue, they were carrying a secret cargo of radar that would be off-loaded in Argentia for installation on the destroyers that were operating out of Argentia. It was very impressive.

It was also restricting and disrupting to the even tenor of the *Pollux*'s normal operation. Nudged and prodded by the stream of messages, Commander Turney, a man who seldom became ruffled, appeared to be a little annoyed.

The *Pollux* had her own guns: a five-incher mounted on her stern and a three-incher on her bow. A "pea shooter," the gun crew irreverently called the bow gun. The *Pollux* had not fired a shot in enemy action in her whole career, and the sailors felt that if they ever did run into the enemy, that little pea shooter wasn't going to be of much help.

The *Pollux* was uncomfortable in other ways. In the crew's quarters, among the regular crew, there was talk tonight of the U-boats, and the general opinion seemed to be that the Germans were having a picnic. Generally there was a continuous game of acey-deucey going on before "lights out," but tonight there was an uneasiness among the men, and it seemed that everyone and his brother were in the heads taking showers. Most unusual on the North Atlantic run in winter. In a system that ruled four hours on duty, four hours off, there was barely enough time for them to grab some sleep, let alone take showers.

No one remarked on it, but practically all who showered put on clean dungarees and shirts. As recruits they had been trained that in the event of injury, cleanliness reduced infection. They were preparing themselves in case of attack or collision. In the cafeteria where the sailors just off duty gathered to get the chill out of their bones and fright of collision out of their system, there was talk also about what they considered to be the stupidity of officers and the Navy in general. Outside was a blinding snowstorm and two destroyers zigzagging somewhere near them. "They're hanging on our bow, and one bad turn on the zigzag is all we need to run into each other," someone growled.

But . . . theirs not to reason why. Still cold, they crawled into their bunks.

Chief Boatswain's Mate Edward Vincent Jabkowsky—"Skee," as he was nicknamed—was an old-timer, a Regular Navy man. He had already begun instructing the young recruits on their way to Argentia, and with the U-boat scare he had told them that in the event of disaster they were to keep a close watch on him. "Follow me," he had told them.

Tonight "Skee" was in sick bay with an attack of malaria.

Vincent Popolizio, fireman second class, was not feeling so well either. Popolizio suffered from chronic seasickness and, whenever the *Pollux* got under way, the big joke was: "Up anchor, down Pops." In warm weather they could always find the suffering Popolizio trying to sleep topside under the lifeboat. Patiently resigned, he lay in his berth.

Lawrence Calemmo, fireman first class, a sailor of Italian extraction in his early twenties, had a definite premonition that this time the *Pollux*'s number was up. It wasn't something that had come upon him suddenly; it had been lurking in the far corners of his mind from the very first time he set foot on her in the Brooklyn Navy Yard, with her brand-new all-over coat of gray paint. He had disliked her instantly. After all, they had been trained for destroyer duty, and he had expected to see a big destroyer, the pride and joy of all sailors. The *Pollux,* as a converted cargo ship, didn't look like a very cheerful home. He had said to his companions: "She looks like a floating coffin to me."

Prophetic words.

Gus Tortorici,[2] a buddy and boyhood friend from the Lower East Side, Manhattan, had looked around and said, "Jesus Christ! What a bucket."

During the following months Calemmo never did shake the feeling that the *Pollux* was a floating coffin, and so overwhelming was his premonition of disaster before this present trip north that he had taken special precautions before leaving the Boston Navy Yard. He had been ordered to install a heating system in No. 4 hold for the number of recruits that were to be transported to Argentia. He had taken it a step farther: as a member of the lifeboat crew and boat engineer of Captain Turney's gig, he was the engine expert, the man who could make engines talk. The lifeboats were powered by diesel engines, which were notorious for not starting in cold weather without preheated air, and Calemmo had constructed heaters by mounting four one-hundred-watt bulbs inside metal boxes with wood bottoms. The bulbs generated heat equivalent to a small space heater; Calemmo then installed a box under the hood of each lifeboat's engine. The makeshift heaters were plugged in for the whole voyage and periodic checks showed they were working well. If or when the U-boats struck, all lifeboats would be immediately operational.

While Calemmo felt that disaster was pending, he had no feeling of personal danger. Whatever happened, he knew he would be all right, but he felt that somewhere in the gray waters of the North Atlantic a torpedo had the *Pollux*'s name on it.

[2] Ratings are not recorded on the list of those who lost their lives. Survivors were able to provide the ratings in some cases.

That night of the seventeenth, as on the *Wilkes*, sandwiches were served instead of a hot dinner, and gradually the crew settled uneasily, fully clothed, in their bunks. Except for Warren Allen "Wag" Greenfield, signalman second class. He stripped to his underwear, crawled into the top bunk, and fell sound asleep. Wag had nerves of steel, and the talk of "Torpedo Alley," as the North Atlantic run was infamously labeled, hadn't bothered him in the least.

Flamboyant and adventurous, Wag, the personality kid, had the gift of getting in and out of scrapes. In his own circle aboard ship, he was No. 1. Stowed below in the tailor shop was the new guitar he had bought in Richmond, Virginia, a couple of months back. It had taken a couple of months' pay, but it had been worth it. It was brought out of storage on trips South; then Wag sat on the hatches at night, played the guitar, and sang in his rich baritone.

Across from him was Isaac Henry "Hank" Strauss, quartermaster third class. Strauss was Jewish, full of pizzazz, and remarkably popular. He was a college graduate as well, which was practically an insult to some of the Regular Navy sailors, and because of it he wound up in the hold more often than not, matching his skill in the boxing area. And since he was rather slight and short, he often wound up on the deck. On one such occasion a lucky blow had felled a hefty opponent, and Hank had been accepted wholeheartedly by the crew.

Since the last trip North, they had been given permission to grow beards, and a goodly number of the crew had done so. One of Strauss' good friends, Boatswain's Mate Second Class Glen Wiltrout, had grown a beard and, just for luck, Strauss pulled it once a day.

The general uneasiness that had prevailed had not bothered Alfred M. Dupuy, storekeeper third class. At twenty-six years of age he had joined the Navy the previous August and discovered he was really an old man by Navy standards. As a member of the Supply Corps, Dupuy had received no training as a Navy man; he was, as the rank indicated, a storekeeper. He had never been aboard a ship before and didn't know port from starboard. Tall, lean, with a sense of humor, a penchant for daring, and a deep, resonant voice that was reputed to carry through any gale, Dupuy, after six months aboard, still didn't know a square knot from a granny knot. To him ladders were stairs and bulkheads were walls and to hell with it. Today Dupuy had washed half a dozen pairs of his skivvies and strung them

across No. 2 hold, where they danced wildly to the ship's movements.

The ship's mascot, an alley cat picked up in some forgotten port,
cared even less about the mood aboard the *Pollux*. It lived the life of
an admiral, but was petted and fed with more love than the men
could dredge up for any officer of that rank. Its nine lives had just
about run out.

If there was anyone aboard the *Pollux* who was not in awe of
Commander Turney it was Lieutenant (jg)[3] William C. Grindley,
navigator, for this was Turney's first command and, to a merchant
Navy sailor like Grindley, who had sailed under many a crusty old
skipper, this fact was obvious.

A very definite and forthright man, Grindley, aged thirty-three,
had been going to sea from the time he had been in high school. Employed with the United States Lines, he had come up through the
ranks to chief officer and had already passed examinations for license as master unlimited, oceans, which was the highest license a
U.S. flag merchant officer could hold. In the school he had been
raised in, he had been taught to love his ship as he would his
mother; thus the ship was called "she." He was taught to obey the
master's commands, and by the time he had climbed the ladder
through third, second, and chief officer, he was well prepared in
every respect for command of his own vessel.

Grindley had seventeen years of seagoing experience behind him
and his professional career was without blemish when he was called
to active duty after the National Defense Act was passed in Congress
on October 15, 1940. He was assigned to the *Pollux* as navigator by
the Bureau of Navigation and made third in command. It soon became evident to him that his experience and rank of chief officer in
the Merchant Navy meant little in the U. S. Navy. It seemed to him
that he was considered just another reservist, to be seen and not
heard, to be put up with for the duration. It took a while to get used
to that, and he felt very much like a fish out of water.

There was a vast difference between the Merchant Navy and the
U. S. Navy. In the merchant ships the captain was God. He made all
the decisions and was fully responsible for the vessel, crew, and
cargo. The same precept applied to the U. S. Navy, but it seemed to
Grindley that Navy regulations were God, and the captain of a U. S.

[3] Lieutenant junior grade is a rank lower than lieutenant in the U. S. Navy.

Navy ship could consider himself in complete command as long as he did not run afoul of them.

With Grindley's seventeen years' experience on the sea and his rise to chief officer, it had come as a shock to him to learn that the *Pollux* was Commander Turney's first command and that his naval career prior to this commission had been essentially engineering, with a bit of duty as a gunnery officer as his only deck assignment.

If Grindley looked askance at Naval Academy graduates in general, he got along well with Commander Turney, who in turn was very satisfied with his navigator.

Grindley was not only the navigator and third in command; he was also deck court officer and senior watch officer and he had to run a training course for the deck watch officers in order that they might qualify as watch officers. As navigator he also had charge of the bridge/navigation personnel, and the communications department, which consisted of the signalmen and the radiomen. In the communications department his right-hand man was Lieutenant (jg) Russell J. Schmidt, who was on the 2000–2400 watch. In addition, Grindley was librarian, ship's service officer, which consisted of the soda fountain, ship's stores, laundry, barber shop, cobbler shop, and the tailor shop—and there were times when he felt like the Merchant of Venice.

Now Commander Turney and Lieutenant Grindley were in the chartroom poring over the charts, and Grindley was not at all happy. He considered it regrettable that they were under escort and tied to the commands of the flagship *Wilkes,* for they must zigzag continually, which made navigating in heavy weather very difficult. On top of that, atmospheric conditions were playing havoc with their navigational aids.

Grindley was beginning to feel very uneasy.

The USS *Truxtun,* the ancient four-stacker destroyer, with a crew of 156 sailors, was much less comfortable than either the *Pollux* or the *Wilkes*. Only 31 feet wide and 310 feet long, she seemed to stand on beam end as the seas worsened. Old as she was, the *Truxtun* was serving on the North Atlantic run because of her exceptionally large fuel capacity, which qualified her for escort duty, and so far she had served well.

She had made several trips to Argentia prior to this one, but had not worked with the *Pollux* or the *Wilkes* before. The *Truxtun* was manned by a strong nucleus of professional sailors who had trained and faced danger together on the old ship. This trip she had fifteen green young sailors who had no sea training at all, and quite likely most of these were seasick as the ship rolled and bucked over the steep waves.

Her master was Lieutenant Commander Ralph Hickox, a thirty-nine-year-old Naval Academy man with a distinguished career. He had taken command of the *Truxtun* in Argentia in October 1941, replacing Lieutenant Commander Harry B. Heneberger. The crew thought Hickox was the best. The navigator and executive officer was Lieutenant Arthur Lester Newman, aged thirty-one, another U. S. Naval Academy man who had joined the *Truxtun* in December 1941.

Hickox was capable and efficient. He made sure that routine emergency drills were held and expeditiously carried out whenever operating conditions permitted. The *Truxtun* might be considered ancient for modern warfare, but her crew were young and eager.

Ensign James O. Seamans, aged twenty-three, a graduate of Harvard with ROTC cruises on the USS *Tillman,* USS *Texas,* USS *Schenck,* and a recent graduate of the U. S. Naval Academy, had stepped aboard the *Truxtun* only a few days before her departure for Argentia. The son of a certified public accountant in Boston, he had grown up near the ocean and spent thousands of hours on and near it before entering the Navy; he therefore did not consider himself a greenhorn, although the senior officers apparently did.

As Seamans was the eleventh officer aboard, there appeared to be no space for him, so he was assigned to sleep in the officers' wardroom mess on the wardroom transom.[4] Oh well, he thought, it was better than the hammocks he had slept in on his training cruises.

He was appointed sonar officer, although there had never been a sonar officer before. Seamans did not wait around to have his every move directed; he decided it was his job to learn about sonar, and set about doing it himself, getting help from the enlisted man who was in charge of it.

Perhaps because he was so self-reliant, no officer took him under his wing during the couple of days he had been aboard, and to date

[4] A seat or couch built at a side of a cabin, having lockers or drawers underneath.

he had not really established rapport with anyone in particular. Once, before leaving port, when the officers were doing their income tax and grumbling aloud, he had offered to help. Since his father was an accountant, Seamans was fairly knowledgeable in this area. They had not accepted his offer.

During duty watch on the bridge that day, Seamans had heard the navigator tell the captain that they had gotten no navigational fix since rounding Cape Sable shortly after 0600 hours. To him it seemed that Lieutenant Commander Hickox and Lieutenant Newman were anxious about sailing so far without a good fix. Seamans also had the distinct impression that they did not want their concern communicated to the officers and men. But Seamans had great faith in the commanding officer and the executive officer, and he gave it no more thought. The main concerns of the officers and crew on duty watch, aside from the *Pollux,* were the U-boats and the possibility of a drifting iceberg, which might do the *Truxtun* in, as one had the *Titanic* thirty years earlier.

At the present time Seamans was sleeping soundly on the hard wardroom transom while Ensign William J. Maddocks, another U. S. Naval Academy graduate, was preparing to take over the midnight watch.

The *Truxtun* was traveling blind. She did not have a fathometer and no soundings could be taken in the deep water with the hand lead at the speed they were moving. They had lost all track of the other ships after nightfall, and their sonar had been unable to pick up the sound of the *Pollux*'s propellers due to the increasing noise of the ocean itself as sea conditions worsened. Because they had lost contact, Lieutenant Commander Hickox had ordered the *Truxtun* to cease zigzagging, although by adhering to the base course as laid down by the division commander of the *Wilkes* he was confident they were still on the port bow of the *Pollux.* They had decreased speed to twelve knots to make allowance for the zigzagging of the convoy.

At 2300 their sonar briefly picked up the propellers of the *Pollux.* After that, nothing. In the radio shack, the radio operator on duty was trying vainly to get RDF[5] bearings on Cape Race, Newfoundland, and Gallantry Head, St. Pierre Island. From the latter

[5] RDF: Radio Direction Finder.

there was no indication that a radio beacon was operating; from Cape Race there was only static.

With the exception of her TBS,[6] which was never that reliable in spite of continual overhauling, all other equipment aboard the *Truxtun* was considered to be in top working condition.

It was customary for the captain and the navigator to divide up the night when in formation and trying to keep station on other ships. Lieutenant Commander Hickox took the first shift up to 0200; after that, Lieutenant Newman took the bridge. One or the other was always available to handle any emergency that might arise that the officer of the deck might not be able to handle alone.

Unknown to their commanding officers and navigators, all three ships had already been subjected to an influence that was setting them northward of their dead-reckoning track. Pitching heavily, the ships steamed onward, their crews oblivious of the fact that they were heading into danger.

[6] Telephone Between Ships: Short-range transmitting voice radio.

3

Earlier, at 0623 hours, the *Wilkes* established her position when Lieutenant Barrett took star sights on Vega, Mizar, Dubhe, Antares, and Arcturus. According to his calculations, they were in latitude 44°30′00″N, longitude 60°28′00″W, roughly 60 miles south of Chedabucto Bay, Nova Scotia, and approximately 30 miles northwest of Sable Island. Her base course at that time was 069° true, carrying the ships on a course parallel to the Nova Scotia coast. The barometer was dropping. The wind was from the north-northwest, force 3.

The navigator did not realize it, but he made a minor error on the star Antares. It was rising and east of the meridian; he calculated it *west* of the meridian. His reported position was approximately 2½ miles southward of his *actual* position. From the time of this error[1] the *Wilkes* would commit a series of errors, each one insignificant in itself, that cumulatively would result in disaster.

The incorrect star fix therefore indicated that the course made good had not been 069° true, but 071° true, which meant a small set, or drift, to the south. It was not unexpected, as far as Barrett was concerned. Nova Scotia chart No. H.O. 99 indicated that the offshore currents set away from land. He had reported it to the commodore and the skipper, but he had made no allowance to correct the southward drift.

[1] To be within five miles of a position as determined by celestial navigation during hazy weather is considered reasonably accurate in northern waters.

Sailing Directions for Nova Scotia also stated: *". . . that as a rule the surface current shifted regular in the direction of the hands of a watch, completing the circle on the average in a period of eighteen hours. The occasions on which this regularity was interrupted and the current direction was observed to shift in reverse way were generally, though not invariably, when fresh to strong winds prevailed."*

In other words the deep-flowing current set *away* from land, but the surface current was generally *toward* the land. The navigator did not give it consideration, but at this time the *Wilkes* was being influenced by the surface current.

It was mandatory for ships at sea to plot their dead-reckoning track and to project their course from each last-known position. Based upon the 0623 star fix, the *Wilkes* was 306 miles from Argentia at 8 A.M. and Barrett calculated the noon, the 1600-hour, and the 2000-hour dead-reckoning positions, which would put the *Wilkes* in latitude 45°29'30"N, longitude 56°46'00"W, roughly an hour's run from the St. Pierre Bank. Because of the heavy overcast and snow flurries, Lieutenant Barrett was unable to take any further sights, and at 1000 hours the wind shifted from north to the east-southeast, force 1—a bad-weather wind.

Then, at 1114 hours, the *Pollux* winked this message:

Do you figure change base course to about 055° at noon and will CDD[2] initiate change of base course.

But Commodore Webb was not prepared to change course for Placentia Bay so soon, and at 1120 hours ordered a signal sent to the *Pollux:*

Will initiate change of course probably at 2000.

Webb, a sailor with twenty-six years of Navy experience, twelve of them as a navigator, studied the proposed course of 055° true as suggested by Commander Turney of the *Pollux* and, from the *Wilkes'* position as established by the 0623 star fix, decided that it would lead the base course of the ships about 9 miles off Burin Island on the west side of Placentia Bay in the middle of the night. That, in his estimation, was too close to land in an area where cur-

[2] Commander Destroyer Division 26 (Walter W. Webb).

rents were so unpredictable; the current along this shore, west of Cape Race, was very tricky.

Sailing Directions H.O. 73 for Newfoundland clearly stated that the drift of the sea and current were "nearly toward the land, especially near Placentia and St. Mary's Bays" and that many wrecks had occurred on this coast owing to the indraft or to the current temporarily setting northeastward. There was a caution: "Mariners approaching Newfoundland in thick weather should use the lead and proceed with caution, as it is *impossible to foretell what current they may have*. On the south coast of Newfoundland the tidal currents are very variable, changing with the locality and influenced generally, both in direction and velocity, by the prevailing winds of several preceding days."

Light winds had been blowing from the north since 0100 on February 16; therefore Webb felt any set would be to the south, away from land.

There was another caution about the current sweeping in on the eastern side of the bays on the south coast: "Westward of Cape Race, the current frequently sets northwestward, *with a velocity of about one knot in the offing*,[3] *but it is variable in velocity and direction and affected greatly by the prevailing wind*. It generally runs in on the eastern side of the great bays indenting the south coast of Newfoundland, and out on their western side. In the offing it is influenced by the wind, and near the shore by the tidal currents."

Since a ship could be set either way, Commander Webb applied the old Navy maxim: "Always split the middle of safe waters," and laid off a course that led directly for Argentia and cleared land to port by twenty miles; to starboard by twenty-five miles. This would lead the ship clear of the eastern shore with its indraft, and made ample allowance for a set in either direction.

He told Kelsey and Barrett, "Once we get into Placentia Bay we're in restricted waters. If we change course to 047° true at 2000 hours, it will lead us up the middle of the entrance of the bay and won't entail a change of course at night." He added, "It will also shake any submarines that may be trailing us."

Webb did not relish entering Placentia Bay at night in heavy

[3] That part of the visible sea at a good distance from the shore, or where there is deep water and no need of a pilot.

weather and low visibility, but orders to arrive at Argentia at 1200 hours on the eighteenth had been explicit, and he intended to follow them. It was a matter of professional pride.

Commander Kelsey and Lieutenant Barrett studied the course laid down, and concurred. Kelsey had checked the sailing directions for Newfoundland for tides and currents and considered the course a good one. The navigator, having read them many times, did not bother to do so this time. His own experience in those waters indicated that tidal conditions and currents were too variable to predict.

By midday the *Wilkes* approached the Artimon Bank, an elevated area of the ocean floor that fell away into the depths of the continuation of the Cabot Strait, and Lieutenant Barrett noticed slush ice drifting southward across the bow of the *Wilkes*. At this time, then, it indicated to him the set of the current was still away from land. He reported it to the commodore and the skipper.

The sky was completely overcast, and the barometer was 29.88 and still falling. Local weather forecasts were not broadcast from Argentia except on request. Since that meant breaking radio silence, the *Wilkes* did not request one.

The winds were light for the most part of the day, and Webb gave no thought to leeway for wind. It did not seem necessary. They were keeping position on a heavily laden cargo vessel which, he was sure, was not too affected by the wind; therefore its effect on the unit as a whole would be little, if any. Besides, the *Wilkes* and the *Truxtun* had left port less than three days before with a full load of oil. Furthermore, at midday there had obviously been a southeasterly current flowing against them, taking ice across their bow, and that current would offset any wind effect from the southeast, with the southerly set she had already experienced the night before. The pilot chart of the North Atlantic Ocean for February 1942, in its information about ocean currents, stated: "The yearly average set of the stream and drift current is shown in small black arrows." These arrows in the vicinity of the *Wilkes'* 2000-hour position tended toward the southwest. With all the evidence pointing to a general southward set, the wind, he felt, would not affect the course.

The wind increased to a moderate breeze and darkness fell early as lowering skies and heavy intermittent snow cut visibility. It was evident they were not going to get another star fix. At 1610 hours

Commodore Webb ordered the message, by TBS, that Commander
Turney on the *Pollux* had been waiting for:

**At 2000 change course to 047 without orders. This course should
lead you five miles off Latine Point.[4] If necessary to change course
later for navigational reasons, do so and notify me of change. At
0800 tomorrow set clock to plus three point five time.[5]**

This order gave the *Pollux* freedom of action during the night in
case she needed to change course. Taking into consideration the
U-boat menace and the possibility of a contact with the enemy during the night, the two escort ships would have to make radical
changes of course and speed to investigate, and they would need to
know where the *Pollux,* as the basic unit, was: Wherever she went,
the *Wilkes* and the *Truxtun* had to maintain station on her.

Plus 3.5 time really went into effect somewhere between the island
of Newfoundland and the Nova Scotia mainland, but it was being
delayed because of the zigzag plan. During the hours of darkness
they would continue to operate on zone plus-4 time.

Information of change of course was signaled to the *Truxtun* as
well, and at 1740 hours the *Wilkes* again signaled the *Truxtun:*

One[6] is conforming to movements of the big ship.[7]

This was to inform the *Truxtun* that the *Wilkes* had ceased patrolling and was conforming to the zigzag plan being used by the *Pollux.*
As the three ships moved northeastward in formation, the wind
freshened and was blowing from the southeast, force 4. It snowed intermittently.

The *Wilkes* was still crossing the deep continuation of Cabot
Strait, approaching the southwest end of the St. Pierre Bank at 1930
hours when Navigator Barrett came on duty and asked for a record
of the soundings. The quartermaster passed him the log and Barrett
was startled to discover that it showed they were in water less than
one hundred fathoms deep. He hurriedly checked Chart No. 981,
which showed that the water over which they were supposed to be
steaming was more than two hundred fathoms in depth, which could

---

[4] On the north side of Argentia.
[5] Three and one-half hours behind Greenwich Mean Time.
[6] USS *Wilkes.*
[7] USS *Pollux.*

mean that they had wandered from their dead-reckoning track. There was a scarcity of soundings on this chart, and in great haste Barrett called Commander Kelsey. Quickly they discovered that the quartermaster had used the incorrect scale of measurement, and the soundings he had written in the log were in error by two hundred fathoms. Barrett and Kelsey corrected the line of soundings and were immeasurably relieved to find that they appeared to verify the 2000-hours position of the ship.

"Nevertheless," Commander Kelsey said, "the scarcity of sound-.ings shown for this area on the chart precludes placing too much faith in this method of checking position." They would have to try to verify their position by radio direction-finder bearings even though atmospheric conditions were far from favorable. "Tell the radioman to try to obtain RDF bearings from stations in this vicinity," he ordered.

They had been joined by the commodore when presently Radioman George Koegler reported back to the bridge and passed the captain a sheet showing the bearings he'd obtained.

"It's not very satisfactory, sir; too much static," Koegler said. They examined the bearings.

From Cape Race: At 1923 hours—obtained RDF bearing at 076°
     At 1947 hours—obtained RDF bearing at 065°
     At 1956 hours—obtained RDF bearing at 069°
From Sable Island: At 1937 hours—obtained RDF bearing at 228°,
        weak signals, broad miasma.

Webb asked, "Is that the best you can do?"

"Yes, sir," Koegler replied, "the Sable Island signal was very mushy, and the Cape Race signal was variable."

The radio signals from Cape Race had been variable indeed. Bearing 076° intercepted their dead-reckoning track on the far side of the St. Pierre Bank, 065° was to the east, but 069° intercepted their DR track much closer. Bearing 228° from Sable Island was to the west of their track.

If the Gallantry Head radio beacon on the French island of St. Pierre, which would be on the port bow as they approached land, had been operating, undoubtedly the RDF would have been able to pick up directions but, unknown to any of the commanding officers

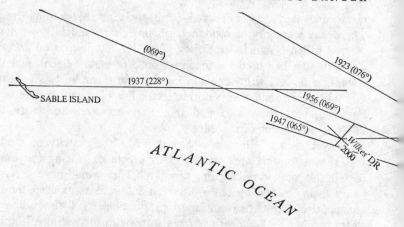

of the ships, that important beacon had been shut down by the French authorities since their last trip to Argentia.

Again Webb took over. He decided that the bearing 069° taken at 1956 hours was the nearest to being correct since it showed a position close to the *Wilkes*' dead-reckoning position, which had been verified by soundings.

"It's not good enough to base a fix[8] on," Webb stated flatly.

"Both stations are over two hundred miles away," Barrett said.

It was agreed that the RDF bearings were not reliable enough to base a fix on; therefore, they would have to be satisfied that their dead-reckoning position was correct, although there was no way it could be verified.

The three men were still poring over the charts discussing course and speed of the ship when the watch changed. Lieutenant Overton Hughlett arrived to take over the 2000–2400 watch at 1945 hours.

It was mandatory for the night watch to relieve the bridge fifteen minutes ahead of time in order to allow for "dark adaptation" of the eyes, which was essential in watch-keeping at night. A warning in an OPNAV confidential letter stated: "Frequently officers and men do not realize how much harm is done by lighting matches, a visit to the charthouse, etc. The eye does not reach its maximum sensitivity in

---

[8] Determination of their position.

The Wilkes' *Bearings at 1923, 1947, and 1956 Hours*

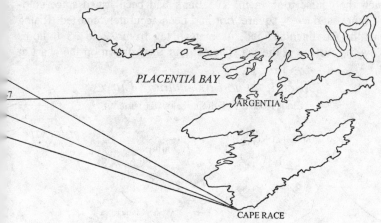

the dark until more than 15 minutes after it has been subjected to a light of an intensity sufficient for reading."

Hughlett checked the chart, noting that the track of the *Wilkes* took them approximately 19½ miles from the nearest point of land on the port side, which was Ferryland Head,[9] a headland jutting into the Atlantic on the west side of the entrance to Placentia Bay. He memorized the track so that he would not have to impair his night vision by entering the lighted charthouse later. He would spend the watch in the darkened pilothouse and on the wings with the look-outs; the junior officer of the deck would keep a check on the crew inside operating the fathometer, the radar, and the radio direction finder in the radio room. As communications watch officer and the one who assisted the navigator in training the bridge personnel, he would be the one to whom even soundings, which were for the benefit of the navigator, would be reported.

At 2000 hours the base course of 069° was changed to 047°, and the three ships headed for the center of the mouth of Placentia Bay. They were now 155 miles from Argentia. Visibility was poor, with heavy snow squalls; the wind had increased to force 5, and the barometer had dropped to 29.40. The plotted dead-reckoning track indicated that they were about 12 miles from the St. Pierre Bank, that

[9] Not to be confused with Ferryland Head on the southeast coast.

great fishing bank about 40 miles south of Newfoundland, over which the course took them. The Bank had been fished since colonial times, and every square foot had been accurately charted. Rising from the Continental Shelf, its plateau lay from 22 to 35 fathoms below the surface of the sea. The contour lines drawn on the chart at

50-Fathom and 100-Fathom Curves

(Cloue Rock is 10 fathoms below the surface.)

MIQUELON

BURIN PENINSULA

PLACENTIA BAY

50-fathom curve

St. Pierre

Cloue Rock

100-fathom curve

ST. PIERRE BANK

ATLANTIC OCEAN

50-fathom curve

100-fathom curve

regular intervals of elevation around the periphery of the Bank indicated where the 100-fathom and 50-fathom depths were; thus mariners could pinpoint their position by soundings when crossing the
contour lines, hence its importance. They would be leaving the deep
water and crossing the 100-fathom line (or curve) south of the bank
very shortly. Because the bank rose steeply on the southward side, it
would be only a matter of minutes before the *Wilkes* crossed the 50-
fathom curve as well, whereas at the northern end of the bank where
the slope was gradual, there was a run of nearly three hours between
the 50-fathom and the 100-fathom curves. Once they crossed the
curves on the southward end the navigator would be able to verify
their 2000 position.

At 2106 hours, on the right leg of the zigzag, course 080, speed 15
knots, the *Wilkes* crossed the 100-fathom curve. At 2112 hours, still
on the right leg, she crossed the 50-fathom curve. Calculating the
course, distance, and speed between the two curves, the navigator
pinpointed on the chart where they had crossed to the bank, and ran
back an hour and six minutes to fix their 2000-hour estimated position.[10] It was 5.6 miles to the eastward of their dead-reckoning track.
This indicated a southward set away from land. *Actually the crossing*
could have been 6 miles to the north or to the south, as the distance
between the two curves did not vary to any extent within 6 miles ei-
ther side of the ship's presumed track.

According to the navigator's calculations, the *Wilkes'* dead-
reckoning track 53 miles across the bank would take 4 hours and
24 minutes before she dropped off the bank and crossed the 50-
fathom curve on the northward side into deeper water.

With the seas building as they rolled over the shallow fishing
grounds it was going to be a rough crossing.

Based upon the *Wilkes'* position crossing the 100-fathom and 50-
fathom curves, Commander Kelsey wrote up the night orders giving
destination, base course, and speed: The *Wilkes* was to maintain her
position on the starboard bow of the *Pollux,* distance 2,000–3,000
yards. They were to cease zigzagging and continue patrolling if visibility improved. They were to make radar search for 30 minutes during each hour, take and record fathometer readings every 15 minutes. Commander Kelsey made note of the fact that the *Wilkes* was

[10] Most probable position.

expected to cross the 50-fathom curve about 0130 hours, and the
100-fathom curve about 0420 hours. He ordered that RDF bearings
of Cape Race and Gallantry Head be taken at 2400, 0200, and 0400
hours. He added a footnote: "After 0400 attempt to pick up land
with radar—range about 20 miles."

Knowing that the *Truxtun* used her sonar equipment to keep track
of the *Pollux* in low visibility and at night, and that it would only be
used effectively if she was directly ahead of the *Pollux,* Commander
Webb decided to give the *Truxtun* her head, either by steaming to
the fore or steaming well clear of her zigzag. At 2120 hours he
notified the *Truxtun* by TBS:

Take any convenient position.

The *Truxtun* returned a "Roger" by TBS. On her own recog-
nizance, she had discontinued zigzagging at nightfall. Not so with the
Wilkes: Zigzag Plan 26 had been ordered by higher authority.

At this time Commander Webb was satisfied that all was well. The
fathometer was working, Hughlett was on the bridge, the radar operator was doing his job, the quartermaster was checking the soundings, and the navigator was still busy with his charts. Making a final
inspection, Webb said, "If by any chance the soundings should shoal
unexpectedly, notify the *Pollux* and the *Truxtun* at once." The water
shoaled along the west side of Placentia Bay and there were small
fishing banks in the bay itself.

Then he went to his cabin just below the bridge and lay, fully
dressed, on his berth.

Because the fathometer gave out a distinctive wave that could be
picked up by submarine, the taking of soundings had been limited to
every 15 minutes, and Lieutenant Barrett, meticulously checking the
dead-reckoning track across the St. Pierre Bank, prepared the
fathometer log for the seamen on the middle watch, jotting down the
time, 15 minutes apart, which they were to fill in. The 0000–0400
fathometer log began at 0008. Since the *Wilkes* was expected to
cross the 50-fathom curve on the northern side of the bank at ap-
approximately 0138, Barrett penciled in *"Expect to hit 50 fathoms"*
opposite that time.

In the normal running of the ship, the record of soundings was for
the use of the navigator in verifying his track and position. When he

returned to the bridge, the track over which the *Wilkes* had traveled would be fairly well defined by the soundings.

At 2130 hours Barrett also went off duty, leaving word with Hughlett that he was to be awakened at 0300. As navigator, he felt he should be on the bridge on the approach to land, which would be about 19 miles on their port beam about 0400.

The three ships steamed onward through the darkness.

Keeping tabs on the *Pollux* by radar was a little like playing tag, according to the bearings picked up by Connolly, the radar operator. Endeavoring to keep within 3,000 yards of her in the heavy seas now buffeting them, radar picked her up anywhere from 3,100 to 4,200 yards.

Hughlett was kept busy directing the continual zigzag changes and keeping a sharp lookout for the *Pollux* and U-boats. While the soundings were taken every 15 minutes and reported to him, he did not deem it necessary to go to the charthouse and lay the soundings on the chart. It was not customary for the OOD on the *Wilkes* to plot positions on the chart during the watch in open water. The captain and the navigator had been on the bridge for the greater part of his watch, and besides, it would impair his night vision.

All seemed well. The *Wilkes* should have been two thirds of the way across the St. Pierre Bank, southward of St. Pierre and Miquelon, the two French islands that hugged the coast of Newfoundland. But all was *not* well.

4

USS *Pollux*
February 17, 1942—2300 hours

Lieutenant (jg) William Grindley, navigator of the *Pollux*, had had no premonition of disaster as Calemmo had, but Grindley's own alarm bells were ringing. After years of making landfalls in all kinds of weather, he had developed a built-in alarm clock, an uncanny sense when things were just not right, and *he had that feeling now*. Something was amiss.

He had been on the bridge since 0400, and during this hour before midnight he was definitely uneasy. Since 1100 hours, his best efforts had not enabled him to absolutely fix their position. To be on the approach to land in low visibility without knowing exactly where one was had to be the dread of all mariners.

Commander Turney had been on the bridge since 0700 and, already harassed by the numerous messages directed at them earlier, he, too, was uneasy that they did not know exactly where they were. It was a dilemma for which Navy regulations made no allowances. Worry had triggered disagreement between the two men, which had not helped.

It had not been a good day since the beginning. At 0620, with his own personal sextant, a German-made Plath, Grindley had gotten three quick star sights, even though the horizon was fuzzy with sea fog,[1] and it was less than satisfactory, but better than no sight at all.

At 1000 hours horizon conditions had not improved but he had

[1] Steam rising off the water.

caught a sun line, and another about 1100, advancing the first line to the second, making it fixed. The interval of the vessel's run and the change in the sun's azimuth were such to give Grindley confidence in this fix, which was further strengthened by the dead-reckoning plot.

Turney had been pleased. "We can rest easier now," he had said.

Grindley, as he had always done, had plotted a new course. Now, when he felt they knew where they were, was the time to lay a course that would be a safe guideline for the approach to Placentia Bay, rather than wait until later, particularly since the weather was not showing any improvement.

Taking into consideration the westward flow of the Arctic current, as specified in the sailing directions for Newfoundland, Grindley had laid off a course from his fix at 1100 hours:[2] 047° true, steering course 055° true allowing for leeway to make the 047° course good, would take them up the middle of Placentia Bay, homing in on Red Island, 6 miles from Latine Point on the north side of Argentia Harbor and 25 miles offshore when Ferryland Head was abeam. In the event that they experienced a westerly set, the radio direction finder on Gallantry Head and Latine Point would definitely lead them in, making a good landfall. Course 055° favored the east side of the entrance to Placentia Bay and would make a better lee for them to run on up to the entrance because the wind, during the morning, had been steadily backing from the north.

Commander Turney was a very careful man; after the reprimands earlier, the last thing he wanted was an error. He had studied the chart. "It's a good, safe course," he had agreed.

"Perhaps even more leeway?" Grindley had suggested.

But Commander Turney had thought 047° true, steering course 055°, was just fine; prudent navigation recommended course changes on fixed positions and he had sent the signal to the *Wilkes* about changing to 055° at noon. The reply came back that the change of course would probably be initiated at 2000 hours.

This could have been considered another rebuff and Commander Turney had not liked it. To Grindley it had been another lesson learned: Never suggest a change of course to the flagship. It was very frustrating. What the hell am I doing here? he wondered.

---

[2] Grindley's navigation was obviously quite different from that of the *Wilkes*, but the *Pollux*'s records were lost and he was unable to recall the latitude and longitude of the vessel position at 6 A.M., noon, and 4 P.M.

Lieutenant Grindley's 055° Course

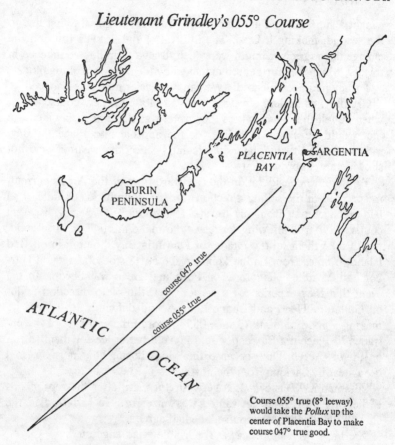

Course 055° true (8° leeway)
would take the *Pollux* up the
center of Placentia Bay to make
course 047° true good.

The noon change of course would have increased the angle from land on the west side of Placentia Bay—the longer the run, the greater the angle. Holding course 069° until 2000 hours was really closing the angle on land, he felt.

Horizon conditions had not improved, and the weather was definitely worsening when, at approximately 1220 hours, Grindley managed to grab a sun sight, but it had not been an exact fix.

"Where are we?" Commander Turney had demanded.

Grindley could give him only the approximate position: "Due to the foggy horizon when taking star sights, our noon position, walked back from the ex-meridian, could be as much as five to eight miles off."

Commander Turney had not liked it.

Grindley had not liked it either, but he had learned in his twelve years of navigating that in the cold, foggy regions of the western North Atlantic, it was par for the course. His RDF bearings from Sable Island, Sambro, and Sydney Low Point had corroborated their position and eased the worry somewhat.

At 1400 hours Grindley had managed to grab one sun sight and had plotted their 1600-hour position. At that time they had been definitely on Artimon Bank; radio bearings, although only approximate, had established it.

Knowing approximately where they were was not very satisfactory, and it was evident to Lieutenant (jg) Jack Garnaus and Quartermaster Henry Strauss, who were on the 1800 to 2000 dog watch, that the captain and the navigator were very worried about their position. Lieutenant Commander John E. Gabrielson, executive officer, had joined them, and all three were huddled over the chart.

Garnaus knew very little about navigation at this time, but he did know that in these waters there was little to navigate by without celestial fixes, and well might they be concerned. . . .

Commander Turney had been relieved as he watched Grindley plotting the course of the *Pollux* toward St. Pierre Bank; once they were on the bank they would know exactly where they were. Navy regulations demanded a 2000-hour position report to the flagship, and by dead reckoning, Grindley had fixed the 2000 DR position at latitude 45°28'00''N, longitude 57°03'00''W, but he had made a notation on the 2000-hour report: "This position could be five to eight miles in error in any direction due to adverse weather conditions while taking sights. . . . Be governed accordingly!"

In midocean, five to eight miles was nothing to be concerned about. Approaching land in bad weather, that distance was something else. Commander Turney was on tenterhooks.

Then at 1610, the *Wilkes* had signaled the *Pollux* to change course to 047° true at 2000, and to notify the flagship if any other change was necessary for navigational reasons.

Turney and Grindley had studied the message. Neither approved of a change of course at such a late hour, but they were learning not to question the flagship.

The flashing message, read by any number of the ship's crew, had been passed around below; their interpretation was: "It's every man for himself."

By late afternoon it had begun to hail and snow, and the ship began to ice up. They had seen no sign of the *Truxtun* since early afternoon, but at 1700 hours had sighted the *Wilkes* close on their starboard bow at about 1000 yards. Grindley had assumed that the *Wilkes* and the *Truxtun* were patrolling when the *Pollux* was on the zigzag course and, convinced that the stormy weather would prevent any kind of submarine attack either on the surface or below, had felt that the two warships should move in closer to them and cease patrolling. In fact, with their speed of 14.2 knots and the existing weather conditions, he had also felt that they should have discontinued zigzagging.

In Grindley's estimation Plan 26 had too many broad changes of course, which made it practically impossible for him to correct the zigzag course for leeway to compensate for the wind and waves on the starboard beam. In the circumstances, since landfall would be made in darkness, it would be more sensible, and assure better dead-reckoning navigating, if he had only to plot the straight lines of the base course.

In his straightforward way he had voiced these thoughts to Commander Turney, bluntly suggesting that they request permission of the escort commander to discontinue zigzagging. Annoyed, Turney had refused. Under Navy rules the senior officer was the one who determined what action to take, and no orders had been received from him, he told Grindley, therefore unless and until he received orders they would continue to zigzag.

Grindley understood his commanding officer quite well. Those needling messages earlier still rankled, and Turney had no intention of stepping out of line and giving the flagship the opportunity to further humiliate him in front of his crew.

Once again the vast difference between the U. S. Navy and the merchant Navy was brought home to Grindley. A merchant Navy skipper would not have been hidebound by regulations; he would have spit on regulations, and on the whole Atlantic Fleet, if there was even the hint of danger where his own ship was concerned.

What did the Commander Destroyers, Atlantic Fleet, sitting behind his gleaming desk, know about steaming through dangerous waters in a storm at sea? How could they lay down such rigid laws that took a man's initiative away from him? It was beyond Grindley. Exercising constraint over his own irritation, he leaned over the chart.

Both Turney and Grindley had been relieved when at 1800 hours definite radio direction-finder bearings confirmed their 2000-hour dead-reckoning position at latitude 45°28′00″N, longitude 57°03′00″W. The bearings had been just clear enough to establish their position, and it had eased the tension slightly, even if dead reckoning was an educated guess.

At 1900 hours visibility had decreased to about 700 yards, and the wind, blowing at force 5, was hurling icy bullets of spray over the bridge. Quartermaster Strauss had been called to the chartroom, where Commander Turney and Lieutenant Grindley had discussed the approach to Placentia Bay. It would be sound navigational judgment to reduce speed at that point, Grindley had suggested; it was what they had done before when approaching Placentia Bay in foggy weather. Commander Turney had agreed and wrote on a piece of paper: "Suggest we reduce speed to eight knots until visibility improves." Then, before he passed it to Strauss to transmit, he had changed his mind and torn the message to shreds. "Better not," he said. "The *Wilkes* seems to be making all the suggestions."

The *Pollux* rolled on. Strauss and the rest of the lookouts rotating on the wings had squinted against the wind, snow, and spume, watching to make sure they didn't run into the *Wilkes* or the *Truxtun*. Wretchedly and unspeakably cold, Strauss was torn between keeping a good lookout to avoid collision or hoping they would collide and go down and get the misery over with quickly.

During the compass checks, which had to be entered in the logbook, Strauss was in and out of the chartroom, where the tension between the captain and the navigator was becoming quite unbearable. Once Strauss heard a snatch of the conversation as Grindley maintained that very possibly there were standing into danger. Commander Turney was obviously angry at finding himself in a situation over which he felt he had no control, and being under constant pressure from his navigator to do something about it. Strauss felt sorry for both men, and angry at the flagship. If they had been left on their own it would have been smooth sailing, storm or no storm.

He left the charthouse with its overpowering tensions and returned to the wings.

Lieutenant Russell Schmidt had taken over the 2000 duty watch. Quartermaster First Class Harold E. Brooks relieved Strauss. "You're in for one hell of a watch," Strauss had told him and went thankfully below to the cafeteria to thaw out before crawling into his bunk.

They approached St. Pierre Bank, which was their only opportunity to fix their position absolutely, but there was a problem of fathometer soundings. Submarines could pick up radiations from the fathometer, and the *Pollux* was under instruction not to use it.

Grindley felt they *must* use it. "It's our only opportunity to find out where we are, sir, and the radiation from the ship is very little, possibly only five miles," he said.

Commander Turney bent the rules a little and ordered the fathometer on. "Keep it running," he told the operator. Then he "caught an hour" on his cabin transom adjacent to the charthouse. There was no question of rest for Grindley. He was a weary man, but he had many hours to go before docking in Argentia.

Being roughly 3,700 yards (2 miles) behind the *Wilkes* and the *Truxtun* in the formation, the *Pollux* crossed the south edge of St. Pierre Bank well behind the *Wilkes,* and Grindley labored over the soundings as the operator passed them along. He knew that, once they dropped off the north edge of the St. Pierre Bank, it would be faith alone that would lead them safely into Placentia Bay. Because of their speed, and because of great depth, uniform bottom, and shoaling close to shore, soundings from. St. Pierre Bank to Placentia Bay were less than satisfactory for navigational purposes. In depths over 50 fathoms the speed of the vessel would have to be reduced to 5 or 6 knots in order for the fathometer to pick up an echo accurately.

Grindley worked diligently over the chart, endeavoring to correct the zigzag course for leeway as the *Pollux* steamed across the Bank. The zigzag made it difficult to get an accurate speed check and course made good, which was regrettable, since it was their only opportunity to chart their course with accuracy, had they been steaming in a straight line.

Turney, back in the charthouse, was pacing between the fathometer and the chart table when Grindley again requested, "Sir, I strongly recommend that we discontinue this zigzagging."

Again Commander Turney refused.

Grindley understood the captain's dilemma, but it did not lessen the danger that might be ahead.

As usual, with adverse climatic conditions, the RDF bearings were coming in poorly, the "null" area was getting broader as they steamed farther north and away from the sending stations.

Heavy seas were hitting the *Pollux* on the starboard beam. Grindley repeatedly went out to the wing of the bridge to get the gauge of the wind and the sea for leeway purposes. It was next to impossible to correct the course for drift by adding leeway as long as she continued to zigzag. It was just a hit-or-miss quantity.

Commander Turney was like a cat on hot bricks, and Grindley had that gut feeling that all was not well.

Goddamn Navy regulations, he thought.

5

At 2330 hours there was a knock on the door of Lieutenant Smyth's compartment. Smyth, fully clothed, lay on the bunk sound asleep. His eyes opened automatically.

"Yes?"

"Time to relieve the watch, sir." The voice of the quartermaster was pitched above the clamor of ship, wind, and sea.

"Thank you."

Here we go again, Smyth thought as he swung his legs over the bunk and planted them hard on the deck to keep from being flung against the bulkhead. God, he was tired. How he wished he could get just one good night's sleep for a change; even a shower would be a blessing, but there was no time for a shower. There was never any time for a shower. With the many duties assigned to him, there was never enough time to sleep. Sometimes he felt he could sleep the clock around.

He sat for a moment, mentally collecting his energies. Was there anything worse in this man's Navy than standing watch in the wild North Atlantic in winter? There was not! Convoy work was dreary, tiresome, and hard and, in his estimation, there were not enough officers aboard the *Wilkes* to man the ship properly. If only the skipper would put Wolsieffer on the watch list occasionally, the rest of us could ease up a bit, he thought. It bothered him that Wolsieffer, as gunnery officer, good shipmate, and all as he was, did not have to stand even an occasional deck watch or assist in training the newly assigned "red asses."[1] Wolsieffer's manning the fire-control tower wasn't doing much good in this kind of weather; the use of No. 2 gun in this storm would be relatively ineffective against a U-boat attack. Oh well, no use wasting precious energy thinking about it.

Bracing himself against the violent motions of the ship, he splashed cold water on his face. He had written a request to return to active flight status the day after Pearl Harbor, and by this time he should have been back in the States taking a quick refresher course. Had Commander Kelsey forwarded it to Washington via the chain of command? Perhaps he doesn't want a new engineer and OOD. I'll have to talk turkey with him next time we put into Boston, he thought.[2]

He really couldn't blame the skipper. As soon as they trained the kids, the powers-that-be pulled them off the ship and transferred them to the many new ships going down the launching ways, leaving only a small core of experienced OOD's. On the *Wilkes,* that boiled down to Hughlett and himself, and they were the ones who had to train the new kids in the duties of the deck watch. His whole life, it seemed, was one round of watch-keeping with snatches of sleep and hastily eaten food.

He reached for his foul-weather gear.[3] God, how I hate this perpetual freezing cold weather, this pitching, rolling deck, and the dreary routine.

Smyth squared his shoulders, thinking, maybe I'll pick up a U-boat tonight and have a chance to make a quick sonar depth-charge attack or ram her on the surface. What the hell, it all counts in twenty.[4]

As the officer of the deck, Smyth's primary job was to hunt subs by sonar, maintain station on the *Pollux,* and follow the designated zigzag plan. It demanded exposure on the wings of the bridge in freezing weather, constant checking of the helm personally for course and speed, alertness for blinker-tube signals, adherence to darkened-ship regulations, frequent reminders to subordinates to

[1] Newly graduated officers.

[2] Smyth's request had been forwarded and approved on January 28, with the notation that no qualified relief was available to relieve him aboard the *Wilkes* before June 1, 1942. He had not been so notified to this time.

[3] Heavy padded windproof clothing.

[4] An expression used to indicate retirement after twenty years' active service.

check below decks, communication with the engine room pertinent to conditions below and so forth, and general supervision of all watch-standers.

Normally, hot coffee was provided in the wardroom for officers going on duty, but tonight there was no coffee; the storm and the *Wilkes'* wild rolling effectively blocked that little comfort. He went out on deck. Snow and a bone-chilling wind knifed at him. Another one of those nights, he thought as he climbed the ladder to the bridge. He gripped the handrails firmly, still feeling the effects of a fall a month before when icy decks had sent him crashing on his back against the coaming guarding the entryway to the bridge.

He entered the lighted charthouse with its light locks that plunged the room into darkness when the door opened. "Good evening, men."

They chorused, "Evening, sir."

Smyth picked up the captain's night order book. Let's see what's in store for us tonight, he thought. Hmmm. Base course 047°, one and three boilers on the line, maintain zigzag Plan 26 on starboard bow of the *Pollux* . . . we're to cross the 50-fathom line about 0130; let's see, that puts us at the 100-fathom mark at 0420 hours.

He studied the chart, noted the ship's present position. O.K.! DRT working? Yep. The dead-reckoning tracer computed and recorded the ship's track on the chart, combining the effects of speed and changes of course and transmitting them to a drafting machine with a tracing pen that inked the course made good. There was a drawback with the DRT: It did not give the true path of the ship during a turn, and with seven turns in each hour because of the zigzag, these inaccuracies had to be taken into consideration.

Smyth noted that Toughie Barrett had prepared a soundings record for the quartermaster to check the track and had added a notation for the QM to check the anticipated time of crossing the 50-fathom curve, and he had a call in for 0300. Well, he thought, just another routine watch; neither the skipper nor the navigator were about, so everything was normal on this landfall. Now his prime concern was to keep the men on their toes, lend an encouraging word in this stinking weather, set the usual example by freezing out in the wings, let young Quekemeyer do his below-decks inspections, and try to keep station on the *Pollux* while looking for the U-boats that had been reported. I sure would like to get a crack at the bastards, he thought grimly.

Smyth memorized the ship's prospective track as laid down by the navigator, and the anticipated hourly positions of the ship during the 0000–0400 watch, as well as all recognizable signals likely to be used during his watch, because he knew he would not be able to re-enter the charthouse during his watch. He would have to remain in control of the conn[5] at all times because he could not afford to entrust bridge operations to Quekemeyer at this stage of his training—not with the threat of submarines and a ship that had to be watched closely.

A note at the bottom of the page stated: "After 0400 attempt to pick up land with radar range at about 20 miles." Well, he thought, that will be Winslow's watch.

No other navigation objects with which to obtain a fix were expected to be sighted during the midwatch, or until Cape St. Mary's light, on the east side of Placentia Bay, which should be sighted at 0530. There was a supplement to night orders concerning low visibility: "In extremely low visibility, close in[6] as necessary to maintain contact."

O.K.! Will do.

Having familiarized himself with the night orders, Smyth initialed it, bracing himself against the tall desk. *Damn!* This bucket never stands still. All right, Smyth, let's get on with it.

After a whole month his back still hurt, and he hoped the wild movements of the ship tonight would not further aggravate it.

He entered the dark, cold pilothouse. Here and on the exposed wings is where he would spend the entire watch. "Hughlett?"

Hughlett replied, "Over here, Chief."

Smyth said formally, "Ready to relieve you, sir."

Just as formally, Hughlett replied, "Base course 047° true, standard speed 15 knots, 139 rpm's adhering to zigzag Plan 26, maintaining station on the starboard bow of the *Pollux*. Boilers one and three in use for steaming purposes. Rough seas, visibility poor."

Smyth asked: "Have you had any difficulty in maintaining station on the *Pollux?*"

"No particular difficulty, although according to the operator she's

[5] To direct the helmsman in the steering of the ship.
[6] On the *Pollux*.

behaved erratically at times. We'd been maintaining station about 2,000 yards on her bow by radar, but the next time I checked station by radar, she suddenly opened up to 3,700 yards. You'll have to watch her."

"O.K.," Smyth said. Midway through his duty watch last night the *Pollux* had kept them on their toes. Instead of continuing the zigzag plan in sequence as laid down for the second hour, she had shifted back to the first hour of the zigzag plan. He had tried to signal her to find out what hour of the plan she was following, but after two attempts he had discontinued because of orders for darkened-ship conditions. He had resumed position by radar and kept a wary eye on her throughout the rest of his watch. He had reasoned that it could have been an error of the OOD of the *Pollux* (or whoever was at the conn) in misreading the hour, minute of the hour, and course change for that hour. Errors happened. It looked like he was in for more of the same tonight.

"Are the skipper and Toughie tucked in?" he asked.

"Yeah," Hughlett replied; "they left about a half hour ago. Kelsey is in the sea cabin and Barrett is below."

All was running smoothly. Smyth said: "I'm going to take a turn around the bridge for a couple of minutes until I get my night vision."

"O.K."

He ducked outside, checking the wings and signal bridge. His green crew were now taking over the watch; lonely young sentinels, already chilled by the biting wind and automatically stamping their feet as frozen splinters of spray and sleet hit them like ice needles. *God! It was cold!* Throughout the watch he would rotate those kids. Keep them rooted in the one place too long and they would lose their effectiveness, such as it was. Signalman Second Class Carl W. Schmidt, a veteran of the Navy, was relieving the signalman of the previous watch; Schmidt would also assist the young lookouts.

Smyth glanced down aft and, with his night vision improving, noted the outline of the hatch cover that now extended to the engine and firerooms. That had been done in December for the benefit of his engine-room crew in order to offset the very real danger of their being washed overboard in heavy seas when entering and leaving the engine room.

First and foremost Smyth was the engineering officer; keeping the ship afloat and operational was his primary mission; the admiration between Smyth and his men was mutual. What a wonderful gang they were.

From the port wing he searched for signs of the *Pollux* and the *Truxtun,* but even with his keen eyesight he could not see beyond the curtain of snow. It looks as though we'll have to depend on radar tonight, he thought.

He went back to the pilothouse. "O.K., I've got my night vision. I relieve you, sir."

Hughlett left and with him went the men of his watch. Smyth had his copy of the zigzag plan tacked to the chart desk in the pilothouse. He would consult it with a small pencil flashlight, suitably shielded, whenever they had to change course. The helmsman had one tacked above the wheel.

Quartermaster Americo Nolfi was in the charthouse, ready to log the fathometer readings every fifteen minutes. His duties were to take care of the quartermaster logs, see that the different officers were properly awakened at the required times, help the officer of the deck, and take compass checks.

In the radar and sonar room aft of the chartroom, Gustav Edward Gabriel, sound operator, sat at the fathometer. His one order on this watch was to take fathometer readings every fifteen minutes. There were no instructions to report the soundings. James R. McPherson, seaman first class, had orders to operate the radar a half hour out of every hour to take bearings on the *Pollux* and the *Truxtun.* The only other special orders were the captain's standing night orders, which stipulated that they were to make any unusual reports to the emergency cabin.

In the radio shack beneath the radar room Ruppert F. Armstrong, radioman first class, sat before the communications system. His chief function tonight was to try to get radio direction-finder bearings.

On the bridge with Smyth was the junior officer of the deck (JOOD), Ensign Henry Quekemeyer, a new graduate of the U. S. Naval Academy. Quekemeyer, aged twenty-three, was of medium height and slender build. Alert, friendly, eager to learn, and attentive to orders, he was good future officer material. As a newly fledged officer, he was, Smyth thought, a little unsure of himself, but because he was so eager to learn, Smyth had more or less taken him under his wing. However, as the chief engineer, he was busy with keeping the plant operational and could only instruct Quekemeyer during the watch.

Although this was Quekemeyer's second trip to Argentia, it was his first under adverse weather conditions; he was still inexperienced in sea duty, a red ass. He was impressed with Smyth more than the other officers because he was the only officer of the deck to outline definite duties. He invariably gave Henry a check-off list and made sure he performed these duties. He felt a genuine admiration for the lieutenant, who seemed impervious to the wintry blasts of ocean wind. Henry himself could not take the cold as Smyth could.

In the gloom of the pilothouse, Quekemeyer waited for his orders. Smyth, pacing back and forth, glancing at the gyrocompass, and mentally noting that the helmsman was holding the ship on course, told the JOOD: "O.K., Quekemeyer, you will see that soundings are taken every fifteen minutes and logged in the quartermaster's log. You will see that radar is operated one half hour out of every hour. See that bearings are taken on Cape Race and Gallantry Head at 2400 hours and at 0200 hours, and you will make a duplicate of zig-zag Plan 26 in case this one I am using gets lost or wet. You will also check the barometer and temperature and see that the lookouts on the bridge are alert at all times."

"Yes, sir," Quekemeyer said.

"You've read the night orders, haven't you?"

Quekemeyer replied smartly, "Yes, sir."

Still pacing, Smyth said, "Well, I don't want you to think I'm treating you like a moron. It's just good practice to always check your JOOD in his responsibilities. Remember this when you qualify to stand top watch."

"Yes, sir, I understand, sir."

"Incidentally, when you make your below-deck inspection, watch your step using the ladders and the exposed decks. In this kind of weather we're ripe for icing conditions and you might lose your footing. There isn't much we can do about it except exercise care. Now, let's get cracking!"

"Yes, sir."

It was still a few minutes before midnight when Quekemeyer passed the order to Armstrong: "Lieutenant Smyth says you're to take bearings on Cape Race and Gallantry Head at twelve o'clock."

Armstrong went into action and Quekemeyer waited.

At 0008 hours Gabriel, assistant to Nolfi, took the first fathometer reading and called: "Thirty-seven fathoms."

Seaman First Class Connolly, still in the charthouse, although off duty from the previous watch, wrote it in the logbook:

Time: 0008   37 fathoms

He said to Gabriel: "Lieutenant Barrett expects the 50-fathom curve will be crossed at 0138."

"O.K.," Gabriel said.

The *Wilkes* buried her bow in white water as she plunged into another wave. Smyth, propping himself against the wing, peered through the driving snow. In this period when radar was not operating, a sharp lookout to port was his main concern. He had no wish to have the *Wilkes* find itself in the path of the *Pollux*.

At 0015 Quekemeyer reported to him: "Armstrong couldn't get any bearings, sir; he says the distance is too great to Cape Race; atmospheric conditions are unfavorable. In fact, sir, he says it won't be any better at 0200."

This news did not surprise Smyth. Past experience had shown him that ranges of any RDF installations varied according to atmospheric conditions, but he said, "Nevertheless, night orders must be carried out, Quekemeyer. See that he tries again at 0200."

"Yes, sir. Incidentally, here's the duplicate of the zigzag plan."

"Thanks." Smyth took it and placed it in his pocket, paced to the port wing. Quekemeyer followed, shivering. "The weather is terrible. Is it always like this, sir?"

"Not always; sometimes it's worse," Smyth told him with grim humor, "but you'll get acclimatized in another crossing or two. I don't think you'll like it, though."

Quekemeyer was sure he wouldn't.

"The important thing is to keep moving and keep your own lookout not only on station, but also to seek out the U-boats." His eyes were trying to penetrate the snow streaking out of the night. He could barely make out the dim figures braced against the ship. "Remember, Quekemeyer, these youngsters acting as lookouts are just kids fresh out of boot camp. They don't have their sea legs and some of them are scared, but they'll make good sailors in due time. Always take good care of your men and you'll discover they'll respond."

"Yes, sir," Quekemeyer said.

"Don't forget that loyalty 'down' is as important as loyalty 'up.' Now, stay out here while I go into the pilothouse to make a change of course in our zigzag plan. It's about that time."

While Smyth checked the zigzag plan with his shielded pencil flashlight and issued orders to the helmsman, Gabriel, in the chartroom, started up the fathometer and took more soundings. Connolly was gone, so Nolfi entered it in the logbook:

Time: 0023   52 fathoms

It did not register with Gabriel or Nolfi that sometime between 0008 and 0023 the *Wilkes* had crossed the 50-fathom curve, which she was not scheduled to cross until approximately 0138. If either one had studied the chart, they would have seen that the ship had crossed an area of the St. Pierre Bank north of their dead-reckoning track where it was much narrower and much closer to land, and would have realized that their ship was off course. There had been no specific instructions as to its importance, therefore no report of it was made to Smyth, who was standing behind the helmsman in the pilothouse waiting for the ship to come steady on course after finishing the left leg of the zigzag. Quekemeyer was in and out of the charthouse.

Since the record of soundings was for the navigator's use, Smyth was not giving any thought to them. According to the dead-reckoning track, they were more than forty miles from land, and he had given young Quekemeyer instructions about bearings and soundings. If anything out of the ordinary happened, Quekemeyer would certainly notify him.

Smyth returned to the bitter cold of the wings after about five minutes and sent Quekemeyer about his duties inside.

At 0030 hours MacPherson started radar, swept, and recorded:

Pollux bearing 295° true—4,700 yards.

Truxtun bearing 335° true—5,000 yards.

He reported the bearings to Smyth.

Smyth did not need to check the points of the compass to know exactly where the *Pollux* was. The formation was good, but she should have been only 2,000 to 3,000 yards from them. Hughlett is right, he thought, the *Pollux* is meandering all over the ocean. But the *Truxtun* too? Radar must be malfunctioning. In any case, he had better close the *Pollux* and try to establish visual contact. He or-

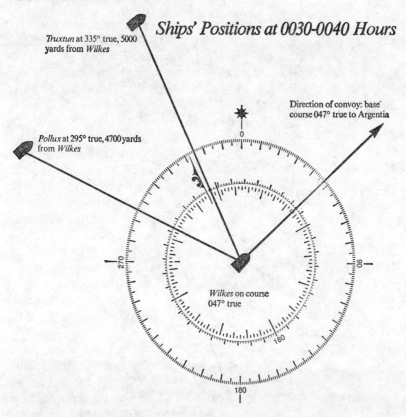

Ships' Positions at 0030-0040 Hours

Truxtun at 335° true, 5000 yards from *Wilkes*

Pollux at 295° true, 4700 yards from *Wilkes*

Direction of convoy: base course 047° true to Argentia

Wilkes on course 047° true

Bearings in the diagram show positions of the *Pollux* and the *Truxtun* in relation to the *Wilkes* from which radar waves emanated and, therefore, do not show the zigzag course as such. Land at this stage (to the north) is beyond the range of radar.

dered the helmsman to come left 10° to gradually close on the *Pollux* at a distance of 2,000 to 3,000 yards.

What with the continual changing of course for the zigzag, Smyth was in and out of the pilothouse. Occasionally the snow ceased and visibility increased slightly. The wind, still force 7, showed no sign of abating as it whistled shrilly through the halyards and around the superstructure. The seas were really pummeling the *Wilkes* as she drove onward; white water lifted over her bow, rushed about the

Ships' Positions at 0105-0120 Hours

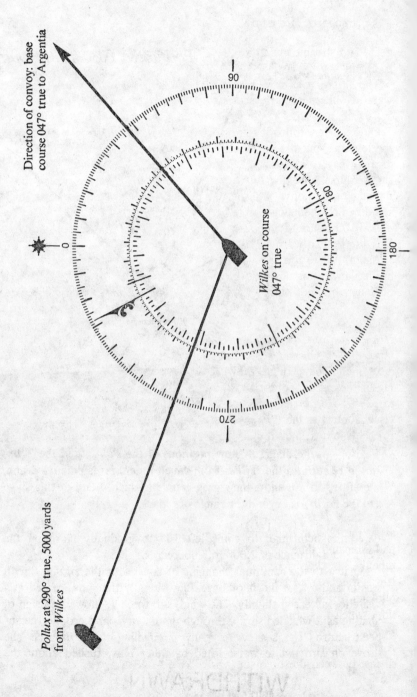

Direction of convoy: base course 047° true to Argentia

Wilkes on course 047° true

Pollux at 290° true, 5000 yards from Wilkes

deck, and streamed over her sides. Smyth noticed she was beginning to ice up.

The *Wilkes* was now beyond the bank and heading into deeper water. Nolfi recorded the soundings:

Time: 0108   85 fathoms

Quekemeyer, following orders, made sure they were recorded in the logbook, but it escaped his notice that the deeper soundings indicated they had passed the 50-fathom curve. Smyth, busy with the ship's course, checking the rpm's, was constantly on the move in the darkened pilothouse and on the wings. Quekemeyer returned to stand behind the helmsman in the pilothouse.

At 0105 hours McPherson started radar, and at 0120 reported to Smyth: "Pollux bearing 290°, distance about 5,000 yards, sir."

Again? We're too far out, Smyth thought as McPherson returned inside. Smyth was not worried about the *Truxtun,* which McPherson obviously had not picked up on radar. Her position was on the port bow of the *Pollux;* she would be there somewhere. The *Pollux* as guide ship was his main concern. She was well within the bearing range as ordered by Commander Kelsey but she was twice the distance that she should be. He went into the pilothouse to the rpm indicator and reduced speed about two knots. They were on the left lag of the zigzag, course 077°, and Smyth ordered: "Come left 30° to 337°." He hurried to the port wing to keep a sharp lookout for visual contact as the *Wilkes* steamed on an intercepting course.

Five minutes later the *Pollux* loomed up unexpectedly at about 2,000 yards. Damn, we closed fast, Smyth thought and stuck his head inside the pilothouse. "Come right 30° to course 007. Quekemeyer, ring up 139 rpm's," he bellowed.

"Aye aye, sir," both men chorused and hurriedly followed orders.

As the *Wilkes* opened up, Smyth returned to the port wing looking aft at the *Pollux.* Had she actually been 5,000 yards away, as radar had indicated? She appeared to be signaling the *Truxtun* by blinker tube; he saw the *Truxtun* replying by blinker light. He had to assume it was the *Truxtun* because through the snow he saw the light only, blinking from the approximate position of the *Truxtun* in the formation, which was about three points forward of the port beam of the *Wilkes.*

He was alert and annoyed. They should not have closed the *Pollux* so fast between the time she was reported by radar at 5,000 yards

and the time she loomed up at 2,000 yards. McPherson had given him readings that were *in excess* of the actual distance by at least 1,000 yards. He'd have to warn him to be more careful with ranges and bearings.

Because of the secrecy surrounding radar, no one aboard the *Wilkes* was aware of its unreliability under weather conditions such as these. Smyth, therefore, felt that it had to be the fault of the relatively green sailor operating it.

He entered the pilothouse and spoke into the voice tube: "McPherson!"

"Yes, sir?"

"Keep a sharper eye on the radar. Especially on the *Pollux*. We should not have closed her so fast."

"Yes, sir."

They had to get back on station. He rang up 145 rpm's to increase speed, and at 0125 hours, back on station, at the designated zigzag course, he reduced revolutions to 139 and returned to the port wing to keep a weather eye on the *Pollux*.

In the radar room, Nolfi had recorded in the log:

Time: 0123   89 fathoms

The *Wilkes* had plenty of water under her keel.

6

It was blowing a gale. The wind, howling through the rigging, spun the snow in a wild pirouette around the bridge, intensifying the unutterable discomfort of the lookouts as the *Pollux* rolled severely. In the charthouse the tension had not eased. According to the soundings, they were slightly northward of their track; not much, but enough to keep Lieutenant Grindley glued to the fathometer and the chart, and to keep Commander Turney pacing nervously. The radio direction finder was useless, and Grindley had tried to gauge their drift from the ship's wings, staring down at the white water creaming against her side. It had not helped. If only they could cease zigzagging, he thought.

The watch changed before midnight, with Ensign Robert Henry "Tex" Grayson, senior officer of the deck, taking over from Lieutenant Schmidt. The skipper and the navigator were trying to determine the ship's position by the readings obtained from the fathometer, which was running continuously. He studied the course. The dead-reckoning track 047° true, according to his calculations, would take them approximately twenty miles off the west side of Placentia Bay and off Cape St. Mary's, on the eastern side, by about twenty-five miles.

Grayson had always attempted to set his own position and check it against the more competent authority of the navigator, and to learn by doing it. Now Grayson matched the fathometer readings with the soundings given on the chart and decided they were to the left of the DR track by about three miles. They appeared to be skirting the little gully that intruded into the St. Pierre Bank, north of their dead-reckoning track.

He said to Grindley: "Is this right, Mr. Grindley?"

If they had not been on duty they would have addressed each other as "Bill" and "Tex." On the bridge was a different matter. Grindley was a little brusque. "That is our position to the best of my calculations, Mr. Grayson." Whatever the difference of opinion between himself and Turney, it would not officially get to the watch.

Grayson went on the bridge, and Grindley continued to work on the plot of their St. Pierre Bank crossing. Turney took time from his pacing to send an order to the gun crews to take shelter inside. "Tell them they must keep on the alert," he said.

Laurence A. Weaver, Jr., storekeeper second class, unmarried and happy that way, was a member of the gun crew of the five-inch gun mounted on the stern of the *Pollux.* He had drawn gun watch from 2400 to 0400, and was quickly numbed by the biting wind and the sleet and snow. Weaver, at age thirty, was another "old" man of the Navy, and he had been a *Pollux* man from the time she had been commissioned.

As the sea hurled icy spray at him, Weaver could not help but reflect what a small world it was. Somewhere up front off the port bow was the *Truxtun* and his lifelong friend, Lieutenant (jg) James Ross Gillie. They had grown up together, gone to Yale together. Gillie had stuck it out and graduated as an ensign. Weaver had not finished. Instead he had joined the merchant Navy for a short time before joining the U. S. Navy, 1st Battalion, 3rd Division of the New York Naval Militia.

He had last seen Gillie on Pearl Harbor Day. The *Pollux,* a very relaxed and easy ship, had been in Boston, and Weaver, on liberty that day, had hitched a ride to Andover where he had bumped into his old friend Gillie and his wife, Betsy. Not having seen each other for a long while, they had spent the day together. Weaver's girlfriend's name was Betsy too, but he had not gotten around to popping the question, even though they had been going together for more than five years. Gillie, he had learned, was assigned to the USS *Truxtun.*

That happy, relaxed day neither of them had heard the news of the
Japanese attack on Pearl Harbor, and when Weaver returned to his
ship he had found it changed altogether. They were officially at war,
and the *Pollux* bristled with guards carrying guns.

From time to time since they had gone out through the submarine
gates at Casco Bay and were met by the *Truxtun* and the *Wilkes* two
days ago, Weaver had tried with binoculars to spot his old friend on
the deck of the *Truxtun*. He had not been successful. Never mind,
they would meet in Argentia, he thought.

Weaver and the other men of the gun watch hung on as the *Pollux*
bucked and rolled; steep seas reared over her. The guns, they discovered, were iced up; the deck was iced up. *God! What a night.*

A seaman appeared. "The captain says you can all come forward
into a protected area, but you have to remain on the alert."

God bless the captain!

The gun watch thankfully clambered off the platform and sought
shelter inside the superstructure. The supply office was just off the
passageway, and Weaver stretched out on the deck beside his own
desk.

Aboard the USS *Truxtun* there were no lookouts stationed forward of the bridge this night because they were taking heavy seas
over the forecastle and it was snowing heavily. The young lookouts
were more efficient on the wings of the bridge, where there was some
protection from flying spray and rushing seas. There had been no
communication with either of the other ships since the message at
1740 hours permitting them to take any convenient position. It was
dangerous to zigzag without being able to fix a position on the guide
ship and, not having radar, the *Truxtun* had ceased zigzagging at
nightfall. By estimating the speed and course of the *Pollux,* they felt
they were still in position on her port bow.

Ensign William Maddocks, assistant engineer and OOD for the
2400-to-0400-hours watch, was prepared for an unpleasant but routine night on the bridge. The officer of the previous watch had told
him there were no lights or land or ships in sight. They had been trying to keep station on the *Pollux* with the sound gear, which had a
listening and an echo-ranging effect. "We had a contact at 2300
hours; we could hear her propellers on the starboard quarter, so
we're pretty well staying in position."

He had shown Maddocks where they were on the chart. Their track was laid out to go right up the middle of Placentia Bay. The 0400 hours dead-reckoning position was expected to be approximately twenty-five miles southeast of Ferryland Head, that last promontory at the entrance to Placentia Bay.

Maddocks read the night orders, noting that the navigator had left orders to be called at 0200 hours and that the radioman was to run the RDF continuously from 0200. Captain Hickox was down in his stateroom for a cup of coffee, but would be taking the 0000–0200 hours watch as usual.

With no fathometer aboard, they had no means by which they could take soundings. They were traveling too fast to use the hand lead, and could only estimate their position by adhering to the base course; therefore Captain Hickox would only be able to estimate the time of crossing the St. Pierre Bank. Nor would he have any way of knowing they were north of their track and about to drop off the north end of the Bank an hour early.

It became much rougher and the *Truxtun* rolled madly, burying her nose under water. The crew on No. 1 gun on the forecastle was ordered to shift the watch amidships on the galley deck on guns Nos. 2 and 3, which were aft of the bridge and a level above the main deck.

The crew thankfully did as they were ordered.

Between 0020 and 0030 (zone plus-4 time), fathometer recorder soundings indicated that the *Pollux* had crossed the 50-fathom curve, dropping off the bank, not into 70 fathoms of water as the plotted dead-reckoning track required, but into 60-fathom depths. They had crossed the St. Pierre Bank an hour ahead of schedule at a narrower track, northward. Soundings indicated that the ship was on the other side of the little gully intruding into the bank, and was now 5 miles northwest of its plotted base track. They had been set 11° to the northwest crossing the St. Pierre Bank—a very dangerous rate of drift.

Commander Turney studied the plot that Grindley had been tracing on the chart. "There must be a small current setting up into the Cabot Strait," Turney observed.

Grindley agreed.

The coast pilot indicated that at times there were westerly currents through the St. Pierre Bank. Even if there was no current, Grindley knew that it was not unusual in low visibility, when navigating by soundings only, to be a little ahead or behind the scheduled crossing of a 100- or 50-fathom curve, or to be a little off course. It was a fact of life, when one did not have landmarks or star sights to navigate by. So taking it all into consideration it wasn't too unusual, in the circumstances, to find that they were where they had not expected to be.

The *Pollux* was following a course that would carry her, not up the center of the mouth of Placentia Bay, 20 miles off land, but west of the center about 12 miles from land—still a good, safe course. Yet, those alarm bells were ringing in Grindley's head as he continued to plot the course made good from subsequent soundings. It quickly became evident that all was not well. As far as he was concerned, the *Pollux* was making just about as much sideways as ahead. Very basic dead-reckoning navigation indicated that unless drastic changes were made, they were heading for a pile-up on the west side of Placentia Bay entrance, as sure as God made little green apples. A course change to 87° or 90° would put the *Pollux*'s head into the drift to westward and take her to safety, but a 180° turnaround would solve all their problems.

He laid it on the line to Commander Turney: "We have been set 11° to the northwest, sir. I recommend that we reverse course and get the hell out of here."

The previous fall, when they had been traveling alone on one of their trips to Argentia in stormy weather, they had anchored one night on St. Pierre Bank. Grindley now urged: "We can return to St. Pierre Bank and cruise around until daylight, and then make our approach to Placentia Bay."

It was what any merchant-vessel master would have done.

Turney was obviously torn by the recommendations of his navigator. If they had been on their own Turney would have been the sole authority and could have readily accepted Grindley's recommendations; but it had been made clear from the beginning of the voyage that the *Wilkes* laid down the courses and made all their decisions and, unless she designated a new course, Turney felt bound by Navy regulations to follow. If he had been given freedom earlier in the day to change course for navigational reasons, there was another reason why he hesitated to do so now: The flagship, with her experienced Annapolis men, her navigational aids, and the magic of radar, had given no indication that they were in any danger.

"It is not possible," he stated. "Besides, if the *Wilkes* thought we were standing into danger they would surely warn us."

Both men were overly tired. Grindley had been on duty for more than twenty straight hours. Turney had been on for seventeen hours. Tempers were short. Grindley flared: "Hell, sir, we haven't seen the *Wilkes* in nearly eight hours."

It didn't matter, Turney snapped, the *Wilkes* had radar, and radar would keep them out of trouble. If they were in trouble, the *Wilkes* would notify them.

"I don't agree with you, sir. The *Wilkes'* radar will be iced up in this weather, the land masses will be iced up, the radar bounce will be very inefficient—two miles at best."

As secret as radar was to the U. S. Navy personnel, Grindley was familiar with it, having seen it in Canadian and British combat ships before being called into the Navy. In January 1940, in Takoradi, Gold Coast, British West Africa, the British heavy cruiser *Yorkshire,* searching for the *Admiral Scheer,* had come into port to fuel up and had offered free-gangway to the crew members of the ship Grindley was on, and they had had a good look at radar and had been told of its drawbacks.

Turney remained adamant.

The gut feeling of danger was stronger than ever with Grindley. The radio direction-finder bearings were useless and, he thought, it was the same old story about electronic navigational aids: The greater your need for them, the more poorly they performed. They had the latest model of Kolister RDF, the very latest on the market, and it still did not seem to function properly.

Commander Turney scowled as the static crackled through the receiver. "Why," he wanted to know, "is there so much static?"

"Because," Grindley told him, "our angle from the sending stations does not make a good triangulation."

"Can't you tune out the static?"

"Hell, I didn't design the damn thing, sir."

In spite of the worry and certainty that they were heading into danger, Grindley felt sorry for Commander Turney. The man was in a tight spot. It *was* a serious offense to break convoy. He might be the skipper of the *Pollux,* but there were many superiors in every port to question his authority, and his career could very well be in jeopardy. But, goddamnit, if Turney's career was in jeopardy, *so was his own.*

It would be presumptuous of him indeed to remind Commander Turney about the message from the *Wilkes* that had given them freedom to change course if necessary since the captain was quite aware of it. But Grindley did say, "I strongly recommend a change of course, sir."

Turney again refused. "The whole thing about the Navy, Mr. Grindley, is that you follow orders."

Grindley had never felt so helpless in his life. As the navigator of the *Pollux* it was his job to recommend changes of course when necessary, but each of his recommendations this night had been discarded. He was a blunt man, and once again pointed out that they had been set 11° to the northwest. "I don't know within ten, twelve, fifteen miles where we are, sir," he said, with barely restrained anger, and again recommended a change of course and a discontinuation of the zigzag.

It was a statement of cold, hard fact, and Commander Turney gave it more worry and consideration before capitulating. They would not discontinue the zigzag, but they would change course 10° to the right.

Grindley was not satisfied. "Ten degrees? With the wind and sea pushing us to the northwest? Sir, that's only adding leeway to the course we're steering. We need at least a 30° change in course, and I recommend that we cease zigzagging."

Commander Turney would not do it. Ten degrees allowed for leeway; it was as far as he would go. In effect, he was not really changing course, but allowing 10° to make 047° good. If there really was danger, he repeated, the *Wilkes,* with her radar, would give them plenty of warning.

It was nearing 0130 hours and the *Pollux* was due to steam on base course when he wrote a message for the *Wilkes* on a piece of paper:

Have changed my base course 10° to the right.

Once the message was sent it was up to the flagship to notify the *Truxtun* of the change in base course.

Grindley had done his best. Simmering with frustration, he made up a new zigzag plan for the helmsman to follow on the new course, 057° true.

Although the *Pollux* had been slightly off course when Ensign Grayson came on duty watch, he did not feel that it was anything to worry about, since Commander Turney and Lieutenant Grindley were working on it. Grayson had been aware of the difficulties in obtaining radio compass bearings, but if whispers reached him of the dissension beween the skipper and the navigator he closed his ears to it.

The watch, if not pleasant, was uneventful. The junior officer of the deck, Walter C. Phillips, chief fire controlman, was standing lookout on the wings with other lookouts, and Grayson, too, had remained out in the bitter cold for the most part, rotating the men so they would not be on the weather side of the bridge all the time. They had seen no sign of the *Wilkes* or the *Truxtun,* and did not expect to in the driving snow.

Grayson was in the charthouse when Commander Turney passed him the slip of paper with the message that he was changing course. He said: "We are changing our course to 057° true to allow for leeway. Send this message to the *Wilkes* by visual signal. Use the small blinker gun if possible."

"Yes, sir." Grayson took the slip of paper. He had been on the daylight watch on the morning of the seventeenth when the nudges and prods from the *Wilkes* had been directed at them. He wondered what their reaction would be to this message.

He called to the quartermaster: "Horner!"

Seaman George Horner, who was also in the chartroom, followed Grayson to the starboard wing of the bridge. He was not a full-fledged signalman, but he had been standing signal watch, along with his duties as quartermaster, for about four or five months. He had learned to send and receive blinker signals from other members of the communications division.

The *Wilkes* was supposed to be on their starboard bow, and Horner had to face into the wind and snow. Black mountains of water, streaked with white, reared above them and fell away as the *Pollux* rolled to port. Visibility, Grayson estimated, was only about six hundred yards.

Bracing himself, Horner turned on the blinker gun and swept it back and forth. It brought no response from the *Wilkes*. "I can't find her, sir," he said to Grayson, who was standing by.

"They must be too far away," Grayson answered, and reported back to Commander Turney: "We can't raise the *Wilkes* with the blinker gun, sir."

The skipper and the navigator were still leaning over the chart table. Commander Turney said: "Then use the big light."

Grayson passed the order to Horner. They did not know exactly where the *Wilkes* was, so Grayson said, "Start aft and swing the light forward; we might catch her in that arc."

It was very rough, and he had to hold Horner so the young man could work the searchlight—a twelve-inch light with a cone that had been adjusted to cut the beam down to six inches.

Horner swept the light from the quarter to the beam and flashed the *Wilkes'* call: "*Dog 441.*"

Two points abaft the starboard beam, through the blizzard of snow, a light answered and was followed by the letter K.[1]

Grayson, holding both Horner and the message, shouted above the wind: "Is that the *Wilkes?*"

"Yes, sir," Horner yelled back.

"Are you sure it's the *Wilkes?*"

"Yes, sir; she answered her call and gave me a K to go ahead."

Lifting the young sailor up to the light, Grayson read the first word, which Horner flashed off, then they waited for a dash from the *Wilkes* to signify she had received that word. Grayson was sure a light blinked at them through the storm, and read off each word until the whole message had been sent, every word receipted for by a blinking light from the *Wilkes*. Horner had no difficulty seeing the light, in spite of the snow and the wild motion of the ship, but the *Wilkes* seemed to oscillate. Her light would be bright and then become dim. What was she doing?

They waited for her to acknowledge with a "Roger" to indicate she had received the message. But the *Wilkes* did not acknowledge.

"I didn't get a Roger, Mr. Grayson," Horner yelled.

"Try to reach her again, and get a receipt before entering it in the logbook, Horner."

Grayson fully expected a reply of some sort from the *Wilkes*—

[1] For King, meaning "Go ahead."

either word that she was conforming to their new course or orders to get back to course 047° true, since, it seemed to him, the flagship had laid down every other course.

Horner again tried to contact the *Wilkes,* but there was no answering light. Presently he returned to the charthouse and logged the message, but did not make a notation to the effect that a Roger had not been received.

Grayson returned to the pilothouse and ordered the change in course to 057° true, and when the *Pollux* settled down, he reported it to the captain and the navigator. Grayson also informed them that they had reached the *Wilkes* with the message and had gotten the dash word by word, but no Roger. He laid the piece of paper with the message on the chart table and returned to the pilothouse. As far as all were concerned, the *Wilkes* had received the information that they were changing their base course.

Now began a long, slow converging of courses as the *Wilkes* held to base course 047° true. It would be delayed by zigzagging, but eventually the *Pollux,* on course 057° true, would cross astern of the *Wilkes,* winding up on her starboard side.

On the *Wilkes,* before the attempt to send the message, Lieutenant Smyth, having gotten the ship back on station on the *Pollux,* had returned to the port wing to keep a vigilant eye out for her. At 0130 hours, from his position on the forward end of the wing, he caught sight of the dim intermittent flashing light on the port beam from the direction of the *Pollux.* Was the guide ship signaling them? He was adept at reading signals, and he watched intently, trying to read what message, if any, was being flashed to them, but in the thick snow, the indistinct flashing light made no sense from his position forward on the wing. There was certainly no continuity of communication. He decided to check with the signalman in the aft position of the wing.

Signalman Schmidt had also seen the blinking light from the *Pollux* and picking up the signal gun had answered with a "King." He did not switch off the blinker gun but kept the gun ray trained on the metal shield of the wing. Through the murk and snow and the seas that reared above them when the *Wilkes* fell into a trough, he saw only one flash, either forward or on what he assumed to be the bow of the *Pollux.* He had seen no other flashing light, received no message.

Smyth approached just as he was laying down the signal gun. "Was that the *Pollux?*" he asked.

Schmidt replied, "Yes, sir."

"Have you received a message from the *Pollux?*"

"No, sir, I just exchanged calls."

Smyth was satisfied. Schmidt had been a signalman for four years; if he said it had been an exchange of calls, that is what it was. It was not unusual for ships to exchange calls as a means of identification in low visibility.

The failure of the *Wilkes* to receive this important message about the 10° change in course added to the inevitability of disaster.[2]

To Smyth, the outline of the high-sided hull of the *Pollux* was a blacker imprint on the black night, and he had the distinct impression that they were on the starboard quarter of the *Pollux* instead of the starboard bow, where they were supposed to be. The *Pollux,* he thought, was up to her old tricks.

He ordered more speed and called to McPherson for a radar bearing so that they could regain position. McPherson started radar at 0135 as the *Wilkes* turned on the left leg of the zigzag, and presently reported:

> *Pollux* bearing 310°—4,700 yards
> *Truxtun* bearing 020°—3,200 yards

While the *Pollux* had changed to base course 057° true, she had at this time turned on the left zigzag, which would be 10° less to the northwest. Gradually over the next couple of hours, the vessel would appear more to the southward on the *Wilkes'* radar.

But for the present Smyth was confused by this sudden change of position. Goddamnit! This is incredible, he thought; only five minutes ago I was in visible contact with the *Pollux,* and now we're already out to 4,700 yards on her bow. Either McPherson is still fouling up and reporting erroneous readings or that contraption called radar is not functioning properly. We'll have to check it out in Argentia.

Meanwhile he'd just have to rely on his own instincts and keep a weather eye peeled to avoid collision. The *Pollux,* he thought grimly, was as cantankerous and independent as some of the merchantmen

---

[2] Smyth, with no access to court records or to the findings of the court of inquiry, was not aware of the importance of this message until informed by the author in 1977.

Ships' Positions at 0135-0150 Hours

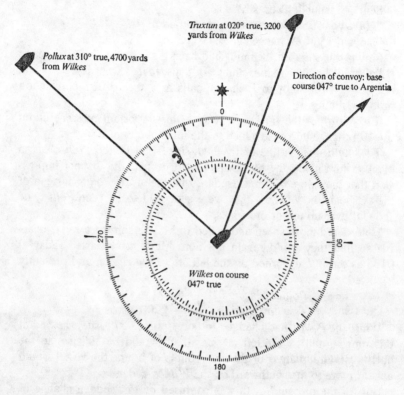

Truxtun at 020° true, 3200 yards from *Wilkes*

Pollux at 310° true, 4700 yards from *Wilkes*

Direction of convoy: base course 047° true to Argentia

0

270

90

Wilkes on course 047° true

180

180

they had escorted across the Atlantic. Many were the times they'd had to call on emergency speeds and abrupt changes of course to avoid collision as they bobbed and weaved in front of, and abeam of, the old hulks they were escorting. Like these old ships, the *Pollux* seemed to be wandering all over the place, and he'd better resign himself to it. He was going to have one hell of a busy watch.

The *Truxtun*, at bearing 020°, was also out of formation, but to signal the other escort ship because she was out of formation was out of the question when she must have complete freedom at all times to maneuver. Now all they needed was for a Nazi bastard to make an appearance. Smyth did not realize that the *Truxtun* had stopped zig-

zagging at nightfall, and therefore whenever they were on a left zigzag when radar bearings were taken, the ship would still be on base
course and would appear to be out of formation.

Spray hurtled across the deck as the wind tore off wavetops and
flung them against the superstructure of the ship. On the starboard
wing the biting wind numbed the faces of the lookouts and seeped
into their cheekbones. Smyth rotated them from the starboard wing
to the more sheltered port wing frequently enough to keep them
alert.

Presently he entered the pilothouse. "Quekemeyer."

From the gloom Quekemeyer replied, "Yes, sir."

"Did you make below-decks inspection?" This was to make sure
no stray lights were showing, and everything else was in top working
order.

"Yes, sir. Everything is shipshape."

"Very well. It's just about time for another RDF bearing."

"Yes, sir," Quekemeyer said, "I was just going to check on
Armstrong."

"Good going. While you're in the chartroom, check to make sure
soundings are being recorded for Mr. Barrett."

"Yes, sir."

Quekemeyer noted that Gabriel and Nolfi were attending to their
duties in the charthouse. At 0138 hours the fathometer had registered 86 fathoms, and Nolfi had jotted it in the logbook where the
notation had been written: *"Expect to hit 50 fathoms."* With no
specific orders about the 50-fathom curve, Nolfi felt he had no
reason to report it.

While Quekemeyer had read about the 50-fathom crossing on
Commander Kelsey's night orders, its importance had made no impression on him; therefore it did not occur to him to check the
logbook or the fathometer, and seeing that all were attending to
their duties, he moved on to Armstrong for the possibility of an RDF
bearing.

Smyth returned to the port wing to keep a sharp lookout. He
dared not forget the likely possibility of a U-boat sneaking up on
them. God, it was cold! He stamped his feet and clapped his hands
to warm them. Occasionally he brushed the snow off his face. The
sea, black and marbled with white, reared above them as the *Wilkes*

rolled over. The wind played the halyards like the strings of a harp, but unlike the harp, it was not a pleasant sound.

The radar bearings that had been reported to him were irksome. He thought: I wish I could take a quick look-see at that screwed-up radar and see for myself exactly what's going on; a couple of minutes inside, out of the wind, would be all right too.

He dared not, of course. Not only would it seriously impair his night vision, which was contrary to orders, but also these kids were still too green to be left on their own at the height of a winter storm, even for a few minutes. As far as Smyth was concerned, they were just bodies; *he* was the real lookout. Schmidt, the only other full-fledged sailor, would be pacing back and forth on the signal platform aft of the captain's cabin, alert for any possible signal from the other ships. Young Quekemeyer, as green as the lookouts in that respect, was just not qualified to have the full responsibility of the bridge while he, Smyth, was inside. What would happen if a U-boat showed up dead ahead for ramming or the *Pollux* loomed up out of nowhere? Nope! There was only one guy he could really trust, and that was William Astrup Smyth. It was his job.

He braced his feet against the careering deck. Would this bucket ever stop rolling and pitching? Lucky for him he kept in shape with the jump rope and a little shadow boxing or he'd be falling on his duff.

Inside, Nolfi was faithfully keeping the log:

Time: 0138	86 fathoms
Time: 0153	83 fathoms
Time: 0208	78 fathoms

At 0210 hours McPherson started up radar and at 0220, having secured radar, reported to Smyth:

Pollux bearing 255°—3,500 yards
Truxtun bearing 305°—3,500 yards

Well, well! The *Truxtun* had eased to port and they were now in good formation.

Armstrong reported that he had been unable to get RDF bearings because of distance and atmospheric conditions. "There's too much static, sir."

"Very well," Smyth said, not surprised at this news.

Ships' Positions at 0210-0220 Hours

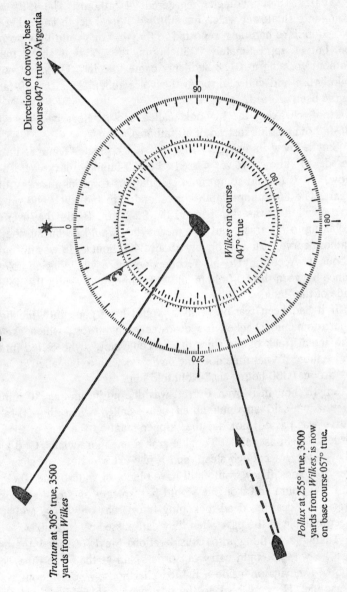

Direction of convoy: base course 047° true to Argentia

Wilkes on course 047° true

Truxtun at 305° true, 3500 yards from _Wilkes_

Pollux at 255° true, 3500 yards from _Wilkes_, is now on base course 057° true.

At 0223 the fathometer registered 74 fathoms. The *Wilkes* was going into shallower water, but still had a good depth under her keel. No soundings had been reported to Smyth, nor would they normally be, but at approximately 0230 hours, the notation about the 50-fathom crossing at 0138 suddenly came to mind. He went into the pilothouse and called through the voice tube: "Has the 50-fathom curve been crossed?"

Nolfi, checking the logbook, called back: "Negative. We got an 86-fathom reading instead of 50 fathoms."

Smyth knew immediately that was not correct. "Damn!" he muttered. "I know we've passed the 50-fathom curve. Let's see now. . . ." He did some rapid calculations from his memory of the chart. The 86-fathom depth corresponded to the track and prospective position of the ship beyond the St. Pierre Bank; they were still adhering to the track, but that meant they would be hitting the 100-fathom curve earlier, probably about 0400 hours. He was not uneasy about it. According to his recollection there was considerable distance between the 50-fathom and 100-fathom curves on the northern side of the Bank.

If it had been feasible, Smyth would have gone into the lighted chartroom and checked the dead-reckoning tracer, which sketched the actual track of the ship, but he could not, so he called into the voice tube: "What time does the navigator wish to be called?"

"About 0300 hours, sir," Nolfi told him.

Smyth thought it over. Barrett was due up in another 30 minutes. He hadn't said anything about being called when the 50-fathom curve was passed; nor did the skipper mention the fact in his night orders. Might as well let Toughie grab a few more winks. God knows they never got enough sleep, and a few extra minutes of sleep were very precious. They would still have plenty of water under their keel at 0300 hours and Toughie would have plenty of time to check the track. Besides, the dead-reckoning tracer was operating, and it had been reliable in the past when they had missed celestial fixes.

Taking everything into consideration, Smyth decided there was just no way he could carry out orders and at the same time do the job of a navigator inside a lighted charthouse—not without trained personnel. He went back to the port wing, eyes raking the night for signs of the *Pollux* abaft the beam, telling himself that they were maintaining station, and if there was anything amiss, the *Pollux* would change course and give them a call.

The *Truxtun* was rolling heavily. During one such roll the forward staywire to the forward lifeboat on the starboard side broke, causing the boat to sway and toss about. It had been hanging from its davits out over the side of the ship in readiness for lowering into the sea in the event of attack and disaster. The deck crew, under Boatswain's Mate Andrew M. Dusak, secured the boat by swinging it in over the deck.

The Navigator, Lieutenant Arthur L. Newman, was called at 0200 hours. He was in the chartroom at 0215 hours and immediately ordered the sound operator to try to pick up the *Pollux* on the starboard quarter. The operator could make no contact, either by pinging or by listening for the beat of her propellers. Newman ordered Edward B. Petterson, chief fire controlman: "Go and check with the radioman to see if he is taking RDF bearings."

Petterson found out that the radioman had been trying without success because there had been too much static.

Having exhausted all means of finding either the *Pollux* or the *Wilkes,* Newman studied the chart. It could be said that the *Truxtun* was lost. Her last contact with the *Pollux* had been over four hours ago. She had no fathometer, no radar, and absolutely no way to corroborate or correct her dead-reckoning position; no way to check anything unless they broke radio silence and talked to the *Wilkes.* Since it was doctrine not to break radio silence, that would not be done.

Newman made a decision to change course. There was one set of rules for the guide ship and a different set for escorts. As the guide, the *Pollux* had to carry out the course and speed precisely as directed by the flag officer. As an escort, the *Truxtun* was free to maneuver in any way as long as she made good the direction the convoy was steaming.

At 0230 hours the navigator came to the bridge and ordered Maddocks, "Change course 1° to the right, to 048° true."

He gave no reason for the change and Maddocks did not question it. Lieutenant Newman had joined the *Truxtun* only on December 27, and they had not gotten to know him very well yet. If he did not volunteer the information as to why he changed course, it would be presumptuous of Maddocks to ask. It was undoubtedly an adjustment to keep them on their dead-reckoning track. Newman knew what he was doing.

Because of orders for darkened ship conditions, there was no attempt to inform the flagship of this change of course by flashing light.

This 1° change of course to the right would gradually take the *Truxtun* to the extreme right of the convoy. Now only the *Wilkes* was adhering to base course 047° true.

Lieutenant Smyth on the *Wilkes* was not aware of it, but the convoy was in the process of a complete changeover.

7

USS *Wilkes*
February 18, 1942—0230 hours

The wind had gone from the southeast to east between 0100 and 0200; now it was going back to the southeast and increasing, keening like a banshee through the rigging, lashing the men on deck with stinging pellets of icy spume. The *Wilkes* pitched more wildly as the sea lifted and dropped her. The snow changed to cutting sleet and back to snow. Occasionally the snow stopped, but for the most part visibility barely extended beyond the ship's bow.

At 0300 hours as the *Wilkes* started on the right leg of the zigzag, Smyth went into the pilothouse and spoke through the voice tube. "Call Lieutenant Barrett."

"Yes, sir," Nolfi replied, and went to awaken the navigator.

At the same time McPherson started radar, secured it at 0306 hours, and reported to Smyth:

> *Pollux* bearing 265° at 2,700 yards
> *Truxtun* bearing 015° at 3,000 yards

Now it was the *Truxtun*. What the hell was she doing so far out of position? Her proper station was between 320° and 340°. And where was Barrett?

He called through the voice tube: "Nolfi!"

"Yes, sir," Nolfi's voice came back through the tube.

"Is the executive officer up and about?"

"Yes, sir."

That was a relief. Toughie Barrett, as the superior officer, would

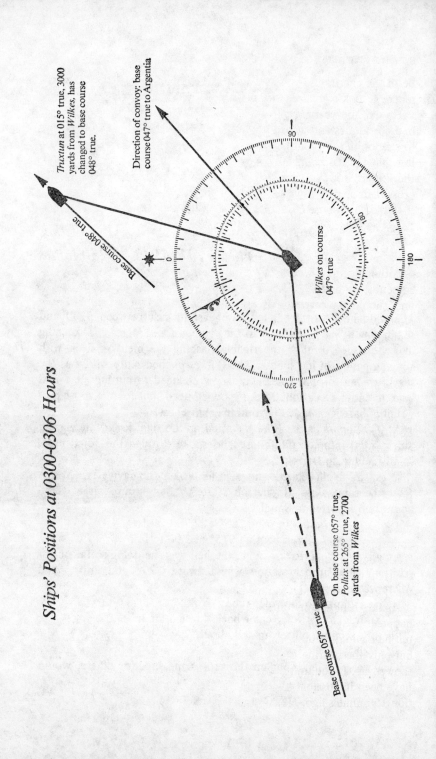

Ships' Positions at 0300-0306 Hours

Truxtun at 015° true, 3000 yards from *Wilkes*, has changed to base course 048° true.

Direction of convoy: base course 047° true to Argentia

Base course 048° true

Wilkes on course 047° true

On base course 057° true, *Pollux* at 265° true, 2700 yards from *Wilkes*

Base course 057° true

be in the charthouse with all available navigational aids at his command. It took a great deal of the burden off Smyth's shoulders.

He did not worry about the *Truxtun;* her captain was experienced in escort duties and would know what he was doing. Smyth's job was to stay on the starboard bow of the *Pollux.* He had no way of knowing that the *Truxtun,* on course 048°, was gradually cutting across the *Wilkes'* bow, and the *Pollux,* on base course 057°, would shortly cross their stern.

In the charthouse Nolfi had recorded the soundings:

Time: 0238	72 fathoms
Time: 0253	56 fathoms
Time: 0308	56 fathoms

Although they were scheduled to cross the 100-fathom curve sometime around 0420 hours according to the captain's night orders, and should have remained in water between 70 and 80 fathoms, Nolfi was not perturbed that the fathoms were dropping steadily—an indication in this area that they were much nearer land than they should have been. In his inexperience he did not equate it with danger. The *Wilkes'* dead-reckoning track as plotted on the chart was 25½ miles from land at this point, and that was where they were sure their ship was.

McPherson started up radar at 0315 hours. He did not find the *Pollux* anywhere abaft the beam, where she should be, between 300° and her last position at bearing 265°, but he continued to sweep and picked up an echo bearing 340° at 8 miles. Was it a ship? At 8 miles it was certainly not the *Pollux* or the *Truxtun,* and land was supposed to be more than 20 miles away. Besides, if land were within range of the radar it would show on the screen in a series of pips. He did not waste time on it. The *Pollux* and the *Truxtun* were his main concerns. He began to search for them.

McPherson found the *Pollux,* well out of position at 190° true, to the right of the *Wilkes,* astern by 3,700 yards. She had converged on the *Wilkes'* track and was now beyond it on a diverging course.

Again, McPherson did not realize the importance of what was happening. Sweeping around, he looked for the other escort vessel but he could pick up no sign of her. Where was she? He swept again, but only the bearing at 340°, 8 miles away, and the *Pollux* at 190° showed up. It couldn't be the *Truxtun* at 340°, he decided; it would have been impossible for her to get that far away from her last position 15 minutes ago. He continued to search.

Ships' Positions at 0315 Hours

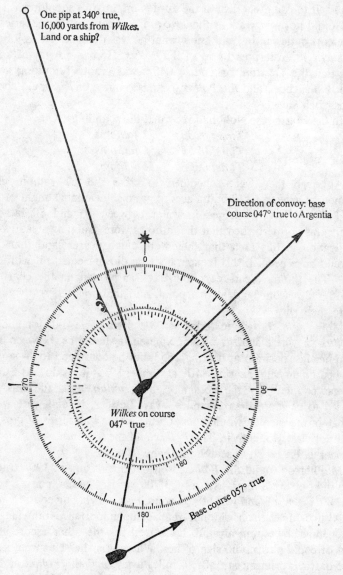

One pip at 340° true,
16,000 yards from *Wilkes*.
Land or a ship?

Direction of convoy: base
course 047° true to Argentia

270

0

90

Wilkes on course
047° true

180

180

Base course 057° true

Pollux at 190° true, 3700
yards from *Wilkes*.

The *Truxtun* was much closer to them than land but, inexplicably, radar did not pick her up as she steamed well forward of the starboard bow of the *Pollux*.

Nolfi recorded in the fathometer log:

Time: 0323 hours   50 fathoms

McPherson was still searching for the *Truxtun* when Lieutenant Barrett arrived in the chartroom. He asked Armstrong: "Any RDF bearings taken on Cape Race?"

"No, sir," Armstrong replied.

"Why not?"

"I've been trying every hour on the hour, sir, but there is too much static."

Barrett accepted that. He turned to the fathometer logbook and noted that the soundings, taken every 15 minutes from shortly after 2000 hours on February 17, did not agree with the ship's track. "Keep the fathometer running," he ordered. To McPherson he said, "Make a search for land." Then he checked the dead-reckoning tracer. It was showing a course well to the north of the dead-reckoning track. He did not notify the division commander, the commanding officer, or the officer of the deck, but began to plot the ship's position.

McPherson made the search for land, and like a beacon, bearing 340° was sending out an echo. "Picked up a bearing 340 at 8 miles, sir," he reported.

Barrett went into the radar room and checked the bearing—a single pip. With the range of radar up to 20 miles, the pip did not indicate land to Barrett; it was undoubtedly a strange ship. He returned to the chartroom and continued to plot the ship's position.

The fathometer was running continuously, as Barrett had ordered, but soundings were recorded only every fifteen minutes. Nolfi recorded:

Time: 0338 hours   55 fathoms

McPherson still had not found the *Truxtun* and at 0340 hours decided he had better report to Lieutenant Smyth. "*Pollux* bearing 190° at 3,700 yards, sir." He said nothing to Smyth about the bearing 340; their primary concern was the *Pollux* and the *Truxtun*.

Smyth asked, "How about the *Truxtun?*"

"I don't have a range and bearing for her, sir."

"Make a search for her," Smyth ordered.

"Yes, sir."

What had happened to the *Truxtun?* And what the hell was the *Pollux* doing? Smyth wondered. They had changed positions, and now the *Wilkes* was on the *Pollux*'s port bow. Was McPherson doing his job properly?

Bearing in mind the earlier miscalculations about the distance between the two ships when he had closed in for visual contact, Smyth said, "Quekemeyer, go in and check McPherson and the radar bearings he's been feeding me."

"Aye aye, sir." Quekemeyer went swiftly into the chartroom. The *Pollux,* he thought, was messing up the zigzag plan again. He passed through the chartroom where the navigator was working on the chart, and took up a position behind McPherson at the radar.

Smyth was thinking that he would have to cut across the bow of the *Pollux* to get back in position if bearing 190 was correct. With the *Pollux* out of position and the *Truxtun* off the radar screen, he did not dare leave the bridge to check on radar himself. Besides, the navigator, his superior officer, was inside and would be on top of everything.

Danger was drawing closer and precious time slipped by as Lieutenant Barrett made up a scale of half-hourly soundings from 2000 hours until about 0330 hours. Because of the sparsity of charted depths beyond the St. Pierre Bank, which averaged only one per 16 square miles, and the ocean bottom's lack of distinctive character, it had been rather difficult to pick out their track. Now he matched his scale of soundings on the chart and made the unpleasant discovery that the *Wilkes* was either north of her dead-reckoning track by 12 miles or south by 20 miles. If it was north and the DRT indicated that it was—she had passed through the gully on the northern part of St. Pierre Bank shortly after midnight and they were on a course that would clear land on the west side of Placentia Bay by about 4 or 5 miles instead of 20 miles. If it was south, they would pass uncomfortably close to land on the far side of the bay.

The navigator was still trying to pinpoint the *Wilkes*' actual position when Ensign Warren Winslow arrived to take over the officer-of-the-deck watch at 0345 hours. Winslow was a Harvard man and came from a good Boston family. Quiet and reserved, he was considered good officer material by Commander Kelsey. Behind Winslow came Chief Gunner's Mate Ted Hunter, who was to relieve Quekemeyer as the junior officer of the deck. The other crew members were making their appearance, one after the other, standing in the gloom of the pilothouse while their eyes adjusted to night vision.

Winslow went into the charthouse, looked at the chart, but saw no evidence that they might be in dangerous waters. The most recent fix plotted on the chart showing the track that cleared land by 4 to 5 miles made no great impression on him one way or the other. He did not discuss it with the navigator or with anyone else. He read the night order book, saw the notation at the bottom of the page about searching for land by radar at 0420 hours, range approximately 20 miles, and initialed the book.

Having familiarized himself with the night orders, Winslow went to the pilothouse where Smyth was waiting for Quekemeyer to report back on the bearing 190.

"Ready to relieve you, sir," Winslow said.

Smyth was a conscientious officer; he could not saddle a relatively inexperienced officer with the responsibility of tracking the *Pollux* and getting back into position. He said, "No. I'm not ready. We're out of position on the *Pollux*. Just stand by until I cross over her bow and get us squared away."

"Aye aye, sir." Winslow, who had been standing deck watches on this trip for the first time, stood by waiting for the situation to clear up.

Smyth was not really worried. The bearing at 190° had to be the *Pollux,* but he did not like being out of position. He cautioned the young lookouts who were taking over the watch: "It's stormy, so keep an exceptionally good lookout."

In the radar room, Quekemeyer had been staring into the radar screen. Hunter was there waiting to relieve him, but he had not turned over the watch because of the confusion over bearing 190. The other bearing at 340° was a very clear-out pip at 6 miles now, and Quekemeyer assumed that it could be land or a ship—definitely not the *Pollux* or the *Truxtun* because it would have been impossible for either of those ships to have steamed that distance since the last bearings taken by McPherson. Most likely, he thought, it was an un-

known vessel because it was just one pip. There was no doubt that
the *Pollux* was bearing at 190°, and he had better tell the chief.

The unpleasant thought of U-boats was intruding upon Smyth as
he waited for Quekemeyer's report. They had had much experience
with the German submarines, and he knew well how they liked to
sneak up and attack from the rear, even in stormy weather. While
the *Pollux* wandered a little, she had never actually gotten so far out
of position.

Then Quekemeyer appeared. "Say, Chief, there is something out
there at 190°."

Smyth was still not satisfied. "Go back into the radar room and
check that bearing again," he ordered.

Quekemeyer ducked back inside.

At 0350 hours the navigator decided to call the commanding
officer. Commander Kelsey awakened instantly when Barrett
knocked on his door. "I think we're north of the track, sir," he said,
and told him about the lack of RDF bearings, but did not tell him
about bearing 340 or advise a change of course.

They went immediately to the chartroom, where Commander Kelsey began to check the data. The 0400 watch was coming on duty
and the door opening and closing turned the light on and off, making
it difficult for his eyes to adjust. The small pilothouse became
congested as seamen squeezed inside. Presently Commander Kelsey
could study the chart and sounding without interruption. Only Nolfi
turned his watch over, to Quartermaster Third Class Robert Francis
Noland; McPherson remained at the radar, Gabriel at the fathometer, and Armstrong in the radio room.

Before leaving, Nolfi recorded:

Time: 0353 hours   47 fathoms

In the pilothouse, Smyth continued to worry about the ship astern
of them. He said to Winslow: "She's shifted from 265° to 190° in
the past half hour. I don't understand how this is possible. Check the
bearing of the *Pollux*."

Winslow went inside. It was quite crowded and he had to work his
way to the radar room aft. McPherson and Quekemeyer were staring
into the radar. "What bearing have you obtained on the *Pollux*?"
Winslow asked them.

As flagship of the convoy, the USS *Wilkes* bore the brunt of the blame. (U. S. Bureau of Ships)

Lieutenant Commander William A. Smyth in 1944, after he returned to the Naval Air Force. (Courtesy of William A. Smyth)

The ancient four-stack destroyer USS *Truxtun,* which ran aground and sank in Chambers Cove, Newfoundland. Only 46 out of 156 men aboard survived. (Navy Department. Courtesy of James O. Seamans)

The *Truxtun* during one of several trips she made in heavy North Atlantic seas a few months before the disaster. (Courtesy of William J. Maddocks)

Part of a newspaper clipping that described the tragedy included a picture of Lieutenant Commander Ralph Hickox, captain of the *Truxtun,* who went down with his ship. (Courtesy of Ena Farrell Edwards)

One of the 11 officers of the *Truxtun* who died was Lieutenant James Ross Gillie (right), photographed with his friend Laurence A. Weaver, Jr., of the *Pollux*. This picture was taken on December 7, 1941, while both were on shore leave. (Courtesy of Laurence A. Weaver, Jr.)

Two of the three *Truxtun* officers who survived: Ensigns William J. Maddocks (left) and James O. Seamans.

Boatswains Mate First Cla[ss] Harry Egner of the *Truxtun*, w[ho] with Seaman Second Class Jam[es] Fex received a Navy Commend[a]tion Medal for getting a lifeline [a]shore.

The supply ship *Pollux* carried 233 men on her last trip. Only 140 of them survived. (U. S. Bureau of Ships. Courtesy of James O. Seamans)

Commander Hugh W. Turney, accepting commission of the *Pollux,* May 8, 1941. (Courtesy of Alfred I. Pollack)

Lieutenant (j.g.) William C. Grindley, navigator on the *Pollux.*

Other *Pollux* officers were Lieutenants (j.g.) George C. Bradley (top) and Jack R. Garnaus (left), and Ensign Alfred I. Pollack.

Five members of the *Pollux* took part in the boat races on the Hudson River, May 30, 1939. Standing, left to right: Joe Janocha, James Ross, and Gus Tortorici. Front row, second and third from left: Sam Nicosia and Larry Calemmo. Of this group, all but Tortorici survived the shipwreck. (Courtesy of Lawrence Calemmo)

George L. Coleman (left) and Vincent J. Popolizio of the *Pollux*.

Pollux crew members: Walter C. Bulanowski (top left), Lawrence J. Calemmo (top right), Ernest L. Califano (bottom left), and Robert M. Collins (bottom right).

McPherson swept and zeroed in on the supply ship. "Bearing 190° true, distance 3,500 yards, sir."

"Is that correct?" Winslow asked Quekemeyer.

"That is correct," Quekemeyer replied.

Nothing was said of the 340° bearing, and Winslow returned to the pilothouse. "Bearing 190° is correct, sir," he reported to Smyth.

It didn't make sense to Smyth. The *Pollux* had capable mariners, but she was way off position. Was radar all that reliable tonight? He said to Winslow: "Did you personally observe the bearing?"

"No, sir."

"Then go back and personally observe the bearing."

Winslow left. After three reports Smyth was reasonably convinced that the object at 190° was the *Pollux* and not a trailing U-boat on the surface. Well, she was the guide ship and he had better get back in position on her starboard bow. He did not wait for Winslow to return; they had ended the last leg of the right zigzag and were steadying on base course 047° when he ordered the helmsman: "Come right to course 070° true."

"Aye aye, sir. Coming right to 070° true."

The bow of the *Wilkes* swung over to the starboard, and Smyth went to the starboard wing to keep a sharp lookout in case the *Pollux* should loom unexpectedly close, as she had been doing since midnight. He was still unaware of the bearing 340, which had come steadily closer. Course 070° was away from land.

Kenneth Herman Shannon, gunner's mate second class, a fifteen-year Navy man, took over the helm. "Present course 070°. Base course 047° true, just steadied to 070° true," he was told.

Commander Kelsey had studied the line of soundings as constructed by Barrett, and laid them on the chart, sliding it either side of the dead-reckoning track. "We could be to the north or to the south," he said. "The north track passes close to land; we had better inform Commander Webb."

Barrett hurried to wake Commander Webb, whose sleeping quarters were beneath the bridge. Since McPherson had not reported any change in the radar bearing in the direction of land, he assumed it was still 8 miles. *Actually, bearing 340° was now at 6,000 yards.*

Meanwhile Commander Kelsey immediately went to the wings to order a signal to the *Pollux* to warn her of possible danger. It was

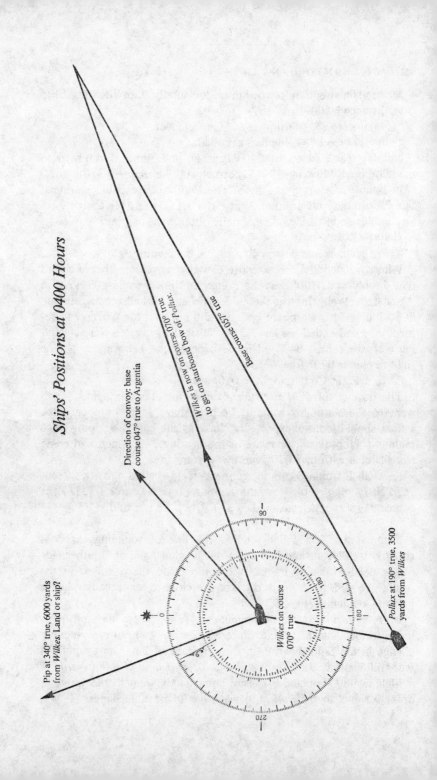

Ships' Positions at 0400 Hours

Pip at 340° true, 6000 yards from *Wilkes*. Land or ship?

Direction of convoy: base course 047° true to Argentia

Wilkes is now on course 070° true to get on starboard bow of *Pollux*.

Base course 057° true

Wilkes on course 070° true

Pollux at 190° true, 3500 yards from *Wilkes*

sleeting and foggy; visibility barely extended beyond the ship's bow as she staggered through the seas rolling heavily against her beam.

Smyth was on the starboard wing, keeping a lookout for the *Pollux* in case he should have to make the decision to increase speed and cross her bow to regain position or come hard right to pass astern. "Morning, Captain," he said as Commander Kelsey approached.

"Morning, Chief. What's the situation?"

Smyth replied: "For some reason or other we're to port of the *Pollux*. I've come right to cross her bow and re-establish position. She's been as erratic as hell the last couple of hours, and the weather's been too gross for me to close her for visual contact."

"Then raise her on the blinker tube," Commander Kelsey ordered.

Smyth passed the order to the signalman: "Call the *Pollux*, Schmidt; she should be slightly abaft the starboard beam."

"Aye aye, sir," Schmidt replied, and began to try and raise the *Pollux*.

They waited, both men unaware of the closeness of land.

Commander Webb had risen immediately. "We're about 12 miles to the left of our course," Barrett told him as they made their way to the chartroom, adding that they had crossed the 50-fathom curve more than an hour earlier than they should have. "We have a radar bearing at 340°, distance about 8 miles."

"Does the radar show anything else?"

"The 340° bearing is a single pip, sir; the only other bearing is at 190°."

Regardless of distance, the two pips indicated to Commander Webb that it was the *Pollux* and the *Truxtun;* the 340° bearing to the left was in the general direction the *Truxtun* would have been. If it was land, radar would have picked it up at least 20 miles off.

When they arrived in the chartroom, Commander Webb studied the chart and did some rapid mental calculations. The ship's position as laid down by the navigator was verified by the soundings recorded by the fathometer. They were 12 miles off course; therefore the radar bearing 340°, at 8 miles, had to be land. Since 2000 hours last night they had been set northward at the rate of a knot and a half, but their position was not an unsafe one. The course they were on took them safely into Placentia Bay, but there were shoals farther in the bay, and it would be necessary to change to the right to avoid them. However, there was ample time for that. "We will have to notify the *Pollux* and the *Truxtun*," he said. There was no immediate danger, and certainly no need to break radio silence. He said to Barrett: "We will have to change course, but fix the position more accurately, if possible, and work out a new course."

Lieutenant Barrett immediately began to work on the more recent soundings, and Commander Webb stepped out into the pilothouse.

On the wings, Schmidt had been unable to raise the *Pollux*.

"Keep trying," Smyth ordered.

"Aye aye, sir."

Commander Kelsey entered the pilothouse, and Lieutenant Smyth, scheduled to check the helmsman's course, followed. At the same time Commander Webb stepped from the chartroom: "Better ease over to the left and get in touch with the *Pollux* and warn her of possible danger to the north," he said to Kelsey. "I'll contact the *Truxtun*." He picked up the TBS.

The situation, as it existed, was far from clear, and it was not to Commander Kelsey's liking at all. A change of course to the left would take them toward suspected danger. He protested: "If we ease over to the left, we'll be heading in the direction of land."

Believing they were well clear of land, Webb commanded: "Ease over!"

It was about 0400 hours, the time that the *Wilkes* would normally come to the left leg of the zigzag course, and Commander Kelsey, following the orders of his superior officer, passed the order to Smyth: "Come left to 007° true."

Smyth, totally unaware of the dangerous situation, was bewildered. They were on course 070° to get back on station on the *Pollux*'s starboard bow, because she had somehow gotten on *their* right. Now they had to come left to 007°, which would take them farther apart. What the hell was going on? Whatever it was, Commander Kelsey had taken command of the bridge and relieved Smyth of the conn. He said automatically, "Aye aye, sir," and passed the order to Shannon.

"Coming left to 007° true," Shannon intoned.

Smyth thought: You're the boss, but this sure as hell isn't going to put us back on station.

Commander Webb was trying to contact the *Truxtun*. The *Truxtun* did not answer, but Webb was not too concerned; it often took time for the TBS installations to get in working order.

In the radar room McPherson and Quekemeyer were staring at the pip on bearing 340 when suddenly it changed to a series of pips ranging from 350° to 020° at 3,000 yards—a good 1½ miles away —that were sending out an alarming number of echoes. Still there was no great reaction to it from McPherson or Quekemeyer.

McPherson said, "That's either a hell of a lot of ships coming this way, or it's land."

"Yeah," Quekemeyer agreed.

McPherson did not report it to anyone because Quekemeyer, the junior officer of the deck, was behind him and aware of it. If anything was amiss it was up to the JOOD to report it. But Quekemeyer did not report it to anyone. He had been ordered to check on bearing 190, which had been of paramount importance, and he was verifying the operation of the radar by McPherson by looking over his shoulder into the radar and personally seeing the bearings and distances as obtained by radar.

At that moment Winslow arrived in the radar room to personally check on bearing 190. He took one look at the pips on the radar screen, noted that they were dead ahead at a distance now of 2,700 yards. The heading of the ship, according to the gyrocompass above the radar, was 007°. He hurried to the captain in the pilothouse.

Lieutenant Smyth had returned to his station on the bridge, where Schmidt was trying to signal the *Pollux* from the port wing now. He was thinking: This is crazy, the *Pollux* is on our stern.

Commander Kelsey was still in the pilothouse when Winslow reported: "There's a bunch of pips on radar from 350° to 020° true, distance 2,700 yards, sir."

Kelsey, who until this minute, at 0405, had been totally unaware of the 340° bearing in the direction of land, assumed that all those pips meant the radar needed decontaminating. He said, "Ask Mr. Smyth when radar was last decontaminated." Then he changed his mind. "But this is not the time. . . ."

He hurried to the radar room and looked at the screen. There were a bunch of pips, all right. It was his first indication of possible danger. He knew that a radar contact could appear on the screen at bearings as much as 020° to the right and left of the true bearing of

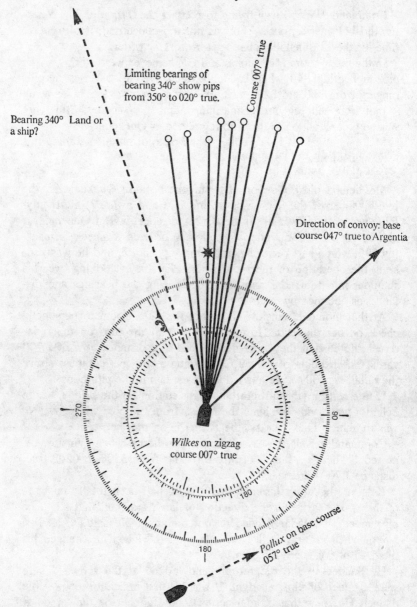

Ships' Positions Shortly Past 0400 Hours

Limiting bearings of bearing 340° show pips from 350° to 020° true.

Course 007° true

Bearing 340° Land or a ship?

Direction of convoy: base course 047° true to Argentia

270

90

Wilkes on zigzag course 007° true

180

180

Pollux on base course 057° true

the object contacted, and he passed an order to Quekemeyer: "I want the limiting bearings as quickly as possible." He hastened back to the pilothouse and out into the wings.

Commander Webb was still trying to contact the *Truxtun* by TBS. Once he thought he had a response, and said into the telephone: "We believe there may be shoals to port."

There was no reply.

Now, in the last moments, there was an awareness that all was not well. The wind, in full cry, wailed stridently; sleet was an opaque curtain. Inside, the young men were silent and apprehensive.

At 0408 hours the fathometer recorded 35 fathoms. Moments later Gabriel reported to Lieutenant Barrett that they were in 17 fathoms of water. Barrett, still trying to fix the position of the ship as ordered by the commodore, said: "Report it to the captain."

Gabriel yelled urgently: "Fathoms dropping, Captain, down to 15 fathoms."

At the same moment Commander Kelsey, standing by the port pelorus, Signalman Schmidt, and Smyth on the forward end of the port searchlight were the first to see the mountain of white looming ahead. Schmidt thought briefly it was an iceberg and yelled: "My God! Look ahead!"

In the pilothouse, Commander Webb had heard the yell from Gabriel and the shouting from the bridge. He bellowed: "Ease her to the right!"

Commander Kelsey burst into the pilothouse, shouting, "Come right to 109! *Stand by for collision!*" Then: "All engines full emergency astern!"

Smyth had raced to the annunciator[1] to execute all engines emergency back full astern. Shannon, the helmsman, his eyes on the gyrocompass before him, called the bearings as the *Wilkes'* bow swung to the right: "Bearings 86, 87, 88, 89. . . ."

The *Wilkes,* losing headway rapidly, grounded at 0409 hours on a bearing between 89 and 90 on the southwest corner of Lawn Head, latitude 46°53'25"N, longitude 55°29'00"W. She had lost headway rapidly and was steaming at 5 knots when she struck. Radar indicated that the land the *Wilkes* had hit was more than 60° to the right of the land picked up by radar. She struck with a rending of metal on rock

---

[1] A mechanical signaling device connected to the engineroom.

that staggered the crew, but came to a stop, upright, caught by the bow.

At the instant of grounding, Smyth sounded "Collision" on the siren, which would alert the other two ships to danger, but the siren was frozen and would not blow.

Commander Kelsey yelled: "Man the searchlights!"

Winslow turned on the 12-inch searchlight on the port wing and trained it ahead on the mountain about 50 yards away. Schmidt turned on the 24-inch searchlight on the starboard wing and pointed it out to sea. He signaled: "Emergency stop."

The *Wilkes* rolled heavily, grating on the rocks as the seas smashed into her. Smyth, knowing that the conn, bridge, and communications were under the direct command of the captain, and aware of his primary duties as engineer officer and damage-control officer, hurried below to direct operations of the damage-control party.

Below decks, her crew scrambled frantically for their foul-weather gear, life jackets, and so forth, and headed topside.

Commander Webb was still on TBS. "*Wilkes* aground, don't know which side," his voice crackled over the radiotelephone. Being very conscious of security even in the direst emergency, he gave the barest details. The *Pollux* and the *Truxtun* would know he meant "which side of Placentia Bay."

He kept repeating the message, hoping that the *Truxtun*'s TBS was in working order. There was no answer. They had rockets, but in convoy rockets were used for submarine warning; to fire them off might draw the *Truxtun* into danger, since she naturally would come full speed to their assistance.

Lieutenant Hughlett, who had been sleeping at the time of the grounding, rushed to the bridge. Commander Webb immediately ordered: "Send an emergency radio signal to Commander Task Force 24 in Argentia. Tell them the *Wilkes* is aground at the entrance of Placentia Bay."

Hughlett ran to give the order to Radioman Thurman,[2] who had taken over from Armstrong. "Send it on the area frequency 2670 kilocycles." This was the area frequency for Base Roger in Argentia.

Meanwhile the *Pollux* and the *Truxtun* had not acknowledged the

---

[2] Thurman's Christian name and exact rank was not included in the court of inquiry, the courts-martial, or the official list from Washington, D.C.

searchlight blinker or the TBS, and Commander Webb rushed to the radio room moments behind Hughlett and ordered Thurman to broadcast on the distress frequency (500 kilocycles), so that the two ships would get it on their radio frequency. While all ships maintained radio silence, it would be monitored at all times for just such emergencies. Commander Webb then returned to the pilothouse and the TBS to continue his broadcast to the *Truxtun*.

Thurman started to send the message but the radio did not seem to be transmitting.

Chief Radioman Koegler ran in, and Thurman yelled: "The commodore gave me a signal to send out, but we're not transmitting."

"Keep sending anyway," Koegler said, "I'll investigate." He ran below to the emergency radio room, but the transmitters there would not operate either. Dashing back to the radio room, he cut all power. "We have to go aloft and see what's wrong."

He selected three men, and up the two smokestacks they went with the wind and sleet tearing at them. The insulators were covered with half an inch of slush ice. It took them 15 minutes, Koegler estimated, to clear the ice off, then he returned to the radio room and turned on the power. The transmitters worked, and the messages went out over the air waves.

There was no reply from the *Pollux,* the *Truxtun,* or from Argentia, but suddenly there was an answer from Radio Station WIM on the Massachusetts coast.

Then they saw a searchlight on the *Wilkes'* starboard hand.

It was another ship, hard aground at the base of a cliff, about 1 mile or so to the eastward. . . .

8

Following the change of course to 057° true at 0130 hours, Lieutenant Grindley kept dashing to the wings to study the drift and leeway. The swell was increasing in size and force, rolling upon their beam and, he was sure, was setting them off to the westward. The wind, force 8 now, lifted off wavetops and flung them over the ship. The deck had grown a thin coating of ice. Sleet cut the night.

Coming on the bridge to take over the 0400–0800 deck watch, Lieutenant (jg) George C. Bradley, twenty-eight, could barely see the bow. The flare of white water beneath her stem was a faint illumination against the black and turbulent sea.

What a lousy night.

He entered the chartroom. Commander Turney and Lieutenant Grindley were leaning over the chart, absorbed in checking the ship's position by fathometer readings. To Bradley they appeared to be very concerned about their position. "It's not a very nice night," he said to Commander Turney, and leaning over the chart table, asked: "What is our position, Mr. Grindley?"

The navigator was a little grim. "Here's where we came off St. Pierre Bank," he said, indicating the track north of the gully on the northern side of the fishing bank they had crossed soon after midnight, "and here's where we changed course to 057° true. This course takes us southeast of Cloue Rock,[1] and about 13 or 14 miles

---

[1] Cloue Rock lies under 10 fathoms of water 7 to 8 miles southeast of Ferryland Head.

from Ferryland Head, at approximately 0400 hours. We'll cross the Cloue Rock 50-fathom line shortly."

Bradley studied the chart, then checked the fathometer to see that the readings corresponded with their position. They did. He noted that the 100-fathom line on the northern side of Cloue Rock was fairly close to the 50-fathom line, and they were now approaching Ferryland Head.

All seemed well. The ship's DR track was certainly well clear of land.

Commander Turney told him: "You will sight land at daybreak, somewhere on the port hand."

Bradley nodded. Tall, thin, quiet-spoken, he had been with the *Pollux* since her commissioning last May. He had complete confidence in the captain and the navigator. Both, in his estimation, were capable and conscientious men.

He read the night order book, initialed it, then entered the pilot-house where Grayson was standing behind the helmsman. Lieutenant (jg) George Bollinger, the junior officer of the deck, had also arrived. He picked up the night order book after Bradley and read it through, adding his own initials beneath.

Having absorbed the pertinent information, and with his eyes adjusting to night vision, Bradley was ready to take over the watch. "Ready to relieve you, sir," he said to Grayson.

Grayson gave him the base course, speed, and other information about the ship's condition, adding: "We changed course to 057° true at 0130 hours to allow for leeway. We notified the *Wilkes* that we had changed course, but we didn't get a Roger at the time."

"Have you seen her since 0130?"

"No."

"Have the skipper and Grindley been in the chartroom all night?"

"All night," Grayson replied.

The men of Bradley's watch were taking their position on the bridge where the sleet was so blinding that Apprentice Seaman Howard Thomas Lewis, the port lookout on the flying bridge collided with the young seaman he was relieving.

"Sorry!" he said. "I didn't see you."

"O.K.!" The young sailor vanished, anxious to get below.

Apprentice Seaman Wayne Brewer, twenty-five, and only two weeks aboard, took his position on the port wing.

As Grayson and his men left the bridge, Bradley said to Bollinger, "Visibility is pretty low so you'll have to do duty as an additional lookout tonight. Take the watch on the flying bridge. You'll have better visibility up there."

"Yes, sir," Bollinger said, and climbed to the flying bridge. Bradley went to the starboard wing to face into the biting wind. The *Pollux* was just ending the last leg of the 0200–0400-hour zigzag; at 0400 they would have to start on the first leg of the 0400–0600-hour zigzag.

Before leaving the bridge George Horner had passed the information about the signal to the *Wilkes* to his relief, Thomas Requa Turner, Quartermaster and Signalman: "I can't say for sure whether we received a Roger, but I sent the signal," he impressed on Turner, and continued, "the *Wilkes* was rolling badly, her light would fade and go out of train, and it was difficult for me to see if the Roger had been sent." Visibility, he stressed, had been bad, and it had been difficult to see the *Wilkes'* light at all.

Unlike Horner, Turner had five years behind him as a quartermaster. He needed no one to supervise him in his duties.

Lawrence Calemmo, assigned to the lifeboat watch from 0400–0800 hours, had reported to the midship passageway where the lifeboat crew for No. 1 motor whaleboat was assembled, fully clothed in foul-weather gear, ready for any emergency. In the stormy weather they had been permitted to remain inside.

Calemmo's first job was to check the boat engine for starting. He opened the water-tank hatch and went on deck. Moving about the deck when it was iced up was not extremely dangerous, but it required know-how, and Calemmo made his way to the starboard lifeboat, sometimes crawling, sometimes sliding on his backside. Another crew member kept a solicitous eye on him until he reached the boat and climbed aboard. The boat was crusted with ice, but Calemmo's main concern was the engine.

The makeshift heater he had installed in Boston was still operating, and the diesel engine came to life immediately. While the engine warmed up, he hacked away at some of the ice coating the boat; presently, deciding that all was well, he secured the engine and worked his way back to the comfort of the passageway. Someone passed him a cup of coffee, and he sat on the deck to relax. The talk floating around was that Commander Turney had been up pacing the deck all night; apparently he knew they were in dangerous waters but he had to follow the leader.

Ernie Califano, his buddy, had just come off lifeboat watch and had decided not to turn in yet. He joined them on the deck for a cup of coffee and a cigarette.

"Gimme a light, Califano," a buddy requested.

"Yeah, me too," said another.

Califano struck a match, lit the three cigarettes, and flicked the match out. "Hey!" someone remarked, "that was three on a match."

"Shaddup and drink your coffee," somebody else growled.

They tried to drink, but the severe pitching and rolling put more coffee on the decks than in their stomachs.

Califano was remembering that a few years back, he and two friends had lit a cigarette on a match while driving in a Model A Ford and shortly after that he had gone through the windshield.

It was an old superstition about three on a match, and Califano didn't go for that kind of stuff, but that accident had been a painful one, and they were in submarine territory. Had he tempted fate?

The forward gun watch under Joe Janocha, boatswain's mate second class, had been quickly drenched as the heavy spray fell upon the open gun mount. Arthur Appel and "Rebel" Thomas Hayward Brown, both seamen second class, were part of the gun watch. Artie was in touch with the bridge through a headset. Because of the freezing spray it had quickly become inoperable, and Artie could make contact only through the earpiece.

They had been there only a short time when orders came from the bridge to get inside the deckhouse for safety. "Check the deck loads on your way aft," they had been told, "and report its condition over the phone from the forward engine room on the main deck."

They did this with alacrity, reporting to the bridge that all was well; then they were inside, standing on the catwalk and looking down into the engine room. They took off their foul-weather gear and hung it over the rails to dry. Appel looked down at the engine-room crew with envy. Not only were they dry and warm, but also they were a damn sight more comfortable than he would ever be during his duty watch.

Somebody went to the galley for a pot of coffee to warm them up, and Rebel climbed down into the engine room.

The captain and the navigator had not permitted their differences to get beyond the chartroom, and officially they would not, but it had been obvious to the preceding watch that something was up. Not being deaf or blind, young seamen in and out of the charthouse knew that the two officers were very worried and disagreeing. It had come to the ears of Wayne Brewer as he settled into the routine of the watch. Below decks it was rumored that Grindley wanted a 30° change to the right, and that the escort commander had permitted only a 10° change of course at 0130 hours. The information, such as it was, had been passed from one watch to another. Scuttlebutt had been further convoluted in the engine room and galley to the detriment of the flagship.

Grindley's instincts were telling him to turn tail and run. The land to port was a brooding presence, emanating warnings of danger to him, and there wasn't a damn thing he could do about it. He could almost *taste* the danger. Their track was taking them past Cloue Rock into Placentia Bay, but the wind and sea had increased and the long, running swells had grown steeper—a sign that they could be in water that was shallower than it should be. If they had been pushed off track by 5 miles from 2000 hours to 0023 hours, how much farther was she off course in the past 4 hours? In his own heart and soul, Grindley felt that the *Pollux* was headed for the beach, and he could only pray that it would be a soft, sandy one. He privately felt they were steaming straight for Lawn Head, 7 to 8 miles west of Ferryland Head.

"I recommend, sir, that we discontinue zigzagging, at least until daylight." He was, in effect, pleading.

Whether it was to ease Grindley's worries or any nagging doubts of his own, Commander Turney agreed. "All right, we'll give it a try." To Grindley he seemed relieved once he had made up his mind. "At 0400 when we come to the end of the zigzag plan, we will remain steady on 057° true. Advise the officer of the deck," he told Grindley.

The navigator went quickly to the wheelhouse. Maybe it was not too late, he thought. "Bradley!"

From the gloom the helmsman, Joseph Meyers, replied, "He's out on the wings, sir."

Normal procedure was to pass the word to the officer of the deck, who would then give the order to the helmsman, but Commander Turney wished to cease zigzagging at exactly 0400 hours, and it was that time. Grindley himself gave the order to Meyers: "You will remain steady on course 057° true."

He then sent one of the seamen on duty out to the wings to inform Bradley. The gossip about their course had not been passed to Bradley, and he did not consider it unusual that they had ceased zigzagging. It was normal procedure, when expecting to make a landfall, to cease zigzagging before land was sighted, and in another 20 to 30 minutes they would be passing the last headland before steadying down to make their approach into Placentia Bay.

He checked the gyrorepeater on the wing of the bridge to be sure when they were steady on 057° true, then walked into the wheelhouse, looked over Meyers' shoulder to double-check the course, and moved on to the starboard wing. It was all quite routine.

In the chartroom, Commander Turney picked up the same piece of paper on which he had written the first message to the *Wilkes* about the change of course 10° to the right. On the other side he wrote: "I am coming to base course steady, speed 12 at 0430."[2] The *Pollux* was still steaming at 14 knots to make the required base speed of 12 knots, but once the message had been relayed, speed would then be reduced. The *Wilkes* and the *Truxtun* would reduce speed too, and all would remain in formation.

Commander Turney personally took the message to Quartermaster Turner. "Send this to the *Wilkes* by 12-inch searchlight," he ordered.

Quartermaster Turner read the message and went to the starboard wing. The *Wilkes* was supposed to be on their starboard bow and he switched on the light, training it in that direction. Snow and rain streaked past the beam, and recalling what Horner had said about the difficulty he had had raising the *Wilkes,* Turner adjusted the cone that had cut down the beam so that a larger beam of light would be seen through the stormy night. He trained the light forward with the idea of calling the *Wilkes* from dead ahead to dead astern.

It was then that he saw two bright lights, approximately two points

2 Because of the zigzag plan, the *Pollux* was operating on plus-4 time in the 3.5 time zone; 0400 hours was actually 0430 hours.

off the port bow. They had the bright blue look of searchlights; one was trained down on the water, the other . . . Turner couldn't make out how it was trained. To his eyes they appeared to be only about 500 to 600 yards away. He switched off the searchlight and ran into the wheelhouse, opened the charthouse door and yelled: "Bright lights ahead, sir."

Everyone saw the lights at the same time. Bradley on the starboard wing thought they came from the *Truxtun,* since she was supposed to be on their left bow, and was seconds behind Turner in the mad dash to the wheelhouse. Lieutenant Bollinger, on the starboard wing of the flying bridge where visibility was slightly less restricted, saw more than the light. Unless his eyes were playing tricks, the light appeared to be trained *on land!* At least, land appeared to be silhouetted against the rays of the searchlight. He moved quickly across the bridge to the port wing. It *was* land. There was no doubt about that craggy outline rising above the lights. He turned to dash below, *and saw a mountain of white rushing toward them.* He yelled, "Land! Dead ahead!" and pounded down the ladder to the wheelhouse.

From the masthead and all lookout positions on the port side came the frantic cry: "Land! Dead ahead!"

To Bradley, it looked as high as the Alps.

Brewer, watching the gray-white mass rushing toward them, wondered if the ship would be turned from her course in time to avoid hitting land dead ahead. If they didn't do something pretty damn quick it would be too late.

In the seconds between the sighting of the lights and the sighting of land, Turney and Grindley rushed to the pilothouse. The glare of lights flashing back and forth caught the two men. Turney said, "Oh, my God!" Then ordered crisply: "Hard right rudder!" and in the same breath: "Sound collision quarters!" Simultaneously he rang up "Full Astern" on the engine-room telegraph.

Grindley cried: "Goddamnit! *I knew it!*"

In the engine room Walter Bulanowski, machinist mate first class, opened the throttle wide to give the engine the full power it needed to reverse, at the same time wondering why they were getting signals to reverse course in the middle of the ocean.

With horns blaring, bells jangling, and bow swinging hard right, the *Pollux* rushed on.

At that moment, in the radio shack, Radioman First Class Oscar

Kemp Cox picked up the message that the *Wilkes* was sending out. He immediately phoned the bridge. Turner answered it automatically, eyes still riveted on the land rushing toward them.

"The *Wilkes* has gone aground!" Cox yelled into his ear.

Turner hung up the receiver just as the *Pollux,* with her engines backing full and with headway checked to about 4 or 5 knots, grounded. It was 0417 hours.

With a great crunching and grinding, 15,000 tons of dead weight crashed upon the rocks with an impact that unhinged bunks and sent the crew spilling to the decks. The *Pollux* reared up several feet, then fell back upon the rocks with a resounding thud, shudders wracking her hull. She quivered, vibrated, and heaved about, listing 10 to 15 degrees to starboard. The bells, horns, and whistles of the general alarm added another dimension to the uproar of a ship in agony.

The *Wilkes* and the *Pollux* were aground. Where was the *Truxtun?*

9

USS *Truxtun*
February 18, 1942—0345–0400 hours

Aboard the *Truxtun* all was strictly routine. About the only thing out of the ordinary that occurred during the 0000–0400-hours watch was when one of the gun captains, who had burned his leg the previous day and was in great discomfort, requested that he be allowed to go below. Ensign Maddocks gave him permission to do so.

Later, Lieutenant Newman, the navigator, ordered Edward Petterson to check on the radioman a second time to see that he was taking bearings. The radioman eventually got a bearing on Sable Island, a little off the port, nearly astern, but with the static, the navigator considered it unreliable.

Ensign Frederick A. Loughridge, torpedo officer, who was to relieve Maddocks as OOD, dropped into the wardroom for a cup of coffee before going topside. The navigator was there drinking coffee and passed on the information that there were no data available, no bearings or soundings to fix their position, but that the ship's distance from land, at this time, would be about 30 miles.

Before relieving Maddocks, Loughridge saw the chart and studied the ship's dead-reckoning track. It was well clear of land. Newman pointed out the 0400 dead-reckoning position, and Loughridge estimated that the nearest land from the track of the ship at 0400 would be no closer than 20 miles. He read the night orders and initialed the book. When his eyes had adapted to night vision, he said to Maddocks, "Ready to relieve you, sir."

"Course 048° true and gyro, speed 12 knots," Maddocks replied.

"The last contact with the *Pollux* was made about 2300 hours on the seventeenth, by the sound equipment. The navigator is in the charthouse; we're steaming on 1 and 2 boilers. Visibility from about 200 to 300 yards, and getting worse." He added, "I'm glad to see you."

"Yeah, O.K., I relieve you, sir."

Maddocks thankfully went below, peeled off the layers of heavy-weather clothing, and crawled into his bunk to get a little sleep before morning twilight. In spite of the ship's rough motion he was asleep in a minute.

A. L. W. Leggett, Jr., radioman third class, came on duty in the radio shack. Walter E. Brothers and William E. Butterworth were also there. Leggett's duty was to guard the convoy emergency frequency, to make sure radio silence was maintained.

Harry M. Egner, boatswain's mate first class, took over the watch from Andrew Dusak. Egner had already been informed of the switch from the forward gun to Nos. 2 and 3 by the messenger waking him, and he had called his crew and gone to the galley for a cup of hot cocoa before braving the elements. With the mug in his hand Egner went on deck, where Dusak gave him the information about weather, visibility, and the lifeboat that had been swung in on the deck earlier.

Having imparted all pertinent information, Dusak left, and Egner posted a lookout on the port and starboard, and took his own position behind the gun, which provided a little shelter. He sipped his cocoa, savoring the hot, sweet drink. He could see nothing beyond the snow and sleet.

"It's a rotten night," he said to his best buddy, Gunner's Mate Second Class William O. Harris. Egner and W.O. always went on liberty together, and W.O. had gotten married only a month ago. Egner wasn't married yet, but his plans for the future included a certain blue-eyed brunette named Dorothy Carney who lived in Philadelphia.

"Yeah," said W.O.

It wasn't a night for conversation. They could only hang on as the ship bucked and rolled, and keep as good a lookout as possible in the circumstances. The old four-stackers were notorious for their rolling, and tonight the *Truxtun* was really outdoing herself.

Lieutenant Newman continued to try to get radio direction-finder

bearings without success, and was standing on the port wing of the
bridge with Ensign Loughridge when the quartermaster[1] reported, "I
saw a light spot in the sky, sir."

Neither Loughridge nor the navigator had seen it and before they
could investigate, both sighted land looming through the sleet, about
200 to 300 yards away on the port bow. A solid gray-white mass, it
towered above them.

Newman shouted, "All engines stop! Full right rudder!"

Loughridge rushed into the pilothouse, rang up "Stop" on the annunciator, and repeated the order for "Full right rudder" to the
helmsman, who was already putting on rudder. Loughridge shouted
to the quartermaster, "Pass collision word."

The navigator took the annunciator and rang up, "Starboard back
full." The general alarm went off, startling the crew to wakefulness
with its clamor.

The starboard engine was backed full and the ship had swung
about 10° to the right, away from the towering cliff, when she struck.
She gave a lurch and seemed to rise up on a ledge and slide along it
for a distance.

"All engines stop!" Newman shouted.

It was 0410 hours, zone plus-4 time. She struck one minute after
the *Wilkes* did.

The *Truxtun* grounded gently enough. To Ensign Seamans,
awakened from sleep on the wardroom transom, it was no different
from the sensation of running gently upon rocks in a smaller boat.
He thought she had struck ice. Maddocks was sure it was ice. They
had passed through ice yesterday; it was not unlikely that they had
met up with more of the same.

Egner had finished his cocoa but was still holding the cup in his
hand when the *Truxtun* struck. He bounced against the gun and
broke the cup. They had hit something. What the hell was it, an iceberg?

He did not give a thought to land. It was the iceberg season and,
he was sure, they had collided with an iceberg. Not a happy prospect
in freezing waters so far from land.

Lieutenant Commander Hickox rushed to the bridge within 30
seconds of the grounding. He immediately passed the word for all

[1] Not identified by Loughridge and not a survivor.

hands on deck, with life jackets on. The crew were already pouring on deck, some dressed for emergency, others not. All headed for their "abandon ship" positions.

The *Truxtun* was aground forward. She was still on an even keel, rocking slightly—a very easy rock—and did not seem to be caught very solidly. The light spot, seen a couple of minutes earlier, was off their port quarter. They recognized it as the reflection of a ship's searchlight. It did not seem to be signaling, but appeared to be sweeping back and forth. Whatever it meant, they had no time to think about it. Their own large searchlight was out of order,[2] and the small signal searchlight was playing on the cliffs towering above them.

They were in a crescent-shaped cove, which protected them somewhat from the heavy seas they had just steamed through. The *Truxtun* was practically leaning against a great rock on her starboard side. About 100 yards from their starboard bow was a cliff sloping to the sea and buried in white water. All around, ice-covered rock loomed above them. Pinnacle Head, a stark landmark for fishermen for miles around, rose straight up for nearly 300 feet on their port quarter. On the left hand, close to the shore, was another huge rock and a scattering of smaller, equally deadly rocks looking like savage teeth through the white water between the *Truxtun* and the sheer granite cliff.

The *Truxtun,* engines now turning over, rocked with the swells that wrapped around the tip of the crescent and rolled into the cove. It was rough, but not as rough as it had been outside.

Seamans had hauled his foul-weather gear over his pajamas, grabbed his life jacket, and rushed topside. His gut reaction was astonishment at the closeness of the surrounding cliffs. With his upbringing on the sea, and his Naval Academy training, he could not stifle the feeling that the *Truxtun* was in a very ignominious position. The sea was running, the wind was blowing, but aground? How? Why?

Ensign Maddocks looked at the cold, gray cliffs and said aloud, "Oh my God! My God! Where are we?"

[2] Not explained if it had been damaged in the grounding or if it had been out of order prior to it.

10

Lawn Head
February 18, 1942—0409–0417 hours

The two escort ships had changed positions. The *Truxtun*, which had originally been on the *Pollux*'s left hand on course 047° true, had gradually switched positions on the 048° course and had gone ashore in Chambers Cove along the coast about 1¾ miles (roughly 3,100 yards) east and to the right of the point of land where the *Pollux* went ashore. The *Pollux*, having changed course from 047° to 057° at 0130 hours, had worked to the right of the *Wilkes*, which had grounded 1 mile or more west of, and on the guide ship's left 0409 hours, the *Truxtun* at 0410 hours, the *Pollux* at 0417 hours. The tide was ebbing, but in less than a half hour, at 0436 hours, it would begin to flood, and it would add more power and fury to the stormy seas falling upon its hapless victims.

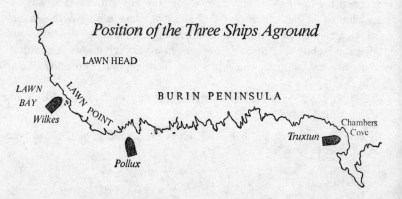

Position of the Three Ships Aground

LAWN HEAD

LAWN BAY

LAWN POINT

Wilkes

BURIN PENINSULA

Pollux

Truxtun

Chambers Cove

PART TWO

Shipwreck

11

USS *Truxtun*
February 18, 1942—0415 hours

Harry Egner's feeling was one of relief as he surveyed the cove. At least they had a chance of survival as long as they were close to land. To have to abandon the *Truxtun* in life rafts and boats at sea would have been the end, he was sure of that.

In spite of the fact that they were hung up on one rock and surrounded by others, Egner and his shipmates had tremendous faith in their captain. They had been in bad storms in Iceland where the ship had dragged anchor all night, and he had used the engines going ahead and backing down to keep them from going aground. In one storm they had lost their boats and liferafts, but he had brought them through. In his thirteen years in the Navy, Egner had sailed with several captains, but Captain Hickox was the best when it came to handling ships. If anyone could get them out of this mess, their captain could.

Having familiarized himself with the situation, Hickox ordered the ship full astern, and with both engines backing, the *Truxtun* slid back a few feet. Her screws hit the rocks and were torn off. With her bow acting as a pivot, driven by wind and wave, her stern swung to port and grounded. She was now firmly entrenched in a nest of rocks, which pierced the hull and released great quantities of fuel oil into the sea. The heavy swells rolling into the cove lifted her and slammed her down with a thud that reverberated around the cliffs. She had a slight list to port.

Then Egner saw a light about 45° off their starboard bow. It was a white light, like the forward masthead navigation light of a ship, about 500 yards distant, he estimated. Lieutenant Commander Hickox and Lieutenant Newman were on the wing and one of them, obviously thinking it was the *Pollux* or the *Wilkes,* shouted, "For God's sake, send a signal; they're coming in on top of us!"

As Egner stared at it, the light[1] seemed to pass them by.

Loughridge was ordered to send a message to the *Wilkes* by TBS. It did not get through. The *Wilkes* was apparently not receiving. An attempt to signal by small searchlight was equally unsuccessful. They did not break radio silence yet. Above all else, radio security took top priority, and they would not reveal the position of a U. S. Navy combat ship except as a last measure.

The seas were lifting and dropping the *Truxtun* on the rocks and rolling her back and forth. The captain ordered the starboard anchor out to hold her bow in position, and the searchlight was played around the cove again. The headland was very steep, but about 250 yards off their port bow, waves were rushing upon a narrow strip of beach beneath the cliffs that appeared less precipitous; it was not much of a beach, but it was better than none.

Orders were passed to the crew to dress warmly and to bring all blankets topside, in case they would be needed if they had to abandon ship,

Seamans went below to the wardroom and pulled on every warm piece of clothing he had: two wool sweaters, an all-weather windproof suit, his heavy pea jacket, pants, and a pair of sheepskin-lined rubber boots over his shoes. He found a pair of woolen gloves and a pair of leather gloves for his hands. Over all that he put on his life jacket, then he gathered the blankets from the transom and went topside.

The crew gradually gathered on the deck, wearing what warm clothing they had been able to find and carrying blankets. Each man took his "abandon ship" position.

Ensign Maddocks, as the assistant engineer, went to his emergency station in the after engine room. His primary concern was to try to keep the pumps and the generators operating. It was quickly evident to him that, as the ship rolled, lifted, and dropped in the heavy seas,

---

[1] Undoubtedly it was the searchlight that Quartermaster Turner on the *Pollux* had switched on to send a message to the *Wilkes,* which was supposed to be on their right, about ceasing to zigzag just before she struck.

the various pumps and other pieces of large machinery were being damaged. Even the keel, the bilge plates, and the frames were buckling and cracking, and water was beginning to trickle in.

The chief engineer, Lieutenant (jg) James Walker Danforth, went to the forward engine room. Danforth's job was to keep the main plant in operation as long as possible, to keep the generators operating so that there was electricity to keep the pumps operating if they were needed to keep down flooding.

Hickox had no alternative now but to break radio silence, but decided to send the message in cryptographic code. Leggett was about to transmit a distress signal when over the emergency signal came the distress call from the *Wilkes* to the *Truxtun:*

Wilkes aground entrance Placentia Bay. Stand by us if possible. Believe we are near Ferryland Point.

Hickox then sent out his own call:

We are on the rocks. Dog tanks holed. Both props useless and rudder out of whack. Am abandoning ship.

Methodically they went about abandon-ship procedure. All secret, confidential, and restricted matter was placed in weighted bags and taken up to the well deck for transfer to the beach. There was no panic. The ship had a slight list to port, and with daylight it would be simply a matter of getting on the rafts or lifeboats and paddling ashore.

Ensign Seamans and a companion[2] watched the machinery in the engine room shake from its foundations. "How long before the boiler rooms flood, I wonder?" Seamans said.

The four boilers—each with its own smokestack—were amidships, and it was a foregone conclusion that it was only a matter of time before the *Truxtun* flooded completely. Yet they could not believe they were in danger: The *Truxtun* was still upright; there was land all around, and eventually another Navy ship would come in and either pull them off and take them to Argentia for repair activity or, if worse came to the worst, they would be taken off.

Presently Seamans stationed himself on the forecastle bow. There was no shelter there, nothing to break the seas, no bulwark, only the

[2] Name not remembered.

lifelines around the edge of the deck. He would not move from his position there until the sea swept him away.

Egner received orders to get out the lifeboat that had been secured inboard earlier. He and his crew tried to get it in position to lower over the side, but with the broken forward stay wire, they had to physically try to swing the bow out and forward in order for the stern to clear the aft boat davit. When the ship rolled to starboard, they would push the bow out, but before they could get the stern out, the *Truxtun* would roll to port and the boat would swing back in, hitting No. 4 smokestack. Egner and his crew tried to get the lifeboat over the side three or four times, but he did not have enough men to hold the bow out. On the fourth try a large hole was knocked in the side of the boat when it slammed into the smokestack. Egner reported it to the captain.

"Try to get the gig in the water," Hickox told him.

Egner and his men went to get the gig over, but the *Truxtun* was broadside to the big rock that was immediately below the gig and it was not possible to launch it. When he told this to Hickox, the captain said, "Try your best to get the boat in the water."

Egner and his crew studied the situation. The seas were rushing upon the rock and surging up around and over it. "If we lower it about halfway, the waves might take it clear of the rock," he told the men.

The Cato brothers, Leo and James, stood on No. 4 torpedo tube, pulling on the boat line as the gig was lowered. The strategy did not work; the gig was smashed into two pieces on the rock.

Well. That was that.

Egner and his men walked away, but the Cato brothers sat side by side on the tube. They remained there, their arms around each other. They were not seen again.

Maddocks, in the aft engine room, watched the machinery fall apart before his eyes. The pounding of the ship against the rocks had smashed in the port side of her hull, causing the room to flood. The pumps could not keep up with the water, and gradually there was more flooding; pieces of machinery began to work loose, breaking off at their foundations. There was nothing to do but retreat before the rising water. The captain ordered the boilers secured and the aft engineering spaces to be abandoned. The steam was let out of the boilers to prevent them from blowing up, and all light and heat were cut off aft. There was a watertight door between the aft engine room and the forward engine room, and Maddocks' crew dogged down the door to make sure the water wouldn't get into the forward engine room, which was still operational under the loving ministrations of the chief engineer.

They were all cold. Egner was belatedly recalling the conversation he had had with some sailors he had met while on liberty in Halifax, Nova Scotia, Canada. They had been shipwrecked, and had grim stories to tell. "Always be prepared and carry a good-sized pocket knife in case you get tangled up in something," they had told him. "Be sure you have a waterproof match box, a waterproof flashlight, and always wear heavy wool clothing, it will keep you warm and help you to float better if you have to go overboard." Another sailor had said he did not have a waterproof match box, but he always carried matches in a prophylactic.

Standing on the deck with the sound of the ocean thundering against the cliffs, Egner remembered too late the advice given to him. He remembered, too, his wallet in his clothes locker, and decided to go below and get it. There were no lights in their living quarters, and the water was up to his knees, but he knew the ship like the palm of his hand and, making his way to his locker, fumbled around for his wallet, two prophylactics, a package of cigarettes, and a box of matches. He put the cigarettes and matches inside a prophylactic, tied the end and, as an added precaution, tucked it inside another one. Then he sloshed his way back through the ship and went topside.

No breakfast could be served, so the cook opened crates of oranges and apples. The chief in charge of the canteen passed out candy. He was an old-timer, honorably retired from the Navy but called back into service at the outbreak of war. They kidded him: "Say, Chief, how are you going to remember who owes you for candy?"

"Yeah! If we get off O.K., you gonna make us pay for it?"

The chief grinned. He had taken all the coins from the change box and put it in his pockets.

"You'd better not fall overboard, Chief, you'll go down like a rock with all that change on you."

"We're gonna keep an eye on you, Chief, and get our share of the loot when we get ashore."

They huddled behind the galley deck, trying to keep out of the cold, and munched on the fruit and candy. Someone joked, "I wonder when the first liberty boat is going ashore."

Sleet, combined with spray, fell over them, icing the decks and making it difficult to move around. The tide was flooding, and the wind was shifting, hauling around more to the south, bringing waves right in on top of them. The *Truxtun* began to pound on the rocks more violently, gradually listing to starboard. She still had power from the forward engine room, which operated the searchlight, but there was little they could do until daylight.

They could not know that in the relative quiet and safety of the cove, *now* was the time to concentrate on getting to the beach.

12

USS *Pollux*
February 18, 1942—0417 hours

As the *Pollux* thrashed about, plates clanging against the rocks, her crew were hurled to the deck. In the forward crow's nest, Seaman Second Class John Harrison Carey was badly shaken up, and as quickly as possible he got down to the deck.

Lieutenant Grindley, regaining his feet, rushed into the chartroom, ran around the table, and glanced at the chart to estimate their position. It had to be Lawn Head, he felt, barely pausing before dashing out on the wing and ducking into Lieutenant Russell Schmidt's room, which was just behind his own quarters. He gave Schmidt the approximate position of the *Pollux* and ordered him to get a message out that they were aground.

The searchlights were turned on immediately, their powerful beams probing the black, sleety night. The port light was trained on the shore; the large 24-inch light was directed out to sea. "Keep it moving back and forth at a moderate speed toward the horizon, to warn other ships that might be coming along behind us," Turney ordered.

"The *Wilkes* is aground too, Captain," Thomas Turner told him.

Whatever his thoughts were about the *Wilkes,* Commander Turney had his hands full with his own ship. It seemed to Grindley that a remarkable change had come over him. The worry of the preceding hours were put behind him; he gathered himself together, became very cool and calm. He was a leader.

The port searchlight revealed that they had hit at the base of a steep cliff. A ledge, projecting from the base, showed black and ugly through the seas hurtling upon it. White water rushed up the rock face, and it looked as if the *Pollux* were trying to climb that cliff as well. She had grounded on a course about 60° from the shoreline.

In the crew's quarters, which had been darkened since "lights out," the men scrambled to their feet, colliding with each other in the blackness. There were cries of "Torpedo!" and "We're hit! We're hit!"

Alfred Dupuy, picking himself up, thought: Oh, Lordy! This is no dry run.

Henry Strauss thought they had been torpedoed until "collision" sounded; then he figured they had run into one of the destroyer escorts.

Over the shouting and confusion, Boatswain's Mate First Class Garrett Lloyd yelled, "Why doesn't someone turn on the goddamn lights?"

The lights came on.

Above them, in the starboard passage, the lifeboat crew tumbled in a heap, Laurence Weaver among them. All were shouting, "We're hit!"

Another crash convinced Lawrence Calemmo that, after many near-misses over the past two days, they had finally collided with the *Truxtun*. "No, we've hit the *Truxtun*," he declared, scrambling to his feet. "Let's go!"

Below, there was a mad dash to get life jackets, foul-weather clothing, and their beloved tailor-made blues, but Warren Greenfield decided to take a look outside first. He rushed up the ladders and looked out through the hatchway to see what the hell was going on. Searchlights revealed white water roaring up a cliff face. Up, up it went, reaching for the black sky, to burst in a cloud of spray before sliding down again. "My God!" he cried, hardly able to believe his eyes.

The ear-splitting alarms, coupled with the severe tremors wracking the ship, were summoning the men to their emergency posts. Lieutenant George Bradley's voice crackled over the loudspeaker: "All hands, man your damage-control stations on the double; this is an emergency. When you have your stations manned, report immediately to the bridge by telephone, or whatever means possible, for further instructions."

There was a rush to the ladders as sailors tried to get topside to their stations. Some were dressed in foul-weather gear; others were not. George Coleman, boatswain's mate second class, was one of those dressed only in dungaree shirt and pants and ordinary shoes and socks, which he would very soon regret.

When the rush subsided, Greenfield hastened below to get into his foul-weather gear, only to discover there was nothing left. His heavy padded coveralls and jacket, heavy woolen helmet, arctic boots, even his gloves, were gone. He dug out what he could find and threw an oilskin raincoat over it all. He came across a flat hat, which was part of their dress uniform, and put it on his head; it would likely take wing at the first good puff of wind, he knew, so he searched for something more practical. He found only a pair of goggles. What the hell, he thought, fitting the goggles over the flat hat and the strap under his chin.

A knife without its sheath lay on the deck, and Greenfield picked it up, thrusting it in the pocket of the raincoat before running topside. Somewhere outside the galley he found a life jacket and struggled into it; then without boots or gloves, he went on deck. With the picture of those waves climbing the cliffs etched on his brain, he had no thought for his new guitar.

Sharing the same compartment in officers' country, Lieutenant Jack Garnaus and Ensign Alfred Pollack were literally bounced out of their bunks when the *Pollux* grounded. Pollack, who had been sleeping soundly, yelled, "What's going on?"

"I think we've taken a torpedo!" Garnaus yelled back. It was a prospect that gave them little hope of survival in the stormy seas assaulting them.

The continual crashing and heaving of the ship told its own story. Both men had slept fully clothed, and they swiftly put on their foul-weather gear. The porthole had been left open while they slept, and almost immediately waves rushed in. Were they foundering? "Let's get the hell out of here," Pollack yelled.

Ensign Grayson's first thought, as he picked himself up off the deck, was the cargo of aerial bombs that had been stacked in the ship's bow. He did not know if they had been grounded, torpedoed, or were in collision, but he felt he had better check the crib of bombs, which could be a menace if they had become loose.

He pulled on his foul-weather gear and, unaware of the true situation, rushed to the main deck forward. Seas lifting over the starboard side of the *Pollux* picked him up and sent him tumbling head over heels back to the bridge structure. As soon as he could find his legs he hauled himself inside and went up to the bridge to appraise the situation.

The sailors coming up from below were stunned by the spectacle confronting them. Through the driving sleet Dupuy saw waves as high as buildings falling over the fore part of the *Pollux* and slamming against the cliff. Calemmo, running on deck to check out No. 1 and No. 2 motor launches, stopped dead. Wow! Was he dreaming? Where the hell did those snow-covered mountains come from? Ten minutes ago they had been surrounded by ocean. Coleman stared, dumfounded. Pollack had the fleeting thought that this might be the end. Garnaus, strangely enough, felt an overwhelming relief; they were in trouble, but at least there was someplace to go if they had to leave the ship. It was a hell of a lot better than sinking at sea with no place to attempt a landing. He gave a fleeting thought to the *Wilkes* and the *Truxtun,* but it was very fleeting.

Strauss and Harold Brooks struggled up the icy ladder to join Turner at the big searchlight. Playing the light on the shore, Strauss was confident they were safe because they were so close to land.

Lieutenant Philip K. Dougherty, chief engineer, a recalled merchant-marine reservist, had already arrived at the engine room and relieved Walter Bulanowski, who hurried to his general-quarters position in the after part of the ship. Dougherty ordered the emergency diesel generator started, in anticipation of having to close down the main plant.

The *Pollux* had four generators: two 250-kw generators; one 250-kw diesel generator in the engine room; and one 5-kw diesel generator in the emergency generator room. Dougherty began to transfer all power to the emergency diesel, but kept one of the turbine generators running. Then he waited for orders.

Calemmo, meanwhile, stopped only momentarily at the sight of the mountains. As a member of the lifeboat crew, and the diesel-engine expert, he must make sure the boats were operational. He rushed toward the No. 1 launch on the starboard side, clambered aboard, and started the engine. The makeshift heater still worked and the engine roared to life, but the launch moved frighteningly in its cradle. A quick check revealed that all the boat gripes were broken—there was nothing to hold the launch in its cradle when the sea rolled over it. Not wishing to be carried overboard, Calemmo did not linger; he was out of the launch and back in the protection of the superstructure when a white-topped wave fell upon the launch and smashed it. He found the No. 2 launch on the port side partially flooded and the engine cold and useless. Once again Calemmo raced for safety as the waves lifted over the foredeck. Shortly after, the port lifeboat was carried away.

The *Pollux,* impaled on a rock just forward of amidships, was hard aground. She had a starboard list up to 10°; her bow was smothered under the breaking seas and was sinking; only her stern was floating free. Commander Turney ordered the engines stopped while they took stock of the situation. He ordered soundings along the starboard side to ascertain the depth of the water over which the *Pollux* was leaning. Under Bradley's supervision, they were taken as far forward as the breaking seas permitted, which was no farther than No. 4 hatch. Strauss and his shipmates, swearing like troopers as the seas hurled spray over them but able to joke about it, took the soundings and reported them to Bradley, who in turn reported to Commander Turney: "There's a heavy undertow, sir, and it's difficult to get accurate soundings, but we estimate between 7 and 10 fathoms."[1] Deep water for a ship in the *Pollux*'s situation.

Commander Turney decided to try to back off. He put the telegraph to "full back." With her propellers thrashing madly, the *Pollux* strained and heaved, but did not budge. Turney ordered the engines stopped.

The seas hitting them on the beam fell over the foredeck and the bow with a devastating force that did not bode well. Her weight, forward of the rocks that had ripped her open, plus the weight of the water falling upon it, would very soon cause the *Pollux* to break in two. When that happened, it was more than likely that she would slide off the reef into the deep water. In her present condition she was still in one piece and salvageable and, with her valuable cargo, Commander Turney had to consider that. "I think that for the time being we had better hold her aground," he said.

His officers agreed.

"We will have to try to get her closer to shore to prevent the bow

[1] Between 42 and 70 feet.

from sinking further, and to make it easier for rescue and possible salvage operations," he decided.

He turned the telegraph to "full ahead."

With grinding, shuddering protests, the *Pollux* was maneuvered to within 20 yards of the ledge, at an angle of about 30°, and there she remained, almost snug against the shore. Her afterpart continued to float; she still had power and seemed to be in no immediate danger.

The officers were checking the ship's personnel, most of whom had taken shelter inside the superstructure after that first numbing look at the scene around them. Far too many were lightly dressed. Grindley gave orders to his ratings: "Get back into the crew spaces, gather up blankets, pea jackets, anything that looks like warm clothing and, if necessary, break into the clothing issues, but do not return empty-handed." How fortunate they were to be in a supply ship and to have winter issue aboard, he thought.

The *Pollux,* not being a combat vessel, had no damage-control officer as such, but Edward A. Stroik, as first lieutenant in charge of the maintenance of the ship, had been designated as damage-control officer. He and his crew gathered at their emergency station in the crew's mess hall, aft of the crew's sleeping quarters, and Stroik reported to the bridge by telephone. "Have a detail go forward and report the extent of damage and whether anything can be done to correct same," Commander Turney ordered. Garnaus and his men went below to check his division aft for damage.

Meanwhile the officers and their crews were going about their abandon-ship procedure. Documents were collected and crammed into canvas bags. All restricted and secret files, which were in the custody of Lieutenant Schmidt and stored in heavily weighted canvas sacks, were placed in pillowcases to facilitate handling. They were placed alongside the main confidential and secret safe, which would also be taken ashore. Most of the navigation records were put in a canvas bag by Yeoman Second Class William J. Ward. Grindley and Turner assisted. "Get everything up to the main deck," Schmidt ordered.

Lieutenant Paul L. Weintraub, the only other U. S. Naval Academy man aboard the *Pollux, w*as the supply officer, and he led the members of his division to No. 3 hold to collect food, water, ship's records, blankets, and other essential items. It looked to Weintraub as if they had run aground in a remote, inhospitable region, and God alone knew how far they were from human habitation. "Take enough food and water for a couple of days, and get every available life jacket aboard," he ordered. There was only one line-throwing gun in the armory, forward, and he sent Gunner's Mate Lee E. Johnson to get it. It was too late; the armory was flooded.

Lieutenant Pollack, as disbursing officer, and his assistant, Storekeeper First Class Paul Enoch Pulver, were gathering records and monies. Navy regulations stipulated that money was to be carried in a canvas money bag attached to a monstrous float with a very long line. It was clumsy and Pollack had always felt ridiculous toting the moneybag with the heavy coil of rope slung over his shoulders, but Navy regs were Navy regs.

They stowed roughly forty-seven thousand dollars in the bag, and vouchers worth another thirty-eight thousand dollars in a leather briefcase owned by Pollack. There were approximately fifteen hundred dollars in silver, which he left in the safe. He might have to carry the moneybag everywhere he went, but he was damned if he was going to load himself with nickels, dimes, and quarters.

The provisions, blankets, clothing, and documents were wrapped in canvas and raincoats and stored on the port side of the boat deck, ready to be carried ashore. Some of the clothing was stored in Commander Turney's cabin, and the odd pint of whiskey found its way there. The captain had put his private supply of cigarettes out for anyone who needed a smoke.

Stroik's damage-control party quickly discovered that the *Pollux* was severely damaged. Her false bottom, which contained the fuel tanks, had been ruptured under hold Nos. 1 and 2, and the structure of the ship had been pierced. Both holds were flooding as the sea flowed in through the damaged hull. No. 1 hold, close to the forepeak, was well under water.

The forepeak, which normally contained part of the ship's supply of fresh water, was flooded. The afterpeak was still watertight, and it gave hope that all was not lost. If damage to the forepeak wasn't too severe, it could be pumped out and they might be able to float her off.

Greatly encouraged, the damage-control party hurried back through the ship only to discover that No. 3 hold was flooding as well, and Lieutenant Weintraub and his crew were prudently retreating before it. Their only hope of keeping the ocean out of the engine room was the cofferdam[2] and the watertight bulkhead, extending from the keel up to the first platform deck, below the main deck. A quick examination showed that the bulkhead was holding and keeping the *Pollux* dry and buoyant aft.

Stroik made his way to the engine room, meeting up with Grayson, who had also been checking on the damage. They entered the engine room; its massive machinery was still humming and giving an impression of comfort and security. Dougherty was told of the conditions forward. "Can you trim the forward peak? If we can lighten the ship forward, we might be able to float her off."

Dougherty got busy. "Try to take bilge suctions forward," he told Water Tender First Class Arthur C. Matthews.

Matthews started the bilge pump, and Dougherty told Water Tender Second Class William Budka, "Go topside and observe the overboard discharge."

Budka rushed topside, but returned shortly to tell the chief that fuel oil was being discharged instead of bilge water. The line to the forward peak must be ruptured, Dougherty decided. At that point the heating coils to the fuel tanks ruptured, and Dougherty ordered the heat shut off forward.

"Can we correct the ship's list?" Stroik asked.

"We can try." During her journey from Casco Bay the *Pollux* had consumed all the fuel oil from No. 5 port tank. "If we can transfer fuel from any of the starboard tanks forward to No. 5 port, it might help." He passed the order: "See if you can get a suction from any one of the starboard double bottoms and transfer it to No. 5 port."

From Nos. 1, 2, and 3 starboard tanks came not oil but a solid flow of salt water. It was a hopeless situation, and Stroik said he had better report to the bridge. He praised the young sailors for sticking by him without fright or panic below decks. "You were all cool, calm, and steady, and I'm proud of you," he told them, then he left to give Commander Turney the bad news.

Dougherty said to his own men, "All right, let's try No. 4." Miraculously they got a suction on No. 4 starboard tank, and began transferring the fuel to the empty No. 5 port tank.

Meanwhile William L. Stanford, shipfitter first class, and assistant

[2] A watertight structure for making repairs below the water line.

to Lieutenant Stroik, was again checking the situation forward with one other member of the damage-control detail. Standing in the storage area of the crew's quarters, two decks below the main deck, Stanford beamed the light of his portable battery emergency light down into No. 3 hold. It looked as if the whole ocean were cascading into the ship. The water was rising swiftly and would very shortly be into the crew's quarters.

The battering of the hull from the outside and the roar of seas rushing into the hold made a combination of sounds that could shake a man to the core, and Stanford and his helper stepped back into the crew's quarters, closed the watertight doors on the port and starboard side forward, and dogged them down. They passed through the empty, littered quarters, stepped into the crew's mess, closed the watertight doors, and dogged them down too. These watertight doors would hold the invading ocean at bay only as long as the bulkhead held. He rejoined the damage-control party. "Phone the information to the bridge," he ordered his helper and then said to the others, "Stand fast while I go below into the engine room to see how the forward bulkhead plates are holding."

A quick exploratory tour revealed that the bulkhead plates were starting to bulge at the seams and water was seeping through.

Lieutenant Dougherty asked, "How bad is it, Bill?"

"Not good. We'll have to try to shore them up," Stanford replied.

He reported it to Captain Turney himself. "Do whatever is necessary, and report back to me whenever possible," Turney replied.

The damage-control crew went below to shore up the bulkhead plates.

It was disheartening news to Commander Turney, who still cherished the hope that his ship could be refloated, but it was evident from the reports of Lieutenant Stroik and William Stanford that all fuel tanks forward had been ruptured, and if the lines were pumping salt water when they should be pumping fuel, they would not be able to trim the ship and float her off. If the watertight bulkhead was weakening, then it was simply a matter of time before the ship was completely flooded.

"We had better prepare abandon-ship procedure," Turney decided.

With a heavy heart he told Lieutenant Commander John Gabrielson, the executive officer, "Rig the cargo nets over the port side aft, and see about getting the liferafts over, or as many as you can get over. Secure them by lines to the main deck." He added, "See that the men are fed as best as possible." Turney also ordered the emergency flares fired. Under the supervision of Grindley, Bradley, and Ensign Edgar D. Brown, Gunner's Mate Johnson fired ten rockets into the sleet-ridden sky. For brief moments the sparkling blossoms of light flared above the clifftops, but there was no one to see them.

The nests of liferafts were encased in ice and the crew began the task of chopping with axes and knives to clear it away before they could be put over the side.

When word was passed to the galley to try to feed the men, the two cooks, Ship's Cook Third Class John Arthur "Dusty" Dunlap and Ship's Cook Third Class Samuel L. Nicosia, started up the stove. Soon ham steaks were sizzling and hungry sailors crowded into the galley. It was not easy trying to cook on a stove with a list up to 10° and the seesawing of the ship; and when the seas started swirling about their knees, it was not really very funny, but the crew were as insulting as ever with their smart remarks about their cooking, trying to make the best of a miserable situation.

Nicosia, plump, unflappable, and, in the eyes of his contemporaries, much wiser than they in many respects, was continually called upon for advice. He had become their overseer, their father. Once he gave advice, it was usually followed. They came to him for money as well, and he gave that too. Now he waved his fork at them: "Shaddup and eat."

Hank Strauss was huddled in the shelter of the bridge. The howling of the wind, the crashing of the waves, the pounding, grinding, jarring, and lurching of the ship, the tortured creaking of the gear as she rolled back and forth was a nightmare of sound and motion, and Strauss was not only motionsick but also heartsick at the scene before him. Someone put a piece of ham steak in his hand. It had an oily fingerprint on it, but Strauss forced himself to eat it. If, by some miracle, they got ashore he would need every bit of food that came his way to keep up his strength.

Lieutenant Commander Sam Bostic, the medical doctor—a veteran of World War I—was another of the fortunate men to get a slice of ham as well as a cup of coffee. Because of the severe rolling of the ship during the night, he had not closed his eyes, and he knew he had a long, grueling day stretching before him.

The officers continued to check the various parts of the ship for damage and flooding. Despite the watertight hatches secured earlier by Stanford, the water on the other side of the bulkhead had begun to seep into the crew's quarters. Grindley discovered it and reported it to Commander Turney, who ordered Bradley and Grayson, "Get a couple of chief petty officers, go below, and get everybody out. Search every compartment and make sure everybody is out."

Those not working at emergency stations were standing or sitting in orderly groups inside officers' country. None of the crew members had returned to their quarters, but as soon as word was passed that it was flooding, several slipped below for some personal effects.

Califano waded to his locker, in oily water up to his knees, for his mother's diamond engagement ring, which he usually wore on a chain around his neck, some family pictures, and his tailor-made blues. He decided to leave everything except the ring.

Greenfield cried out, "Holy smokes! My guitar!"

The bo'sun in charge, James Earl Dunn, said, "You *would* think of something like that."

Greenfield rushed below to retrieve it. The lights were still on, operating on the emergency generator, and he jumped down the ladder to the first deck, started down the ladder to the crew's quarters, but stopped dead when he saw the oil-crusted water creeping upward. He turned and bolted topside.

Sam Nicosia was still cooking when the word was passed; Artie Appel had a couple hundred dollars in his locker and decided to go below to get it. "I've got a hundred down there too," Sam said.

"You gonna come?"

A sea boarded the *Pollux*, rushed up the deck into the galley and around Sam's knees. "Are you kidding?"

Appel went below and got his money.

Strauss went below with Chief Quartermaster Robert G. Conine and brought up two cartons of cigarettes. Many others collected their beloved blues. Later, when the water was much higher, Nicosia went below and got his money. Janocha also went below to get his wristwatch, which had been a gift from his wife, and a handful of cigars.

The more daring ones dug out pints of liquor they had smuggled aboard on their last trip to the Caribbean, strictly as a protective measure against the bitter winds of winter in the North Alantic. Nicosia slipped five pints inside his jacket.

Gray daylight revealed towering breakers spilling white water over them. One behind the other, white tops streaming before the wind, huge waves crashed around and on top of them, so that the whole Atlantic Ocean seemed to be tumbling upon them. They were lying beneath a cliff with an overhang; the extremities of the snow-covered ledge at its base were heavily iced. The cliff was probably not more than 75 feet high above the ledge, but its face was sheer. Waves reached for the clifftop then fell back, surging across the narrow stretch between ship and shore, to slam against her port side. She was being pounded so heavily it was impossible for the men to keep on their feet without holding on.

Her bow was about 40 feet from the ledge, her stern about 200 yards from the shore. Lying parallel to the shore, they could not see the jagged rock face of the land extending eastward behind the headland, buried in the wild wave; but westward, the shore was a series of ice-covered slopes and crevices, beyond which was the ridge of Lawn Head that Bollinger had seen silhouetted against the beam of the *Wilkes*' searchlight. Rock islands were scattered in the mouth of the bay, visible through the sleet because of the heavy surf climbing them.

The *Wilkes* had run into a little indentation under the cliffs in the lee of the the headland and, to a degree, was protected from wind and sea. But the *Pollux,* trapped at the base of a headland facing south, was exposed to the battering force of the ocean.

13

The *Wilkes* was caught by the bow on a rocky shelf at right angles to the shore, roughly 50 yards from a great snow-covered embankment. Protected as she was, the swells, propelled along the shore, caused her to roll heavily.

After the grounding, searchlights revealed jagged rocks on each end of the shelf, but none were close enough to cause injury to the *Wilkes'* structure. Commander Kelsey ordered the engines stopped in order to keep her on the shelf until the extent of damage, and depths of water around her, could be determined.

Depths ranged from 20 feet forward up to 70 feet aft. Damage was severe enough. Eight of her forward compartments had been fractured and were entirely flooded; two more were partially flooded. One fuel-oil tank was leaking. She was down by the head slightly but not listing. Quickly Commander Kelsey ordered the crew to begin efforts to lighten ship forward. "Move all provisions, all ready-service ammunition, and all accessible portable weights from forward aft," he told the officers. He ordered fuel oil pumped overboard from the leaking forward fuel tank. Boats and rafts were made ready for instant lowering. Crew members not so employed were assembled aft.

A steady stream of sailors hustled back and forth, depositing all portable cargo aft. Topside, the port anchor and 30 fathoms of chain were dropped overboard to lighten the bow. As the crews labored on deck, damage-control parties were below shoring up bulkheads and hatches; the pumps were operating on the flooded compartments with no success.

The wind was shifting southward, bringing the seas to bear more directly upon the *Wilkes* and causing her to bounce and roll in an alarming manner. There was real danger that as the storm center passed, it would blow more from the southwest and perhaps blow her broadside onto the beach.

The engines were started. Commander Kelsey ordered the engine room by telegraph to back the port engine from one third to full astern to compensate for wind and sea, which were threatening to swing her sideways onto the ledge. Only boiler Nos. 1 and 3 had been in use for steaming; now Kelsey ordered No. 2 boiler lighted in No. 2 fireroom, to give her more power for backing off. It would also help in case water had gotten into the fuel lines operating to Nos. 1 and 3. Lieutenant Smyth, operating on the same wavelength, had already taken the initiative and ordered boiler Nos. 2 and 4 lighted off. As a further preventive measure against being driven ashore, Commander Kelsey directed that they try to haul the starboard anchor aft, using the towing hawser, in the event it would be needed to drop over the stern and hold her fast.

All efforts to back off the ledge were futile, and it was conceded that until the tide began to flood, there was no likelihood of the *Wilkes*' getting free.

The attempt to haul the anchor astern was abandoned. Every ten minutes they tried to back off the shelf with the crew assisting by rushing from midship to the fantail, hitting the rhythm of the ship each time the stern dipped and adding their combined weight, totaling more than 30,000 pounds. Back and forth they ran, to no avail. Smyth, popping on deck now and again to keep an anxious eye on the props, prayed furiously: "Get us off! Get us off!"

Finally, at 0710 hours, with the port engine backing full to offset the seas that were rolling upon them from the south, and subsequently with all engines churning at full speed astern, the *Wilkes* managed to back clear of the ledge into deep water. It was too risky to try to haul in the port anchor, and they had slipped it at the 90-fathom detachable link.

While the lifeboat crew were swinging the gig to the inboard position, the *Wilkes* rolled viciously, and the guys were wrenched from the hands of the sailors. The gig crashed on the bilge pad and was damaged beyond repair. They now had only one lifeboat.

The *Wilkes*' bow was sheared at the 9-foot mark and her bottom plates were curled like an opened sardine can, almost to No. 2 turret. She limped out of Lawn Bay and hove to, 1,000 yards offshore from the *Pollux*.

Commander Turney and Lieutenant Grindley on the *Pollux,* standing at the port aftercorner of the bridge deck, had intermittently watched the flagship maneuvering to free herself. In a voice charged with emotion, Turney said, "Thank God she's free; they so desperately need destroyers for the war."

Grindley had a different thought: What a lucky bunch of stumble-bum bastards!

Commander Kelsey ordered a message by searchlight, which Signalman Crowley sent:

Wilkes badly holed forward. Will lie to near you as long as possible.

The *Pollux* flashed back:

Damage as far aft as No. 3 hold. Fast aground. Do not believe can get off without salvage assistance. Am going to try to land crew on beach.

The *Wilkes* lay off and waited.

14

Lawn, Newfoundland
February 18, 1942—0730 hours

Along the ice-covered arms of Lawn Bay, tucked behind a promontory, the picturesque fishing village of Lawn lay a good ten miles by land from Lawn Head. Houses perched on the rocky shoreline had their own coating of ice from the spray and sleet. White water exploded on the west side of the bay, and even in their protected little corner the ocean was quite disturbed; fishing skiffs bobbed wildly at their moorings.

Joseph Manning, a middle-aged fisherman, had gone to early church—for this was Ash Wednesday—had eaten breakfast, and had gone to the wharf to attend to his skiff. It was sleeting and snowing alternately when two youths came up to him. They were from Webber's Point, a couple of miles along the west arm of the bay. "Mr. Manning, there's a ship ashore on Lawn Point. We saw her," they said.

Manning looked at them with skepticism. "Now then, me sons, how can you see across the bay to Lawn Point in weather like this?"

"When it let up a little, we could see her. She wasn't against the shore—we could see the water between her and the Point."

Manning squinted across the harbor. He could barely see Webber's, which was no more than two miles from Lawn; how could they see five or six miles up the bay to Lawn Point? He didn't believe them.

"We seen her," the youths insisted.

The lads seemed earnest enough, but in his own day Manning had played many a trick on the older men in the community, and it *was* too thick a day for anyone to be able to see clear up the bay to Lawn Point. On a stormy winter's day it would be a long journey on a fool's errand to go through ten miles of woods on the say-so of two young rascals like that.

The two youths told their story to others in Lawn, but reaction was the same. Nobody believed them.

15

The barometer was still falling.

With the rising tide, the sea grew more boisterous. The wind was force 8 and the *Pollux* was taking severe punishment as she thumped about, further weakening the plates around the gaping hole where she was impaled. She was flooded to the deck plates forward, and her weight would eventually break her in two; there could be no doubt about that.

Sleet, wind, and stinging spray bedeviled her, but most fearsome of all was the ocean slamming against the cliffs, and the millrace it created between ship and shore. At first it had been pure white, but as the fuel oil flowed from her it had become an ugly yellow-brown. Wreckage was tossed about in the heavy current.

Lieutenant Dougherty reported to the bridge that they had lost the suction to No. 4 starboard tank after 2½ hours of pumping. "It hasn't made any difference to the ship's list, sir, she's still showing a starboard list of 8½°."

That had been evident all along.

The ledge at the base of the cliff seemed to be the only place where they might land. About 25 feet above sea level, it looked humpy, with holes and small crevices showing under the snow, and it was sheltered, to a degree, by the ship's bow. To the left, the sea cut into the ledge almost cutting it in two. It was joined by a narrow ridge, close to the face of the cliff. High-water line indicated that only the top part of the ledge was above water at high tide. The problem was how to get there and, with the probability of the

More of the *Pollux* crew: James M. Ross (top left, Elliot Portraits), William Stanford (top right), Thomas J. McCarron (center left), William C. Heldt (center right, courtesy of Isabel Farrell) and Laurence A. Weaver, Jr. (bottom left, Elliot's Peachtree Studio).

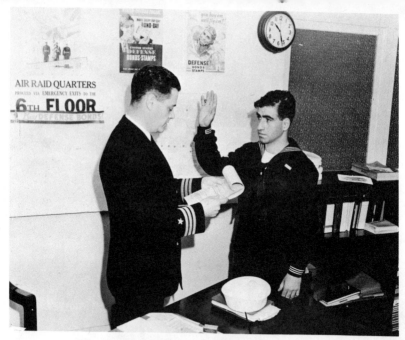

Isaac Henry Strauss receives his commission from Commander Hugh Turney after the disaster.

Warren "Wag" Greenfield (left) and Alfred M. Dupuy on shore patrol in Boston after the shipwreck. (Courtesy of Warren Greenfield)

Only the bow of the *Truxtun* remains above water in Chambers Cove the following day. Pinnacle Head, fishermen's landmark, towers darkly over the wreck. (Ena Farrell Edwards)

The broken remains of the *Pollux* off Lawn Head. Wreckage and fuel oil fill the cove in the foreground. (Ena Farrell Edwards)

The bow of the *Pollux* had just broken off and was disappearing beneath the sea when this rare photo was taken by Donald W. Cady from the port wing of the bridge. (Courtesy of Isaac Henry Strauss)

Cady also took this picture of sailors clustered beneath the boat falls, watching Garnaus, Greenfield, Calemmo, Lloyd, and DeRosa trying to reach the cove in the whaleboat. In the foreground is the section of the ledge reached by the sailors who swam ashore. (Courtesy of Isaac Henry Strauss)

This aerial view shows the ledge to which the *Pollux* sailors swam, the overhang on which the Newfoundlanders stood to pull the men up by rope, and the cave in which Calemmo, Lloyd, and 18 other men spent the long, bitterly cold night. (Derek Brown)

This is the ravine to which survivors had to walk after being hauled up over the cliff. They huddled around a smoky fire until all the men were rescued, then started the long trek to Iron Springs Mine. (Derek Brown)

A close-up of the cove where the *Pollux*'s whaleboat capsized and the cave that offered refuge to 20 of the shipwrecked sailors. (Derek Brown)

A view of the same cove and cave (dark shadow at right) from above. The rocky plateau to which Garnaus, Greenfield, and DeRosa climbed is just above the cave. The cove is still strewn with bits of wreckage. (Derek Brown)

Lifelines, attached to the *Pollux* rail, still trailed over the ship's side into the oil and wreckage when Ena Farrell took photos of the wreck on Saturday, February 21. (Ena Farrell Edwards)

Chambers Cove. The sheer cliffs are as high as 300 feet in places. The *Truxtun* was trapped between the two large rocks offshore, and men had to swim through oil, wreckage, and crashing breakers to reach the beach at right. Many died in the attempt. (Derek Brown)

At low tide, the beach is littered with driftwood, and some of the boulders are still crusted with fuel oil. The ledge in the left foreground is where Beau Parkerson stood for hours sending messages to the *Truxtun*. (Derek Brown)

The recess at the north end of the beach offered slight protection from the wind and sea. Newfoundland rescuers had to climb over the small oil-coated cliff in the foreground with the sailors on their backs before scaling another cliff to the top. (Cassie Brown)

Pollux breaking in two, it was a matter of urgency, they believed. The boats on the starboard side, including the captain's gig, could not be launched because of the heavy seas breaking upon them. Only No. 3 motor launch and No. 2 motor whaleboat, both on the port side aft of the bridge, were in a position where they might be put over.

The crew had cleared the ice from one of the rafts and were struggling to push it up the slanting deck. The raft, made of balsa wood and covered with canvas, could hold 15 men and, with the ship jerking around like she was, it was a monumental task shoving it up the tilting, icy deck.

It was taking a great deal of time and Commander Turney ordered the exec, Lieutenant Commander Gabrielson, to launch the No. 3 motor launch. Because of the starboard list, the launch was hanging in over the deck, and this created another problem getting it launched.

"Use the cargo boom of No. 5 to lift the boat out of its cradle and lower it into the sea," Turney ordered. The dynamos were still running, and the power was still being supplied to No. 5 hold. It should be relatively easy.

The winches were put into operation and, with a group of sailors holding a guideline to control the movements of the boom, the 30-foot boom swung up and over the heads of the sailors pushing the liferaft aft. Another group of sailors boarded the lifeboat, and Chief Machinist Mate Irving Smith, in charge of the lifeboat crew, also got aboard.

Calemmo, pushing on the liferaft, became aware of the commotion around the motor launch. They were *his* babies! He abandoned the raft and scrambled across the icy deck to find out what was going on. The launch was ready to be lifted off its cradle and Chief Smith was trying to start the engine. Nobody could handle those engines like Calemmo, and he shouted, "You get out, Chief, I'll take it."

Smith got out and Calemmo jumped aboard. The engine roared to life under his touch and the launch was ready to be picked up off the cradle. The timing had to be just right, and there was a few seconds' pause to allow the waves to break, then the boom lifted the boat about six feet off the cradle and began to swing it over the side as another wave rolled the ship to port. The boom swung out of control, snapping the guideline and whipping the launch out over the sea in an arc. Back and forth it swung, out and up and around as the ship heaved about; then as the *Pollux* slammed back to starboard the boom jerked violently inboard, hauling the lifeboat behind it.

The crew in the launch reacted as they had been trained to do in such emergencies; they ducked and held their heads. In over the deck the boat swung, to crash into the captain's gig sitting in its cradle on the starboard side. Men and launch were still suspended from the boom, six feet above the sloping deck, and swinging erratically and dangerously with the surging of the ship. The sailors working about the deck, pushing liferafts, had to halt their activities and keep a safe distance. Grayson ordered the lifeboat lowered and presently it was brought down on the hatch.

"Jump!" Grayson roared.

The lifeboat crew jumped out. Not one had been injured. "Well," Calemmo said as he surveyed the wreckage, "that knocks out two more boats."

Attempt No. 1 to get ashore had failed.

By this time the No. 1 motor whaleboat on the starboard side, aft of the bridge, had been battered by the sea and had broken in half. Only No. 1 motor whaleboat, hanging from its davits on the aft part of the port wing of the bridge, was still in one piece.

A group of sailors, Strauss among them, decided that maybe they could get a plank across to the ledge. Lumber was stowed in the after hold in the charge of Storekeeper Third Class Howard Flechsenhaar. As they staggered up the passageway with two-by-fours and other size planks, young Flechsenhaar chased after them. "Hey, fellas, wait a minute, *wait a minute!*" he yelled, "I've got to write all this down. How many pieces are you taking? What size are they?"

They left the young storekeeper in a flap, anxiously trying to count the pieces of lumber for which he was responsible.

For all their efforts, the planks were useless.

At 0800 the barometer reached a low of 28.85, and from here on it would begin to rise.

The *Wilkes* flashed a message at 0803:

Are you getting your crew ashore?

The *Pollux* replied:

We have not been able to get a line ashore yet but we are endeavoring to.

Again they turned their attention to the liferaft. About twenty men including Calemmo, pushed and heaved up the tilted deck until the raft was in position to be shoved over. A heavy line was attached to it and secured to the ship's railing. Other men stood by with lifelines and attached them to the railings, among them George L. Coleman and his buddy, Boatswain's Mate First Class George Marks.

"O.K.! Let her go!" Gabrielson ordered.

"Let loose the liferaft," Marks yelled.

Aided by a heave from the ship, the raft went over. It disappeared in the boiling seas and popped back up to crash against the ship as the seas surged up her side. It was now a matter of paddling ashore, towing a line, and rigging a breeches buoy—not a simple or pleasant task, in the circumstances, but not an impossible one. A great crust of oil restrained the wild seas, and had gathered in an eddy between ship and shore; wreckage was trapped there as well. A tarry slime covered the shoreline.

Lieutenant Bradley, who had grown up on eastern Long Island, was used to cold weather and rough ocean, therefore he was less intimidated by the seas rushing between ship and shore; the *Pollux* provided a good lee, and the water was not all that rough, he thought.

Bradley asked Commander Turney: "Permission requested to board the liferaft, sir."

The raft, with its wooden grating bottom attached by rope netting, offered a cold, wet, and hazardous journey to shore. It was definitely not suitable for the North Atlantic in winter, but there was no alternative. Commander Turney reluctantly gave permission.

Quartermaster Third Class Rex E. Copeland and Seaman Second Class Bill McGinnis, a cheerful, happy-go-lucky young man, volunteered to go on the raft with Bradley. They had lines attached to their life jackets in the event they got ashore or had to be hauled back to the ship. All wore their heavy foul-weather gear. The plan was to get as close as possible to shore and swim the rest of the way, if necessary.

They waited on the cargo nets, draped over the ship's side, until the raft rode up on a swell, jumped in, and down they went in a smother of oily foam.

The breath was almost shocked from their bodies by the bitter cold of the sea as it enveloped them—for a moment Bradley thought he was finished—but the adrenalin was running, and they were cool, calculating men. They grabbed the paddles as the raft rose on the crest of a wave and hurled shoreward, but they were carried back to the ship as they met the seas falling back from the cliff. Forward they went again paddling furiously, and again the undertow swept them back. Again and again they tried, but to no avail.

Bradley, who felt that their efforts should have taken them to the shore, discovered the line from the raft to the ship seemed to be hopelessly entangled in the floating wreckage. They could not expect to overcome the fierce undertow *and* the wreckage, he thought, and fearlessly throwing himself into the sea, began to try to work his way through the sludge and debris toward the shore. But it was a formidable barrier, and the undertow carried him back to the raft. Totally without feeling by now, he climbed aboard with the help of Copeland and McGinnis, and they were hauled back to the ship. The three men forced their numbed bodies up the cargo nets where ready hands reached for them and dragged them, exhausted, onto the deck.

They were taken to the sick bay, given a good stiff drink of whiskey, had hot showers, and changed to dry clothing. Bradley discovered that both his knees were badly bruised.

Attempt No. 2 to reach shore had failed.

Ensign Al Pollack and Lieutenant James Boundy, along with Lieutenant Commander Sam Bostic, the medical officer, had watched Bradley struggling through the oil and wreckage to get a lifeline ashore. Boundy was one of the passengers on the *Pollux,* bound for the administration staff of the USS *Prairie* in Argentia, but he and Pollack were old buddies, having done duty in Washington, D.C., before the *Pollux* had been commissioned.

If the three men had been less encumbered by clothing, Pollack was sure it would have been relatively easy to get ashore. The ship *was* very close to shore. It made sense, Boundy thought.

Should they try to swim a line ashore? Pollack wondered.

Small, bouncy, and considered quite a guy, Boundy, who was in his thirty-fifth year, was more than willing to try.

"It's pretty rough," Pollack said, "but with less gear I'm sure we can do it."

"Right!" Boundy agreed.

"Swim trunks?"

"O.K. with me."

Pollack turned to Bostic. "What do you say, Sam? Do you think we could make it?"

"I think you're damn fools," Bostic said bluntly.

They knew the maximum period a man could survive in the North Atlantic in the wintertime was no more than a few minutes, but they were *so close*.

"You're really going to try it?"

"Yep!"

"That's pretty cold water," Bostic told them. "You'll need something to protect you."

A bo'sun's mate spoke up. "I know where I can find a can of grease, sir."

"Then get it," Pollack said.

They went below, stripped, and put on their swim trunks. Pollack did not stop to consider the reason for such a seemingly rash decision. At this moment it was important to get a line ashore, so they could all get off the ship and head for safety. Someone had to do it.

The bo'sun's mate spread the grease liberally over their bodies and on their faces, and over that they put on life jackets. Harold Brooks was greasing himself up to swim ashore with the two officers; Brooks was a signalman, and a signalman would be needed ashore to communicate with the ship. Hank Strauss joined him; he was a state-champion diver and an excellent swimmer. "I'm a better swimmer than you are," he told Brooks; "I think you should let me go instead." Brooks was his boss.

At about this time Lieutenant Dougherty reported to the bridge that they had gotten the suction on No. 4 fuel tank and were transferring fuel to the empty tank on the port side, and was on his way back to the engine room when Pollack spotted him. "Hey, Chief, do me a favor?"

The chief engineer looked at the tall young man, recognizable under the grease only by his voice. "Sure, Pollack."

Pollack picked up his wristwatch, which had been given to him by his parents on his twenty-first birthday; a tie clip, which had belonged to his great-grandfather; and his wallet, which had been given to him by his sister, Jean. Besides his money, the wallet contained the "lucky" dollar bill put there by Jean when she had given it to him. "Take these, Chief. If we ever meet again, give 'em back to me; if not, and you're a survivor, send them to my folks, will you?"

"Sure." Dougherty took the articles and stuffed them in his pocket.

Pollack and Boundy went topside while Strauss continued to argue with Brooks, at the same time stripping and greasing himself up.

Against the backdrop of ice-covered cliffs and raging ocean, the two officers presented an incongruous picture, but there were plenty of smart remarks even in this grim moment.

"Going for a swim, sir?"

"Swim trunks!"

A few shrill whistles rent the air.

"Some guys have all the luck."

Pollack and Boundy, understanding the irreverence that concealed the men's true feelings, made a few smart remarks back. "Come on in, the water's fine."

Lifelines were tied to their life jackets, with another eighteen-foot line tying Pollack and Boundy together. The two men had no fear. They were young and strong, in peak physical condition, and buoyed up by the excitement of it all.

The raft was beating against the ship just below the cargo net, and the two men went to Commander Turney. "Request permission to get aboard the raft and get a line ashore, sir."

Permission was granted.

Pollack and Boundy decided not to wait for the signalman; the extra weight in the raft might be a hindrance. They went down the cargo net and dropped into the raft as it rose up on a swell. Their bodies were instantly numbed in spite of the heavy coating of grease. Grabbing the paddles, they vigorously stroked for shore. Forward they hurtled, then backward, caught in the eddy that had thwarted Bradley, Copeland, and McGinnis, each surge of the sea sweeping them toward the shore, the backwash dragging them back toward the ship.

They kept at it, arms straining, adrenalin pumping, but making no headway until the raft crashed against the ship and the two men went flying overboard. Pollack's breath came in quick, short gasps, then his arms and legs moved automatically, pushing against the crust of oil. Boundy was working his limbs steadily. The oil fouled the air around them, and the wreckage, flung about by the strong current, was a threat to life and limb. No matter how determinedly they worked their way through it, the sea flung them about like playthings and, their vitality depleted, they let themselves be carried back to the ship. Shaking with cold and exhaustion, they got up on the cargo net, a feat that others would not be able to duplicate later.

The men above were hauling the raft back to the ship and, as the two men began to pull themselves up the net with numb and frozen hands, the raft crashed against the ship again, hitting Pollack's right leg. He barely felt it, and continued to climb.

Bostic was waiting for them with some medicinal alcohol, and there were jokes about that. "What a guy won't do for a drink of whiskey."

"Make mine straight, sir."

"Yeah! Likewise."

"Just a sip," Bostic cautioned the two shaking volunteers.

Pollack and Boundy immediately went below. Pollack was limping and his right leg was badly skinned. As they tried to nurse life and vitality back into their bodies, Pollack said grimly, "After that, I'm sticking with the ship, no matter *what* happens."

Boundy was still shaking. "Yeah!"

They did not remove the grease, nor did they dress. They put on their arctic boots and their heavy "goon" jackets over their swim trunks and went topside. The "goon" jackets were heavily padded and came down below their knees. Later, Pollack would puzzle over why they did not dress, but he had no answer for it.

Attempt No. 3 had failed, and it was obvious now that, in spite of the close proximity of land, getting ashore was not going to be all that easy.

Strauss had come to the deck too late to go in the raft with Pollack and Boundy. He was greased up, but had wisely put his clothes back on and was ready for whatever action was to come.

It was waiting for him.

A group of his buddies were on the deck just forward of the bridge, trying to throw a grapnel hook to the ledge. The hook was heavy and fell short, for the most part, but occasionally it landed on the ledge, only to slide off because the outer edge of the ledge had been worn smooth by the sea. Phillip Jewett, Charles Killelea, Feroll Myron "Hoot" Gipson, and Glen Wiltrout muttered a few expletives as the hook refused to catch.

"One more try," said Wiltrout.

On that last try the hook hitched into a crevice. They pulled it taut and tied it to the rail. There was jubilation. *They had a line to the ledge!* Not a very good one but good enough, perhaps, for a slight man to go across and rig a proper line.

Who would volunteer to go over on the line?

Strauss looked the situation over. He was a slight, short man and, if he went over, there would not be too much strain on the rope. Under his clothing his body was already greased up, so he was the logical candidate. From where they were, just forward of the bridge, it was no more than sixty or seventy yards to the ledge; not too far for a man to go hand over hand. The yellow, greasy waves piled up on the ledge, but if he was swept off the line, well, he could swim that distance with his hands tied behind his back, if it came to that. Besides, if he was ever to get back to his wife, Jo, he had to do something.

"I'll go," he said.

He went to Commander Turney, who had been watching. "Request permission to go down the line to the ledge and take a line over, sir."

Commander Turney refused. It was too precarious.

Strauss persisted. "It seems to be the only possible way to get a line ashore, sir."

Turney thought it over and gave his permission.

Strauss returned to his buddies. "O.K., Hoot," he said, "let's go."

Wiltrout and Gipson tied a line to his life jacket. Jewett and Killelea crowded around. "If you can't make the ledge, we'll haul you in, Hank," they told him.

"O.K.!"

Trailing a lifeline, Strauss went hand over hand above the raging ocean toward the ledge, and the sailors on the superstructure watched admiringly. Geez, Califano thought, he looks like a goddamn acrobat.

Strauss made it right to the ledge. But as he was getting ready to reach his foot out, a great sea rose up and broke over him. Down he went among the rocks, and was dragged under. He was instantly paralyzed by the freezing cold water, but his life jacket brought him to the surface just as he thought his lungs would burst. He was unable to move his limbs but his brain was working overtime. Why weren't they pulling him in? They had promised to haul him back to the ship, but nothing was happening. From where he was in the water, that sixty to seventy yards to the ship was suddenly a very great distance away. He screamed at them to pull him in. Then he began to lose consciousness.

His friends were hauling frantically, but the rope was coated with oil, and their numbed hands could not get a firm grasp. It was Wiltrout who wrapped the rope around his body and, turning around and around, and being turned around by others, acted as a winch to bring Strauss to the ship.

Strauss was dimly aware of being inched up the side of the *Pollux* and hearing Gipson shouting, "Heave, ho! Heave, ho!" Then Strauss lost consciousness completely until he was hauled over the rail. They rushed him inside to the sick bay, where he was given a drink of medicinal alcohol, stripped of his wet clothing, rubbed briskly to bring life back to his body, and given dry clothing.

Attempt No. 4 had failed.

It was getting up to 0900 hours.

The ship had lightened considerably forward as the fuel leaked out, and the bow had ridden up to within twenty feet of the ledge. From the group of officers huddled on the bridge studying the situation came the idea of rigging out the No. 2 cargo boom, then the men could easily shinny down the boom on a rope ladder to the rocky shelf. Technically, it was simple. "The boom is about fifty feet long; it should easily reach shore," someone said.

There was no power forward; therefore the boom would have to be lifted out of its cradle by manpower. A crew went forward, Strauss among them. They quickly manhandled the boom up and lifted it clear of the cradle. The barrage of waves quickly drenched them so that their clothing froze solidly. The ship pitched wildly, nothing was standing still, everything was coated with ice, including the boom, yet Strauss again volunteered to try to get to the ledge. Permission was granted and he clung to the rope ladder attached to the end of the boom. Once it was over the ledge, he would climb down it onto the rocks and rig a lifeline.

The boom, hauled by guidelines, swung smoothly out over the sea toward the ledge with Strauss clinging to it, but their calculations were out. At its nearest point it was still a good ten feet from the ledge.

Commander Turney sent an order for the men to haul the boom and Strauss back over the deck. "It isn't possible for him to reach the shelf that way," Turney said.

They did so, and all went below to strip down and put on dry clothing. There would be no further action from the bow.

Attempt No. 5 had failed.

Strauss knew now that there was a real possibility that this was the end. They might be close enough to land to reach out and nearly touch it, but they might as well be a hundred miles from it, for all the good it did. Before he changed into dry clothing, he slipped below to the crew's quarters, waded to his locker, and took out the picture he had of Jo. If they found it on his body, she would know he was thinking of her at the very last.

Despite the best efforts of the damage-control parties, the forward bulkhead plates, which kept the ship buoyant aft, were steadily weakening. Water trickled through the ever-widening seams, and it became evident that it was only a matter of time before the ocean burst through. Stanford reported it to the bridge.

They secured the watertight hatches in all the machinery spaces
"Secure the hatches," Commander Turney said.
forward, and on the passageway leading into the engine room itself.

Commander Turney called Dougherty: "Damage control reports the bulkhead is weakening. Secure the engines and remove all unnecessary personnel."

They began to let the steam out of the boilers and hot water out of the tanks to circumvent an explosion if and when the forward bulkhead collapsed. Incredibly, the fuel line to the emergency diesel generator had not yet ruptured, and Dougherty selected his two leading petty officers, Robert C. Ashbridge and Joseph P. Neville, to remain below with him while everyone else was ordered topside.

The men cracked jokes to keep up their spirits, but it was apparent to all now that they were face to face with death. Artie Appel, Sam Nicosia, and the ship's baker, William DeRosa, wearing the white duck pants of the baker, had been raised in the same part of New York City and had gone to elementary school together. Now they made a pact: If any of them did not make it, the others would tell their parents how they had died.

They sealed it with a handshake.

16

The sea showed no signs of moderating, although the sleet let up occasionally, giving the men on the *Pollux* a view of the bleakness of the coastline. The *Wilkes* stood off, pitching heavily in the stormy seas, as her crew prepared to float rafts to them.

Lieutenant Jack Garnaus had made an inspection of his area aft and throughout the ship. As the seas, falling with numbing explosions upon the quivering hull, rushed into the holds, the fleeting thought occurred that there might not be a spring wedding as planned for himself and his fiancée, Margaret Huntling. He firmly put it out of his mind, and came on deck in time to see Pollack and Boundy come aboard. He was surprised that, with his own background of college swimming, lifeguard work, and Red Cross examiner, which everybody aboard was familiar with, they had not called on him.

He noted that the boats forward and starboard were either gone or taking a bad beating from the seas. About the only remaining boat for practical use was the whaleboat in his division area, portside aft. His division petty officer, Garrett Lloyd, and Wag Greenfield, who generally stood signal watch during Garnaus' OOD watch, were standing by the boat.

Garnaus looked at the whaleboat carefully. "It's still in pretty good shape," he said to them.

"Yeah," Lloyd replied.

"Are we going ashore?" Greenfield was shuffling about to keep warm.

"I think we should try it."

"What the hell, we may as well try something." Greenfield was dressed more warmly by this time, having picked up some officer's foul-weather outfit from the heap of clothing collected from the ship's stores. He had not found a Navy helmet and still wore the flat cap, strapped to his head with the goggles, and he had no gloves or arctic boots.

They studied the shoreline. About sixty feet to the left of the ledge and the overhanging cliff, the shore was less steep, but appeared to be a solid sheet of ice. Facing them, a small cove cut diagonally into the rocky slope, slanting upward to a dead end about twenty feet above sea level. Beyond the cove was another indentation in the shoreline, then the land continued upward and extended up to the ice-covered ridge of Lawn Head. Across from the ledge, a small rock island about thirty feet offshore provided a comparatively quiet basin at the foot of the slope, but a nest of rocks blocked the basin and the cove. Seas funneling between the ledge and the rock island heaped up and fell upon the shore. Great globs of congealed oil were splattered everywhere. The men realized that they would have to try to run the last lifeboat over that nest of rocks; it was the only place they might get a line ashore.

"If we can make a landing in that little cove, we'll be able to pull a heavier line to shore. It can be used to ferry the rafts to shore," Garnaus said. Lloyd agreed.

"Can we pick up a crew?"

"Count me in," Greenfield said.

"Me too." William DeRosa, startling in his white duck pants and wearing a foul-weather jacket, had clambered into the whaleboat before any of the leading seamen, clustered nearby, were aware of what was going on.

Now they needed a man to work the engine. "I'll get Calemmo," Lloyd told Garnaus.

Calemmo was with a group that was trying to push another raft along the slanting deck. Lloyd came up to him. "Larry, we're going to take No. 1 boat ashore. I'll coxswain if you'll be my engineer."

Calemmo did not hesitate. "O.K." he said. Lloyd had about

twelve years of Navy service behind him; he worked his men hard but treated them fair and square.

When they reached the lifeboat, it was to find Ernest Califano aboard trying to start the engine. He was having trouble.

"What the hell are you doing?" Calemmo asked mildly.

"I'm gonna take this thing over to the cove," Califano told him.

"Naw! I'm gonna take her over," Calemmo said. "Get out, I'll get her started."

Califano grinned at his friend. "O.K." He was not going to argue with the expert.

Having collected a crew, Garnaus and Lloyd went to Commander Turney and requested permission to go ashore. Turney hesitated. So far, four unsuccessful attempts had been made to get across that narrow stretch of treacherous sea. But Garnaus pointed out, "It's the only boat still in one piece, sir. If we can get it launched without breaking it up, it's the best chance we have at getting a line ashore."

"If the boat can be launched, then permission is granted," Turney said.

They all assembled near the boat. "O.K., men, let's get our signals together," Garnaus commanded.

Greenfield already had his signal flags. A sailor handed Garnaus a knife. "You'll need it, sir." Lloyd and Calemmo briefed each other. "You're going to have all you can do to keep the boat on course, Chief, so you control the steering and let me handle the throttle and clutch as I see fit, O.K.?"

"O.K., Larry."

A light line held by a bo'sun's mate was attached to Garnaus' waist so that when he reached land a heavier line could be attached to it and hauled over; then he took his position in the bow of the whaleboat. Greenfield and DeRosa came out, then Calemmo at the engine and Lloyd at the tiller. It did not occur to them to tie lines to their life jackets in case the boat capsized.

The boat was unleashed and lowered slightly to await the proper moment for dropping into the sea.

Gus Tortorici, Calemmo's boyhood buddy, leaned over the side and offered Larry his flashlight. "Here, take it," he yelled.

"No," Calemmo said, "you keep it, Gus. Where I'm going I won't need one." As far as Calemmo was concerned, it was a matter of getting ashore quickly and finding help as soon as possible.

"O.K., buddy. I wish you luck."

Calemmo would never see Gus again.

As the boat inched downward, Greenfield looked up and saw white faces lining the ship's rail and over the rush and roar of the sea heard voices shouting "good luck" as the boat was slowly lowered. As he looked toward shore, the waves were coming down between the cliff and the ship; everything was white water—like a devil's cauldron, he thought.

Calemmo started the motor, which roared to life instantly as the seas rushed up the ship's side to meet the boat. Immediately it partially flooded and Calemmo kept the engine racing to keep it from stalling. He could not engage the clutch until the boat was unhooked from the falls, a hazardous and tricky job with it rising and falling crazily with the sea. If hands or fingers detaching the boat were not pulled away at the exact moment, they could be torn off.

Swiftly Garnaus detached the forward hook, and Lloyd the aft hook. Calemmo waited for the signal from Lloyd, engaged the clutch, and suddenly they were in the sea's power. The boat shipped more water, as they were carried forward and backward with Calemmo racing the engine to fight the push and pull of the surf and Lloyd struggling to keep the bow aimed at the little cove. Calemmo kept his eyes riveted on Lloyd, whose movements coincided exactly with his, engaging and disengaging the clutch; they were operating on the same wavelength. Aft of the *Pollux*'s stern a great wave picked the whaleboat up and tossed it like a rubber ball over the nest of rocks into the cove where it smashed on a great ice-covered rock. Garnaus, Greenfield, and DeRosa were thrown out on the port side and landed in waist-deep water below the steep slope; Lloyd and Calemmo were pitched out on the starboard side into the cove, also landing in the surf up to their waists.

All fought to overcome the terrifying pull of the sea. The current was sweeping strongly westward, and Garnaus' first thought was that they might be carried away. By rapid scrambling he managed to get up on the shore. Greenfield had never felt anything like this in his life. The icy water was like a hand holding him in a paralyzing grip. Both he and DeRosa wore only Oxford shoes, which had no gripping power on the slippery surface, and they could barely inch their way up the rocks. Garnaus grabbed first one, then the other, and helped haul them up. He could not see the other two men as they hauled themselves out of the black slime and crawled upon the oil-slicked boulders in a desperate effort to escape the icy seas that were chasing them into the cove. Walls of ice reared above either side of the narrow cove, and at the top of the incline was another wall of ice, but behind a protrusion in the left corner Lloyd and Calemmo found a black, triangular cleft in the rock. They crawled into it and found a small area of level ground. It was dark and still inside, and bitingly cold.

"You O.K., Larry?" Lloyd asked.

"Yeah. You O.K.?"

"I'm O.K."

Calemmo's hand was bleeding slightly, and he had lost his right shoe. After he had rested a few minutes, he poked his head outside the cave to look for his shoe, and saw it halfway to the shoreline. He made his way down over the rocks, retrieved it, put it on, and crawled back to the cave. They did not know what had happened to their three companions.

Both Garnaus and Greenfield had taken their knives and were hacking their way up the icy slope. Greenfield was so intent on the task at hand that he did not see or look for Garnaus, who was ahead on a slightly divergent track.

Garnaus was the first to reach a small plateau or level area halfway up the slope, about forty feet above sea level. It was on the rim of the cove, above and a little forward of the cave where Lloyd and Calemmo were huddled. On the other side of the cove it sloped more steeply upward for another forty to fifty feet and leveled off behind the headland under which the *Pollux* lay. Looking around, Garnaus spotted a boulder; true, it was sheathed in ice, but so was everything else. Here, then, he decided, was as good a place as any to warp a line ashore.

Greenfield, followed by DeRosa, reached the plateau. Greenfield had been wondering where the hell Garnaus had disappeared, and now he wondered how Garnaus had made it to the plateau ahead of him. "Where are the other guys?" he asked.

Garnaus told them they were in the little cove below but, looking over the edge, Greenfield saw no sign of his friends. He stared out at the *Pollux:* The waves breaking over the ship exploded against the superstructure on the starboard beam, a fearful backdrop for the crew clustered on the port side of the bridge. All eyes on the ship were riveted on them.

Garnaus cut the light line from his life jacket and they began to pull in. The line draped over the side into the cove and Lloyd and Calemmo, hearing the voices of their shipmates, crawled out of the cave to give a hand. As they continued to haul in the light line, the men on the *Pollux* attached a heavier line to the other end of it. A crust of solidified oil made the line difficult to handle and it kept slipping through their numb hands.

The wind whistling down the slope was bitingly cold. Sleet stung their faces and hands. DeRosa, his duck pants saturated with water and oil, was shivering violently. The foul-weather gear that Greenfield had put on did not fit well. His regular foul-weather gear fitted like coveralls, while the outfit he was wearing separated at the waist and gave less protection. Body heat, generated in the excitement of getting ashore, began to dissipate.

The heavier three-quarter-inch line seemed to weigh a ton. It was being swept westward by the current, and fuel oil and floating wreckage added to the problem of hauling it in. Before they got the heavy line to shore, their strength gave out. They had managed to pull in over three hundred feet of the light line through the oily muck, but the heavier line needed for a lifeline floated in the wreckage somewhere between ship and shore. Nevertheless, for what it was worth, a lifeline of sorts connected the *Pollux* to land. They secured it around the boulder. "As long as it doesn't slip off, it might be of some use later on," Garnaus said.

Below them, Lloyd and Calemmo returned to the shelter of the cave.

When it became evident to those on the ship that the men on shore had stopped hauling on the line, signals were flagged from the bridge:

Pull in the three-quarter-inch line.

His body trembling with exhaustion and cold, Greenfield took out his flags and signaled:

We can't pull anymore. We do not have the strength.

They had to find shelter before they froze to death. Garnaus took a quick look to see if they could move along the shore to a point

nearer the ship. There was no way across the ice-covered rock wall
—they would have to persevere upward. Hacking at the ice, the
three men continued their climb to the top. It was much steeper than
the lower slope, but once again, Garnaus forged ahead diagonally
across the cliff, becoming slightly separated and out of the line of vision of Greenfield, who could concentrate only on the holes he was
chipping.

Near the top the slope was not as steep, and Garnaus was the first
to reach the crest. From where he was standing on the knoll only the
stern of the *Pollux* was visible. The view overland was disheartening.
Bleak, snow-covered hills stretched as far as the eye could see. He
was on the knoll of the promontory under which the *Pollux* lay.
Humps of rock sloped gently downward about a hundred feet to the
overhang, which fanned out and slightly upward. Flying spume,
caught by the wind, was being flung upon the clifftop. White-capped
waves rushed toward the shore. The *Wilkes* was standing by, still
unable to help the stricken ship.

He took a quick exploratory trip across the promontory and down
the other side, only to be brought up short by a great chasm that cut
into the shoreline eastward. Concealed by an overhang, it fell for a
hundred feet at least. Savage seas thundered into the chasm, sending
an explosion of spray up over the headland. Garnaus backed away.

His eyes swept a great barren hill gradually rising another few
hundred yards behind the promontory. There were no formations
that could offer shelter, but near the top was a shallow ravine filled
with dwarf trees. A little closer there was a clump of trees, around
which the snow had drifted. It could provide a little protection.
Other than that, there was nothing. The hills rolling east in a seemingly endless line were equally stark. He cautiously skirted the east
side of the headland, seeking a way to the ledge. There was none.

When Greenfield and DeRosa reached the clifftop and looked
around for Garnaus, he was nowhere in sight. They hastened to a little ledge on the side of the great hill below the ridge, to try to get out
of the wind, which was cutting them to the marrow. Greenfield
figured that they were worse off than if they had stayed aboard the
Pollux. On this godforsaken, wind-scoured cliff they could freeze to
death in short order. DeRosa, frozen and dazed, had curled up in the
snow.

Greenfield thought about the line they had secured. Pretty soon the men on the *Pollux* would be hauling the liferafts to shore. "I'd better tell 'em to send over some dry clothes and blankets, and some food," he told DeRosa.

He sent a signal asking for blankets and clothing because they were freezing to death.

The signal came back: *"Hang on."*

But nothing seemed to be happening as far as Greenfield could make out. The line trailed over the ship's side, and apparently they had not taken the slack out or tried to ferry the raft across on the line. What in God's name was wrong with them? Why wasn't somebody doing something about that lifeline?

He could not stand the ice-cold wind, and he returned to DeRosa. At the same time Garnaus came looking for them; there was a slightly better place up the hill a bit, he said.

Dragging DeRosa, they made for the clump of trees, up to their knees in snow at times, and fell into the shelter. Greenfield began to shiver uncontrollably. "Now what do we do?" he asked between chattering teeth.

First they had to concentrate on DeRosa, who just lay in the snow and showed no inclination to move. They tried to get him moving. "Come on, DeRosa," Greenfield urged. "You can't just lie there."

". . . cold," DeRosa mumbled.

Greenfield himself was cold. God! he was cold. "You gotta move about, DeRosa, or you'll damn well freeze to death," he warned.

Garnaus decided that he had better see what could be done for the men aboard the *Pollux*. He returned to the ice-capped promontory close to the overhang and inspected it more closely. A large crevice of broken rock sloped steeply down to the extreme west end of the overhang. It, too, was encased in hard, wet, gleaming ice, and he dared not attempt to traverse it.

He knew he was clearly visible to the men on the bridge of the *Pollux* and, unaware that the line-throwing gun was in the flooded armory, he waited for them to shoot a line across. Very quickly it became evident to him that this was not what they were going to do. While he was puzzled, he did not waste time in useless speculation, but felt he should try to find a way to the ledge below. Once there, he had no doubt that they would get a line to him. However, the shoreline to the east offered no way to the ledge either, so Garnaus decided he had better get back to the shelter where he had left Greenfield and DeRosa. The *Pollux* seemed to be in no immediate danger.

On board the *Wilkes* they had watched the antlike figures of Garnaus, Greenfield, and DeRosa on the hilltop, and they signaled to the *Pollux:*

Do you believe entire crew can get ashore?

The *Pollux* signaled back:

We have five men ashore trying to establish rescue. Believe there is nothing you can do. Suggest you proceed to port and do what you can to hasten help to us.

The *Wilkes* asked:

Do you want to send boat to us? If so, will stand close. We have but one small boat.

The *Pollux* replied:

We have no boats left.

The situation was desperate. The handful of men ashore were unable to help. The one line they had made fast was fouled in wreckage and congealed oil, making it impossible to ferry the liferaft ashore. Large cracks had developed in the forward deck between cargo holds Nos. 2 and 3 and she could not hold together much longer, yet the wild seas precluded any further attempts to get ashore at present. At 0947 the *Pollux* sent a message to the *Wilkes:*

We cannot land men on beach. Request help be sent from shore. Please transmit.

Back to the meager shelter Garnaus went to find Greenfield swearing at DeRosa and massaging his limbs, but DeRosa did not appear to have much desire to exercise. Garnaus, deciding to try to find better shelter for them, left again.

Greenfield, furiously intent on keeping DeRosa alive, was aware that Garnaus had come back, then was aware that he had left. Where the hell had he gone now?

Calemmo and Lloyd, having recovered their strength somewhat in the cave, communicated by hand signals with the *Pollux,* and learned that the other three had made their way to the top of the cliff. They thought that they should try to join them and help in whatever rescue work was being effected.

A projecting end of a great slab of rock forming one side of the cave slanted steeply upward. On a summer's day it could have been traversed easily with rubber-soled footwear, but today it was a sheet of hard ice, as were the walls. They were trapped; nevertheless they tried, and Calemmo received another small injury to his arm.

The cave protected them from the wind but it was unutterably cold. Over the roar and pounding of the sea they could hear the sound of the ship's hull smashing on the rock as she was lifted and dropped by the waves. To Calemmo, who had grown up on the Lower East Side in Manhattan, the *Pollux* made a noise like the dropping of an empty oil drum from about fifty feet onto a concrete slab. He said to Lloyd, "Jesus Christ! Listen to that."

Time and again they crawled out of the cave and looked toward their ship and the men clustered against the port railing. They were *so close,* yet that small stretch of ocean was filled with wreckage, fuel oil, and a heavy undertow. A deadly combination.

Calemmo and Lloyd could do nothing except wait.

Attempt No. 6 had failed.

17

USS *Truxtun*
February 18, 1942—0630–0945 hours

Because of the storm, daylight came late. The crescent-shaped cove, which faced west, still protected the *Truxtun* from the fierce waves that were falling upon the *Pollux* farther along the coast, but the wind was steadily shifting to the south, bringing the sea around with it, and the waves wrapping around the tip were smashing the *Truxtun* with greater force. Oil from the ship coated the cliffs and was propelled by wave action toward the little beach in the far southeast curve of the crescent, where it had congealed into a tarry morass, effectively flattening the waves there. In that quiet corner the sea was beginning to curl and break on the edge of the oil slick.

On their stern, Pinnacle Head, with its sheer rock wall up to 300 feet in height, curved to join the stark granite cliff forming the northern end of the semicircle that was Chambers Cove. Where it merged it had a slope that was very slight and offered no means of escape. A sandspit jutting out from the tip of the crescent to the big rock about 60 yards off the *Truxtun*'s port beam, and a strip of shingle at the base of the sweeping stone wall more than 200 feet high off the *Truxtun*'s port side were disappearing beneath the rising tide. The straight gray precipice merged with a bulging mass of pink rock in the center of the crescent. Where it joined there was an overhang, like a great platform, at the top. To the right of the pink rock was the small beach they had seen by searchlight earlier, approximately 250 yards off their port bow, which might offer sanctuary. From the

Truxtun's position in the cove, the line-throwing guns were inadequate for reaching the top of any of the cliffs.

Southward, on the farthest end of the beach, the cliffs ringing the
cove seemed less sheer, with many bulges and crevices, and along
the top of that particular section the men could see *a fence*. It had to
be a farm, they reasoned, and help was as near as that farm. It
cheered them considerably.

With the lifeboats gone the rafts were now their only hope and it
was decided to launch them and get on with the abandon-ship procedure. Each raft, which could hold fifteen men, was equipped with a
small wooden barrel of fresh water, food, paddles, and first-aid
equipment. There were three on either side of the ship, mounted
above the main deck, outboard of the superstructure and rigging, so
that they could be dropped into the water and held alongside the hull
while sailors slid onto them. It worked fine in open water, but the
rocks, the listing of the ship, and the worsening seas created a
difficult set of problems.

The three rafts on the port side slid over the sloping sides of the
ship, hit the water, and turned upside down. On the starboard side,
one raft smashed upon the great rock beside her; the other two
bounced off and were being battered against the ship by the combers
falling upon her.

A group of sailors hauled the upside-down rafts to the port bow in
preparation for boarding and paddling to the beach; the remaining
two, on the starboard side, could not be utilized because of the angry
sea. "Try to maneuver them around the stern," Lieutenant Commander Hickox ordered. Once in the lee of the port side, there
would be less difficulty in getting the rafts to the port bow.

The crew began to drag the first raft around the stern but huge
waves tore the lines of the raft from their hands, and off it went to
become part of the debris washing from the ship. It was decided to
leave the other raft where it was, for the moment. Later the sea
would carry it away.

Other crew members were collecting what three-inch manila line
or wire cable they had on board and running it out on the forecastle
in preparation for getting a lifeline ashore.

On the main deck, aft of the galley deck, Harry Egner, W. O.
Harris, and others had been arguing about the best way to get to the

beach. It was obvious to them that they were in a life-and-death struggle. They had seen a couple of young sailors who worked in the engine room standing barefooted on the deck; the steel deck had peeled the skin from the soles of their feet, and they had left tracks of blood as they moved around. Some who had rushed on deck without footwear or adequate clothing had already frozen to death. Egner had seen one sailor remove the shoes of a dead man and put them on his own feet. It had been rather foreboding.

The oil slick on the water in the cove had a quieting effect on the turbulent sea, and Harris appeared set on swimming ashore. "I can work through the oil to the beach," he said.

"Don't do it," Egner said.

"I can do it," W.O. insisted.

"The water is too cold and rough; you'll never make it."

W.O. was confident. "Sure I can."

"Look at it," Egner reasoned. "Look at the waves breaking on the cliffs. You'll never make it."

Harris would not listen. He had made up his mind, and before anyone could stop him, he jumped over the side.

Egner was stunned. He searched the water, but saw no sign of his friend. A few others followed W.O. and began to swim toward the beach, but a wave took them toward the oil slick, where they disappeared from view. Then, before his horrified eyes, they were lifted on the oily crust of a great wave and carried up the steep rock face— up, up they went, nearly to the top, then the seas dropped back with a crash. Staring incredulously at the towering cliff where his shipmates had been dashed to their deaths, Egner felt very strange, as if a part of him had been cut away. Just like that, W.O. was dead. He could not believe it.

In these moments between life and death, other men on deck had picked up empty apple and orange crates and thrown them overboard in the remote possibility that it would help those in the water. The crates were carried shoreward and presently were caught in the oil slick and pushed along the cove toward the beach.

Egner and his shipmates, still unable to believe what had happened, stepped back into the shelter of the superstructure.

Unaware of the drama aft, sailors were hauling the upside-down rafts to the bow under the orders of Ensign Howard W. Taylor. Ensign Seamans was still on the bow, and having seen the rafts turn over when they hit the water, he had privately thought that they were poorly designed. They could not be used in their present condition, and the men were trying, unsuccessfully, to right them. One sailor jumped overboard to try to heave a raft over, and was paralyzed by the frigid waters. Hastily Ensign Taylor ordered a lifeline tied to his life jacket, and he dived into the water in an attempt to save the hapless sailor. He was too late; the waves had swept the other man away. They hauled Taylor aboard, and he went inside to change.

As the men continued to try to turn the rafts upright, Seamans decided they were going about it the wrong way. He told them, "Get a couple of grappling hooks and throw them over the far side; pull on the lines and the raft can then be tipped upright."

In his foul-weather gear he was not identifiable as an officer. Being new aboard the *Truxtun,* he had not, heretofore, had cause to assert his authority. They did not know him and they ignored his order.

He barked, "I am Ensign Seamans and I'm telling you, *do it!"*

A chief petty officer recognized him. Quickly the grappling hooks were thrown, and without a great deal of difficulty, the first raft was righted.

The chief petty officer reported to Commander Hickox that No. 1 liferaft was ready. Hickox came to the forecastle. Now they needed an experienced, dependable sailor to take the raft ashore and establish a lifeline.

Egner, still pondering the fate of his best friend, was huddled out of the wind behind the galley when someone called, "Boats,[1] you're wanted on the forecastle."

He hurried forward. The captain and several crew members were there. Hickox asked him, "Do you think you can paddle a liferaft and tow a small line to the beach?"

Egner knew from past experience how difficult it was to handle a Navy liferaft, even in calm water. The bottom of it was a grating attached to the round inflated sides by a rope netting, and it would sink at least a foot in the water when the first man boarded, so that he would be standing or sitting in icy water. Normal procedure in calm water was for them to sit on the side of the raft and paddle; in

[1] Nickname for boatswain's mate.

rough weather it was almost impossible to handle. He looked toward the beach. Steep waves rushing into the cove were breaking on the edge of the oil slick, but inside that the sea was relatively quiet under the weight of the oil. It would be a rough, wet journey.

He said, "If I had a man to help me, I think I could make it, sir."

"Take as many men as you need," Hickox told him.

It was a fifteen-man raft, and Egner looked over the men about him. No one in his right senses wanted to pit his puny strength against the fury of the ocean trapped within the confines of that cove, and he felt he needed only one good man to help him. He spotted Seaman James Fex. Fex worked in Egner's division; Fex was about twenty, big, strong, dependable, and he took orders readily.

"Fex?"

James Fex stepped forward. "I'll go, sir."

With the good wishes of their shipmates the two men slide into the raft. It was not possible to sit on the side and paddle; they would be tossed overboard promptly, so they knelt on the grating. Egner thought his heart would stop with the shock of the icy water as they sank to their waists.

Up they went, and down and sideways, as they leaned over the side and started to paddle furiously. Their arms working like pistons, they began to inch away from the *Truxtun*. They could not head directly toward shore because the waves would sweep them against the cliff in short order; therefore they had to paddle in the direction of the open sea and let the wave action take them toward the beach as it had taken the fuel oil. The sea reared over them and slid under them, oil and salt spray fell upon them. To compound their difficulties the light line they were towing made it difficult to make headway as oil adhered to it, adding to the drag of the undertow. Egner and Fex paddled like fury, trying to keep the oil and salt water out of their eyes and the raft from being carried to the cliff.

From the battered, complaining *Truxtun,* as she worked to and fro on the rocks, the men watched intently as the two sailors slowly made their way through the heavy sea. Ensign Seamans was mentally willing them to succeed.

Time lost all meaning. Egner was sure his arms, which were going on their own volition now, would fall off, and he wondered how many hours ago he and Fex had left the ship and if they would ever reach the beach. The raft was sluggish, undeniably heavier and coated with fuel oil, as they were. His lungs whistled; the stench of oil made him want to retch. Would they make it?

It seemed like forever, but in half an hour they reached the beach, jumped out, and hauled the raft up on the shore so it would not drift away. They had to slog through a foot of black, gelatinous oil, but it was good to feel land beneath them. As the wind cut through their wet clothing it seemed to draw the very life from their bones.

There was no time to think about it. They signaled the *Truxtun* that they were ready to pull in the line. A three-inch line had already been attached to the light line they had towed ashore, and the two sailors began to haul it in. The heavy line quickly became unwieldy with fuel oil. Egner and Fex were numb with the cold; their arms were so tired and weak from the strenuous paddling that they had to stop to rest periodically. Each time they paused, the men aboard the *Truxtun* signaled them to hurry. It was not possible; they could haul in about fifty feet of line, then they had to stop to recuperate. After an interminable length of time they had the heavy line on the beach, walked it around a big rock set back from the water's edge, and secured it with a couple of half hitches. The lifeline from ship to shore was established. At last they were able to sit and rest and look around. What they saw was not very encouraging.

Behind the bulging pink cliff face at the north end of the beach was a small recess that was not visible from the ship. Around and above the recess the rock wall rose straight up. On the south end of the beach there was a definite slope to the cliff but it was sheathed in ice. A smaller cliff, made up of an outcropping of jagged rocks, separated them from the less sheer cliffs that might offer access to the top. A narrow strip of shingle, liberally sprinkled with rocks, ran along the base of the shoreline.

Aboard the *Truxtun* the second and third rafts had been turned upright with the grappling hooks, and had been ready and waiting for the lifeline to be secured. The ship had continued to list steadily to the starboard as the seas lifted and dropped her. Each time she thudded upon the rocks the men were bounced severely about, yet there was a reluctance to leave her. Clustered along the port railing, they had all witnessed the agonizing struggle of Egner and Fex to reach the beach and, even if they now could haul themselves hand over hand on the lifeline, it meant getting soaked to the skin in freezing temperatures. Therefore there were no eager volunteers for the next raft.

Eventually ten men, clutching their blankets as ordered by the captain, slid down the rope onto the raft under the supervision of Chief Fire Controlman Edward B. Petterson. One of them was eighteen-year-old Edward L. Bergeron, seaman second class. A line was attached to the raft so that it could be hauled back to the ship.

The waves had grown steeper with the rising tide, hurtling up the cliff in a display of force that struck fear in the bravest heart. Over the wavetops and into the troughs, up to their chests in water, the men hauled themselves hand over hand to the beach. Their arms ached with the strain as the tidal flow pushed the raft toward the cliffs, but once they reached the oil slick it was easier, although the oil fumes were overpowering. They made it in about fifteen minutes and jumped ashore into the muck with the help of Egner and Fex.

Those on the forecastle began to haul the raft back to the ship. It was more difficult than they had anticipated. Fighting wind, sea, and the natural clumsiness of the raft, plus the added impediments of wreckage and fuel oil, the relatively simple process of getting the raft to the ship's bow proved to be arduous and time-consuming. Lieutenant Commander Hickox decided to offset this. Fewer than a half-dozen men were preparing to go ashore in the third raft, which was about ready to shove off, when he sent for Ensign Loughridge and told him, "You will go to the beach on this raft to supervise the landing of the men." Loughridge was also told to hold the raft on the beach until the next one came over with more men, then he was to tie the two rafts together, if possible, and loop them to the lifeline; they would haul both rafts back to the ship at the same time, which would save time and get the men ashore more quickly.

Loughridge picked up the rope needed to tie the rafts together, slid down into the raft, and began the arduous journey to the shore. Others prepared to board the raft that had just been towed to the ship.

It was still sleeting occasionally. The rising tide was forcing the men on shore back against the rock wall and, by the looks of it, high tide might very well inundate the beach completely.

If there was a way up over the cliffs, it had to be at the far end with its bulges, crevices, and slope. A handful of sailors went over to

explore the possibility of climbing to the top and finding help. Chief
Petterson and Seaman Bergeron were among them.

They examined the icy slope and Bergeron decided to try it. With
his knife he hacked handholds in the ice and began to work his way
diagonally up the cliff. Up he went, keeping his body flat against the
rock, hacking away, not pausing to rest or look back. Chief Petterson, carrying a light line, followed.

Too frozen to do anything but watch, the men below kept their
eyes on the young sailor as he chopped furiously at the granitelike
ice, inching steadily across and upward, with the older man following. Presently, both disappeared over the top.

If Bergeron and Petterson expected to find any sign of a farm-
house, they were bitterly disappointed. It was bleak, bare, and wind-
scoured; ahead of them stretched empty, uninhabited coastline. The
fence that had been visible from the ship enclosed a small piece of
land; from the edge of the cliff the land sloped into a ravine, and at
the very bottom was a small shed. On the other side of the ravine a
wire fence wandered across the land.

The two men hitched the line around a knob of ice, in case others
wished to follow them up the cliff, and then slid down the ravine,
leaving a trail of black, greasy oil. They reached the shed, opened
the door, and stumbled inside. It was no more than ten feet square
but it contained a small amount of hay, which they put around their
wet, freezing bodies while they rested and caught their breath.

Petterson was exhausted, but Bergeron appeared to be quite fresh
and less frozen. "I'll go find help, sir," he said.

Petterson said O.K., and told the young man to follow the wire
fence.

Bergeron left the hay shed and quickly disappeared into the driving sleet.

On the beach, Egner and the others were trying to keep warm.
Some of the orange and apple crates that had been thrown overboard earlier had been tossed upon the shore and, remembering the
matches and cigarettes he had put inside the prophylactic, he took
them out. They were still dry. Egner ordered the men to collect the
crates and break them up for firewood.

He took out his knife and made fine wood shavings, then knelt, re-

moved his gloves, carefully built the fire, and lit it. As wet as the
wood was, it burned. There were not that many crates, and the fire
did not last long, but they huddled around it, convincing themselves
they could feel the heat of it.

The third raft, with Loughridge aboard, was grounding on the
beach when Egner, whose boots were filled with water, sat beside the
remains of the fire and removed his boots in order to pour the water
out of them. The five men leaped ashore, but when Loughridge tried
to get out, his foot caught in the netting and he fell head first into the
sea. Still held by the netting and unable to free himself, he was swept
back and forth in the filthy surf, his head under the raft.

Egner saw it. Jesus! The man would drown or smother in the fuel
oil!

He dropped his boots, ran out into the water, and, while the others
held the raft, worked Loughridge's foot free. They dragged him up
on the beach, spitting oil and salt water. "Thanks," he mumbled.

Recovering, he took command. "When the next raft comes in we
have to tie them together and attach them to the big line so they can
be pulled back to the ship at the same time," he told Egner, explaining how difficult it had been to get the first raft back to the ship. This
way the tide would not sweep the rafts toward the shore, the rescue
operation would proceed more efficiently.

Privately, Egner did not like the idea. He did not think it would
work at all, but orders were orders.

The next raft, which had been the only one returned to the *Truxtun,* had ten volunteers this time. It could hold more, but unless they
were ordered to go ashore, the men shrank from deliberately going
into the sea. As bad as their situation was, the ship seemed to be
solidly set in the cluster of rocks and likely would ride out the storm.
Ensign Seamans was not tempted either; officers were the last to
leave the ship unless ordered to go ashore.

They cast off, towing the rope that had brought it safely back to
the ship the first time, and reached the beach without mishap.
Among those on the beach now were W. E. Butterworth, the young
radioman; Signalman Third Class Clifford H. Parkerson, "Beau" to
his shipmates; and Mess Attendant Third Class Lanier Walter Phillips, a black man.

As ordered, a rope was looped to the lifeline; the two rafts were hitched together and tied to the loop. The raft that Egner and Fex had reached shore in was still on the beach. It had no towline connected to the ship and was therefore out of operation. Egner and the others, up to their waist in oil and water, secured the two rafts to the line, then signaled to the ship to haul away.

Twisting, turning, and bouncing, the rafts plowed through the oil-crusted water. The waves swung them round and round, wrapping them around the lifeline, and about fifty feet from shore they fouled.

No amount of pulling on the lines could get the rafts to the ship; they were apparently too tightly wrapped around the lifeline. Lieutenant Commander Hickox decided there was only one thing to do: Untie the lifeline on the beach and haul the rafts and line back to the ship. It would mean another long, difficult struggle, such as Egner and Fex had gone through, to establish another lifeline, but it was the only alternative.

Hickox sent for a signalman. Aboard the *Truxtun,* Signalman First Class Walter W. Brom was *the* signalman. Weatherbeaten, strong, and resolute, he was experienced, capable, and highly trained—the model of a Navy signalman.

"Tell them to untie the three-inch line," he was ordered.

Brom took his position on the port wing and signaled with his flags. Parkerson, on the beach, read the signal. "The captain says we're to untie the lifeline," he reported to Loughridge.

Whatever the feelings of Egner and Fex, who had just about torn their guts out to get this line ashore, they followed orders and untied the lifeline to the ship. Since the rafts were thoroughly fouled on the line, it was, Egner thought, the only way they would get the rafts back to the ship, and there was no reason why it would not work.

But it did not. The lifeline got caught on the rocky bottom of the cove and fouled too, and no amount of tugging could budge it. The men on the *Truxtun* were stranded, but on a more ominous note, the wind was shifting more to the westward, bringing the seas rushing straight into the cove and surging more and more upon the deck of the *Truxtun.*

On the beach the men huddled in the little recess, out of the wind and the sleet, moving about to keep their circulation going. About twenty-four men had come over on the rafts, and it was crowded. They were aware that a couple of men had gone over the top of the cliffs as reported by those who watched them, but that seemed hours ago. Had they gotten lost on this barren coastline?

Egner's body was without feeling. His gloves had disappeared after he had lit the fire, and his galoshes had either been swept away by the rising tide or some other survivor had claimed them. He had given no further thought to it because, up to now, he had been too busy to think about anything but he sure as hell was aware of the cold now. His hands were two frozen appendages; his arms and legs had stiffened like boards from the tremendous exertion of paddling ashore. He was numb from head to toe.

Ensign Loughridge had been keeping the men on the move; now he spoke up: "Men, there's nothing you can do here. I think some of you should try to make it up over the cliff to see if you can find out what's happened to the men who have gone ahead."

Loughridge himself could not attempt to scale the cliff; his orders had been to stay on the beach and, looking up at what was facing them, the majority decided that they preferred to wait for rescue. They were too clumsy and weak with the cold to attempt it on their own.

Egner decided he would try. At least it was action of some sort.

About seven of them started for the far end of the beach, including Phillips. None of them was sure exactly where Bergeron and Petterson had gone up, and they clambered over the small jagged cliff, looking for easy access to the top.

Phillips called to Egner, "I think this is where the other guys went up, Boats." He was standing at the foot of a ravine, which narrowed to a small ditch running straight up to the top of the cliff. It was steep but it had enough of an incline for them to make it without too much danger, they thought. Phillips, who was taller than Egner, went first.

It was more precipitous than it looked, and they had to lie flat and work their way up with great care. Less than halfway up, Egner's hands and feet were not co-ordinating. His hands were useless, the fingers were numb and bent like claws, and he had to push himself up by his elbows.

"Come on, Boats," Phillips encouraged.

Slowly Egner edged upward, wind and sleet battering his body. He was so tired and cold he could easily have gone to sleep right there. Was he going to make it? Up to this time he had been too busy to think about *not* surviving, but at this moment it became a distinct possibility. Help me, God, let me get to the top, he prayed silently. He thought of his girl. If he was ever going to see her again, he *had* to get up that cliff.

Putting an elbow on each side of the ditch, he pushed himself up. Help me, God! Help me!

After an interminable length of time—and each second a prayer on Egner's part—they neared the top. The crevice they had so painfully climbed petered out three to four feet from the top, and from there it was sheer and ice-covered.

Egner's tall companion hefted himself over the edge and disappeared, while Egner stared in shock at those last few feet. In his condition he could not possibly make it over that glassy top; his body was too frozen, his hands lifeless.

The black face of the sailor appeared over the edge. "Come on, Boats!"

"I can't," he croaked.

"Damn it, Boats, if I can make it, so can you."

Egner had come through a lot, but just below the clifftop his body refused to co-operate.

Phillips, lying on his stomach, extended a hand. "Come on, Boats, grab my hand."

By sheer willpower Egner lifted a stiffened arm and clawlike hand, and Phillips' hand closed firmly around it. In a few moments Egner was over the top.

"Thanks, buddy."

"O.K."

They saw the shed in the ravine below them, and Egner lay on his back and slid down the hill. Phillips was right behind him. The tarry slime of oil was liberally smeared on the shed and the ground in front of it. Egner opened the door and found the other four or five men who had scaled the cliffs as well. They lay in the hay, trying to get warm. Chief Petterson was still there. "I sent Bergeron for help," he told Egner.

Egner decided to look for help on his own. Maybe Bergeron had not been gone long, but to those waiting for rescue, it seemed like an eternity. Maybe the boy was lost. At any rate he had better get moving before he froze to death.

He moved off up the hill on the other side of the ravine, following the wire fence. A few others, including Phillips, went with him.

There were mixed feelings aboard the *Truxtun* when the rafts and the lifeline had fouled. It was one thing to have a choice to go or stay; it was another to realize there was no longer a choice. They had tried to lower the remaining gig, but it had smashed in two. Whether they wanted to or not, they had no alternative now but to remain aboard.

The waves had become increasingly violent, exploding upon the big rock on her starboard beam, rolling over her bow and stern, and rushing up her tilted deck. Steep waves, passing inside, thundered up the cliff, leaving ugly black smears of fuel oil high up on the rock face. It was evident that the flooded stern was in danger of breaking off, and all personnel still remaining at their stations aft were ordered to the forward section.

Despite the fierce grinding of the ship on the rocks as she was lifted and dropped with a force that banged their teeth together, the forward engine room was dry and, under the ministrations of Chief Danforth, the generators were running normally, keeping the pumps operating. As long as she had power there was a feeling of security that it would get no worse and the U. S. Navy would soon be on the scene to take care of the situation. They had an unshakable faith in the Navy.

With binoculars, Ensign Maddocks had watched Bergeron hacking his way up over the cliff, and the cheering word was spread that help would soon be at hand. That fence running across the cliff *had* to mean that there was a farm nearby, and at any moment they expected to see men with lines and maybe boats. There was a general feeling of optimism; but it didn't last long.

Seamans said, "I believe it's letting up."

"Yeah!" agreed another. "I believe it is."

It was not, of course; it was wishful thinking on Seamans' part, but he could not bring himself to put into words the fact that the *Truxtun* was finished.

Yet, in their minds, it was a foregone conclusion that before too long the ship was going to break in two in the after engine. The feeling was strengthened when Commander Hickox passed the dreaded word that anyone wishing to try to swim for the beach might do so.

There it was, facing them: Sink or swim!

There was no great rush to abandon ship. The beach was a long way off, and most did not have the heart or the will to deliberately jump into the icy ocean when they knew that survival in it was probably less than five minutes. They could see that the fuel oil quieted the heavy combers near the beach, but the prospect of swimming diagonally across those fearsome waves and against the powerful tidal influence sweeping in around the cliffs was frightening. Yet some realized if they could reach the fuel oil safely, with know-how it *could* provide sanctuary.

Some knew there *was* no other way. Empty crates went overboard, and so did a few sailors.

Edward Bergeron had not wasted any time in his search for help. He had run along the coast, not breaking any records because of the ice crust but keeping up a steady jog. This part of the coast was less steep, and to his left up the incline, scrub brush sheathed in ice lay over on the ground. On his right the seas fell madly upon the shore, spray hurtled in over the land. On a summer's day it was possible to find, buried in the gorse, seashells that had been hurtled up over the hills in a storm.

Presently the land sloped downward and, through the snow and sleet, he saw a cluster of buildings and a mining rig about a half mile inland. There was a river in full flood between him and the buildings, and he staggered along the side until he came to a bridge. He crossed it and, like a drunken man, made his way toward the buildings.

18

The sleet was thinning and letting up occasionally, a sign that the storm was passing. The wind had gone around more to the southwest and the sea was assaulting the *Pollux* from abaft the beam, but still falling upon her, working her savagely back and forth with such force that it was only a matter of time before she broke in two.

The fuel service line from No. 2 hold had broken at 0940, contaminating the fuel in the storage tank, forcing Lieutenant Dougherty to switch all power to the turbine. The bulkhead plates were still holding, and the turbine ran on the power that had been generated by the diesel.

The cracks on the forward deck continued to widen and the crew, huddled on the superstructure, watched in quiet desperation as she began to disintegrate beneath their feet. They knew there was no one to help them and they could not help themselves. The *Wilkes* could not get closer; indeed, many of the older seamen wondered if she was not already too close. It would not take much for those furious seas to drive her in on top of them.

Hank Strauss was too busy to dwell on their situation. Onshore, Wag Greenfield had asked for blankets, clothing, and food, which could not be sent over to them because of the fouled lifeline, but the boat they had gone over in had its emergency rations, and now Strauss tried to communicate this to Calemmo and Lloyd, who occasionally appeared at the water's edge in the cove. Either Lloyd or Calemmo did not read his message or the broken whaleboat was out of reach. As far as Strauss was concerned, they did not seem to get the message.

As the tide began to fall, the powerful undertow, combined with the ebbing tide, dragged at the *Pollux*. She started to list more to starboard. The weight of the flooded forward section was too much; another large crack opened from port to starboard, just forward of the bridge.

At 1045 hours, water spraying over the turbine in the engine room told Dougherty that it was time to leave. "That's it, men, secure the generator," he ordered. Robert Ashbridge lifted the safeties on No. 1 boiler; Joseph Neville lifted the safeties on No. 2. The steam hissed out. The two men preceded Dougherty up the ladder.

They were now without power. The *Pollux* was completely dead.

A U. S. Navy plane had flown over, and the *Pollux* signaled the *Wilkes*:

Please tell plane to get help from the beach.

The *Wilkes* transmitted the message to the plane, and then passed along the information to the *Pollux* that help would arrive in two hours. The flagship was cautiously maneuvering even closer to the *Pollux* when Commander Turney ordered a warning signal sent:

Ship is breaking up, set at your discretion.

The *Wilkes* replied:

We are standing in and will attempt to float liferafts down to you.

Liferafts were eased toward them, but the seas took them past her stern.

It was almost midday when the bow of the *Pollux* broke off. As it separated from the main section, an incongruous sight emerged. There, for all to see, were Alfred Dupuy's line of skivvies, still strung across the hold, quite black with fuel oil but unmistakably recognizable for what they were.

"Goddamn!" drawled Dupuy.

As fraught with danger as the moment was—for the *Pollux* could have slid off into deep water—there was a momentary lifting of the pall of despondency that had settled upon them: There were wisecracks and laughter. Then, as the seas between the ship and shore became more frenzied, gloom returned. They watched the bow swing to starboard and its after part begin to pound against the rocks. Cargo, spilling out of the section that had broken off, was swept into the oil slick and smashed against the shore. For Dupuy it brought to mind his studies of Dante's Inferno—the frozen rain of hell, the dirty water, the putrid slush that waited. . . .

William Stanford was increasingly uneasy: The pounding and buckling of the stern increased, and he did not like the feel of it. He slipped aft and, with his emergency battery light, examined the cold, dark after part of the ship. Near the bottom, the hull plates were starting to split and water was already running in. As far as he was concerned, the *Pollux* would be in three pieces before very long.

He hurried topside and reported his findings to Commander Turney.

"Thank you, Bill," the captain replied. He had aged considerably in the past few hours.

Stanford headed aft again, followed by Dougherty. "What are you up to now, Bill?"

"Why don't you follow me and find out, sir?"

Stanford, a careful, reliable sailor, was greatly respected by the officers. "O.K., buddy, that's just what I'm going to do," Dougherty replied.

They stopped by a repair locker on the main deck, where Stanford picked up a bolt cutter, then they headed for the deserted doctor's office in the sick bay. Two cabinets, containing whiskey and medicinal alcohol, were heavily padlocked and, without explaining to Dougherty, he cut the padlocks off without difficulty and began removing the bottles. "We're going to need this," he said, and Dougherty agreed.

They put the medicinal alcohol in containers, secured them tightly, and took them to the bridge. The whiskey was brought forward too. "We might be needing this, sir," Stanford told Dr. Bostic.

"Undoubtedly," the doctor agreed.

The bow of the *Pollux* had disappeared beneath the waves. The sea was abating slightly but it remained quite turbulent between ship and shore despite the crust of oil. The crew, huddled together amidships, were drenched with flying spray in spite of the heavy overcoats passed to them by the ship's officers. They had been grounded for more than six hours. Where was the Navy?

Dupuy, with his two buddies, Storekeeper Third Class Fred Brehm and Storekeeper Third Class Frank Hak, jiggled and danced to keep their blood circulating. "Goddamn! It's cold!" Dupuy allowed.

George Coleman had remained with his buddy, George Marks. Somehow Coleman had missed out on the heavy clothing. He wore only dungaree shirt and pants, and was dancing and clapping his hands to keep warm—not so easy to do when the ship was listing more severely. As the tide fell, she was dragged farther over on her side.

Edward Jabkowsky, still weak from malaria, kept strict control of the young recruits. "If word comes to abandon ship, follow me," he told them.

Great waves continued to suck and pull on the *Pollux,* trying to haul her from her precarious perch. It was a nerve-wracking situation, but they could do nothing but wait and pray. Then in one heart-stopping moment, the stern swung to port, jammed on the rocks, and she took another heavy list to starboard. One more like that and she'd turn right over, spilling them into the sea or taking them to the bottom with her.

Strauss felt they were finished, and there was nothing more to worry about. He was quite resigned to the fact that he might not see Jo again; yet he went into the chartroom and checked their location so that if, by some miracle, he could get ashore, he would know in what direction to head. The whole idea of planning ahead like this was ridiculous, he knew, because if he did get ashore he could not possibly survive on that desolate coast. Nevertheless, he studied the wave action toward the shore to see where the waves would sweep him to the rocks, even if he might be insensible from shock and the freezing water.

The ship gave another ugly, groaning lurch to starboard, and Strauss heard a crash from below. A hasty check in the officers' wardroom showed the water pouring in through the starboard side. He rushed to the bridge and reported it to Commander Turney.

Turney, looking old and haggard, discussed the situation with Gabrielson, Weintraub, and the other officers with him. "I think it would be well to tell the crew that those men who wish to attempt swimming ashore, or getting ashore on floating wreckage, have permission to go overboard." He added, "May God go with them."

The word was passed down the line. Many received it as it was given, and decided to stick with the ship. An equal number of men translated it to "Abandon ship!"

Jabkowsky was the first over the side, and there was a general movement toward the ship's railing among the younger sailors. It was what they had been waiting for. They all had life jackets; they were young, strong, and confident they could make it. "Let's go! Let's go!" they cried.

Lifelines were attached to the ship's railing, and they began to slide down the side. Some went down the cargo nets.

With tears in his eyes, Turney again called: "May God go with you."

Wayne Brewer was among those who went down the cargo net. He was not anxious to go overboard, but the order he had heard was "abandon ship!" and orders were orders. Reluctantly, he eased down the ship's side and let the sea take him. Instantly it paralyzed his body and swept him into the oil quagmire.

In the cove it was Garrett Lloyd, keeping vigil on the *Pollux,* who first saw the sailors swarming over the ship's side, their orange life jackets vivid splashes of color against the dark hull of the ship. He yelled, "Larry, is that Skee going over the side?"

Calemmo looked. "Sure it is." He recognized Jabkowsky—everybody recognized Jabkowsky, the old-timer who had been instructing the recruits. They were actually abandoning ship! They watched with mounting excitement as the sailors shinnied down the lines and dropped into the sea. "Holy mackerel! Here they come!" he yelled.

The two men made their way down the incline over the rocks, as close to the water's edge as they dared, and waited.

Bo'sun George Marks ordered the liferaft hauled alongside, and slid down into it. Coleman, about ready to follow Marks, hesitated. Dupuy, Brehm, and Hak also hesitated to take that awful step although it looked so *easy.* The sleet, the heaving sea with its stinking cap of fuel oil, did not look so difficult to any man who could swim, and it was not far. . . .

Strauss, having been in the water, was rooted to the deck. Should he go? The ocean was pouring into the *Pollux* and it was probably a matter of minutes before he had *any* choice, yet he could not bring himself to voluntarily enter the water again. He said to Grindley, "I don't want to go in, but should I?"

Grindley himself had decided he would stick to the ship until she rolled off into deep water. "Keep your eye on me, Strauss," he said. "Don't leave the ship unless I leave."

"O.K.," Strauss said. He had great respect for Grindley who, he was sure, never slept, never rested.

Down the lifelines went the sailors, some sliding all the way down before relinquishing their grip on the rope, others dropping from halfway down. Some went gingerly down the cargo nets; still others dropped into the liferaft with Marks. All were shocked breathless by the viselike cold that immobilized their bodies.

The kapok life jackets had no leg straps but did have chin straps. However, a large number of the recruits had neglected to tie the chin strap. Depending on the angle the sailors hit the water, many of the life jackets became death traps as the force of the water pushed them upward, jamming the men's arms in an upright position above their heads. They drowned immediately and were carried forward to disappear under the ship amid wreckage and oil, or were carried into the oil slick.

Above the roar and tumult of sea and ship, a voice screamed, "Mother! Mother! Mother!"

Another voice shrieked, "Oh, God! Shoot me! Shoot me, please!"

Before the realization of what was happening could hit home, the *Pollux* gave another heavy shift so that her starboard searchlight was under water. There was no doubt about it now; the next one would send her under. Sailors who had been uncertain about going over the side now made a concerted rush for the ship's railing, Ernie Califano, Peter Manger, and Bob Collins among them.

Strauss watched Glen Wiltrout who, an hour or so earlier, had used himself as a winch to save him, jump over with a cigar in his mouth. Bill McGinnis and Rex Copeland, who had made the first attempt to get ashore by raft with Lieutenant Bradley, followed Wiltrout. Chester McKay was behind them, and Feroll Gipson, James

Henry Strauss made a sketch of men abandoning ship, as he saw it from the deck of the *Pollux*.

Dunn, Charles Killelea, and Tommy McCarron were right behind McKay. Gus Tortorici, Christian Protz, Jr., and Johnny Simcox, all personal friends of Strauss, went over together. "Hell, we can make it," they said.

Stewart Pond, seaman first class, was about to go down the boat falls when a dying sailor cried out, "Don't come in, Pond!" Pond returned to the deck.

Yeoman William Ward grabbed the bag with the navigational records, slung it over his shoulder, and jumped. Ward and records went down like rocks.

McGinnis struggled for a few minutes, waved to the ship, and went down.

Strauss was rooted to the deck with shock.

Not wanting to be carried to the bottom with the ship, Dupuy did not linger. "Hell!" he said to Brehm and Hak, "I'm goin'."

Cries and pleas for help were heard as men were immobilized by the freezing water.

"God! Oh, God!"

"Throw me a line, in the name of God!"

Some tried to crawl back up the cargo nets, but their bodies were too numbed to make it.

Walt Bulanowski watched his best friend, William Budka, go over the side. Budka, paralyzed with the cold, looked right into his eyes as the sea rushed up the ship's side. "Don't come in, Walt!" he cried, and in the next minute was carried into the malodorous oil slick between the ship and shore, where he disappeared. It was now very evident that the morass of congealed oil was a death trap; once the current carried a man into it, he went down as though in quicksand.

Bulanowski was devastated. Budka was to have been best man at his wedding in a few weeks' time. Galvanized into action, he and Joe Janocha began to throw empty ammunition boxes over the side in the vain hope that they would be of some help. Then Walt knelt on the deck and prayed to God to save him and his shipmates. Never in his life had he prayed so hard and so sincerely.

Others began to toss overboard everything that came to hand; anything for the men to cling to. Even paravanes—torpedo-shaped machines, fitted with apparatus for severing the moorings of sea mines —were thrown into the sea. One of them became activated and, its arms sawing back and forth, began to cut a deadly swath through the struggling sailors before it was caught in the oil slick.

Unable to move, Brewer was at the mercy of the waves propelling him through the sludge, wreckage, and choking oil fumes, toward the raging shoreline, where a yellowish brown comber flung him against the ledge. A shipmate, Apprentice Seaman James R. Edenfield, had already been deposited on the lower part of the ledge, where he sat hunched over, looking down upon the life-and-death struggle of his shipmates. Brewer did not have time to force his arms and legs to move so that he could scramble to safety, before the undertow dragged him from the shore. He did not struggle—could not struggle —as the sea pummelled and jostled him about; his body had been anaesthetized by the frigid water, but his mind was crystal clear. He had to be prepared when the next opportunity presented itself to get ashore.

As the sea carried him back and forth Brewer witnessed a seemingly irrational act as Edenfield, who was safe and sound on land, stood up and jumped back into the raging ocean. It was such a wild and reckless act, Brewer could not help but wonder if his shipmate had lost his senses. At the same time, he was unable to concern himself with Edenfield, or any other sailor who, like himself, could only pray to be lucky enough to be thrown upon the shore.

Back and forth he was swept until a great wave cast him into the cove where Lloyd and Calemmo were waiting. This time Brewer was ready; he crawled out of the mire, up the incline, out of the reach of the sea, and lay gasping for breath. He had lost his right shoe and sock.

Like the others, Dr. Bostic was riveted to the deck by the carnage before his eyes. He watched sailors being carried around in the water —even the most powerful swimmer could not make headway against that undertow—noting that only those lucky enough to be picked up by a wave and carried in to a place where they could land were going to make it. Even so, the majority of these who had been thrown upon the rocks were either stunned or killed outright. Others were brought back by the sea and smashed against the iron side of the ship. He felt heartsick.

The raft was still tied to the ship, and Marks, McCarron, Dunn,

and a couple of other sailors were up to their waists in water, ready
to cast off, when Dupuy slid down into it. The moment his feet hit
the water he knew he had made a mistake. A bad mistake. It damn
near took his breath away as it rushed up his body like ice fire. If it
had been possible for him to climb that rope, he would have done so.
It was cold! Dear God, it was cold!

Bob Collins missed the raft, plunging into the sea beside it, and
McCarron hauled him aboard.

"Let's go!" someone bawled as they reared and plunged against
the ship's side.

"We gotta cut the line first."

"Who's gotta knife? Anyone got a goddamn knife?"

There was considerable swearing as the frantic sailors searched for
a knife. A hand, wielding a knife, slashed at the line, and they
shoved off. Great waves picked them up and threw them down; the
current swept them forward and hauled them back in spite of the furious paddling of all aboard.

Forward and back they were swept, pitting their strength against
the powerful current rushing between ship and shore. It was madness
to think they could overcome that millrace, but the adrenalin was
running high, giving them a sort of superhuman strength.

Around them, others were being propelled toward the shore, black
blobs popping up through the yellow-brown muck. As numb and unfeeling as his body was, McCarron's mind was alert. He saw the captain's steward, Rente Jacinto Ricaf—nicknamed "Ricafente" by the
gang—clinging to a piece of wreckage with one hand and hanging
onto his steward's cap with the other. "Ricafente" was a Filipino
who worried constantly about his family in the Philippines, but right
now he appeared to be most concerned about losing his cap.

About seven or eight times the raft nearly made it to the shore, but
each time the undertow carried it right back to the ship. How long
they had been tearing their guts out, Dupuy did not know, except it
seemed to be an exceptionally long time, which irritated him. Jesus
Christ! They were playing Ping-Pong and Yo-Yo on the goddamn
raft and getting nowhere.

"Hell!" he said to everyone in general, "I'm goin'!"

On the forward sweep of the raft, at its closest point to the shore,
he flung himself overboard.

At that moment a wave spilled them all into the sea. The raft fell over on McCarron, forcing him under. His life jacket kept pushing him up, and after a couple of tries he got away from the overturned raft and was swept shoreward and westward by the current. He did not struggle or try to swim, but guided himself toward the shore; then he was in the thick of the fuel oil and wreckage, being pounded by the waves and hitting against the debris. . . .

Dupuy quickly discovered that it was not possible to swim through the tarry oil and debris cluttering the shoreline; he could only work his way through it. Oil clogged his nose, mouth, ears, and got into his eyes until he thought he would smother in it. A wave flung him against the base of a rock. Having expended so much energy on the raft, his body, with its extra coating of solidified oil, felt as if it weighed a ton. A few other black blobs were already on the rock, sitting or lying in various stages of exhaustion.

Dupuy could not move. "Men," he croaked, "give me a hand."

They looked at him, but made no effort to help. That made Dupuy mad enough to give him the incentive to crawl; that, and the sound of the waves roaring back toward shore—that was a hell of a lot of incentive for getting out of the reach of that goddamn surf.

He scrambled up on the rock, unaware that somewhere along the way the sea had sucked his shoes, socks, and gloves off. Since his hands and feet were totally without feeling, it made no difference.

It was impossible to recognize one oil-coated sailor from another as they huddled miserably on the rock, coughing and retching fuel oil. He wondered if Brehm and Hak had made it. Over the roar of the ocean he yelled at the nearest sailor, "Have you seen Brehm?"

The sailor croaked, "He didn't make it."

Dupuy was shattered. "Oh, my God!"

Perched on the reef, half frozen, blackened with oil, and the sea hurling spray upon them, the sailor grinned at Dupuy, his teeth startlingly white against the tarry slime covering him. Jesus Christ! It was *Brehm!*

Others who had crawled upon the rock were Joseph Quinn, Melvin Bettis, a passenger for the USS *Prairie;* Pete Manger, Ernest Califano, Robert Collins, John Baumgarth, Henry Drag, Eugene Gieryn, Frank Hoffman, Robert Herlong, Barnett Glazer, and Thomas Hukel. The lifeless bodies of their shipmates were already being battered against the rocks. They were out of their misery, at least.

In the little basin at the foot of the slope where Garnaus and his crew had gone up earlier, the water was comparatively quiet, and Dupuy could see men standing up to their chests in water, crying for help and a line. Hell, *he* didn't have a line to throw!

Well, they had made it to the shore. What next? They were on the far end of the ledge, which was joined to the main part by the narrow ridge of ice-covered rock. Above them, the cliff rose another seventy to seventy-five feet, jutting out like a giant seashell. Where did they go from there?

Dupuy looked at the *Pollux,* leaning at a crazy angle over the deep water. It sure looked warm and safe, and he wasn't all that certain he'd made a good decision in leaving her, but it sure as hell was too late to reconsider. There was no way back now.

His companions were lying on the rock, their movements becoming heavier and clumsier as the cold sapped what little vitality they had left. Dupuy's clothes were frozen, he was frozen, and he knew that in very short order he and his companions could freeze to death. Had they gone through all that just to die?

Well, there they were. He himself was so tired and cold—so *goddamn* tired and cold—he had to rest.

Damn! It had all looked so easy.

Wiltrout had been swept out to sea, but his body would be deposited upon a rock along the shore, and would be recovered within a few days.

With tears streaming down his face, Commander Turney was watching his men struggling valiantly toward the shore when the *Pollux* was struck by a sea and thrust back to a more upright position. The order was sent immediately to stop anyone else from swimming ashore.

Over one hundred men had gone over the side. More than eighty had died within minutes.

19

Garrett Lloyd and Larry Calemmo, watching the exodus from the *Pollux*, saw men die as the frigid ocean shocked the life from their bodies. Calemmo saw the life jacket fly right off one sailor who had dropped from a lifeline.

The bizarre sight of dead comrades floating in the debris with their arms jammed above their heads by life jackets was devastating, but they had little time to dwell on it. The current was sweeping some of the survivors in their direction, and they were grabbing the line that had been brought ashore earlier by the whaleboat. With the line to guide them, they were pulling themselves into the cove.

Lloyd and Calemmo were waiting for them. They could not stand at the water's edge and try to drag their shipmates ashore because the surf funneling between the big rock and the ledge was too powerful; instead they lay on their stomachs in the water, protected somewhat by the rocks, and inched their way to the blobs lying helplessly in the muck that had piled up there. Calemmo locked his hand on a sailor's upper arm and yelled, "Now you do the same to me."

A hand locked around his upper arm and Calemmo heaved and strained to haul the man out, but he was inert, his normal weight increased by fifty to sixty pounds of congealed oil adhering to his body.

"Come on," Calemmo panted, "you gotta help." His own reserves would not take too much of this.

The man could not help. "Give it a try," Calemmo encouraged, but the man did not budge.

A wave engulfed them, filling Calemmo's eyes, nose, and mouth with oil. He gagged, but kept a grip on the sailor's arm. "Move!"

The sailor did not budge. "If you don't help me, I can't help you. Let go," Calemmo yelled.

The sailor croaked, "Try again, Larry. Try again. Help me, don't leave me here."

Calemmo tried again and again, but the sailor could not or would not help. "Goddamnit, *move!*" roared Calemmo.

After one more valiant effort it was beyond Calemmo's strength to drag the man's dead weight ashore, and he let him go. There were others who needed his help.

Two men, Gunner's Mate Third Class William Wood and Wayne Brewer crawled ashore on their own, but most of the survivors who had been thrown upon the rocks were too frozen and helpless to make it without assistance. Calemmo and Lloyd locked arms with them all and, with their help, dragged them ashore.

Calemmo found himself locking arms with Tom McCarron. After a few minutes of pushing and pulling, McCarron gave up; his body was completely without feeling and he did not have the strength, or the will, to continue the struggle. "Let me go, Larry, let me die," he said.

Calemmo gasped, "Come on, you Irish bastard, *push!*"

"Leave me alone," McCarron said. He was too exhausted; his body too numbed to care about living; it did not seem worthwhile to make that extra effort.

"You son of a bitch, push!" The string of insults continued until McCarron responded in anger. Calemmo nursed the anger, calling him every unprintable name he had learned on the streets of Manhattan until McCarron, in righteous anger, began to move. Presently he lay out of the reach of the sea.

Eighteen men had swum to the cove. They were: Storekeeper First Class Norman Mongeau, Gunner's Mate second class Edward Thomson, Mess Attendant First Class Leon Dawson, Apprentice Seaman Wayne Brewer, Seaman First Class Arthur P. Malone, Storekeeper Third Class Frank J. Hak, Apprentice Seaman David W. Jalanivich, Seaman First Class George W. Johnson, Seaman First

Class Thomas McCarron, Mmsth1c[1] Phillip L. Jewett, Storekeeper First Class Ever L. Hanson, Mess Attendant Second Class Tommie Harris, Mess Attendant Third Class James H. Foster, Storekeeper Second Class George Trojack, Apprentice Seaman James R. Edenfield, Apprentice Seaman Burt C. Jordan, Seaman Second Class James C. Enfinger, and Gunner's Mate Third Class William Wood. Sixteen of these men were hauled out by Calemmo and Lloyd. On the other side of the nest of rocks that had smashed their whaleboat, several bodies floated about in the oil and wreckage. Calemmo and Lloyd turned their attention to the survivors, prodding and pushing them, making them crawl up the incline on hands and knees. Eventually they were all in the cave, where they rested.

Aboard the *Pollux,* George Coleman was rooted to the deck by the dreadful scene before him. His ears still rang with the cries of the men who had died. When the raft had overturned and the struggling sailors had been carried about by the steep waves, Marks had looked straight at him and called, "Don't come in, George. In the name of God, don't come in." Before Coleman's horrified eyes, Marks was swept forward and sucked under the ship.

He could hardly believe that in a matter of minutes all these men had perished. If ever there was a hell, it had been there before him as his shipmates had fought a losing battle against the violent seas.

Now, less than thirty feet from the ship, he saw a black blob struggling toward the shore. Pray to God he makes it, George thought fervently, but in the same moment the sailor turned toward the ship, raised his right arm in a salute, and went under.

After that, there were no more shouts and cries, and Coleman felt a fear come upon him. It was not the fear of dying—death was almost a certainty—but as a reasonably devout Roman Catholic, he feared for his soul. Was his soul in the state of grace? He didn't know. "Help me, Mother of God," he prayed silently.

He stood there, thinking over his life and mentally confessing his sins to God; then he made an Act of Contrition.

Standing there on the icy, windswept deck, ill clad against the elements, George felt an inner peace come over him. He turned to go to the bridge, where everyone else had gone but, for some reason,

[1] The author has been unable to find out, through other survivors, the breakdown of this rating.

changed his mind and went to the stern of the ship instead. He was unaware of the cracks in the ship's hull plates astern or of the imminent danger to anyone going aft. The stern was high out of the water and buckling back and forth in an alarming manner.

Rounding the base of the five-inch gun platform, he saw a young sailor, all by himself, staring pensively out to sea. He was about eighteen, blond, with blue eyes; a typical clean-cut American boy. George did not recognize the young man and assumed it was one of the recruits they were taking to Argentia.

"What are you doing back here?" he asked. "You'd better go forward."

"I wanted to be alone for a while with my thoughts," the young sailor replied.

George understood that very well. He did not leave the young man, but waited quietly, staring off at the *Wilkes* trying to float rafts to them, and at another ship,[2] a tug by the look of it, which was steaming toward them. Was it the Navy?

The wind had gone around more to the westward and the *Wilkes* had eased around with it, coming as close as possible to them, but her rafts, appearing on the steep wave crests and disappearing in the troughs, appeared to have fouled.

Suddenly there was a heavy vibration and shuddering as the stern began to break away. A great crack, three feet wide, opened across the deck, amidship of No. 3 cargo hold, and the stern took a 12° list to port. The *Pollux* lay askew, with a severe starboard list forward and a port list aft.

There was shock and fright for a heart-stopping moment until it was apparent the stern had not totally separated; then they scrambled madly toward the edge of the crack, seeking a way to get across to join the rest of the crew amidships.

There *was* no way.

George and the young sailor could not get a firm footing on the icy deck and, if they did recklessly jump, they might very well slide right down the steeply slanting deck on the other side, right into the sea, or into the black depths of the broken ship, which would also be the end of them. Furthermore, they were blocked from the view of the bridge by a high bulkhead and the gun platform. They were trapped. So far the stern was buoyant, but as the split widened and the sea

---

[2] The USS *George E. Badger*.

flooded her, as it inevitably would, the stern would sink. It was as simple as that.

The young sailor showed no sign of fear. "What do we do?" he asked.

"We'd better try to get their attention," George said.

They yelled, hoping the men on the bridge would hear, but the noise of the ship, sea, and wind drowned their voices. Presently, having shouted themselves hoarse, they stopped wasting their breath.

They eased back from the edge. The slick coating of ice that lay over everything made it difficult for them to move about. The hatch of the cargo hold was so slippery they could not sit on it; the deck was tilted, but a flat vent on the deck at the very stern gave them some stability. They sat on it, talking about rescue, which didn't seem very probable in the circumstances. They were strangely calm.

George realized he was beginning to freeze. At a trim 168 pounds, he was in peak physical condition, but in thin dungaree shirt and pants, his body was growing numb. He began to clap his hands, rub his ears, and tap his feet until a little warmth stole over him. "You do the same," he ordered his companion.

As they made an effort to keep from freezing, the young sailor wondered if they would get out of this alive. George had no answer, no words of wisdom to pass on to the young man, who showed a stoic acceptance of whatever fate had in store for him. George himself had no fear. He was ready for whatever was facing him. Many of his friends had died a short while ago, and he could not quite believe it had happened, but the *Pollux* was breaking up around them.

The stern continued its list to port, and George felt they should do something to try to save themselves. "Let's see if we can get somebody's attention," he said.

Again they yelled at the top of their lungs, but nobody came to rescue them, and once again they gave up. George studied the sea. The tide was still ebbing, and the waves were coming in long, long swells at a slant, and sliding off the stern to rush forward. They had moderated, but had they moderated enough for him to attempt to swim ashore? A lifeline, attached to the stern railing earlier in the day, trailed to the angry sea, and George weighed the possibilities again. The stern was slowly but surely filling with water and ready to capsize. Nobody knew they were on the stern and it was likely nobody ever would. Death was a certainty if they lingered much longer. He really had no choice but to try to swim ashore. "We can't survive back here," he told the young sailor. "I'm going to try to swim ashore."

The sailor did not move or say a word. His face was a mask as he watched George put a leg over the railing, then he said, "Hey, Boats, could I please have your cigarettes and matches? When you go overboard, they'll only get wet."

Clinging to the railing, George looked at the sailor. His face was deathly white, the blue eyes seemed startlingly blue. Could he leave this boy alone? Another thought crept in: If he went overboard, would he make it to the beach?

He climbed down from the rail. "I'll have a smoke with you," he said.

They settled back on the vent and lit up. Within a minute four sailors with lifelines appeared around the bulkhead on the other side of the gap. They had seen George from the bridge when he had climbed the railing to go overboard.

A line was thrown, and George put it around the young sailor. The deck was very slippery, but they found a pad-eye[3] about eight to ten inches from the crack, where they could place a foot and take off. "At the count of three you jump and we pull," they were told.

Within moments the young sailor was across, and George followed.

He never did find out the name of the young man who, in a way, had saved his life, just as George, in a way, had saved his.

---

[3] An eyebolt with a plate at the end to distribute the strain over a larger area.

20

St. Lawrence, Newfoundland
February 18, 1942—0800 hours

The outport of St. Lawrence on the southeast corner of the Burin
Peninsula was a peaceful, happy community. It had been a poor
fishing village until the opening of the fluorspar mines by three en-
terprising Americans in 1933, when most of the fishermen had laid
aside their fishing gear and picked up the trappings of miners. More
recently the Lavino Mines had opened and had started operations
close by. If the St. Lawrence people had not gained a firm hold on
prosperity in the years between, they considered themselves better
off than many other fishing outports in Newfoundland.

They were devoutly Roman Catholic and genuinely respected their
Church. Hard workers, they had few luxuries and a true consideration for their neighbors. It was, in general, a happy place and if
life was not overly exciting, they were reasonably content.

February 18 was Ash Wednesday and the savage sleet and wind
storm had not kept them from Church. They had fasted before going
to Mass, where Father Augustine Thorne had put the smudge of
ashes on their forehead, and the miners had returned home, eaten
their early-morning meal, and then made their way on foot over the
rough dirt road to the mills, a mile or more outside the community,
or on to the Iron Springs Mine, a couple of miles beyond that, or to
the Director Mine, a few miles farther inland. Chambers Cove was a
couple of miles to the west of Iron Springs Mine.

The coastal steamer SS *Kyle,* carrying passenger and freight for
various outports along the south coast of Newfoundland, had

steamed into port during the night. Her master, Captain Tom Connors, had decided to wait out the storm in the sanctuary of the harbor. Two of his passengers were nurses: Margaret O'Flaherty and Mrs. Vincent (Cecelia) Reddy (known up and down the coast as "Reddy") were en route to their nursing stations along the coast.

St. Lawrence had a couple of small general stores, which opened at 9 A.M., and it would be business as usual. The children went off to school, young mothers began their household chores, some of the single girls went to work. Except for the storm, which provoked mild exasperation and an anxiety because of the extremely slippery conditions, people settled into the routine of an average day.

But this day would be like no other in their whole lives.

The Iron Springs Mine, owned by the St. Lawrence Corporation of Newfoundland, was managed by an American, Donald A. Poynter, currently in New York on business. A quiet, soft-spoken Newfoundlander, Howard Farrell was the assistant manager who was at this moment on his way home from Mass. It was a little after eight o'clock. The mine had just started its early-morning shift, and Albert Grimes, the pump man, was busy checking the pumps that kept the mine dry. His boss, Rupert Turpin, the mechanical supervisor, was checking the overall mechanical operation. René Slaney, the mine captain, was in his office. By chance, Louis M. Etchegary, the mill superintendent, was at the mine this morning, and outside, Mike Turpin, Sylvester Edwards, and Tom Beck were loading a couple of trucks with fluorspar to transport it to the mill.

It was Mike Turpin who saw the figure of a man stumbling toward them, obviously in an exhausted state. It was such an abnormal sight that the three men ran to meet him. The man was covered with a thick coating of congealed oil. "Can you help me?" he gasped.

"Yes, my son. Where do you come from?" Mike asked. He was a tall, well-set man who liked to keep his hand in fishing now and again.

Edward Bergeron pointed along the coast. "I've come from a warship; she's on the rocks in a cove under cliffs. There's over one hundred men on board, and they need help." He added, "I came up over the cliff."

They knew that had to be Chambers Cove, and God help any ship trapped there when the wind was from the south and west, as it was today. Those who still fished gave the Chambers Cove area a wide berth on such days.

They helped the young man to the mine house, a large building with a big iron stove and a couple of rooms with tables where the miners ate their lunches and took their breaks. In a matter of minutes Louis Etchegary, René Slaney, Robert Turpin, and Albert Grimes gathered around the young man, who repeated his story. They knew there would be no rescue from the sea—not with the wind and waves coming around straight into the cove—and by the look of the young sailor, rescue was a matter of urgency. Mike, Syl, and Tom took off immediately for the cove. Turpin carried a line.

"Get all the ropes you can find," the supervisor told Grimes.

"We'll need men," Slaney said.

"Get a few of them up out of the mine," Etchegary advised, "and phone Howard Farrell; he'll take it from there. I'll go on over to Chambers Cove." He had already looped a rope around his shoulder and was going out the door.

Slaney told Rupert Turpin, "Spread the word. Call Howard and tell everyone to get horses and sleds and get to Chambers Cove as quickly as possible. We'll go on to the cove and see if we can help."

Actually, no man there had the authority to take men out of the mines. Any interruption in the mining process could impair production of a commodity needed in the making of steel, so necessary for the war effort; but in such an emergency the Newfoundland men made their own decisions. They had learned, after generations of coping with the treacherous sea, that their only defense was caution, and a united front when peril threatened. In the circumstances, the mine was secondary.

As the preparations got under way, young Bergeron quietly left the building and was heading back to Chambers Cove, following in the tracks of Mike, Syl, and Tom, who were cutting across the hills in a direct line toward the cove. There was no road. Years before, a couple of families had braved the keen winds and the fogs to try to farm the gentler slopes along the coast, but only traces were left of those hardy souls who had given up the unequal struggle to accept the security offered by the mining company, and the convenience of community living.

It was rough traveling through the brush and small trees, but the distance to the cove was considerably less. In little more than a half hour they reached the ravine and the hay shed. Mike counted four men, black with fuel oil, huddled under a coating of hay. "Are you all right?" he asked.

"We're all right," one answered, "but there are others on the beach and on the ship."

The three men hurried up the hill and stood on the clifftop. Wind, spray, and sleet drove at them so fiercely they had to shield their eyes against it. To a man who had been born and brought up close to the sea, the *Truxtun* was a heart-wrenching sight. Sleek, gleaming, her big guns ready for action, she looked beautiful but pitiful as she lay at a forty-five-degree angle between the two rocks with the seas exploding over her. At least a hundred men were clinging to the safety lines on her port side. White water cascaded into the cove, breaking upon the edge of the oil slick that extended thirty feet from the shore. Wreckage and life rafts heaved and tossed in the oil strung from the ship, and sailors were clinging to the flotsam. As the wreckage overturned, or was torn from their grasp, the sea swept them toward the cliff.

Where Bergeron and Petterson had come up, there was a light handline looped around a knob of ice. Mike picked it up. He would not trust it to hold around the ice. "You stay here, Tom, and hold onto the rope. Syl and I will go down to the beach," he told Tom Beck.

Tom stationed himself on the incline, well back from the cliff's edge, and grasped the rope while Mike eased down the slippery cliff to the beach below, making use of the holes chopped in the ice by Bergeron. He could not help but marvel at the daring and endurance of the young sailor who had hacked his way to the top. Syl Edwards followed. There were a few men in the water close to the beach and Mike waded out up to his hips, threw them a line, and hauled them in. Minutes later, Louis Etchegary came to the clifftop, and he, too, worked his way down the cliff while Tom Beck held the line.

Ensign Loughridge and his bedraggled, frozen men, crammed into the recess at the far end of the beach, were overjoyed at seeing the Newfoundland men. "Thank God!" Loughridge said fervently.

"Help is coming," Louis told him, "more men and ropes, and horses and sleds."

"The captain will be happy to know that," Loughridge said, and ordered Signalman Parkerson to signal the *Truxtun* that help was on the way.

Word of the disaster spread very quickly. Theo Etchegary, the strapping twenty-eight-year-old chemist at the mill (and son of Louis, the mill superintendent) received the news in a phone call from an excited Rupert Turpin, and spread the news to the merchants in the community; then he commandeered a truck driven by young Alan Farrell, whose helper was Theo's sixteen-year-old brother Gus, and the three took off for the Iron Springs Mine. The merchants took it from there, alerting the townspeople.

At the mine, Theo paused long enough to collect a stout rope, but Gus and Alan, impatient to see the action, took off like a couple of deer. A young fellow, Charlie Brinston, followed Theo as he set out across the hills, but he was quickly left behind.

Captain Connors of the SS *Kyle* put to sea and steamed along the coast to Chambers Cove in an attempt to effect rescue from the sea.

Halfway to Chambers Cove, Theo met René Slaney and Rupert Turpin, with a couple of blackened, oil-soaked survivors they had met wandering across the hills. Harry Egner and Lanier Phillips had emphasized the gravity of the situation, and Slaney and Turpin were going back to the mine to get more men.

"I'll go on," Theo said, and presently he came upon the oil-smeared shed in the ravine and, hearing voices, he poked his head inside. "Don't stay here and freeze; walk to the mine. It's not far," he told the shivering sailors. "There'll be food and clothes for you when you get there."

The sailors made no move to leave. "There's nothing you can do here, and there's plenty of help coming for your friends," Theo said. "It's better for you to start walking; at least it'll keep you warm."

The men got stiffly to their feet, stumbled out of the shed, and moved clumsily up the side of the ravine. "It's not far," Theo called, then he climbed the hill to where the lone figure of Tom Beck was keeping vigil.

It was difficult to look into the teeth of the wind laden with sleet, spray, and spatterings of oil, but Theo's eyes were drawn to the huge warship heeled over on the rocks, the seas smothering her, the men clinging to her port railing. Straight out, along the coast a mile or more, he saw another ship[1] standing off. He did not question in his mind what a ship was doing there, but he knew it would be of no assistance to the one trapped below.

In the heaving water between the ship and shore, a few sailors, like tiny black bubbles in the gummy oil, were trying to cling to a couple of rafts or wreckage, but the waves swept everything from their grasp. One man tried to crawl aboard a raft but it tipped and slid away. He disappeared for a long moment, then popped up and made another try. It was a painful sight to watch, and Theo, wasting no more time, took his coil of rope, passed it to Tom Beck to hold on to, and prepared to lower himself over the edge.

Beck, shouting above the uproar, told him, "Your dad and Gus are down on the beach."

"All right," Theo called back. By the time he had worked his way down the cliff, more sailors had made their way to the shore, had been hauled upon the beach, and were being forced to their feet to keep moving. All of them were exhausted from cold and exposure. Theo put his jacket around a scantily clad youngster. One sailor had lost his shoes and socks and one of the Newfoundland men removed his own warm woolly socks, put his rubber boots back on his bare feet, then knelt and put his socks on the feet of the young man.

The combined noise of the wind roaring into the cove and the seas hammering the cliffs was overwhelming. Thank God for the fuel oil, Theo thought. It not only quieted the seas here, but it protected the beach as well. How lucky for the sailors. However, the tide was still rising and would shortly be at its peak, leaving only a strip of five or six feet of beach for them to work from.

Ensign Loughridge explained to them the abortive attempt to get the liferafts and the lifeline back to the ship, and Theo, Sylvester, and Mike immediately began a search of the shore for the line, while Louis Etchegary ordered young Gus to gather fuel for a fire. The wet, frozen men were reeling from exhaustion, and Loughridge had to speak sharply to them to keep them on the move.

Gus scrounged around the rocks and crevices, picking up pieces of driftwood and wreckage that had been thrown up on the beach, including an oil-soaked life jacket. After a great deal of difficulty, a smoky fire was lit, and although it gave little heat, the physical evi-

---

[1] The USS *Wilkes*.

dence of a fire perked the men up and they shuffled over to it. All except one, a youth, very little older than Gus, who lay on the shingle.

"Get him moving, Gus," Louis Etchegary ordered his son. Like the other Newfoundlanders he was busy dragging around a survivor himself.

Gus went to the young man, knelt, and put his arm around the tarry form. "Come on," he encouraged, and carted him to the fire. Round and round they walked. "What's your name?" Gus asked.

"Butterworth. Bill Butterworth," the youth mumbled, his body shaking with weakness and cold.

It struck Gus that this was no mere adventure; this was stark truth, life and death, and total involvement in it.

Heedless of the wind and sleet on his own body, Gus took off the old jacket with a sheepskin lining that he was wearing and put it around Butterworth. "It'll keep you warm," he said. Presently he had to leave the youth to search the shoreline for more wood for the fire.

By now more men had arrived from the mine and worked their way down the cliff to the beach, making it very crowded. Among them were Abe Pike, Leo Loder, Henry Lambert, Dave Edwards, George Carr, Fred Walsh, Neil Tarrant, Charlie Pike, Arch Pike, Alfred Turpin, Gregory Edwards,[2] and Phil Edwards. Dozens of other men were gathering on the top of the cliff, ready to give a hand in any way they could.

Theo and his two companions had slogged through the muck along the shore, but found no line. They could see the fouled liferafts about fifty feet off from the beach, but closer, at the edge of the oil slick, was the raft the men had been trying to climb onto. It was still in the same position, twisting and turning, appearing and disappearing as oily waves engulfed it.

Theo yelled above the din: "If that raft's got a rope attached to the ship, we might be able to free it and then we'll have a contact with the ship. Do you think we can haul it back to the beach?" If they could possibly get a line from ship to shore, there need not be

[2] Later Gregory Edwards would write a song about the shipwreck.

any further loss of life; no need for those desperate men to try to swim that treacherous stretch of water.

Sylvester Edwards was a fearless man. "We can try, if you like."

The waves in which the raft was bouncing around were running four and five feet and it would not be easy to control. Theo and Sylvester tied ropes around their waists and, as their companions held the other end, began to wade out to it. The scum of oil was about a foot deep, and so tough they could barely get through it. The frigid water burned as it crept up their legs, thighs, and bodies, then mercifully numbed them. The bottom of the cove, farther out, was rocky and rough, and they felt their way carefully, Theo ignoring the alarmed shouts of his father. Soon the waves were rolling over their shoulders, but they reached the raft, only to find it firmly snagged to the bottom. They tugged at it, trying to drag it toward the shore, but it bounced and dipped, and stayed where it was. Because of the thickness of the oil, they dared not explore beneath the raft, and eventually they had to return to the beach without it.

They continued to range back and forth along the shoreline, searching for the lifeline which, they reasoned, could be snagged on rocks closer to the shore. At the same time they kept a close watch on the *Truxtun,* waiting for her men to make the first move. They could do nothing until then. A feeling of helplessness and inadequacy swept over them.

Theo made his way out onto a ledge on the base of the pink cliff and saw the SS *Kyle* backing cautiously to within five hundred yards of the entrance to the cove, but the seas were huge and the ship could go no farther. It was foreboding. If Captain Connors couldn't help it was certain that no other ship could.

Wisely, Connors steamed back to St. Lawrence Harbor, where he ordered his crew to gather ropes, axes, and ships' blankets and get overland to Chambers Cove.

Gus went to find more firewood and when he returned he discovered young Butterworth lying dead on the beach. "You may as well put on your jacket, Gus," one man advised; "he dropped a little while ago."

Gus did not know Butterworth, and their brief association did not warrant any personal feeling, but he had felt a kinship with the young man and in a rush of emotion he wept as he tended the fire.

As cold as he was, he could not bring himself to take his jacket from the young sailor . . . not yet.

There was enough manpower on the top now to start bringing the survivors up the cliff. They were in no condition to work their way up by themselves, not even with ropes strapped around them, but that problem was not difficult to solve. The ice would permit them to be more or less slid *up* the cliff. A rope strap was hitched under the arms of the first man, and with seven or eight men hauling on the line, the limp form was eased over the glistening surface without any apparent difficulty. Yet there were many protuberances on the cliff face, and being too bone-weary to assist in any way to avoid them, he was bruised and bleeding when he was pulled over the top. He was immediately taken to the shed in the ravine to await the arrival of a horse and sled to take him to Iron Springs. The second man was also battered by the time he reached the top. Someone went down the rope to tell them what was happening, and there was a consultation. It was impossible for anyone to go up with the victims, so they would have to find another way.

There was only one other possibility, and that was on the other side of the craggy little cliff jutting out into the sea. The miners were familiar with the ravine that Egner and Phillips had used; they would have to use it to *carry* the survivors to the top. It meant literally carrying the men over the smaller cliff as well.

"Let's get 'em up," Abe Pike said to Mike Turpin.

Aided by George Carr, they began their backbreaking task. With the survivors on their shoulders they made their way over the small cliff into the next cove; then they strapped a rope around themselves and the sailors and, digging their toes in on either side of the narrow ravine, they inched their way up. It was easy on the survivors—but killing work for the rescuers.

21

St. Lawrence
February 18, 1942—0930 hours

Upon learning of the magnitude of the disaster, Howard Farrell closed the mine for the day and sent the men out to the cove to assist in every possible way in the rescue of the American sailors. He directed a number of them to collect every piece of rope they could find; others were told to scour the community for food and clothing and bring it to Iron Springs. The district nurse, Sadie Ash, was brought there as well.

Most of the women of St. Lawrence had heard about the shipwreck but were unaware of the true dimensions of the disaster. A ship being ashore did not necessarily mean a tragedy in which they would be involved. At one time direct involvement had meant bereavement; now there was only a stirring of curiosity. They tended to their babies and did their housework. Some did not know what had happened until trucks began loading up with foodstuffs from the stores and word began to spread about the American warship and the number of men who had already lost their lives in Chambers Cove. Even so, it would not occur to the women of St. Lawrence to venture over the hills to the scene of the disaster.

There was one exception: Howard Farrell's nineteen-year-old sister, Ena Farrell, worked in the office of Hollett's General Store. Among her own age group she was a leader. She had just a little more daring, was more definite in her opinions, and, for a circumspect young lady, had a tomboy streak. She also had a sense of history. An American warship was breaking up on their doorstep, much dramatic action was taking place, *somebody* should have a record—a picture—to show what was actually happening, she felt.

Her mother had given her a box camera for Christmas, which may have cost all of five dollars, but it took good pictures, and she had several rolls of film, and was probably the only person in St. Lawrence with a camera and film. Would Howard let her go?

As adventurous as she considered herself to be, she was not daring enough, in the circumstances, to go to the scene of the disaster without obtaining her brother's permission. It would be no place for a young girl. So, for the time being, she contented herself with handing out food and blankets and everything else the truckers demanded, while she kept an eager eye out for Howard.

At Iron Springs, as the survivors began to arrive, it became evident that they presented a problem that the miners were unable to tackle. Not only was their clothing saturated with oil, but also their frozen bodies needed a good scrubbing down and a warming. An appeal went out to the women to come to the mine house with their galvanized tubs and soap and whatever clothing and blankets they could find; spare mattresses would come in handy as well.

The women rose to the occasion splendidly. They collected their husbands' spare clothing, stripped the blankets from their beds or dug out extra ones; teen-aged girls were called to look after babies; more food was gathered from the cupboards, and with their tubs and clothes they were picked up and taken to Iron Springs. Among them were Violet Pike, Effie Haskell, Florence Etchegary, Josephine Turpin, Julia Skinner, Loretta Walsh, Theresa Saint, Ethel Giovannini, Dorcas Turpin, and Clara Tarrant. Clara, whose husband, Patrick, worked at Director Mine, left orders with her children, Ella and Carmel: "Keep a good fire going and keep everything hot; we have to be prepared for the Lord knows what."

"Yes, Mom," the girls said, and Clara climbed into a truck and went off to Iron Springs.

Fortunately there was plenty of hot water at the mine house, but as the shivering survivors began to thaw, they simply could not get enough heat into their bodies. The stove was being used to heat pots of soup and boil kettles of water for coffee and tea, so the Newfoundland men lit many small fires outside the mine house, ringing them with rocks which, when heated, could be used to warm the limbs of the survivors.

The women set to work to restore life and strength to the *Truxtun*'s semiconscious sailors, laying them on the table and stripping the clothes from their bodies. The oil had seeped into the pores of the skin so that they looked black all over. Those who returned to consciousness to find themselves mother-naked on the table were too sick to care as the Newfoundland women scrubbed, scoured, and rubbed life back into their frozen limbs and dressed and fed them like children.

Ena, having passed out the last tin of soup, the last package of coffee, the last blanket, closed the store. She wanted more involvement in this tragedy and, commandeering a horse and sled, began going from door to door gathering additional clothing and food. She persuaded the local president of the Women's Protective Association to donate all the woolen goods that had been knitted for the Newfoundland soldiers and sailors serving in the European conflict. Many a pot of home-made soup she carried carefully to the sled and brought to the truckers, who kept returning to St. Lawrence for more supplies. At the same time she carried her little box camera, ready to snap any unusual happening within the confines of St. Lawrence.

Howard Farrell, directing the rescue operations, had dashed home for a belated breakfast when Ena buttonholed him. "Can I go to Chambers Cove and take pictures of the wreck and rescue?" she asked.

Howard, a gentle, retiring, straitlaced man, was shocked at her request. For his young sister to go take pictures of the carnage was unthinkable. "You mustn't," he told her, "not today." Then he took off for Chambers Cove.

Despite her deep disappointment, Ena abided by her brother's decision, but *tomorrow,* she thought, she would get her pictures, come what may.

Father Augustine Thorne stood on the clifftop, the wind whipping his cassock against him, and raised his hand to give general absolution to the hapless sailors clinging so valiantly to life.

Like the other men gazing down upon the wreck, Howard Farrell experienced a feeling of helplessness. There seemed to be no way to save the hundred or more men still on the warship. It was heart-rending to see an occasional man swept away and dashed against the cliff, but even as he watched, a plan began to formulate in his mind. . . . If they could get enough rope to reach from one side of the cove to the other, and drop it right over the *Truxtun,* they would have a line from ship to shore. A breeches buoy could be rigged and not one more life would be lost. They would need up to five thousand feet of rope to skirt the cove and get well to the west of Pinnacle Head on the far side, but Farrell felt it could be done. He passed the order to the men to begin tying the ropes together.

Captain Connors and his crew arrived very soon, having dropped Nurses O'Flaherty and Reddy at Iron Springs with the other women. His men assisted the miners in tying the ropes together, and when every piece had been secured, more than a hundred men began to skirt the cliff, leaning against the wind with the rope on their shoulders. It was taken right around the cove to the far side of Pinnacle Head, but when it was released to fall across the wreck, the updraft of the furious winds hitting the cliff wrested the rope from their hands, and blew it upward and in over the land.

What a bitter disappointment. . . .

The *Truxtun* continued to take a severe pounding, falling more and more over on her side. The after part had broken off completely, and each huge wave pushed the stern farther away. The crew had watched the metal tearing apart, but heard no sound of it over the ear-splitting noise of wind and sea. They could see hundreds of people lining the clifftops and looking down upon them, but where was the help? Where were the small boats to take them off? *Where was the U. S. Navy?*

The tide had reached its peak and was falling. The wind had shifted to the west and was blowing directly into the cove, bringing forty-foot waves with it.

On the forecastle Ensign James Seamans began to feel that it was all a nightmare. Was this really happening to him? Shipwrecked on an American warship with the wild ocean crashing, men dying around him, and people on the cliff watching them. Was he going to die? The whole scene was unbelievable . . . the smoky fire on the beach . . . the tiny figures climbing the cliff . . . it was like the Hardy novels he had read in his youth.

But this was no Hardy novel. The raging sea, the trapped men, and
the battered ship were stark and real, and they were all looking death
in the face. Despite this, there was no outward sign of fear or panic
among his shipmates. Undoubtedly, he thought, they were too occupied with the physical act of hanging on for dear life. Seamans was
no less occupied.

At 1100 hours a Navy plane flew over, circling the cove. There
was a wild, unreasoning surge of hope. *They had been found!* Ships
would appear on the scene at any moment and, in some miraculous
manner, save them. Their spirits rose. At least the Navy knew where
they were. But in his heart and soul, Seamans knew the Navy could
not help them any more than the Newfoundland men could.

When Chief Danforth reported that water was entering the forward engine room and the forward fire room, Captain Hickox ordered all boilers and generators secured and all machinery spaces
abandoned. There was no more power . . . the *Truxtun* was a dead
ship now. . . .

The sleet had finally ceased with the shift in wind, and the sky was
not as gray, but it was still bitterly cold. The order was passed
along: "Keep moving your hands and feet." Presently the captain ordered whiskey to be broken out and passed around. Each man took
a swallow, and it took the chill off momentarily. The fiery trickle
gave Seamans the impression of heat. How unusual, he thought, a
Navy man-of-war, and men drinking on the forecastle. He knew the
captain had to be desperate to permit it

For a few minutes the warming drink took them out of the quiet
despair that had stolen over them. Damnit! What were they doing
here waiting for the sea to carry them away? How the hell had they
gotten here in the first place? Why hadn't the *Wilkes* alerted them
when she had run ashore? However, such thoughts quickly passed—
there was no room for anger and resentment in the circumstances.
"The Navy will get us off," someone said confidently, "they're on the
way. You wait and see."

They had supreme confidence in the U S. Navy. It looked out for
its people. Any moment now a ship would heave to and send in rafts
or life boats. . . . Somehow, the Navy would save them

Fuel oil was still pouring from the *Truxtun* as the seas filled her.
The men aboard her waited, for what they knew not. From time to

time someone went overboard, whether by accident or design was debatable. If they were lucky they made it to the beach, where the Newfoundland men waited for them, but most of them were paralyzed by the frigid water, carried into the quicksandlike mass of oil too soon, and were smashed against the cliff.

The communications officer, Lieutenant (jg) J. R. Gillie, was ordered to send for Signalman Brom. "Tell them," Hickox directed Brom when he arrived on the steeply tilted bridge, "to get boats to us."

Bracing himself on the port wing, Brom sent the signal: *"Send us boats."*

On the strip of beach the Newfoundlanders waited for more men to swim ashore. Getting the survivors up the cliff was incredibly arduous. Eight or nine men were hauling on the line to bring up the combined weight of two men. The oil that clung to them added an extra fifty pounds to each man.

Lionel Saint, a man of middle years, and his son-in-law, Ferdinand Giovannini, made their way down to the cliff with a bottle of liquor. "This might help to revive them," Lionel said. It was a generous gesture because liquor was a rare commodity—one had to travel two hundred miles to the capital city of St. John's to get a supply. The bottle was passed around with grateful expressions from the men.

Lionel and Ferdinand then assisted the other Newfoundlanders with the rescue work. Gradually the crowd on the beach became smaller as Mike Turpin, Abe Pike, and George Carr, aided by Leo Loder and Gregory Edwards, carried the men up to the top. It was obvious to them that the *Truxtun*'s position was becoming more desperate. The forward part of the ship was well over on its side, her bridge and four funnels were buried under a blanket of white foam, and the stern was well separated from the rest of her. Pretty soon she'd be flat on her side.

Young Clifford H. Parkerson, the signalman, had refused to leave the beach because he was the only link with the ship. When Brom began to signal, he passed the information along to Loughridge and the Newfoundlanders: "They're asking for boats, sir."

Boats? It wasn't humanly possible to launch boats in the wild seas climbing the cliffs, and by the time the seas quieted, it might very well be too late to help anyone if they stayed aboard. "Can you answer them?" Theo asked.

"Yes, sir."

"Tell them it isn't possible, under the conditions, to get a boat down the cliff. Tell them they will have to swim . . . that many of their men have made it safely to the beach." God knows there had been few enough, but they *had* made it.

Parkerson sent the message, and still the signal came back:

Please send a boat.

Were they getting the message? the Newfoundlanders wondered. Could the signalman on the ship make out the black, oil-covered form of Parkerson against the oily beach? Theo picked up one of the *Kyle*'s white woolen blankets, clambered out on the ledge of the cliff, and laid it over a protuberance. "You stand in front of that, Beau; they'll see you for sure. Tell them to jump and swim with the waves . . . to keep OUTSIDE the point where you're signaling from. Tell them to keep well off from the point."

Parkerson sent the signal, then read the signal from Brom: "They still want a boat," he reported.

It was evident to the men on the beach that the *Truxtun* would be inundated pretty soon. They're wasting their chances," Theo told Loughridge.

"Tell 'em to jump, Beau," one sailor advised.

"Tell 'em to slide off. Tell 'em not to wait to be washed off," said another.

Parkerson stayed at his post for the next two hours, urging those on the *Truxtun* to swim ashore. Whatever the messages were that passed between himself and Brom, the gist of them was that the sea was too rough for swimming, and the men did not want to risk it. Who could blame them?

The *Truxtun,* just about completely flooded and lying almost on her side, rose less with each wave, and began to break at No. 3 stack, almost dead center of the ship. Then the mast snapped off . . . and the forward section broke in two. Above the roar of surf and wind the men could not hear her breaking up, but it was no less frightening to witness the soundless destruction of their ship. She was in three pieces, with all her crew on the forward section. As she began to settle deeper in the water, the waves surged more and more upon the deck, drenching the sailors clinging to the safety lines, taking a man here and there whose numbed hands could no longer hold on.

Ensign William Maddocks, like everyone else, concentrated on hanging on. He knew that eventually he was going to have to swim to shore; nevertheless he could not deliberately bring himself to let go, even though he knew he should make the attempt before he became too frozen and numb to use his limbs. Whichever, it was not much of a choice. . . .

As these conflicting thoughts ran through his mind, he had been observing his shipmates who had either slid or been swept off the ship. They were being carried into the oil, getting covered with it, no longer recognizable as men, just little mounds of black slime in the great pool of filthy oil. Some disappeared completely; others were driven toward the cliff; a few made it to the beach. He was too busy trying to survive to wonder if the captain or the navigator were still alive. He had not seen or heard from them since taking orders and relaying them to Danforth. He didn't even know if Danforth was alive.

Suddenly Maddocks was hit by a wave and found himself clawing desperately at anything and everything to keep from going overboard —then in another split second he thought, Let it go. He had to swim sooner or later . . . better now!

Since he was already wet, the water did not feel that much colder but, for a moment as it closed over him, he experienced panic before he automatically began to move his arms and legs in the breast stroke. Here and there he saw an arm lift as a sailor tried the overarm stroke—almost a physical impossibility with the life jackets they were wearing. Maddocks, in peak physical condition and a good swimmer, grew more confident with every stroke that he would make it to the beach. Then, despite his best efforts, he was in the fuel oil, bobbing like a cork on the ponderous oily waves. It began to cover him, getting into his mouth, his nose, his eyes. The fumes were overpowering! He began to choke and a prickle of fear touched his brain; his confidence quickly ebbed. There was a real possibility that he could choke to death on bunker oil—it was blinding him so that his eyes smarted and burned. It made him work more aggressively. The breast stroke helped to keep the oil away from his face and made it possible for him to breathe.

The oil got thicker and he continued pushing against it, working his way through it, shoving aside the debris that had collected—life jackets . . . liferings . . . pieces of wood. It was like a huge stew, getting thicker with each wave, and he was a part of it. He kept on blindly, working, working his way through the quagmire until it seemed he had been in it for hours. Presently, through a haze of exhaustion, he realized he had been thrown upon some rocks beneath a towering cliff. They were heavily coated with the oil, and he lay in a bed of it, almost completely covered.

He just lay there, looking up through oil-blurred eyes, not conscious enough to draw attention to himself, but after a while voices, or a face, seemed to impress itself on his consciousness. . . . Had he heard voices? Had he really seen a face peering over the cliff at him?

A rope with a loop on the end of it was lowered to him. Maddocks, his training asserting itself, automatically got up, put his foot in the loop, and was hauled up the cliff. It was a long pull and he had many an unpleasant encounter with jagged outcroppings, but hands were soon dragging him over the top. Maddocks looked down at the *Truxtun* lying askew in the surf. Through his red-rimmed, blurring eyes he could still see his shipmates clinging to the side of the hull. Then he was put on a sled and he let himself drift off.

He had been carried past the little beach and landed on some rocks strewn beneath a big bluff, and his ascent on the rope was not seen by the men who were busily directing other sailors who had been swept off the ship at the same time. They had gone out into the water as far as they dared, almost to the edge of the oil slick, forming a human chain back to the beach. One sailor working his way through the sludge was one black glob of oil. Only his eyes were visible, fastened on them with a burning intensity. They encouraged him with gestures, pressing forward until the waves of muck and debris were rolling over their shoulders.

Finally he was near enough for them to hook their hands into his life jacket, and the moment the sailor felt contact with them, his eyes closed and he went limp. They carried him to the beach and up the cliff.

Henry Lambert dragged a struggling sailor ashore, then had to hold him down as he raved in a delirium, shouting for his mother.

He thrashed about the beach, heedless of the cuts he was inflicting upon himself, and Henry, with the assistance of Abe Pike, had to forcibly restrain him.

"We'd better get him up, quick," Henry said to Abe.

They had to wait until Mike Turpin returned with the rope, and by that time the young sailor had died.

Then the Newfoundlanders waited—Mike, Leo, George, Abe, Henry, Dave, Fred, Neil, Charlie, Phil, Theo, and Syl, just about as soaked and covered with oil as any survivor—for the next sailors to come. Others were examining the black jelly along the shore, which was deep enough to cover a man completely if he was flung upon the beach. The fire was still going, but now the men were burning some of the blankets that had been thrown down. Ensign Loughridge and a few men had remained on the beach; young Parkerson was still at his post on the cliff signaling the *Truxtun* and urging the remaining personnel to swim ashore and to stay away from the cliff, but he was totally exhausted.

Seaman First Class Roscoe Jim Brown, aged twenty-three, was clinging to the boat boom, which normally was on the port deck below the bridge. With the *Truxtun* lying on her starboard side, the boat boom was about the highest perch one could find—but it was not high enough to keep the seas from surging over Brown. It was very clear to him that the time had come for him to make a move. If he was to survive, he had to make that swim to the beach—*now!*

It was going to be a long swim and he thought he had better remove his galoshes first, but found he could not move his fingers to unlock the buckles. Ensign Gillie was also clinging to the boom, and Brown asked, "Will you unlock my buckles, sir? I'm going to try to swim to the beach."

Gillie obliged and Brown, stepping out of his galoshes, unhesitatingly jumped into the water. Once over the initial shock he swam steadily toward the corner of the crescent, his eyes glued to the smoke from the fire, which was carried upward by the wind. Caught up in the fuel oil and nearly overpowered by the stench of it, he felt a faintness come over him, yet something would not let him give up, and presently he got his second wind. How long he was swimming he did not know, but a wave picked him up and flung him on the beach. Before he could gather himself together, he was sucked back with

pieces of wreckage and debris, then once again hurled upon the
beach. He lay there, barely discernible in the thick layers of oil.
Hands grabbed him, turned him over, and a voice said, "This one's
dead."

Brown opened his eyes.

A great wave rose up and inundated the *Truxtun* completely. To
Ensign Seamans it was like sitting under an icy waterfall. When it
passed he looked about, gasping, and saw about thirty men in the
water. One or two were swimming. A few shouted for help—he
couldn't hear them, but he could see their mouths moving. Most of
them seemed to be paralyzed and were kept afloat only by the life
jackets. They were quickly carried into the oil and dashed against
the cliff.

Another huge wave smothered the ship and when the tons of
ocean water had fallen away, Seamans saw another number of men
floundering in the sea—about twenty this time, he estimated. Again,
only a few men tried to swim; the others were simply bobbing up
and down like lifeless corks, unable to move their limbs in the frigid
seas. They, too, died against the gray cliff.

Because of the ebbing tide, the sea at long last began to lose some
of its momentum. Its power was no less, but its reach up the cliffs
was gradually diminishing. The strip of beach off their port beam
was beginning to emerge. Also emerging were the broken bodies
under the oil. . . .

Survivors were making their way to the beach, forcing their way
through the black sludge toward the Newfoundland men who still
formed a human chain to the beach. John Arthur Shields, fire controlman third class, kept his eyes on the big young man who was encouraging him with shouts and gestures. Shields' ears were clogged
with oil and he could not hear what the man was telling him, but he
watched the oil-grimed figure with a prayer: "God, let me get to
him." He concentrated on the man, following his every gesture, gradually nearing him until the man lunged for him. Shields remembered
only the hands on his life jacket, then he lost consciousness.

Radioman Lovira Leggett remembered only the face of a youth
leaning over him as he returned to consciousness on the beach. It was
Gus, and he put his jacket around the young man.

Others followed Shields, all heading on a dangerously close course

This is the ravine that Harry Egner climbed, pushing himself up with his elbows because his hands were numb and useless. It is higher and steeper than it looks in this photo, and the top has eroded considerably in the past 37 years. (Derek Brown)

Heavy seas at the height of the storm made it almost impossible to lower a dory over the cliff in the left foreground, but the Newfoundlanders did it as the tide fell and rescued the last three men left on the *Truxtun*. (Derek Brown)

Thirty-five years after the disaster Andrew Ferrie (left) and Fred Edwards of St. Lawrence stand beside what is left of the fence that the crew could see from the deck of the *Truxtun*. (Cassie Brown)

Ena Farrell walked to Chambers Cove the day after the tragedy and took this picture of the derelict *Truxtun*. (Ena Farrell Edwards)

All that remains of the *Truxtun* today is a piece of rusty iron on the beach. (Cassie Brown)

The first survivors to scale the cliffs at Chambers Cove took refuge in this hayshed. The dark stains on the shed and snow are from the fuel coating the *Truxtun* men. (Ena Farrell Edwards)

This was Iron Springs Mine, where the shipwrecked sailors were revived and cared for by the women of St. Lawrence. All traces of these buildings have disappeared. (Ena Farrell Edwards)

Newfoundlander Pius Turpin (extreme left) and American salvage team haul up the decoder from the wrecked *Truxtun*. In this manner did the Newfoundlanders rescue American sailors the day before. (Ena Farrell Edwards)

to the sharp base of the bulging cliff on the north end of the beach. Like a traffic cop, Theo was directing them off from it. Like obedient children, they changed course, keeping their eyes on him . . . eyes so vividly blue or brown or gray followed his every movement with such intense concentration and complete trust, it touched him profoundly. Eye contact was broken only when the swimmers felt the hands of the men on their life jackets.

There was no more signaling between ship and shore. Brom, who had stayed at his post for hours, had been swept away. Parkerson was back at the smoky fire, walking in a circle with the few remaining survivors who were waiting their turn to be taken up the cliff. He had valiantly refused to leave the beach in the remote possibility that he would be needed.

Suddenly he fell and began to shiver violently. They rushed to him, covering him with blankets and rubbing his body, but the shivering continued. Then, as suddenly as it began, it stopped. Parkerson called, "Mother!" Then he died.

Gus had wept when young Butterworth died; the St. Lawrence men in particular were deeply touched by Parkerson's death. He had not been merely a survivor; he had been a part of their team.

Wherever it came from, whether it had been brought ashore by some sailor, or maybe swept off the ship, an American flag lay on the beach. It was badly stained with oil, but they covered Beau Parkerson with it.

Back on the top of the cliff, Lionel Saint had made his way to Pinnacle Head where he could look down on the *Truxtun*'s deck. He and his son-in-law Frederick Giovannini noticed debris and an oil slick drifting toward Chambers Cove. It was coming along the coast. . . . Had another ship gone ashore?

Saint began to walk toward Lawn Head.

22

Lawn
February 18, 1942—1300 hours

Earlier, the people of Lawn had learned through the telephone switchboard connected to St. Lawrence about the wreck of the *Truxtun* in Chambers Cove. Well, well! The ship the boys from Webber's Point had seen must have been standing by the *Truxtun* in Chambers Cove, which was less than a couple of miles from Lawn Head. They rationalized that the ship had probably steamed up around the Head for some reason.

Then about midday, a report said that another ship was also ashore at Lawn Point. It was true then! The two young fellows *had* been right about a ship on Lawn Point.

Lawn Point was a good ten miles away over mountainous hills and thick woods, much closer to St. Lawrence. Should they go? It would take them five or six hours to get there, and most likely they were rescued by now. Would they be going on a fool's errand?

"We'd better go," Manning decided.

They had already eaten dinner at noon, and did not think of taking food. They collected ropes, axes, and flashlights, harnessed up five horses, and started off. The rescue party consisted of ten men: Joseph Manning, Jim Manning, Fred Edwards, Clarence Manning (a youth), Alfred Grant, Andrew Edwards, Martin Edwards, James Drake, Robert Jarvis, and Thomas Connors.

Halfway there, Fred Edwards felt unwell and they sent him back with the youth, Clarence. Fred had two slices of brown bread, which he gave to them, and they shared it among the eight of them.

It was a rough climb over wild country which heretofore had only felt the tread of a few hunters, and the first time that horses had been brought over the hills. Their greatest worry was getting there before dark, and there was still the uncertainty that they might have come on a fool's errand.

23

USS *Pollux*
February 18, 1942—1100–1430 hours

On the cliff above the *Pollux,* Jack Garnaus was unable to find better shelter from the piercing wind. The dwarf trees in a slight depression farther up the hill were little better than the clump of trees they now huddled under and, having satisfied himself about it, he returned to the promontory. His next act, which he knew was of the utmost importance, was to try again to get to the ledge below in order to rig a line and get his shipmates ashore. Somewhere there had to be a way down. Again he skirted the chasm on the other side of the cliff but this time eased his way down to the shore only to find that on this side of the promontory, sheer rock rose abruptly from the sea. There *was* no way to the ledge beneath the overhang.

Back on the promontory, he went as close to the edge as he dared but the overhang glinted evilly with ice and effectively prevented him from getting close enough to see what was going on below. He was, therefore, unaware that the men of the *Pollux* had tried to swim ashore. Another ship had joined the *Wilkes,* and they were exchanging signals; still another ship[1] was approaching. If there had been a dozen ships offshore, they could still have done nothing in the heavy seas pounding the shore, Garnaus thought. It was frustrating.

As he was returning to the little clump of trees that sheltered Wag Greenfield and DeRosa he saw a couple of men approaching, and for one brief joyous moment he thought that help had arrived. It was

[1] The USS *Kite.*

with mixed feelings that he saw they were two oil-soaked survivors. One was Seaman First Class William Heldt, a man from his own division. "Is that really you, Heldt? Where the devil did you come from?"

"I came up the same way you came up," Heldt said, explaining that the ship had slipped with the change in tide, and the captain had given the men permission to get ashore on their own if they wanted to try. "I hit that heaving line you brought ashore, and came up the way you did."

"I've been looking for a place where we might get close enough to catch a line," Garnaus said.

"I don't think there is one," Heldt said, looking around at the bleak hills. "What do we do now?"

"I don't know," Garnaus confessed, "there's no sign of life; I don't know how far we are from people who could help us."

The first thing to do was to get out of the cutting wind. Heldt and his companion[2] each carried an extra fifty pounds of congealed oil on their persons, and they were exhausted. They followed Garnaus to the small grove and found Greenfield still working on DeRosa.

The presence of two more men gave Garnaus and Greenfield moral support. If these two had made it, it was possible that others could. With that hope in mind, Garnaus left them and made his way back to the clifftop to see if there were any developments. He found it difficult to totally accept the fact that there was no way to the ledge, and this time he approached the edge more directly, cautiously easing his way down the slippery incline.

It was very treacherous, with only a few snow patches, and taking out the knife, Garnaus sat and eased himself toward the overhang. Suddenly he began to slip toward the edge, and in fright he dug the knife into the ice. It caught in a crevice and halted his downward slide over the cliff. Scrambling wildly, he worked his way back to more level ground.

Garnaus was breathing heavily, his heart pounding from fright and exertion. To relax he took many deep breaths. Jesus Christ! That was too close for comfort. The thought crossed his mind that mountaineers, alpinists, and the like must be more than a little crazy. They would never have to worry about Jack Garnaus crowding their field.

[2] Thought to be Seaman First Class Hubert Joseph Greene.

He saw that the *Wilkes* and the other ship were still standing off, unable to do much for his shipmates. What was happening below? Would more men find their way to the cliff like Heldt and his companion? God help them if they did.

He began to walk back to the shelter. He had explored all possible avenues of getting close to the *Pollux,* and there had been none. Should he take off overland to try and find aid? Would there *be* any aid close enough to save them in this desolate land? Perhaps a short exploration along the coast would give him an idea if there was a town or a village nearby. He thought about it as he slogged through the snow. It was already afternoon, and what with the limitations of early darkness, unfamiliar terrain, plus the snow and ice, he could not hope to get far. Yet he felt he really had no alternative, and he had better get a start as soon as he consulted with his men.

Garnaus was halfway back to the group of survivors when he saw the tiny figure of a man coming over the hills from the east. Help had arrived! It had to be help! Pray God it was help!

He hurried forward. As soon as they met, Garnaus said, "Thank God! Can you help us? Is help nearby?"

There was help, the man told him in the soft dialect of the Newfoundlander, but it was a five- or six-mile walk over the hills to the Iron Springs Mine. He explained that he had seen an oil slick and wreckage floating along the coast toward Chambers Cove where they had been rescuing the poor men from the *Truxtun,* and had come along to see where it had come from. They were still working on the *Truxtun,* he added.

Garnaus was shocked. The *Truxtun!* He had quite satisfied himself in his mind that she had somehow missed trouble, but all three ships had run ashore!

"Not many saved from the *Truxtun,*" said the man, who gave his name as Lionel Saint from St. Lawrence, which was a couple of miles from the cove where the *Truxtun* lay, he said.

As shocked as Garnaus was, the situation of his own shipmates was his primary concern. Briefly, he told Saint about their own misfortune. "We will have to return to Iron Springs Mine to get help for them," he added, "but I have some men who will have to come with us."

The Newfoundlander went to the clifftop to take a look at the *Pollux* while Garnaus went to the clump of trees to get the men under way. DeRosa was slipping badly, seemingly more dead than alive, but they got him to his feet, and the trek over the hills began. Even with the Newfoundlander leading the way, they had a good three hours' walk ahead of them.

On the bridge of the *Pollux* they were trying to get a line to the men on the far end of the ledge. Several men had made efforts to catch the rope, and Melvin Bettis had gone dangerously close to the edge at the risk of being carried away by the seas, but the rope was too short, too heavy, and the west wind was too strong.

They were temporarily frustrated until Lieutenant Grindley ducked below and dug out a fishing line he had bought in St. Thomas, in the Caribbean, on their last trip South. He cut off the telephone receiver of the TBS and attached it to the fishing line. "Let's try this," he said.

But first they had to persuade the men to cross the narrow ridge of rock to the main ledge closer to the ship. They began to shout and wave their arms to rouse the men who had curled up and lay on the rock or sat with their heads resting on their arms.

It registered on Alfred Dupuy that those on the ship's bridge were signaling to them with shouts and gestures. Their voices were only fragments of sound over the booming seas, but their gestures were unmistakable. They wanted someone to cross over to the big ledge.

No one seemed inclined to risk crossing the ridge, but they sure as hell were getting nowhere fast by staying where they were. "Come on, men, we've got to give it the old college try," Dupuy croaked.

Their bodies were too frozen and clumsy to maneuver the ridge, they told him.

"Well, hell, I'll go then," Dupuy said. It did not occur to him that what he was about to do would later be considered heroic. It was merely something that had to be done because there was no one else to do it. He approached the ridge cautiously, pushing his hands down to seek any slush hole or crack that might make him lose his balance and send him tumbling into the sea and oil in the ravine. It was less formidable than it looked and he crossed safely. A little gully cut through the rock; humps, holes, and crevices under greasy slush gave him good hold, but for the most part, the outer edge of the ledge was a solid sheet of ice. With the wind swooping along the shore, he had no intention of setting foot on it. He went as far as the

ice permitted, then stood up. In his bare feet, with his clothes
sheathed in ice, Dupuy waited for the line.

Aboard the ship they watched Dupuy making his careful way to
the big ledge, and when he finally stood, feet apart, some were sure
they could hear his teeth chattering over the wind and the sea. With
the telephone receiver tied to the fishing line, Grindley swung it
about his head like a bola, starting with a small loop and letting it
ease out until he had a loop about fifteen feet in diameter. When he
felt the circle had enough momentum to reach the ledge, he let go.

Straight as an arrow it shot toward Dupuy, who caught the
receiver and nearly fell over doing so. He stood there like a zombie,
as if he did not know what to do with it. They shouted, "Don't drop
the line! Whatever you do, don't drop the line!"

Dupuy could barely hold the receiver. His hands were totally without feeling and would not close around the fine fishing cord, so he
clumsily put it between his teeth, crawled to the top of the ledge, and
began to pull in the line between the flat of his palms, using his teeth
to keep the line taut. It was a painfully slow process, and from the
bridge they watched prayerfully as the fishing line crept over the sea.
It seemed an eternity before the slightly heavier line they had
patched to the fishing line was inching across the sea. Then a two-
inch line was patched to that one and began its agonizingly slow
journey toward shore.

Dupuy, unable to close his hands around the heavier line, had to
continue hauling in with his palms and teeth. His body might be slow
and clumsy, but his mind was clear. Hell, a drink of whiskey would
put a bit of life back into him, he was sure, and pausing in his la-
bors, he put his hand to his mouth and threw back his head to indicate that a drink of whiskey would be appreciated. The hint was
taken. A bottle of whiskey was attached to the line and went dancing
over the sea to the ledge. Still holding the rope between his teeth,
Dupuy reached for the bottle, clasping it between his palms, but to
his chagrin his fingers could not unscrew the top. Awkwardly he
tapped the bottle on the rock; if he could break the neck he could
get that life-warming drink. Then he stopped. Better not. With his
luck he'd probably drink glass and die. Hell, he'd come too far for
that.

He laid the bottle carefully aside and continued to haul in the line with his palms and teeth. The heavier line was more cumbersome, and Dupuy was weakening. Where the hell were the other guys?

After an eternity he felt that he had enough line and, holding it in his jaws, he crawled to a rock jutting out of the ledge, walked the line twice around, pulling it as taut as he could. Then he lay on the ledge and rolled the line around his body and, taking the rope once more between his teeth and his palms, braced his bare feet against rock.

From the bridge they pulled the line taut and found that it would hold.

At this point Bettis crawled across the ridge and gave Dupuy a hand securing the rope around the rock. "Where were you?" Dupuy croaked.

They tied four or five granny knots around the rock. At last, they had a line from ship to shore.

A breeches buoy was quickly made by Bill Stanford, Chief Gunner's Mate Jabin Berry, and Harold Brooks. The line looked safe and strong enough as it stretched over the sludge and wreckage tossing about between them and the shore, but had the half-frozen men on the ledge tied it securely around the rock? Was it taut enough?

To make sure the rope would hold, Captain Turney ordered a heavy load of canned food and dry clothing to be sent over. It reached the ledge safely, but they needed a man who would, in effect, risk his life to see if it would hold a man's weight.

Ensign Edgar Brown, a strapping six-footer with the build of a football player, volunteered. If the line held up under Brown, it was solid enough for the rest of the crew.

Dupuy and Bettis waited as the hefty young ensign prepared to come across. Dupuy watched in admiration. Goddamn! That sure was one helluva brave guy. Who was to say the line they had hitched around the rock would hold? If it didn't hold, he was one dead ensign. Sure as hell he was dead!

"I don't suppose," Dupuy said to Bettis, "his weight will make the line sag enough to put him in the water."

"It might," Bettis said.

They moved as far down the ledge as possible to be ready in such an eventuality, and when Brown began to slide toward them, the line did sag somewhat. Dupuy and Bettis put their shoulders under it and lifted. Brown went very close to the water but did not get wet.

The line was established. It was about 1430 hours. From here on, it was simply a matter of getting ashore and making their way overland.

So they thought. . . .

24

Adam Mullins, a carpenter employed in the mill, had not been to Chambers Cove. He had seen the unusual activity as trucks rushed back and forth between Iron Springs and St. Lawrence, but he was busy with his work and did not take the time to find out what it was all about until Howard Farrell, the assistant manager, had asked him to get to the cove to help.

Adam, aged forty, had been a fisherman in his early years, and considered himself one of the few seamen left in the community. "Have they got any dories over there?" he asked.

"No," Farrell replied. "It's pretty rough in the cove."

Adam had fished the coast and had great faith in the dory, which was generally accepted by fishermen for its ability to ride the heavy seas; therefore he did not go to Chambers Cove immediately, but commandeered a truck and four or five men to go to the harbor to pick up a dory. Soon they arrived at Iron Springs, where the dory had to be transferred to horse and sled in order to get it across the river and to Chambers Cove.

Before long the boat was on the clifftop awaiting more favorable circumstances for rescue operations. The only point near the wreck where it might be launched was on the slope of the Pinnacle, where it joined Chambers Cove. The sea was still rough, but Mullins began to recruit volunteers for the attempt to take the dory to the wreck as soon as it became possible.

The tide had fallen and now there was plenty of shingle exposed beneath the cliff that had claimed so many victims. The wind was beginning to drop, but the seas continued to pound the *Truxtun*. Incredibly, a number of men were still clinging to the safety lines, Ensign Seamans among them. For no logical reason, considering the interminable length of time his body had been punished by the seas, he still had hope that he would survive. Whatever he felt about the others still on board the ship, he knew that it would soon be Jim Seamans, alone, against the sea.

Meanwhile, he held on.

A voice, carried by the wind, echoed around Chambers Cove: "Help me! Save me!" Strong and vital, it bounded and rebounded against the cliffs.

They heard it on the beach and on the clifftop, and they could see the blackened figure of the sailor, saved from certain death by the grace of God and the falling tide, clinging to a rock offshore at the base of the cliff that had claimed so many lives. Even so, each time the oily waves smashed upon the shore, his legs flew up in the air.

How were they going to get to him? No man had ever gone down over that straight wall, and few were foolhardy enough to risk being dashed against the bare rock, as they certainly would be, with the wind still blowing into the cove.

Henry Lambert, aged twenty-five, was not overly tall, but he had a tough, wiry frame, and he was totally without fear. "I'll get him," he said.

As a boy he had lived close to the cove, and knew that the only way to get that man was to go down, not over the straight face but over the overhang where the gray wall joined the pink cliff. It was a big overhang, projecting well out over the rock face, and would give him plenty of room to compensate for the wind—but it was a good two-hundred-foot drop.

He left the beach, where the men were still in the water encouraging a lone swimmer toward them, was hauled up to the top, and made his way to the overhang. He had a rope around his waist and he carried another around his shoulders. Half a dozen men let Henry

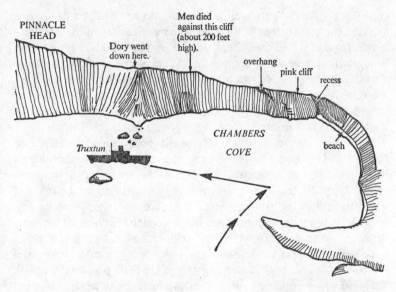

down. The wind, rushing upward, swung him about but he reached
the shingle without a scratch or a bruise. Bodies were strewn under
the black, jellylike mass that blanketed the strand and there was a
great ledge twenty feet high projecting from the base of the cliff at its
center, and Henry had to clamber over it and down the other side;
like the beach, it was slimy with oil. The sailor, continually being
buried in surf and oil, watched him, his arms wrapped around the
rock. Henry took the rope he had brought with him, tied it around
his waist, and fired it out to the sailor, who caught it, hitched it
around himself, and let Henry pull him ashore.

The exhausted man could not climb the big rock, and Henry literally had to haul him up over the ledge and lower him on the other
side. Slipping and sliding over oil and battered bodies, he guided his
companion to the rope, and presently they were hauled to the top.

Seamans still held on. There had been no communication with the
bridge; it had been every man for himself. Whether the captain or
the executive officer were alive or dead he did not know and, in
truth, he had no thought for them other than believing they were still
on board. He had not seen them, but no word had passed along the
line that they had been washed away. The ranks had thinned steadily

until there were only six men left on the forecastle. If the seas were quieting somewhat, they still fell in green avalanches upon the *Truxtun*. A big one rolled over them, and when they finally emerged from it Seamans turned to his companion. "That was one son-of-a-gun of a wave," he gasped. He was holding on with one hand and one foot, when another one fell upon them. It tore him from the safety line, throwing him straight up, somersaulting him two or three times as it carried him overboard.

The ocean was so unbelievably cold it nearly drew the life from his body. He popped to the surface in a trough and found himself looking under the *Truxtun* as she lay on the rocks. He toyed, momentarily, with the idea of somehow getting back on board, but when the following wave inundated her completely, Seamans discarded the thought; he must head for the beach. He had instinctively begun to swim, pushing at the oil with the breast stroke. He was quite skilled at that stroke, which was less tiring than the crawl and more suitable for rough waters. Although his body was totally numb, his mind was surprisingly lucid; as rough as the seas were, it was not that difficult after all. Had everybody else found it so easy?

Suddenly, his life sped by kaleidoscopically, and then sped back. It jolted him. Only men who were about to die, particularly by drowning, were privileged to see their whole life flash before them in such a manner. Was he dying? He would not die! He must not die! I must make it to shore! he told himself fiercely. The oil, he realized, had just about suffocated him. After each effort to push it aside, the stinking mantle folded around him again. He swam more aggressively. He could not die here in the wintry seas. His parents had worked hard to put him through school; *he* had worked hard to get through his schooling; therefore it could not be wasted here in the cold, cold waters of the North Atlantic.

His cool, analytical mind reasserted itself. This was no way for Jim Seamans to die. He *would not* die! Keeping himself perpendicular to prevent the oil from smothering him completely, he swam diagonally downwind across the waves.

He was thrown into shallow water, into the congealed crust of fuel oil, just another bit of black, gummy flotsam from the shipwreck. He tried to stand but was swept back into deep water by the receding wave, turned upside down, and cast a little closer to the water's edge. He again tried to stand in the tarlike oil, but could not. He tried to wave, but was again pulled back into the sea, and the third time was thrown upon the beach. He did not have the strength to crawl out of the water; his stomach was churning from the fuel oil he had swallowed, and he could barely see, but he was determined not to be swept back into the sea. He lifted an arm and shouted. A man hurried toward him and grabbed him. Seamans said, "I'm all right. I'll get up."

Then consciousness fled.

He was lifted onto the shoulder of the man, taken up the cliff, laid on a sled, covered with a blanket, and within minutes was on the way to Iron Springs.

At this same time Theo Etchegary, as close to the edge of the oil slick as possible, was directing two more survivors to safety. They had been swept dangerously close to the base of the cliff, and he had waved them off. The first man kept his burning gaze on Theo as he signaled him to go farther offshore. "Out! Stay out!" he bawled.

The first survivor changed direction and went offshore, but the one behind him waited too long. Before Theo's horrified eyes, a sea washed the hapless sailor against the cliff and sliced his head off.

The broken pieces of the *Truxtun* had separated so that the seas were breaking between them. The port wing of the bridge had been swept away, taking all who had sheltered there. Only three men could be seen clinging to the wreckage. They were making no attempt to swim for shore.

Now, with the sea in a more restrained mood, the dory was brought into action. With a dozen men on the clifftop holding on to a good stout rope from the Newfoundland steamer the SS *Kyle*, Adam Mullins, Howard Kelly, Charlie Pike, and Dave Edwards[1] were eased down over the steep slope with the dory. Kelly was to anchor himself on the shingle and hold a rope attached to the dory stern while Mullins, Edwards, and Pike would row over the heaving seas, throw another rope to the survivors, and get them off the wreck. Kelly would guide the dory back to shore.

With Mullins standing ready to throw a line, and with the other two men rowing, the dory bounced over the oily seas as Kelly paid

[1] A man from Lawn.

out the line. Edwards and Pike were not fishermen but were reasonably skilled in the use of the dory, and it was no great distance to the wreck.

Soon they were close enough to throw a line, which one of the sailors caught and tied to the rail. Mullins had a brief view of twisted bodies as the dory rose and fell on the waves, then a great sea rose up, rolled over the ship, and stood the dory on end. One sailor was washed overboard, the other, Fireman Second Class Edward McInerney, was washed into the dory, while Charlie Pike was washed out. The last sailor, Seaman Second Class Donald Fitzgerald, was still clinging to the safety line on board. When the sea passed, the dory was swamped, the oars were gone, but Mullins, Edwards, and McInerney were aboard the dory and Charlie Pike was clinging to its side.

The truculent seas, the swamped condition of the dory, and Charlie Pike clinging to one side made it impossible for them to take off the last man. They would have to get back to shore and make another attempt as soon as they could empty out the water and get Charlie to shore.

They signaled for Howard Kelly to haul them back. Adam Mullins had not relinquished the line that had been tied to the ship's rail, but paid it out, keeping the dory under control as they were hauled shoreward.

The last sailor, Donald Fitzgerald, watched with mixed emotions as the dory receded. He had seen both his shipmates swept overboard by the last wave and thought both of them were dead; safety, which had been so close, had been torn from his grasp. He was the last live sailor on the *Truxtun,* and he did not want to stay with her a moment longer. He decided it was now or never, and taking one last look around the dead ship with its dead bodies, he grasped the line that Adam Mullins was paying out, and began a hand-over-hand journey to safety.

The dory, with Charlie Pike clinging to its side, made it safely to shore. Fitzgerald also made it when a sea picked him up and hurled him, insensible, to the strand. McInerney was fine.

It was about 3 P.M.

The *Truxtun* ordeal was over.

On the beach the last survivors were hauled ashore, the last one taken up over the cliff. Mike Turpin felt as if his back were broken.

Theo Etchegary was suddenly struck with a great weariness that spread from his feet upward. The vitality that had permitted him to operate in and out of the frigid ocean for the better part of six hours left him suddenly; he was chilled to the marrow of his bones.

Men were wading through the oil slick searching for bodies, examining every bump protruding above the muck. Again, Theo was overwhelmed by a feeling of inadequacy. They had been able to save so few—so very few. What a waste of human lives. He went to the ravine and indicated to the men on top that he wanted to be hauled up. Halfway up he saw his oil-soaked jacket; it had obviously slipped off a survivor as he was being hauled up the cliff. Theo was too tired to make that extra effort to retrieve it. He took one last look at the scene below. The tide was nearly out, the seas were moderating, and in a few more hours it would be peaceful in the cove, but the black, gummy slime of oil desecrated the pristine beauty of this wild place, and tragedy had forever claimed it for its own. Chambers Cove would never be the same.

Most of the survivors were ill; practically all of them were in a semiconscious condition and came to their senses to find themselves naked, on a great table, surrounded by women who were trying to scrub their chilled bodies clean. Then they were dressed in an assortment of clothes, given hot soup, put into trucks, and bundled off to the homes of the people of St. Lawrence.

It was crowded and noisy in the mine house as the Americans retched and coughed up fuel oil. The women were up to their ankles in crude oil, and the stench of it was overpowering.

Clara Tarrant said to two of her companions: "Let's go over to Chambers Cove and see if there are any more survivors."

The women needed no urging and soon they were on their way. It was a far cry from the sleet storm of the morning. The sun breaking through the overcast glanced off shimmering, ice-coated trees; a cold brisk wind made them walk with lowered heads.

Halfway there they met Father Augustine Thorne and stopped him. "Are there any more survivors, Father?" Clara asked.

"Just one, Clara, he came hand over hand on the line." He told them the story of the rescue attempt and the subsequent result. "He's been semiconscious ever since. They're waiting for a horse and sled to bring him in."

Having imparted that information, Father Thorne continued on to Iron Springs. He had comforted many a dazed and frightened sailor this day, and his cassock reeked of oil.

Clara and her friends went on to the cove, arriving upon the clifftop and taking in the sad scene below. Many men were working on the beach; others seemed rooted to the rim of the cove as if hypnotized. Clara, looking for the survivor, saw two men bringing him, weaving on rubbery legs, over the sloping hills. She and her friends hurried toward them, reaching them just as Fitzgerald collapsed. Clara made a grab for him. "My God, don't let him fall," she cried.

Don Fitzgerald was more dead than alive. His jaws were clenched, his tongue protruded. He was covered with oil.

A horse and sled driven by Jack Lundrigan was cautiously approaching the far side of the ravine from Iron Springs. Clara waved and shouted: "We have one more survivor, Jack."

The men dragged Fitzgerald down into the ravine and placed him on the sled. Lundrigan went off with him.

Clara wasted no time. "Let's go back," she told her companions, and set off at a brisk pace. She feared that the men at Iron Springs might think the young man was dead—and well he might be by the time Jack Lundrigan could get him across the frozen land to the mine house.

She was right. The nurses could detect no heartbeat in Fitzgerald's body when he was taken into the big room and laid on the table, and he was presumed dead. They left his body there temporarily.

Totally exhausted, Theo Etchegary arrived at the mine house, having hitched a ride on Tom Molloy's sled. The buzz of voices, the wracking coughs, and the stink of oil enveloped him as he stood by the table where Fitzgerald lay. "This one is dead," someone told him.

He certainly looked dead. The jaws were clamped together. The tongue, badly bitten, was hanging out of the mouth. There was no sign of life. Theo, still affected by the great loss of life, tried gently to put the tongue back in the mouth. Something about the feel of the man prompted him to call Nurse Sadie Ash. "Are you sure he's dead?"

Nurse Ash put her head to Fitzgerald's chest, listening intently. "I believe there is a heartbeat, Theo," she said after some minutes.

Theo was galvanized into action. "Let's try artificial respiration," he said, and turning Fitzgerald over began pressing rhythmically on the back. Presently the body beneath his hands jerked convulsively, a drop of blood came from the nose. . . .

Clara Tarrant arrived at Iron Springs as they were cutting the clothes off Fitzgerald. Huge blisters the size of eggs covered his legs; someone was trying to pry his jaws open, with little success. Clara picked up a blanket and wrapped it around him. They continued to rub and massage, but he showed no signs of consciousness.

There were no more survivors; the mine house was a disaster area, and night was approaching when Howard Farrell asked the women to take the remaining sailors into their homes.

"I'll take *him*." Clara pointed to Fitzgerald.

"He's just about dead already. Why don't you take another?" someone asked.

"Everyone else is all right," Clara snapped; "they're able to speak for themselves. This one needs someone to look after him." She had the very strong feeling that Fitzgerald would die unless she was able to get him under her care. It was strange that she should feel this way, but she did. They put him on a stretcher, lifted him in the back of a truck with her, and off they went.

Her daughters Ella and Carmel had followed her instructions; a great wave of heat met them as the men brought the young sailor into her kitchen. They hauled the couch near the stove and laid him upon it. Fitzgerald had shown little sign of life until they opened the oven door; as the heat flowed over him he began to shake.

"Thanks be to God he's alive," Clara said. "Children, kneel down and say the rosary."

As her daughters prayed, Clara poured camphorated oil in soup plates and dinner plates and set them on the back of the stove to heat. She had only one hot-water bottle and used heated bricks to warm their beds on cold winter nights, and now every brick they could find went on the stove or in the oven. Soon they were rubbing the shivering man with the heated camphorated oil, wrapping the bricks and plates in towels and packing them around his chilled body.

The blisters on his legs were rather nasty-looking and Clara sent her daughters to the store for Mecca ointment, then sterilizing a darning needle she broke the blisters, covered them with the ointment, and bandaged his legs to the knees.

Fitzgerald showed no signs of returning to consciousness, and Clara felt for his pulse. "It's faint and flickery, but it's there," she told her daughters.

They continued their ministrations.

25

St. Lawrence
February 18, 1942—afternoon

The U. S. Navy had finally arrived. Lieutenant Charles R. Longenecker, junior medical officer of the USS *Prairie,* Argentia, and
Medical Corpsman Haralson,[1] of the USS *Brant,* who had been commandeered along with Elmon R. Pittman, Ray L. Miller, Stanley
Barron, and James E. Cupero, under the command of Lieutenant
Commander George W. Ashford, had flown over the *Truxtun* lying
in Chambers Cove, and over the *Pollux.* They had seen the *Pollux*
men on the clifftop and had signaled the *Wilkes,* lying offshore, that
they would reach the site in a couple of hours. From the air, it
looked as if the two ships lay less than two miles apart, and they had
reasoned it would take them no more than a couple of hours to
reach there after they had landed in St. Lawrence Harbor. The *Truxtun*'s crew obviously had all the help they needed, while the *Pollux*
lay helpless and unaided.

It had looked to the men in the plane that the *Pollux* was snug
against the land, and she had been in one piece. Certainly she
seemed to be in no imminent danger. Before leaving Argentia there
had been some question of food and clothing for the survivors but,
as someone pointed out, the *Pollux* was a supply ship and undoubtedly there was plenty of everything available to the crew. Therefore
they carried only limited medical supplies in their corpsmen bags,
which was standard equipment on rescue missions of any kind. Each

[1] Christian name not established by the court of inquiry.

man also carried a limited amount of pure grain alcohol as a stimulant.

Their arrival in St. Lawrence went virtually unnoticed because the townspeople were so busy with the *Truxtun* survivors. When Lieutenant Commander Ashford tried to organize a rescue party he met with failure. There was no one in authority left in the town, and the women, thinking that these Americans were talking about the *Truxtun,* informed them that the men were already being rescued. There was no alternative but to walk to the *Pollux* on their own.

They set off briskly and walked the three miles to Chambers Cove, bypassing Iron Springs and arriving in time to see the dory attaching a line to the *Truxtun.* They stayed briefly, passing the information along about the *Pollux.* Lieutenant Longenecker left two of his corpsmen, Pittman and Cupero, to look after the *Truxtun* survivors, and they continued on over the hills toward Lawn Head.

26

Lawn Head
February 18, 1942—1430–1630 hours

As the evacuation of the *Pollux* began, Lieutenant Garnaus and his men, guided by Lionel Saint, lurched and weaved over the hills, dragging William DeRosa between them. It was rough going because at times they were hip-deep in snow, and sliding over icy slopes at other times. The sky was brightening, sending forth an occasional ray of sunshine as the brisk wind pushed the storm farther east.

DeRosa was leaning more and more on his companions as his frozen limbs refused to function. Then, on a hill in the middle of nowhere, he gave out completely, his six-foot frame sprawling in the snow. No coaxing could get him to his feet; he seemed unable to put any effort into it. His companions, as wet and almost as frozen as DeRosa, knew their own reserves were running out.

It put Garnaus in a predicament that required a further decision he did not like to make; yet it was his responsibility to get help for the crew of the *Pollux* still trapped, as far as he knew, on a ship that was breaking up miles from the help they so desperately needed. "It's getting late and DeRosa is slowing us down," he said. "I'll go on ahead with Mr. Saint and try to get help back for DeRosa and the rest of our men on the ship."

Wag Greenfield, William Heldt, and Hubert Greene were distressed to see their brawny young shipmate lying helplessly in the snow, but he was much too heavy for them to carry over the hills stretching before them. Heldt and Greene decided it was too bitterly cold to linger and soon took off after Garnaus and Saint.

Greenfield knelt, put DeRosa's arm around his shoulder, hefted him to his feet, and began to lug him through the snow. He reeled under the dead weight of his friend for half a dozen steps, then fell, with DeRosa on top of him. He struggled from beneath the still form and got up. "DeRosa," he panted, "get on your feet and walk."

A mumble came from DeRosa but he did not move, and Greenfield knew he did not have the strength to carry him any farther. After working so hard to keep his shipmate going, it had come to this. It was almost unbelievable that DeRosa, whose reputation for toughness was unsurpassed, was giving up. He yelled, "Damn you, DeRosa, you gotta walk."

This time DeRosa did not answer. Greenfield slapped his face. "You're so goddamn tough, you guinea bastard, get up off your ass and walk!" he roared.

He piled on more abuse, which normally would have had DeRosa up and fighing, but it did not work this time. DeRosa lay there as if he were dead already.

The drone of an airplane sounded over the wind. It was a PBY from Argentia, flying low over the hills, heading directly for them. Greenfield waved frantically, a wild, unreasoning hope replacing his rage and despair. Maybe they had blankets, or clothing, or *something* to drop for DeRosa. But the plane lumbered on, to circle over Lawn Head where the *Pollux* lay, and Greenfield made one last effort to get DeRosa moving. There was no response, no movement to indicate he had heard.

Greenfield left him. Time seemed to stand still as he floundered through the snow. The sun slipped in and out of the clouds, causing the bright glitter of ice crystals to hurt his eyes, which were already irritated by the fuel oil. Up to his hips in snow one minute, his feet flying from beneath him the next as he hit a patch of ice, he struggled on, his Oxford shoes offering no protection to his numb and lifeless feet. He fell often, and each time it was more difficult to get up. You gotta keep movin', Wag, you can't quit, he told himself. Just pick 'em up and lay 'em down.

His thoughts were disconnected. There were a lot of his buddies back on the ship who needed help. Where the hell did Garnaus go? Garnaus was always disappearing. Where did Heldt go? God, he was thirsty!

He ate snow. Somewhere he had heard that it would increase your thirst, but what the hell was a fellow to do? There was no other sensation in his body except the raging thirst; all else was deadened, like wood. He scooped up another handful of snow and ate it. It parched his mouth. He wanted to rest but dared not. Keep goin', Wag, if you stop you freeze to death, he told himself.

On he went, lucid enough not to wander too far from the coastline but staying away from the ice-glazed cliffs, then after forever, he came over a hill, and off in the distance he saw the *Truxtun* lying on her side, under cliffs, in a crescent-shaped cove. He cried aloud, "My God! My God!"

The *Truxtun* seemed to be broken into bits and pieces; waves were rushing straight into the cove and were breaking white over her. About a quarter of a mile from Greenfield, a group of people were standing on the cliff looking down upon the wreck.

As shocking as it was to see the *Truxtun* so battered, he was too exhausted to think of anything but his own overwhelming weariness. He staggered on, waving his arms until they noticed him, then he sank into the snow, unable to walk another step.

In the group was an American wearing the familiar trappings of a U. S. Navy corpsman. "Where did you come from?" he asked.

"The *Pollux,* she's ashore back there." Greenfield waved in the direction from which he had come. "I left a buddy back there in the bush. He's in bad shape."

The Navy corpsman yelled to someone, and a Newfoundlander came with a horse and sled. At the same time the corpsman whipped out a needle, forced back the frozen, greasy sleeve, and bared Greenfield's arm. It was black with fuel oil and, as the needle was prepared, Greenfield could only think of the fact that his arm was dirty. It was dogma in the Navy that cleanliness reduced infection, and this guy was going to stick a needle in his dirty arm. He asked blankly, "Aren't you going to clean my arm?"

The corpsman plunged the needle in and Greenfield yelled. The needle must have had a bloody square tip! He was put on the sled, only vaguely aware of his surroundings as the horse jogged over the snowy hills. They came across another group, Heldt among them, and he too was put on the sled with Greenfield; then all went blank.

About this time, Lionel Saint walked into Iron Springs with Jack Garnaus and electrified the people with the news that another U.S. warship was wrecked at Lawn Head.

Many men who had already spent hours in the water and climbing the cliffs with helpless men on their shoulders departed again, this time for Lawn Head, as soon as they learned of the other shipwreck.

The men working the Director Mine were unaware of the drama going on a few miles away until Patrick Tarrant came to get some dynamite, shortly before the four-o'clock shift was due to take over. There had been no communication between the Director Mine and the Iron Springs Mine, and Tarrant stared in amazement at the extraordinary activity. "What's going on?" he asked.

He learned in short order that two ships had gone ashore, that horses and sleds were still bringing survivors in from the first ship, and that fresh men were needed to go to the second ship at Lawn Head.

Without further ado, Tarrant returned to the mine, and soon men were pouring from below. Laden with tins of juice and soup, ropes and axes, Patrick and a group left immediately for the *Pollux,* while plans were set in motion to collect more food and supplies to take to Lawn Head.

On Lawn Head, the abandoning of the *Pollux* was going smoothly. Immediately after Ensign Brown had landed, the whiskey bottle was opened and passed around. Dupuy took a good swallow, passed it to Bettis, then it went the rounds among the others who had been sufficiently aroused from their lethargy to cross over to the main ledge.

Each man leaving the ship in the breeches buoy carried something: ship's records, blankets, food, clothing, and other supplies that would maintain them while on the shore. Each sailor carried a flashlight in his back pocket because it was apparent that they were miles from habitation, and it was going to be a long walk throughout the night, across the hills. There was a ragged cheer for each man landing on the ledge

Only a few had gotten across when the watertight bulkhead, forward of the engine room, finally gave way, causing the ship to cant more severely as the ocean flooded through her. The sharp list made the removal of personnel exceedingly difficult, and to speed the process, it was decided to rig a second line from the flying bridge, with Grindley and Bradley handling the lines, while Russell Schmidt took

charge of getting men in the chair. Navy regulations made it mandatory for officers to wear .45-caliber pistols during abandon-ship
procedure,[1] and all officers and gunners' mates wore them. Commander Turney strapped on his sword.

Dr. Bostic arrived on the ledge with a five-gallon container of medicinal alcohol and ministered sips to the freezing men. "Just a little," he cautioned. They knew better than to take more than that. At
190 proof, it would blow your head off.

During this operation another plane flew over.

The *Wilkes,* the USS *Kite,* and the tug the USS *George E. Badger*
were still standing by helplessly, their best efforts to get rafts to her
having been circumvented by the westward flow of the current. Nor
could they move closer to shore to rescue the men there. Both
ships were unaware of the heavy loss of life the *Pollux* had sustained
when her crew tried to swim ashore and, observing the crew going
to the beach in the breeches buoy, Commander Webb felt that the
situation was well in hand.

The *Wilkes'* own condition was keeping the damage-control parties on the alert for any breaking down of the bulkheads, leakages,
or further damage to the skin of the ship. She was holding her own,
yet Webb felt they dare not take unnecessary chances. While favorable winds prevailed, he decided to get the ship to port. They signaled
the *Badger:*

**Stand by *Pollux* and crew. Rescue them from the beach if
weather conditions permit. *Wilkes* proceeding Base Roger.**

At 1540 hours the *Wilkes* steamed slowly away. They kept a
sharp lookout for the *Truxtun* but did not see her. They did see
the USS *Brant* along the coast and assumed the ship was standing by the *Truxtun,* but they did not investigate.

Those aboard the *Pollux* were too busy to notice the departure of
the *Wilkes.* In fact, a surprising number of the ship's personnel had
not seen her after she had freed herself from the rocks. Huddled in
the shelter of the port side of the bridge, they had no desire to face
into the weather to see what the other ship was doing. Now they
were lined up, waiting their turn to get to the safety of land.

[1] A custom dating back from sailing-ship times.

Each man reaching the ledge immediately gave assistance to the soaked, freezing men who had swum over. Under the supervision of Bostic, they were given dry outer clothing and laid close together, to conserve body heat, in a shallow depression on the highest part of the ledge, then covered with blankets or overcoats until they could be taken to the top. Bob Collins was unconscious, and so was Pete Manger.

Alfred Pollack, clad in swim trunks, goon jacket, and arctic boots, went over with the canvas moneybag, float, and fathoms of rope. Paul Pulver followed with the briefcase full of vouchers. Gradually there was standing room only on the ledge, and footing was treacherous.

Finally a handful of men were left on the ship, and Commander Turney ordered Lieutenant Grindley ashore. Now that the danger was past and they were headed for the beach and safety, Grindley's own plight was very clear to him. He was in trouble. As the navigator, it was likely the loss of the *Pollux* could be laid at his door. He thought, "Your ass is in a great big jam, Grindley, you'd better get your charts and work books." He ducked into the cold, wet chartroom and gathered the remainder of his work books together, but they were too bulky and heavy; he'd never make it to the beach with all that tied to him. He left them, but picked up the chartroom copy of the 2000 hours report of February 17, stuck it in his pocket, and went across to the ledge.

Only Turney, William Stanford, and Jabin Berry were left. Turney gestured for Stanford to leave.

"I'll go last, sir," Stanford volunteered.

"That is my privilege, Bill," the captain replied. "You go now, then Chief Gunner's Mate Berry, and then I will leave. That is an order."

The words were spoken firmly and gently.

Berry said, "O.K., Bill, you first."

Stanford went; then Berry. The men on shore watched in silence as their captain got on the breeches buoy. His sword hitched in the rail, was torn from its scabbard, and dropped into the sea as he slid down the rope toward them. They all gave a rip-roaring cheer as he stepped on the ledge. Stanford then cast off the breeches buoy, severing all ties with the *Pollux*. It was about 1630 hours; almost twelve bitter, soul-searing hours since they had struck—but it was behind them; they were safe on land.

Their optimism was short-lived when the officers made the shocking discovery that they were up against sheer rock with no place to go. They could not believe it. Grindley examined the cliff face. It was broken and bumpy with a slight alcove on the extreme east end where a group of men huddled, and the edge swept up in a rough curve to where the overhang merged with the cliff. It would not be impossible to get up there, Grindley thought, except for the fact that it was solidly coated with oil. Even so, he tried to find handholds and toeholds but was unsuccessful. There was no other way off the ledge, and by the look of the high-water mark, there would not be all that much room at high tide. It was just about low tide now, and soon the water would be rushing back upon them. In six hours' time it would reach its peak and, if the seas were as bad as they had been throughout the day, it was not likely that one man would survive.

They looked longingly at the *Pollux:* broken, lopsided, groaning, and complaining as she thudded upon the rocks—but so safe and comfortable in comparison to the ledge.

Someone said, "Where in hell is the Navy?"

The *Badger* and the *Kite,* having seen the crew going ashore on the breeches buoy, had steamed for St. Lawrence Harbor to start some of their crew overland.

27

Despite the knowledge that their position on the ledge was perhaps even more precarious than it had been throughout this long and harrowing day, the morale of the *Pollux* crew did not falter. A rough count estimated 122 men crowded there. Some had huddled against the cliff to remove themselves as far as possible from the spray mushrooming over them. Alfred Dupuy was moving about to keep warm. Where he was standing there was a hole filled with slushy snow up to a man's knees and, no matter how he tried to avoid it, he stepped into it time and again. It was enough to make him damn near cry. Reason told him that from the ledge the cliff was no more than seventy feet high, but it *looked* to be four hundred feet high.

A gully carved by the water ran along the base of the cliff, cutting diagonally through the ledge. As the tide rose, the seas would race through this gully and spill over, making the shelf even more hazardous for the men. From the eastward side of their rocky perch they could see the waves still rushing against the land. Westward, the ridge of Lawn Head was silhouetted against the fading sky.

Up to now, Ensign Pollack had lugged around the cumbersome money bag with its float and fathoms of line. "To hell with this," he declared, and hacked off the line and float. He left only enough to secure the bag and briefcase together, set it in a niche, and ceased to worry about it. So much for Navy regulations.

Others picked up the worry for him. "Hey, Paymaster, where's your money bag?"

"Don't worry about it."

But they did.

"How much you got there, Paymaster?"

"There's forty-seven thousand dollars there in cash. You want to look after it?"

Geez! Right there at their feet was forty-seven thousand dollars belonging to the U. S. Navy. The idea of so much money lying about excited the imagination. Holy smoke, forty-seven thousand bucks! Califano thought in awe, but someone would have to account for the money to the Navy, and who would want that formidable responsibility?

"I wouldn't touch it with a ten-foot pole, Paymaster."

They avoided the money bag like poison.

As cramped and slippery as the rocky surface was, George Coleman continued to clap his hands, rub his ears, and jump up and down to keep warm. Suddenly, up ahead of him there was a cry of alarm as a man slipped, fell, and began to slide down the ledge. He was grabbed by another sailor who fell too, but whose hands locked under the first man's chin. Both began to slide over the edge, but the third sailor in the line grabbed him by the leg. When all three began to slip down a fourth sailor grabbed the third by both legs. He, in turn, was firmly held by the men behind him. It all happened in a matter of seconds and the men spread-eagled on the ledge were unable to move one way or another. The first man was hanging over the edge, held only by the hands locked under his chin. The sailors strung along the ledge grabbed each other and, like a great chain, strained backward in an effort to pull them all back to safety, but each time they hauled back, they, too, slid closer to the edge. Now the dead weight of the sailor being held by the chin was too much for the second man, and within a few minutes his hands began to slip in spite of his efforts to hang on. The first sailor[1] dropped into the sea, and, released, from his weight, the human chain of men was able to ease the others back to safety.

Another shipmate was gone . . . twilight was deepening . . . there was no help in sight . . . the tide was rising . . . all Navy ships had disappeared. . . .

[1] This was either Winson Aloysius Edwards, Floyd Lee Edwards, or Edward Henry Tholen.

They had to close their minds to their desperate situation. Hank Strauss and a few of his shipmates began to sing an old World War I song: "There's a Long, Long Trail Awinding." It was picked up by all and gradually their voices swelled over the pounding seas.

It was Ensign Grayson, standing on the perilous outer edge of the ledge, who saw the line of men silhouetted along the ridge of Lawn Head. "It's Garnaus! It looks like Garnaus!" he yelled. "He's come back with a team. The Navy is here!"

They gave a cheer.

It was not the Navy, but the eight men from Lawn. They looked down upon the *Pollux* with mixed feelings. She was like a big island, Joe Manning thought. Slewed over, the seas breaking upon her, she was a dead thing.

There was still enough light for them to see wreckage, fuel oil, and bodies drifting about the sea, but aboard the *Pollux* there was no sign of life. From their position they could not see the men clustered on the ledge in the shadow of what they called the Big Head. It was desolate and dreary—no place for men in the dead of winter, with night on their heels.

Joe Manning said to his companions, "I don't see a man alive."

The ridge was a sheet of glittering ice and the five men who had horses moved slightly inland to a little copse of wood in a small ravine about three hundred yards along the crest of Lawn Head, where they hitched the animals in its shelter—the ravine that Lieutenant Garnaus had surveyed earlier The other three made their way to the shore. Manning picked up his ax and was making his way down to where the ship lay when one of the men who had gone down to the shore ran toward him, waving his arms and shouting: "Get your rope, Joe, everyone bring ropes, they're ashore under the Big Head, and they're wavin' to us."

They were all familiar with the Big Head. They either fished offshore from it or hunted sea birds around it. It was, without doubt, the worst possible place on Lawn Head that a ship could hit.

They held a brief consultation to decide on the course of action—not that they had a choice—there was only one place that they could work from: A gully of broken rock sloped steeply down the west side of the Big Head and, as if by Divine Providence, narrowly split the overhang. This was the only place from which it was possible, in the circumstances, to effect the rescue. It would be reasonably easy for the survivors to work their way into the split once they had been hauled up to it.

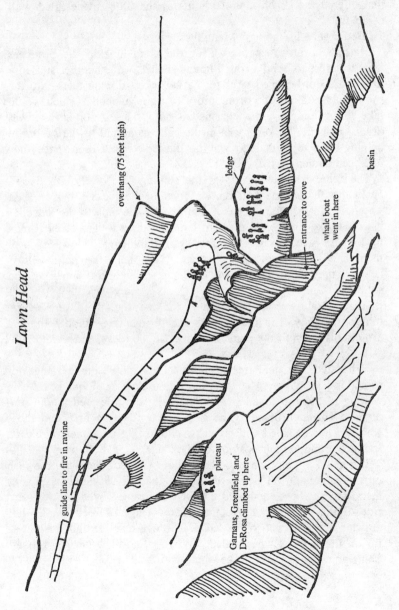

Lawn Head

overhang (75 feet high)

ledge

entrance to cove

whale boat went in here

basin

guide line to fire in ravine

plateau

Garnaus, Greenfield, and DeRosa climbed up here

It was going to be a long night and they had much to do before they could begin the rescue operation. The wind was rising again and snow was beginning to drift—a bad combination. The only place that offered the slightest protection was the little ravine filled with dwarf trees.

"Better get a fire going," Manning suggested.

Martin Edwards began to clear the area, limbing the branches from the trees to build a rough bough shelter, while another started a fire, and a third lopped trees to use as stakes, driving them into the snow patches along the promontory to rig a guideline, which would take the sailors past the chasms on both sides. Another line was draped over the broken rocks in the gully as an aid to the sailors in helping them to work their way up the ice-covered rocks once they had been hauled up from the ledge.

The other five headed down the sloping side of the Big Head, hacking with their axes at the ice crusting the rocks, working their way down to the cleft. There would be one line only to the ledge, as it would take the five of them to haul the dead weight of each man up the cliff face. Spray, exploding against the ledge below, fell over them and kept icing up the rocks. "God help the poor fellows below," they said. Their own clothing was quickly saturated and solidly frozen.

Alfred Grant was the first man on the line; the others were behind him, in the gully. The last one was anchor man. He wrapped the line around his body, firmly planted his feet on the rocks, and waited.

Exhausted, wet, and freezing, the sailors waited on the ledge for something to happen. There would doubtless be a medical team waiting at the top to administer first aid, they decided, and Commander Turney ordered, "The sick men will go up first, and those who are less disabled will go next." Following that, men would be sent according to their position on the ledge.

It seemed a long time since Lieutenant Grayson had seen the men on the ridge, and all traces of daylight had disappeared when they heard voices above them and a light was beamed over the westward side of the overhang above the narrow ridge of rock Dupuy had crawled across to get to the ledge. The overhang did not jut out as far on this side. A voice called, "We're going to try to get you up. Shine your light so we can see where you are."

Captain Turney's emergency light was beamed upward. As the last man off the ship, his position on the ledge was on the extreme east end.

"We can't get you up from there. You'll have to come over here," the voice yelled.

The ridge would not give them much room in which to operate. It also meant that the men would have to jump the little gully that cut through the ledge when their turn came to go up the cliff—risky enough in the darkness.

It was William Stanford who was across first. He couldn't see the men on the clifftop, nor could they see him. "We're ready," he yelled. "Have you got a rope?"

"We've got plenty of rope, but there's room for only one man at a time," the disembodied voice came down through the rocks. "We're dropping the rope now."

The rope snaked down, was caught in the beam of Commander Turney's light, and Stanford grabbed it.

"Stay where you are," he told the men. "There's room for only two or three men here, so just a couple of men will come over at a time, and *only* when I tell you."

The sick men were helped over the gully, Stanford tied the rope around the first man's chest, tugged on the rope, and he was inched upward.

Slowly the dead weight of the sailor was hoisted. There were several projecting rocks near the top, but the young man was too numb to push himself away from them. He was scratched and bruised before the Newfoundland men got him up through the cleft in the overhang. The wind struck him, cut him to the marrow as he took one unbelieving, horrified look around. Where was the Navy? Where was the shelter?

Joe Manning said, "Come on, young feller."

Grasping the rope that led them up the steep gully, Manning half carried, half dragged the young sailor up the icy rocks to the top of the promontory. Here there was no protection at all from the wind.

The sailor's teeth were chattering. "Where are you taking me? Is there a house?" The wind felt as if it were shriveling his bones, and he thought he would die then and there.

Manning told him as gently as possible; "I'm taking you to a little copse of wood; that's where you have to spend the night."

The top up.

Hauling men up the cliff looked like this to Henry Strauss.

The sailor moaned, "Oh, God!"

"We've got to get the others up before we take you anywhere. Never mind, we've got a bit of a fire going, and help will soon be here."

They reeled up the long incline to the little fire and the bough shelter in the ravine. The young man fell down beside it, and Manning went back to the overhang.

The officers had lined the young men up along the ledge. Lieutenant Bradley was up front on the outside edge of the gully; other officers took their positions down the line to protect the men, if possible, against the tide, which was rushing back upon the ledge. Behind them the *Pollux* was a noisy, complaining presence.

The ailing sailors were barely able to stand on their feet as the rope was hitched around their chest and they were hauled up the cliff. There was speculation among the officers that these men might need assistance once they got to the top. "We should send someone up to look after them," said one.

George Coleman was still rubbing his hands and ears, and jumping up and down. An officer asked, "Who is that man back there jumping up and down?"

"That's Boats Coleman, sir."

"Bring that man forward."

Coleman was passed along the ledge by the men, each one holding him firmly so that he would not slip off. The officer looked him over. "You look healthy and strong, Boats Coleman. How do you feel?"

"I'm alert, sir," he replied. "I'm still warm. I've been jumping all the time."

"Good! I want you to be the next man up the cliff and give those men up there a hand. Over you go."

"Yes, sir." Coleman leaped nimbly across the little gully and Stanford tied the rope tightly around his chest. In a few minutes he was being lifted up the cliff. Being more agile than those who reached the top ahead of him, he was able to push himself away from the projecting rocks and had no difficulty getting through the overhang. "I'm to give you a hand," he told the men as they helped him up.

"You come with me," one of them said, and George, following the actions of the rescuer, grasped the rope and crept up over the slippery rocks behind him. He flinched when the wind pierced his thin dungaree shirt and pants as they reached the top. On the ledge there was no wind.

"Follow this line," the man told him, indicating the rope tied to the guideposts, "don't go to the left or right because there are gulches on either side, and you can fall off the cliff, you understand?"

"I understand."

"Now we'll go up to the fire."

George followed through the black night, shaking with the cold. At last they reached the shelter where a few flames were licking at some green trees.

"Now then, my son," said his guide, "you come back with me and bring the others to the fire accordin' as we get 'em up."

"O.K., sir."

"Remember," the man cautioned as they returned to the clifftop, "don't let them go to the left or the right of this guideline."

"I won't, sir," George said, and waited in the top of the gully of broken rock out of the wind, to take the next survivor up to the fire.

Alfred Dupuy went up early. For the second time he had lost his shoes—in that damn sinkhole, he suspected. Not that it mattered, because his feet were like two sticks of deadwood anyhow. He sure appreciated getting off that ledge, and felt pretty good about the whole thing as he crawled up over the rocks until the howling wind on the clifftop struck at his body. *My God! It was cold!* It pushed needles of ice into his bones; they throbbed with the agony of it.

Somebody took him to the ravine. It sure as hell wasn't much of a fire, he thought as he pushed his dead, frozen feet toward it.

Because of his badly skinned leg, Ensign Pollack was sent up early. The money bag and the briefcase went up behind him, and he waited patiently for them at the overhang, then he crawled up the gully and went to the shelter. He was still limping.

Blankets, clothing, and an assortment of boots and shoes were sent up for the men. Dr. Bostic, who had followed the ailing and injured, kept administering sips of medicinal alcohol.

Back and forth Coleman went, about fifteen times, guiding men to the fire. Presently he was so exhausted he could hardly stay on his feet. He rested for a while by the fire, and from then on just went halfway down the hill. Other survivors were helping to guide their shipmates to the fire, and the path, by now scattered with various objects, seemed to be fairly well defined.

When Ernest Califano was hauled to the top, one of the Newfoundlanders guided him up over the rocks and put his hand on the guideline. "Just follow this rope, my son; it'll take you to the fire," he was told.

Half blinded by fuel oil, he groped his way through the black night until he was at the end of the line. It *was* the end of the line, but where the hell was the fire they were talking about? He took a couple of steps, tripped and fell, sat up, and discovered he was clutching a pack of cigarettes. "Well," he thought wryly, "if I have to go, at least I'll have a cigarette first." The only thing was that whoever dropped the cigarette forgot to drop matches. Oh well, he really didn't want a smoke.

He sat there and tried to get his bearings, but the wind and cold further depleted all sense of direction. His eyes were burning, and if somebody didn't come along soon, he'd damn well freeze to death.

He began to shout and someone came and guided him to the fire.

A crescent moon slipped in and out of the racing clouds, drifting snow whirled around them. It had grown colder.

The fire in the ravine had grown as the number of survivors increased. Martin Edwards and some of the other Lawn men were steadily chopping trees to keep it replenished. Ice on the branches all but put out the flames, but the warm smoke took some of the bitter chill from the air. At the rate the fire was eating up the trees, they would soon be out of fuel, and would be forced to range farther afield. In spite of the bough shelter and the fire, they were unspeakably, indescribably cold. They were ravenous too. What they would give for a cup of hot coffee.

The money bag was lying in the snow near the circle of men, and Pollack joked: "I'd give forty-seven thousand dollars for a cup of coffee right now."

"Yeah!"

"Who wouldn't?"

A cuppa coffee, they thought longingly.

Dupuy, sitting by the fire, occasionally got up and shuffled around. Where was the help they needed? What were they doing here on a godforsaken windswept cliff, freezing, starving, and dying? "Where," he cried in anguish, "is the goddamn Navy?"

There were a few murmurs: "Yeah! Where *is* the goddamn Navy?"

Ensign Brown, who had also been sent up from the ledge, was ordering the more energetic sailors to help their shipmates get from the Big Head to the fire; he prodded the men to get up and walk around. Dr. Bostic had run out of medicinal alcohol and, like Ensign Brown, kept nudging the men to their feet. "Keep moving, lads! Don't fall asleep."

"I'm tired, Doc," a sailor mumbled.

"You're dead if you don't keep on the move."

Bostic and his fetish about keeping moving, Pollack thought wryly, as they scuffed around in a circle. "They said help was coming, but where the hell is it?" he asked. "Where is the Navy?"

"In my estimation the best thing to do is to walk to town," Bostic said. "At least you won't be tempted to lie down and sleep."

Pollack thought it over. Wearing only his goon jacket and boots over his swim trunks, his body was totally without feeling, but the heavy coating of grease protected him somewhat from the biting wind, and he was definitely fresher than most of them. He had put a lot of effort into surviving, and to sit around the fire was dangerous. If he was going to die, he'd rather die moving. "But where the hell is this town? Can we find our way in the dark?"

"If you follow the shoreline you have to come to it eventually," Bostic reasoned.

They talked it over. The little ravine was quickly being depleted of its trees. What would happen when there were no more? It looked like they would have to go to find help.

Lieutenant Bollinger staggered into the circle, soaked from the continual barrage of flying spray on the ledge and numbed with the cold. When Pollack announced he would walk to St. Lawrence, Bollinger decided he would go too. Four or five others got to their feet, eager to leave. Dupuy joined them, then changed his mind. No, no, no, he told himself. Still in his stocking feet, he thought it wiser to remain.

The small group left the fire with the good wishes of their shipmates and disappeared into the windswept darkness.

Pollack left the money bag with Paul Pulver.

The plight of those on the ledge was becoming more desperate as the tide rose relentlessly. It began to race through the gully along the base of the cliff, cutting through the rock between Stanford and the men and spilling like a waterfall over the ledge. They thanked God for the *Pollux,* a stone's throw away—even now she afforded them some protection. Some, but not enough. Each wave loomed closer, like some monster out of a nightmare.

The shelf was icing up worse than ever, and they were compelled to kneel or lie flat, clutching with unfeeling hands to pieces of projecting rock. Not all had flashlights, but those who did switched them on and stuck them in their back pockets. Commander Turney kept swinging his light back and forth and encouraging his men.

Then James Thomas Hill slipped and went over the ledge. "Jimmy! Oh my God!" someone screamed.

They heard him shouting for help and saw his flashlight blinking on the sea, then it disappeared. They trained their own lights on the sea, but the yellow surf rushing at them was all they saw. Even if they did see him, what could they possibly do for him?

They linked arms and prayed Walter Bulanowski held on to his shipmate, Harold W. Eaves. Larry Weaver had never been an overly religious man, but now he prayed right along with them. His thoughts were very much with Betsy Butler. He suddenly realized how very dear she was, and vowed to himself that, if he got out of this, he would not waste any more time; he would propose to her the minute he saw her. Joe Janocha, Artie Appel, Sam Nicosia—they clung to the rocks and prayed too.

Stanford called, "O.K.! Two more men can come over now, one at a time, and *be careful!*" This had been his litany throughout the night.

Lieutenant Bradley was still at his post on the outer edge of the gully, alert and watchful as the men jumped. One man leaped and made it safely. A couple jumped behind him, colliding in midair, tumbling into the gully just as another wave rushed through. Bradley threw himself face down into the gully with arms outstretched and grabbed a piece of rock projecting from the other side, using his body as a dam to keep the men from washing away.

It was in vain. Both were swept over the edge, screaming for help, but what could be done for them in the blackness of this wild night?

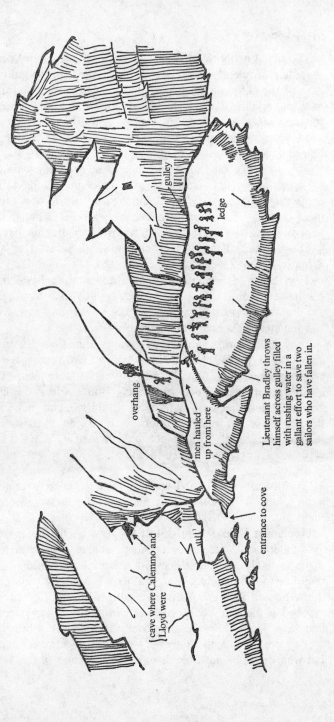

Lawn Head

guley

ledge

overhang

men hauled
up from here

Lieutenant Bradley throws
himself across gulley filled
with rushing water in a
gallant effort to save two
sailors who have fallen in.

entrance to cove

cave where Calemmo and
Lloyd were

Stanford and the other sailor grabbed Lieutenant Bradley by the arms and pulled him over to where they were standing. He was bleeding profusely from the inner side of his arm. They ripped open his sleeve, saw the blood flowing, and quickly applied a tourniquet above the elbow.

"Up he goes to Dr. Bostic," Stanford said.

They tied Bradley onto the rope and yelled to the men above. "This man is bleeding badly, get him to Doc Bostic, he needs emergency treatment."

"We'll look after him." The voice sounded faint against the roar of the ocean.

As Bradley was hauled laboriously up the cliff, the men prayed more fervently. Some began to sing another old World War I song, their voices sounding thin and reedy. Others joined in: "It's a Long Way to Tipperary. . . ."

On the clifftop, Joseph Manning had long ago relieved Alfred Grant at the outside position on the rope. Their hands were blistered and bleeding, their arms were nearly torn from their sockets as they hauled the dead weight of survivors up the cliff, but there could be no thought of resting. They knew what it must be like on the ledge below when those hauled over the cliff's edge had pleaded through chattering teeth, "Hurry! Hurry!"

28

St. Lawrence
February 18, 1942—7 P.M.

It was a happier scene in St. Lawrence where survivors had been left in the care of the women. Warren Greenfield had returned to consciousness after the shot of morphine had worn off to find himself stark naked on a table in a big, rough room, surrounded by women who were washing him. "Holy smokes!" he yelped, but the women, ignoring his embarrassment, continued to scrub. Presently he was given long underwear, more makeshift clothing, and hot soup, and a while later was taken to the home of Howard and Isabel Farrell. Bill Heldt went with him. Both young men were cheerful despite frostbitten hands and feet, and happy to be alive, but now and again lapsed into periods of brooding over their shipmates. Who had made it? Who had not?

The St. Lawrence men who had not already left for Lawn Head were meeting with the American officers aboard the USS *Brant* to plan the rescue strategy. More food, more clothing were needed; every available horse and sled had to be utilized. Homes, shops, even the ships in the harbor had to dig into their stores for food and clothing. It would take hours to organize.

Howard Farrell was in charge of the rescue operations and was therefore attending the meeting aboard the *Brant,* and Isabel took the two survivors next door to the Farrell family home—the "big house," with its large, comfortable living room and fireplace. Howard's brother, Aubrey Farrell, a merchant, lived there with his bride, Sue, as did Ena, her younger brother Cecil, and sister Marjorie.

The sight of leaping flames immediately raised the spirits of the young men. Staring pensively into the fire were John Shields and Stanley "Ski" Kendzierski from the *Truxtun*. Despite two or three washings, both sailors bore traces of oil. Ski looked as if he had a black eye, but in reality the oil had seeped into the pores of the skin around his right eye.

Greenfield brightened at the sight of a guitar owned by Cecil. He picked it up, strummed it, then burst into song: "Oh give me a home where the buffalo roam . . ."

The Farrells were a musical family; Ena went to the piano and Cecil picked up the violin. There was a piano accordion that Cecil played as well, and so did one of the Americans, who picked it up and began to play along with them.

The cheerful fire, the warm, happy atmosphere of the big house were very different from the setting at Lawn Head where their shipmates shivered around the smoking branches of ice-covered trees.

Ena played a few bars of a popular American song and Greenfield joined in, singing out the lyrics loudly.

A surprising number of survivors had bounced back within a few hours and were brought to the big house, where the cheery atmosphere revived them even more. John A. Brollini and Arthur Perrault from the *Truxtun* were among them. Perrault had been taken into the home of René Etchegary.

In spite of the cheerful mood, a deep pall of gloom occasionally settled over the men as they reminisced about their shipmates who had not made it. Once Shields wept and Brollini emotionally proclaimed: "I'll get even if I have to drink the whole Atlantic Ocean."

"Yeah!" everyone agreed wholeheartedly to this absurd and unrealistic likelihood.

Ena and Cecil brought them back to the present by playing a lively Newfoundland jig.

In Clara Tarrant's home Don Fitzgerald was muttering in a delirium. Unconvinced that Edward McInerney had been saved, he raved about his friends who had been with him in the last minutes aboard the *Truxtun*. Clara and her daughters had continued to rub him with hot camphorated oil, trying to clean off some of the black grease on his body. Once he opened his eyes and asked, "Is this Boston?"

"No," Clara told him, "you're in St. Lawrence, Newfoundland."

Through stiff lips he said, "I want to say I'm O.K."

Clara was a quick-thinking woman. "You want to send a message to Boston to let someone know you're all right?"

He nodded.

"Your mother?"

"Yes, my mother."

"We'll let her know," Clara soothed.

The lucid moment passed and Fitzgerald sank back into an incoherent rambling, but Clara was satisfied that he would make it.

An element of mystery now raised its head. Some of the *Truxtun* men were troubled, obviously having something of great importance on their minds. In their weakened condition it had become too great a burden to bear even though they had made a pact aboard ship to keep it among themselves. Here and there from the tormented men came a story of suicide; they had heard a pistol shot from the vicinity of the bridge and discovered that the navigator had shot himself rather than attempt to swim to shore.

The story spread like wildfire around St. Lawrence, and yet another story circulated: It was the captain who had shot himself.

This story of suicide would sweep Base Roger at Argentia later, and would be discussed endlessly by the men when they sailed back to Boston on the USS *Tarazad*.

The rumor also spread to the capital city of St. John's the following day. In 1974, when research was started, it was still alive in the minds of all who were a part of the tragedy.

Washington, D.C., would not be able to verify the rumor.

In the kitchen of Leo and Lillian Loder, Ensign James Seamans drifted in and out of consciousness. Because of the oil and water he had swallowed, he was continually throwing up.

Lillian's mother had come to help her tend the young man, whose frostbitten hands and feet were terribly swollen. It was normal practice to "rub out" the frostbite with snow, but Lillian could not bring herself to do it. "The poor man has been out in the cold and snow all day," she told her mother. Instead, they rubbed lots of Mecca ointment on the frostbite and covered his hands and feet with bandages.

The only heat in the house came from the kitchen stove, which meant it needed constant attention. Leo was on his way to Lawn Head with a group of men to aid the crew of the *Pollux,* so Lillian and her mother prepared for an all-night vigil.

Only forty-six of the *Truxtun*'s crew members survived. One hundred and ten men had died against the cliffs of Chambers Cove.

29

Lawn Head
February 18–19, 1942—2100–0030 hours

Assaulted by the razor-edged wind, crawling on their hands and knees along the ice-capped cliffs, Pollack, Bollinger, and the other men followed the sound of the sea. They knew they were adding unnecessary miles to their jouney by following the contour of the land, but they had agreed among themselves it was better to do that than get lost in the trackless wasteland.

They had stayed inland as much as possible in the early stages, and on the slope of the first hill had stumbled upon the body of DeRosa. In the circumstances they were too apathetic to feel too much shock, and had continued on, but the wind was carrying the sound of the sea away from them and they were forced to move closer to the edge of the precipice, where they could hear the booming surf. When they weren't on their hands and knees they were up to their hips in snow and the strain was beginning to take its toll. Pollack and Bollinger conferred. "We're wasting a lot of energy needlessly."

"Yeah! We should take turns scouting while everybody else rests."

"We should also take turns breaking trail in the snow." They had remained bunched together, each one making his own way through the snow. They should follow in each other's footsteps and conserve energy.

It was agreed that was what they would do but so exhausted were they, it was necessary for them to stop every ten minutes or so and rest.

Alonzo Walsh and Celestine Giovannini of St. Lawrence (right) helped the Americans bring up two bodies from the beach. One of them was still uncovered when this picture was taken. (Ena Farrell Edwards)

Canvas-covered bodies lie on the clifftop awaiting transportation to St. Lawrence. (Ena Farrell Edwards)

Newfoundlanders haul drowned American sailors out of the ravine and over the hills to St. Lawrence. The hayshed and fence are in the background. (Ena Farrell Edwards)

Some days later, Newfoundlanders were still lowering themselves down the cliff in the search for bodies. (Ena Farrell Edwards)

Other men of St. Lawrence brought victims of the shipwreck to the harbor in their dories. (Ena Farrell Edwards)

Four grateful survivors from the *Truxtun* pose for a photo outside the Farrell home. John A. Shields (left rear), Stanislaus J. Kendzierski (front left), and John A. Brollini (holding Ena's pet dog); the name of the fourth American is not known. (Ena Farrell Edwards)

Left to right: Howard Farrell, assistant manager of Iron Springs Mine; Bill Heldt of the *Pollux;* Isabel Farrell, Warren Greenfield (*Pollux*), and a Navy corpsman, thought to be Pharmacist's Mate Third Class Stanley Barron. (Ena Farrell Edwards)

A horse-drawn sled bearing a coffin is guided down the street by Newfoundlander John Kelly. (Ena Farrell Edwards)

Many men and women of St. Lawrence form the funeral cortege following the flag-draped coffins to the cemetery. (Ena Farrell Edwards)

Father Augustus Thorne says prayers for the dead before burial. (Ena Farrell Edwards)

A chill wind lifts the American flag held by American sailors over the common grave of their countrymen in St. Lawrence Cemetery. (Ena Farrell Edwards)

A sad sight: three more coffins on the way to the cemetery. The recovery of bodies continued for months after the disaster. (Ena Farrell Edwards)

Ena Farrell stands beside a great granite stone that marks the grave site of the American sailors. The plaque reads: "In Memory of the Officers and Enlisted Men of the U. S. Navy Who Lost Their Lives in the Disaster of the USS *Pollux* and USS *Truxtun* February 18, 1942." (Ena Farrell Edwards)

An oil-coated American sailor who helped recover the bodies of men lost on the *Truxtun*. (Ena Farrell Edwards)

Gregory Edwards of Newfoundland, who wrote a song about the wreck of the two ships. (Courtesy of Mrs. Ronald O'Brien)

Commander Charles R. Longenecker, medical officer from the USS *Prairie,* who aided in rescue work.

The hospital that the U. S. Government presented to the people of Lawn and St. Lawrence in grateful recognition of their heroic efforts to save the lives of the shipwrecked Americans. Without them, many—perhaps most—would have died. (Courtesy of Cathleen Barnier)

Somewhere along the way they met up with Lieutenant Commander Ashford, Lieutenant Longenecker, and the medical corpsmen who, having climbed seemingly endless hills themselves, were wondering if *they* were going to make it. Only Lieutenant Commander Ashford's encouragement had kept them going. The *Pollux* survivors were given stimulants, encouragement, and directions, and Longenecker left Pharmacist's Mate Miller with them. As they crawled and staggered through the drifting snow Pollack thought of his home in sunny California and wondered, numbly, "What in hell am I doing here?"

And . . . "Where the hell is the rest of the Navy?" Nearly a hundred men dead, and so far a handful of Navy men were sent to help them when the whole bloody United States Navy should have been marching over the hills to rescue them! Why weren't they?

The U. S. Navy *was* marching toward Lawn Head—not in droves —but a sprinkling of men from the USS *George E. Badger* and the USS *Brant,* assisted by the St. Lawrence men, were coming in groups, loaded with blankets and a small amount of food. The same men who had spent the day in the freezing waters of Chambers Cove were leading the way.

Not too far behind Lieutenant Commander Ashford's group were Henry Lambert, Patrick Tarrant, Alfred Turpin, and Mike Turpin; in another group were Joseph Turpin, Clem Slaney, Rupert Kelly, Lionel Turpin, David Slaney, and Rupert Turpin.

But the biggest drive had not started yet. While the women ministered to the wretchedly ill sailors being brought into their homes, their men were collecting what food and blankets they could find and preparing their horses and oxen for the rescue trip. There were no trails to Lawn Head; they would have to take axes and blaze the way.

The crowd swelled around the fire in the ravine. "Who is it?" was the question as each figure lurched toward them. Each man who had a best buddy still on the ledge prayed he had not been swept away by the rising tide.

Bradley was in a very weakened condition and Dr. Bostic had strapped his arm and tied him to a small tree to prevent him from falling over or lying in the snow. Checking him frequently as he moved through the circle of men, Bostic encouraged him: "You're O.K., George."

Commander Turney had finally ordered Lieutenant Dougherty up. The Newfoundlanders had helped him up to the windy clifftop, put his hand on the guideline, and told him, "Follow the rope, sir; someone will meet you on the other end and take you to the fire."

Dougherty, really old by Navy standards, was exhausted and eager to get to the fire, wherever it was. He stumbled along to the end of the line, but no one was there to show him the way. Where was he? He could see no reflection of a fire in the black night, yet reason told him it had to be somewhere ahead. He headed away from the guideline, floundering around in the heavy snow, and quickly had the feeling that he was lost. At that moment he stepped on a patch of ice, slipped, and fell, twisting his left ankle.

He lay there waiting for the sound of a voice, footsteps, anything, but only the wind howled at him. Dougherty did not waste any time. Mentally blessing the old Navy regulation that had put a gun in his possession, he fired a couple of shots in the air. Within a couple of minutes two men of the Newfoundland rescue party found him and assisted him to the shelter.

Each man who came staggering to the fire reported that conditions below were getting increasingly worse. The sea had swept food, clothing and records from the ledge; the gully on the ledge was a millrace, encroaching more and more upon the space left to them. Lieutenant Weintraub kept a close watch on the time; high tide was approximately 2230 hours, roughly in another hour, and the possibility of complete inundation was not unlikely. But the rescue operation could not be rushed.

Time dragged endlessly for those waiting their turn to be taken up the cliff. Now and again they were startled to see lights bobbing on the sea. These were the liferafts, equipped with emergency lights, that were being swept off the *Pollux,* but they soon disappeared.

Chief Pharmacist's Mate Robert George "Doc" O'Connor, retired from the Navy but recalled in 1939 to serve on the *Pollux,* was knocked down by a wave. Dazed, he lay there as the sea toyed with him. Strauss grabbed him and half dragged, half carried him to where Stanford was tying men to the rope.

O'Connor was next to go up and Strauss was not far behind.

Higher and higher rushed the waves until they began to break across the ledge. Then, at the peak of the tide, a sea picked up Ensign Francis Xavier Clarke, a young officer just out of Harvard, and swept him away.

As soon as Ashford, Longenecker, Haralson, and Barron arrived, they were immediately absorbed in the large circle of men around the fire, and many sailors were unaware that the Navy had arrived. There was little they could do except dole out sips of the medicinal alcohol to the exhausted men, and that disappeared quickly.

The Newfoundland men arrived right on their heels. Henry Lambert, Patrick Tarrant, Alfred Turpin, and Mike Turpin went straight to the clifftop. "Just what we need—fresh men," Manning said, and gratefully relinquished the rope. There were still about thirty men to bring up the cliff.

The small supply of food was soon gone. Cans of soup and juice were shared, as far as they would go. The majority of survivors didn't know that there had been any kind of sustenance at all. "More help is coming," they were told. "Food and clothing and horses and sleds—it's all coming behind us."

Sam Nicosia doled out sips of his own supply of whiskey to his shipmates who lay in the snow.

Dupuy had sense enough to get up and shuffle around occasionally. None of the meager supply of food had reached him, and he was not aware that any had come with the rescue party, but he had a raging thirst. Oh for a drink of water! He found an empty can, packed it with snow, and placed it close to the fire. Where the can came from he didn't question; he just kept adding snow and watching it very carefully as it melted. After an interminably long time the can was two thirds full and he was reaching for it when someone passing between him and the fire inadvertently kicked it over. Dupuy stared at it with frustration and dismay.

Lieutenant Weintraub went up the cliff at 2300 hours, and was brought to the fire. By now, more Newfoundlanders and some of the

U. S. Navy personnel were waiting at the top to take survivors up to the ravine.

Ensign Grayson went up soon after and, seeing that Dupuy was without shoes, took off his arctic boots: "Put 'em on, Dupuy."

"I thank you." Dupuy stuck his lifeless feet into the boots while Grayson trudged around in his shoes.

Commander Turney, Navigator Grindley, and Shipfitter Stanford were the last three on the ledge. Stanford tied Grindley to the rope and up he went. When it snaked down again Stanford, whose admiration of Turney was boundless, said, "Captain, be my guest. I'll tie you onto the rope and send you topside, and when the rope comes back I'll tie myself on, and that will be the end of this little drama."

As weary and frozen as he was, Commander Turney was deeply moved. Stanford had been a pillar of strength with his expert handling of the men and the line during the past six or seven hours. He said courteously, "Shipmate, I thank you, but remember, I am the captain and I go last, so up you go."

Stanford was concerned. What did the captain remember about tying the proper kind of knot that would hold him until he was hauled up over the cliff? "Skipper, I'll agree under one condition: You'll tie me into the rope as I show you, and you'll have to do so until you do it right a few times, or no agreement. I don't intend to lose you now if I can help it!"

"O.K., Bill."

With the ocean snarling at their feet, they went through the process of tying Stanford to the rope until both were satisfied that when the captain's turn came, he could tie himself safely. Stanford gave a tug on the rope and was pulled up the cliff. He waited at the top until the commander was hauled up. It took a while, because he was a heavy man, and the Newfoundland men wheezed and grunted with every pull. Henry Lambert's palms had been stripped of flesh. At last Captain Turney came up through the crevice and thanked them. He was barely able to stand. Then he saw Stanford. "What are you doing here?"

"Waiting for you, Captain—what do you think?"

Captain Turney replied, "Thanks, buddy. We'll go together and join our shipmates."

He and Stanford staggered off toward the hill, guided by the New-foundlanders.

It was approximately 0030 hours.

The *Wilkes,* nursed along by her damage-control party, was crippling up Placentia Bay toward Argentia.

30

Lawn Head
February 19, 1942—0300 hours

In the black little cave on the shore, Larry Calemmo roused and muttered, "Are we ever gonna get out of here?"

Altogether there were twenty men in this little black hole, and not even the most energetic of them had been able to scale those icy walls during the daylight hours.

Lloyd had kept a sharp eye on them throughout the day, yelling at them if he thought they were falling asleep. Occasionally someone crawled outside to look at the battered wreckage of their ship. Gunner's Mate Wood had tried to fire a shot in the air to draw attention to their plight, but the mechanism of the automatic .45 was stiff with congealed oil. At times Wood had shouted, but no one heard.

Darkness had brought its own strange sounds to bedevil them— the rush and roar of the sea, the *Pollux* clanging on the rocks and moaning as the seas forced air up through her.

The day had been very long and no one had come to rescue them. Had Garnaus, Greenfield, and DeRosa gotten through? Was everybody else lost? They wondered if they were the only survivors.

The cave was not very comfortable. There was snow on the ground and ice on the rock sides, but at least the wind and sea did not reach it. They had taken a couple of life jackets, shredded the kapok, and, with a Zippo lighter produced by Wood, eventually got a fire going. Little globs of fuel oil prolonged the life of the fire, but its true value was psychological rather than physical. Now and again they crawled outside to scrounge for driftwood. What they found was wet and covered in oil, but it ignited and burned fitfully.

All were wet and covered from head to toe with thick, greasy oil. Tom McCarron, clad only in dungaree pants, shirt, and life jacket, was grateful for the insulation it provided his chilled body. It clung to them, inches thick, and they were recognizable only by their voices. They were black, shapeless forms, hunched over a tiny fire—only the whites of their eyes distinguished them from the blackness around them.

Suddenly, one of the young sailors who had been in a daze began to shout incoherently. They tried to calm him down, but he did not heed them. On and on he raved, his voice raised in garbled prayer until Lloyd yelled, "Shaddup!"

It was an order, but for the first time it did not have any effect; the sailor was beyond reasoning. Another sailor threatened: "You wanna go back into the water?"

They were all getting upset now. Here they were, barely hanging on to life and reason, and the young man was not helping the situation. Yet they knew he was not in his right senses and any one of them could have been behaving in the same manner.

The sailor appeared to be oblivious of his companions, and suddenly demanding that the fire be put out, he scattered the pieces of burning wood with his hand.

It was the last straw. Gunner's Mate Wood drew his useless gun, at the same time threatening to shoot the young sailor. The fire gave no heat, no real light, and it was not really worth the effort it took to scrounge for driftwood, yet it did flare up occasionally, and if a man was not too stupefied with the wet and the cold, he could see the comforting outline of another human form, or the flash of an eye. In that flickering fire, then, was their own hold on reality and on life.

The sailor calmed down, not because of the gun, but because he had depleted his last reserve of energy.

Phillip Jewett had been sitting motionless for some time. The sailor next to him gave him a nudge. "Wake up, Jewett!" Jewett fell over. To all appearances he was dead. As the slow hours dragged by, others fell over, seemingly dead, despite Lloyd's shouting, until there were six still forms: Foster, Jewett, Mongeau, Hak, Hanson, and Harris.

McCarron began to doze and Lloyd, ever watchful, yelled,

"McTavish, you goddamned Irishman, keep your eyes open! Don't go to sleep!" It was a peculiarity of Lloyd's that his own personal nickname for McCarron was "McTavish."

McCarron roused and mumbled "O.K.!" He leaned back against the icy side of the cave; he was really exhausted and could hardly keep his eyes open. "Maybe," he thought, "if I could turn around every once in a while and lick the ice, it would keep me awake." It took considerable energy to even turn around, but he found that it did make him wake up. He kept licking the wall now and again, even though it parched his mouth.

There was no conversation, no idle speculation about what, where, or why. Eventually the last life jacket had been burned; the last piece of wood. They were freezing to death and they had no desire to remain awake. Lloyd no longer had the energy to shout and yell at them. He turned to Calemmo, groped for his hand, and muttered, "Good-bye, Larry, I guess I won't be seeing you anymore."

Calemmo murmured, "I guess not. Good-bye, Lloyd." It did not seem terrible or frightening that they were all going to die—he was too unutterably weary to do other than accept it.

"Good luck."

"Good luck to you, too." The cold, black stillness of the cave was the stillness of death.

Calemmo put his arms on his knees, wearily rested his head on his arms, and fell asleep.

McCarron felt very, very drowsy in spite of licking the icy wall. If he could sleep . . . just for ten minutes . . . just for a little catnap . . .

His eyes closed and the sound of the sea and the *Pollux* faded.

31

Lawn Head
February 19, 1942—0300 hours

To his dying day, Joe Manning would never forget the scene before him on the bitterly cold hilltop: the smoky glare of the fire, the injured, draped in blankets, sitting and lying on the snowy ground, their faces seeming to change in the dancing shadows cast by the flames. Men shuffled in a great circle around the fire, some more vigorous than others, helping their shipmates, and above all this the bite of the wind as it howled across the hills, hurling icy blasts into the shallow ravine. To Manning it paralleled many of the descriptive scenes he had conjured up while reading *Pilgrim's Progress* during his school days.

There were no jokes cracked now. Pete Manger lay dead, eyes staring sightlessly into the fire; they could get no life into the still form of Gunner's Mate Schuster; and many others were unable to move because of frozen limbs. Each man had but one thought: to stay alive till daylight and rescue, and their mental energies were directed to that one great effort.

Other Newfoundlanders had arrived from St. Lawrence in twos and threes, mingling with the survivors and passing out the bits and pieces of food they had brought with them; walking the survivors around the fire and scouring the hills for firewood. "We'll guide the men who can walk into St. Lawrence as soon as day breaks," they told Commander Turney. "By that time the rest of the rescue party should have arrived to take care of the injured and the dead," they said.

Firewood was getting quite scarce now, and some of the survivors as well as the Newfoundlanders were scouring the ravine and beyond, bringing back great armloads of trees. When thrown onto the fire the small Christmas trees, as the Americans called them, blazed up quickly, then sent forth billows of smoke to hang over them like a pall.

Before leaving the *Pollux* Popolizio had grabbed a Very pistol that had been lying on the deck. Now someone took it from him, shot flares into the tangle of smoldering wet trees and, for a brief period, the trees burned brightly, sending forth an intense heat. Once the flames died down they made the discovery that, if anything, the heat from the fire made them feel colder. Unless one could practically crawl into the fire, it did very little to keep them warm.

On the periphery of the ring of men shuffling about, Grindley and Grayson decided to start a fire of their own. They found a discarded, sodden life jacket, shredded it, and soon had a small fire. It wasn't much of a blaze, but soon they had their own little circle of men.

Strauss had found Grindley in the crowd, and kept close to him. To a degree he had leaned on Grindley throughout this battle of life and death and, having taken his advice, had so far survived. It followed naturally that where Grindley went, Strauss was not too far away, which was a lucky decision for the young man.

It was now a matter of waiting for daylight and transportation.

Califano was shoeless and just about blind. His thoughts were very much on his friend, Larry Calemmo . . . Larry who was always yelling at him. Had they gotten his friend up from that cove yet? he asked.

"Not yet," he was told, "but don't worry, he's O.K."

From around the circle other voices were asking the same questions about missing friends: "He's probably gone off to get some Christmas trees," or "He's probably walking around someplace" were the stock replies.

Bill Stanford and another survivor had wandered slightly beyond the periphery of the fire and thought they heard a cry for help above the wind. They hurried down the hill toward the cliff edge, and were joined by one of the Newfoundland men who had also heard the voice. "Let's have a look," he said.

They scouted around the cove where Calemmo and the others were, flashed their battery lights into all the nooks and crannies along the shore, but saw no sign of life and heard no more cries for help. They returned to the fire. "As soon as day breaks, we'll take a good look around for any more survivors," the Newfoundlander told the two sailors.

They went back to the fire.

George Coleman, in his thin dungaree shirt and pants, was still jumping occasionally and moving about the circle, rousing those who had lain down to rest. Many had frostbitten feet and could not move; an astonishing number were without shoes and boots. "You gotta move or you'll freeze to death," was the warning cry.

They found Paul Pulver lying beside the money bag and briefcase, seemingly dead. Coleman grabbed an arm, others grabbed his other limbs, another took Pulver's face in his hands, and they massaged him for up to half an hour before he showed signs of life. They hauled him to his feet and dragged him around the fire, more dead than alive.

Nicosia still doled out sips of whiskey. Those who could, went off into the night with the Newfoundland men in their unending search for firewood. All were fighting to survive, and all were afraid to sleep in spite of the overwhelming desire to close their eyes. Henry Strauss was a little delirious; the piercing cold penetrated the very core of his being and he had lain down to sleep because not enough oxygen was flowing to his brain to keep him awake, and alive. He had remained with Grindley and Grayson, and now and again Grindley had to drag him to his feet, bounce him around, and slap his face to shock him out of his lethargy. But now, in the early hours of this bitter morning, even Grindley, who had been without sleep for nearly forty-eight hours, had fallen into a doze.

Strauss, in his delirium, decided he had to go home to see Jo. Blind with fuel oil, he could not see where he was going, but the overwhelming urge to see her was foremost in his mind. Nobody was more important to Strauss than Jo . . . he got up and lurched off into the night.

Grindley awoke with a start—whether it was that sixth sense of his, the bitter cold, or the strict self-discipline that would not permit him the luxury of leaving his body vulnerable to the elements, he never knew. He missed Strauss immediately and staggered off into the night in search of him. How long he had dozed, and how long Strauss had been gone, he had no idea, but he did know that he had to find him pretty damn quick or the lad would likely freeze to death.

Grindley thought he would freeze to death himself as he prowled the hill up to his waist in snowdrifts and was about to fall on his face many times. Finally he heard Strauss calling: "Jo! Jo! Hurry, Jo! Please come and get me, Jo!"

He was almost buried in a snowdrift and Grindley, grabbing him by the life jacket, actually dragged him up the hill to the fire. Strauss did not doze off anymore than night.

It was getting close to 0400 hours when Ensign Brown, unaware that a party had already scouted the ravine, decided that something should be done about their shipmates in the little cove. "We should try to get them up to the fire," he urged.

No one heeded him. They barely had the strength to stay alive, let alone face that awful hill and the steep, ice-covered cliff where Garnaus and his crew had landed.

"They're your shipmates!" Brown yelled, "Are you gonna let 'em freeze to death in the cove?"

They heard and understood, but were physically unable to do anything about it. Besides, to search that little cove on an unfamiliar shore in the windy, bitterly cold darkness was asking for more trouble.

Those Newfoundland men who were close by listened. Till now most of them had not known that other men had gotten ashore in the cove and were still trapped down by the sea. They decided they would get them. They moved off, followed by some of the anxious sailors. As they trudged down the hill a small party of U. S. Navy men arrived. "Lots of help just behind us," they reported, and learning that more men were being rescued by Newfoundlanders, they went to help.

Calemmo was awakened by the sound of rocks and ice falling. He raised his head, barely able to see through slits of eyes, and saw the vague outline of a giant of a man. It was a miracle, he thought, an angel from heaven . . . or God himself? Gradually, realization came over him that they had at last been rescued. A Newfoundlander had been lowered into the cove, and was shining his light into the cave. Groggily those who were not insensible awakened to the fact that help was at hand, that they had not been forgotten after all.

A rope was tied around the chest of the first man and up he went, sliding easily over the wall of ice. At the top a couple of his shipmates took him by the arms, and all three, staggering like drunk men, went up the hill to the fire.

Foster, still sitting with his arms around his knees and head on arms, was dead, and Harris, Mongeau, Hak, Jewett, and Hanson were thought to be dead as well, and were left until last.

McCarron came to his senses as he was being hauled up the steep incline. Two men helped him to the shelter, removed his sodden life jacket, threw a blanket around him, and told him to get near the fire. The heat of it made him realize how deathly cold he was. He saw his friend Pete Manger, lying on the ground, staring into the fire. "How's Pete?" he croaked.

"He's dead," they told him.

In spite of all he had gone through, it was a shock.

Calemmo was the last of the mobile survivors up the hill. All he could think of as he was pulled to the top was food and a warm shelter; the windy, bleak clifftop nearly killed him then and there. There was no food or shelter in the ravine either, but a place was made for him at the fire, where he fell down and went to sleep. Nothing could keep him awake.

Brewer was taken to the fire where it was discovered that there was no dry clothing left for him. "We'll fix you up," Dr. Bostic promised.

Brewer, a southerner, was transfixed by the bitter wind as it cut through his saturated clothing. For the first time in his life he was achingly conscious of every bone in his body; never had he experienced the cold as he experienced it now. Could he survive it?

Quickly, Dr. Bostic gave him an injection of some kind, and, wrapping and tying a piece of torn blanket around Brewer's bare foot, indicated that he should lie in the snow. The sailor did as he was ordered, and the rescuers packed snow around his body to protect him from the wind. By the time they had finished, he might not have been exactly cozy, but no wind touched him. Two or three others who did not have the benefit of dry clothing were also wrapped in snow.

Once the unconscious men had been hauled up the steep incline, makeshift stretchers were made with blankets to carry them to the fire. The strain on the sailors, already weakened by long hours of exposure, was killing, but somehow, somewhere, they found the reserves to drag or carry their shipmates to the fire. As each one was brought to the shelter, all crowded around to see who had been saved. At 1650 hours, by Dr. Bostic's watch, the last sailor had been brought to the ravine.

Hak was laid beside Dupuy, and the Navy rescue party, under Dr. Longenecker, and Dr. Bostic, were vigorously massaging the insensible men. It kept Mongeau, Hanson, and Jewett alive, but Tommie Harris died, and Hak drew his last breath with his head in Dupuy's lap.

The group of sailors led by Pollack and Bollinger had floundered through snowdrifts all night and, in spite of the biting cold, not one had fallen by the wayside. Because they followed the coastline they had not met up with any of the rescue parties behind Commander Ashford's group, who were traveling farther inland in a reasonably straight line toward Lawn Head.

It was a nightmare journey that Ensign Pollack thought would never end but at dawning they sighted the distant lights of the Iron Springs Mine and staggered toward it.

Even at this hour there were a few women at the mine house ready to look after them. Pollack was given coffee, and clothes for his deadened body. Presently they were put into a truck, taken into St. Lawrence, and dropped off at various houses. Pollack was taken into the home of Albert Grimes.

Dawn had brightened the sky, and the men from Lawn, being as cold, hungry, and exhausted as the men they had rescued, decided to head in the direction of St. Lawrence with as many survivors as could fit on their sleds. They would have to blaze their own trails through the woods and ravines stretching ahead of them, but they did not anticipate any great difficulty.

They brought the five horses and sleds to the circle, tied an injured man to each sled, and quietly took off. Because of severe frostbite, Dupuy was one of the first to go.

This brought the men out of their lethargy and started a general

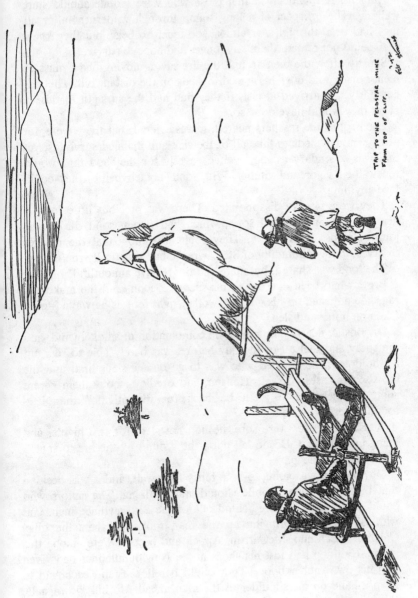

TRIP TO THE FELDSPAR MINE
FROM TOP OF CLIFF.

Henry Strauss' impression of the trip to Iron Springs Mine by horse-drawn sled.

movement. It was decided that those who were mobile should start walking. The prospect of a long tramp through wilderness after all they had been through was almost too much to bear, but they knew they could not remain there any longer and hope to survive.

Shortly after, the men around the fire saw a moving black mass of men, horses, and dogs harnessed to sleds on the distant hill. The rescue party had arrived at last. If they had had the strength to raise a cheer they would have done so.

Even so, as the rescuers neared, it was evident that there were not nearly enough sleds to take all of the sick and maimed survivors, yet that was secondary as they waited eagerly for the food that would renew their vigor and vitality. With food in their bellies they could face anything.

They were bitterly disappointed. There was precious little food—dry crackers and canned soup, which had frozen solid during the journey across the country. They could not know that the meager reserves of the community of St. Lawrence had practically run out.

The food was shared, but many did not receive a mouthful.

Brewer had been dug out of his snowy cocoon, and the makeshift rag shoe adjusted on his grossly swollen right foot as he waited to be taken on horse and sled.

Dr. Bostic, nearly blinded by the combination of smoke, wind, and the spray and fuel oil of the day before, was barely able to see, but as the doctor, he decided who was to go on the sleds first, and the most severe cases—Jewett, Hanson, and Bradley among them—were soon on their way. "We'll be back for the others," the Newfoundlanders promised.

"O.K.!" His eyes were sore, he had not slept for two nights, and being utterly spent, Bostic fell upon the ground by the fire to snatch a few minutes' sleep.

Obviously it was going to be a fairly long wait, and it was decided that those who were mobile should start walking. The sailors who could walk formed a line behind one of the St. Lawrence men, and with Bill Stanford bringing up the rear, took off across the hills. Calemmo, Califano, McCarron, Appel, and Nicosia were among this group. Califano had lost his shoes and a Newfoundlander had given him his own rubber boots. They could barely see, and each had to keep a hand on the shoulder of the man ahead. Up hill, down dale, through the snowdrifts they weaved, stumbled, and fell, too tired to care if they lived or died. Nicosia kept going up and down the line, administering the last of his whiskey to his faltering friends.

Henry Lambert led another group of survivors, some of them with only socks on their feet and wearing thin dungaree pants and shirts. He got them to within a half mile of the Iron Springs Mine when one of the sailors fell. "I can't go one more step," he mumbled. A couple more sank into the snow and could not be persuaded to continue. Henry hauled them into the shelter of some scrub trees and promised he would be back for them shortly. They were close enough to the mine that a truck could be brought almost to the spot.

Having guided the others to Iron Springs, he returned with help to find the first man sitting, staring unseeingly ahead, holding for dear life onto a little tree, and they could not break his grip. Henry whipped out his sturdy pocket knife, hacked the tree off, and brought man and tree to the truck. They carried him into Iron Springs Mine with his hands still frozen into a viselike grip around the little tree.

Brewer, being mobile, had been ordered to walk, and he had been with Henry Lambert's group when it left the fire. He had gotten down the hill a few hundred yards when he discovered that his makeshift rag shoe was gone, lost somewhere in one of the snow drifts they had plowed through. Brewer kept going because that was the only thing he could do, but he fell behind the others, and very soon realized that his other shoe and sock had disappeared. He was now completely barefoot.

A slight, young American Coast Guardsman, who had been one of the rescue party, had brought up the rear of this group of survivors. He had kept an eye on Brewer, falling behind with him. Now he took off his heavy pea jacket and offered it to him. It did not go near Brewer's hefty 6 foot frame. "Then take my arctics," he urged, and swiftly removed his heavy arctic boots.

Brewer gratefully tried to force the boots on his feet, but they were too swollen, and the boots were too small. "I thank you anyway," he said. His hands and feet were so black and swollen he wondered what he had done to bruise them so.

They trudged on through the snow, over hills, into ravines, following the track of the others until they came to Chambers Cove and the hay shed in the ravine, where a welcome sight greeted Brewer's tired, sore eyes: A man was there with a horse and sled. In short

order Brewer was sitting on the sled, his grotesque feet stuck out before him, while the Newfoundlander trotted along by the side of the
horse, which had the unlikely name of "Maude," encouraging the
animal as it hauled its burden over the difficult terrain.

The man took Brewer to his home where his wife cut off the sodden uniform and covered the American with a variety of dry clothes.
He could not eat, but got down a swallow of coffee, and presently
the Navy came and took him away.

At Lawn Head they were loading the sleds with the remaining survivors, so many that Grindley wondered if the tough little ponies
would be able to make it over the hills.

It was decided to leave the dead men and return for them
later, and satisfied that all would be transported, Commander Turney and the executive officer, Lieutenant Commander Gabrielson,
sharing a sled, began the long, cold ride over the unfriendly hills.

But the sleds were too crowded, and Grindley said, "I'll walk in."
In spite of the lack of sleep and rest for more than forty-eight hours,
he felt he was in better physical shape than most.

Bostic and Longenecker, old friends from earlier times when Longenecker had been Bostic's junior doctor in the Sixth Battalion, decided they too would walk in with the sleds.

"I'm going to take a look at the *Pollux* first," Grindley decided.

A young sailor, one of the kids just out of boot camp, joined him.
"I'll walk in with you, sir," he said.

The fire was still smoldering; wisps of blue smoke rose lazily in
the air. The ravine, shorn of its greenery, was dotted with tiny tree
stumps and littered with debris; the snow, beaten down under the
shuffling feet of the survivors and rescuers, was black with fuel oil.
The bodies of the dead sailors had been laid side by side.

Before leaving, Grindley covered the dead bodies with a few oil-
soaked blankets and other discarded clothing. In this wild, desolate
country there were bound to be wolves,* and he did not want them
desecrating the bodies. The few rags he placed over the bodies
would not have done any good, but at least he had made the gesture.

With dawning the wind had dropped considerably, but by the look
of the sky, Grindley knew they were in for a "blue norther"—bitter

* There are no wolves on the Island of Newfoundland.

winds and dropping temperatures, and it was definitely no time to linger on an open hillside. "Let's go, pardner," he said to the young sailor.

Grindley walked to the clifftop and looked down at the ship and the few battered bodies still floating in life jackets and pounding against the rocks. The superstructure was still upright. Goddamnit! If they had stayed put, not one life would have been lost. A great anger grew in him, an anger at the system that had led to the destruction of the *Pollux* and the death of her crew, both victims of the system. "One fool leading another fool," Grindley thought. A great sadness filled him too. With a little common sense this scene of death and destruction could have been prevented.

Silently, he turned and left.

They followed the sled tracks up over the hills and into the ravines. Grindley was completely numb from the waist down. They could see the smoke of the town rising above the next crest when his companion gave out.

"You go on, sir."

There was a lean-to shack up ahead, and Grindley got the young man to it. "I'll send help back," he said.

He walked into Iron Springs, alerted the people there of the young man in the lean-to, then walked on into St. Lawrence and aboard the USS *George E. Badger*. A quick going-over by the ship's doctor revealed frostbite, but no frozen limbs.

The young man in the lean-to was picked up, but Grindley never saw him again and never did learn his name.

32

St. Lawrence
February 19, 1942—Morning

Ensign Al Pollack, in the home of Albert Grimes, was thawing, and from head to toe Pollack's body was wracked with agonizing, excruciating pain. He lay on his stomach on a daybed in a little living room, his arms hanging over the sides, and shook so uncontrollably they had to hold on to him to prevent him from falling to the floor.

A Navy doctor had come by and given him morphine. It hadn't helped. "I can't give you any more, it'll kill you. You'll have to ride it out."

Pollack thought he was going to die, but the doctor comforted him. "If you're thawing, you're going to be all right. It's the guy who doesn't feel it we're worried about."

His body one great pulsating mass of intense pain, Ensign Pollack rode it out, crying like a child.

The liferaft had damaged the nerves in his leg. His limp would never disappear.

Lieutenant Bradley was carried aboard the USS *George E. Badger*, where he had to have several stitches in his arm. Lieutenant Dougherty, who had a broken ankle, also received medical attention.

Paul Pulver, whom Coleman and others had brought back to life on Lawn Head, later told Coleman a strange story. As he was freezing to death, he had met some of his dead relatives, he said. They were reaching for him, and he for them; their fingers had been a mere inch apart when he began to be brought back to life. He had not wanted to come back, he told Coleman.

As strange as the story was, it comforted George. It reinforced the Christian belief that when people did cross the Great Divide, they were met by their loved ones.

Harold E. Brooks, quartermaster first class, had arrived at Iron Springs on one of the sleds. He was so blinded by wood smoke that his eyes showed no whites, no pupils; they were an opaque gray.

Having gotten ashore on the breeches buoy his body was not as begrimed with oil, but his clothing was saturated, and he had somehow lost his footgear. They had put on an assortment of dry clothing; found a shoe for one foot and a gaiter for the other before Theo Etchegary and Alan Farrell put him in a truck with several others and went seeking a home for them.

Clara Tarrant had not slept at all. She had sent her daughters to bed around 4 A.M. but had kept watch over Don Fitzgerald, applying the heated bricks and plates to his thawing body. He had rambled on about his friends, rousing occasionally for hot coffee, and she was more than pleased with his progress. After daylight, a neighbor, Mrs. Slaney, came in to help.

Patrick had come home about 9:30 A.M. Wet, cold, and exhausted after helping to haul the men up over Big Head and keeping the survivors moving around the fire, he had fallen into bed and was sleeping soundly.

Theo and Alan came to her door about midmorning. "Can you take a man?" Theo asked.

"I can," she said promptly, "give me the sickest one you've got." Sure, I'm a fool, she told herself, but in the next moment when she saw Harold Brooks with his blank eyes, one bare foot in a shoe, she bustled toward him. "Come in, come in. Can you see at all?" She guided him to a chair.

"No, ma'am," Brooks replied, "I'm smoke blind." He explained further: "I *think* that's what happened. We were all around the wood fire . . . I didn't realize there was so much smoke."

The two women brought the galvanized tub into the kitchen, filled it with hot water, and between them got Brooks into it. They found the corner of a woolen Navy blanket across his chest. "I was afraid of getting penumonia," he explained, "I've had it before."

"Don't you worry, you won't get pneumonia," Clara said briskly.

They scrubbed him down as much as they could, hauled another couch from the parlor into the kitchen, dried and dressed Brooks, and guided him to it. He lay back as they packed heated bricks and plates around his body. Don Fitzgerald roused now and again to awareness of what was going on.

Clara fed them hot soup, and as Brooks showed an inclination to doze off, she said to him, "I'm going to put some drops in your eyes."

"Are you a nurse, ma'am?" he asked drowsily.

"No, I'm not a nurse, but I have some silver nitrate, which is good for babies' eyes, so it'll help your eyes."

She dropped the silver nitrate into his eyes and presently he slept. When he awakened four hours later, there were pinholes in the layer of gray covering his eyes. "I can see you," he cried, and added, "you look just like I thought you would."

Clara laughed and put more drops in his eyes.

It was past midmorning when the *Pollux* survivors who had walked from Lawn Head entered the mess hall of the Iron Springs Mine. They were stripped and cleaned off as much as possible by the St. Lawrence women, most of whom had not slept at all. A few had snatched an hour or two and had hurried back to the mine house to be on hand when the *Pollux*'s crew arrived.

They cleaned the sailors who badly needed it, despairing that their skin would ever be white again. Violet Pike vigorously scrubbed a sailor but could see no noticeable difference in the color of his skin. "My dear," she panted, "I can't seem to get the oil off."

The sailor groaned, "That's all right, ma'am, it won't come off. My skin is black."

Violet Pike was flabbergasted. She had never laid eyes on a black man in her whole life.

Nearby, Sam Nicosia chuckled heartily.

Larry Calemmo was given dungarees, shirts, two left boots, and a captain's blue uniform coat. He hastily refused the captain's coat, but was firmly made to put it on because there was nothing else.

Presently, those who were not too incapacitated were taken by

truck to the *Brant,* and Calemmo realized he was being given preferential treatment. First the truck driver had taken him up front in the
cab, out of the wind, and as he went to board the ship the skipper[1]
ran down from the bridge and put his arm around him. "This way,
Captain," he said.

Calemmo, barely able to keep his eyes open because of the oil,
said, "I'm a fireman first class, sir."

The skipper laughed, then indicated that he should follow his shipmates.

Later in the day the Navy came for the survivors. There was a
great tugging on the heartstrings. Most of the women were young
matrons and they had looked after the sailors as they would their
own children. The survivors clung to them as they would to their
mothers. They *were* their mothers.

James Seamans was still desperately ill, and Lillian Loder walked
beside the stretcher to the ship, holding his hand. Before they parted,
she took off her beret and put it on his head.

Clara Tarrant was not having it. The Navy had come to take Fitzgerald and Brooks aboard ship. Brooks was mobile and, after the
silver-nitrate treatments, his eyes were totally clear. Don Fitzgerald
was still sick and weak. "He's not strong enough to be moved yet,"
she stated; "you've got plenty of men to carry aboard, leave him with
me for another night; tomorrow he'll be better." She still had that ur-
gent feeling that he needed her.

In the face of such persuasion the U. S. Navy conceded that perhaps Fitzgerald would be better off under the ministrations of Mrs.
Tarrant for another day. They took Brooks with them and promised
to return tomorrow for Fitzgerald.

It was fairly late on Thursday when Ena Farrell, with her box
camera and her friends Julia Skinner and Ethel Giovannini, left for
Chambers Cove to record for posterity some of the action taking
place there. She had snapped some of the survivors outside her
home, and after the Navy had taken the young men away, the three
girls had skied over the hills to the scene of the disaster.

[1] Lieutenant Commander Lamar N. Wise was captain of the USS *Brant.*

The sea was much quieter today, lifting beneath the heavy layer of oil along the shoreline, yet resounding around the cove. The cliffs were coated with ugly black streaks of oil. The *Truxtun*'s forward section, lying on its starboard side, was awash; there was no sign of the stern or midsection.

The U. S. Navy was there with the Newfoundland men, searching the shoreline for bodies under the gelatinous coating of bunker oil covering the shore. This would go on for weeks as the sea gradually gave up some of the dead. The Navy was concerned about secret papers and, in particular, the decoding machine, which might conceivably fall into enemy hands. It was all very hush-hush.

There was not enough time for the girls to ski to Lawn Head for pictures of the *Pollux* today, and having taken snapshots of the activities they headed for home.

Wearing a captain's coat, Calemmo was due for more preferential treatment as they disembarked from the USS *Brant* onto the USS *Prairie* in Argentia some eight hours after leaving St. Lawrence. The whole ship's company assembled to watch them come aboard.

Calemmo approached the ladder and started up. His eyes were sore and only half open, and he was looking straight ahead. As he neared the top of the ladder he saw a few pairs of highly polished shoes, and above that were uniforms with a ton of stripes on them. Waiting on the landing was an admiral who hurried forward, placed an arm around Calemmo's shoulder, and said, "How are you, Captain, how do you feel?"

Larry said, "Sir, I'm a fireman first class."

The admiral dropped him like a hot potato.

It happened again in the dispensary when the doctor, a three-striper, made a fuss over him, but the doctor laughed when Calemmo told him his rank and, discovering Calemmo was Italian, went off and got him a large salami sandwich, a piece of apple pie, and a cupful of brandy.

Boy, what a meal that was!

At 2300 hours that night, Phillip Jewett died. He was the last one claimed by the tragedy.

PART THREE

The Court of Inquiry

33

Base Roger, Argentia
February 20, 1942

The *Wilkes* was the villain of the piece, as her crew were quick to learn. When she limped into Argentia at 0411 hours on February 19 and tied up at the tender, Commander Webb and Commander Kelsey were greeted brusquely by Rear Admiral Arthur LeRoy Bristol, Jr., Commander Support Force, U. S. Atlantic Fleet, ordered to rest up, and told to have their reports in by 0800 hours. The preparations for a court of inquiry had already begun.

Having gone without sleep for twenty-four hours and having less than four hours to put a solidly comprehensive report together was a formidable task, but both men submitted their statements to Vice Admiral Bristol within the allotted time.

On Friday, February 20, the inquiry got under way aboard the flagship USS *Prairie*. It was presided over by Captain Gail Morgan, USN; other members of the court were Captain Robert Fleming, USN; Lieutenant Commander Douglas P. Stickley, USN; and Commander George D. Martin, USN, as judge advocate. Lieutenant Commander John R. McKinney was ordered as counsel to assist the judge advocate, and Lieutenant W. H. Johnsen, USN, was ordered to assist the judge advocate in working up the reckoning of the ships. Reporters were William S. Edwards, Chief Yeoman, USN, and Calvin R. Underdown, Chief Yeoman, USN. Acting Pay Clerk Harvey R. Lampshire, USN, was detailed to act as assistant to the judge advocate.

Commander Webb, Commander Kelsey, Lieutenant Barrett, and

Lieutenant Smyth, having a concern in the proceedings, were named "interested" parties. The court, after reading the statements of Webb and Kelsey, arbitrarily offered them in evidence for the purpose of reading the reports into the record, and designated the two men as defendants. As such they would not be required to testify at the inquiry on the grounds that their testimony might incriminate them, which meant that, depending on the outcome of the inquiry, there was the distinct possibility—if not certainty—that they would face charges of negligence and have to bear the disgrace of a court-martial.

Both men requested counsel, and on the following day, with the permission of the court, Commander Webb introduced Lieutenant Commander Archibald G. W. McFadden, USN, as his counsel. Commander Kelsey introduced Lieutenant Commander Llewellyn J. Johns, USN, as his counsel. Lieutenant Smyth was unable to find a counsel to represent his interests—rather intimidating when rumor had reached them that a group of officers, looking down upon what was left of the *Pollux,* had said: "We're gonna get those guys. Somebody is gonna get it for this."

Commander Kelsey questioned the legality of introducing the reports he and Commander Webb had hastily put together into evidence, and objected to their incorporation in the record when he and Webb were available as witnesses, but the court announced that the objection was not sustained.

Lieutenant William Smyth was the first witness to be interrogated. Traditionally the prospect of looking down the long green table was something to be dreaded, and when Smyth saw the cold, stern faces of the board members he had the gut feeling that all was not going to go well for them. Fleetingly he wondered what constituted the background of the president of the inquiry, prior to this court. Had he ever commanded a convoy or passed through any dangerous and treacherous waters, worrying about the elements and the U-boat threat? It wasn't likely.

The court asked questions that permitted none of the worries and anxieties of Smyth's watch to be recorded. He explained in detail the difficulties of maintaining station on the *Pollux,* which, according to radar bearings, wandered considerably. Neither the board members nor the *Wilkes'* crew were aware at this time that radar could have been at fault.

"Were any reports made to you of the depth of water or readings of the fathometer, and how often during the watch?" the court asked.

"No readings were reported to me," Smyth replied: "however, at 0230 I asked the quartermaster the following questions: (1) if the fifty-fathom curve had been crossed; (2) the time the navigator wished to be called. I received the following answers: (1) negative, about eighty fathoms; (2) about 0300. I knew negative was in error because the statement about eighty fathoms confirmed in my mind that we had passed the fifty-fathom curve and were adhering to the ship's track according to the night orders and my recollection of our position on the chart."

In detail, Smyth recounted his actions on the bridge. Having no idea at this time that the *Pollux* had actually sent a message to the *Wilkes* at 0115 or thereabouts, and unaware of the significance of it, he told the court of the exchange of calls. At this time the court did not know of its significance either. Eventually the court asked some very pointed questions: "Did you check the navigational position of the ship at any time during the watch?"

Smyth explained the procedure of studying the ship's position and where she was scheduled to be at different times *before* taking the watch. "During darkened ship conditions the officer of the deck cannot afford to impair his vision by looking at a steady light or lighted chart for any time," he told the court.

"Did you have your junior officer of the watch check the navigational position of the ship at any time during the watch?" the judge advocate asked.

"No, sir," Smyth replied, but did not explain that the junior officer of the deck was inexperienced in this area.

"Did you have anyone else check the navigational position of the ship during the watch?"

He replied that he had not.

"Were you making any allowance in steering for leeway due to wind or sea?"

"No, sir. I adhered to the assigned zigzag plan on base course 047 true."

The court asked, "Was the navigational position of the ship fixed at *any* time during your watch to the best of your knowledge?"

"Yes, sir, I believe it was," Smyth replied. "I had the navigator called at 0300. I checked the quartermaster at 0315 and asked him if the navigator had been called. I received an affirmative answer. At 0345 when Ensign Winslow entered the charthouse I looked in and saw that the navigator was in the charthouse at the time and appeared to be taking fathometer readings."

The court deliberated, then informed Smyth that his testimony indicated a probability that he did not take positive action either to plot the position of the ship by all means available or to determine positively that someone else was doing this during his watch. "You are advised at the present time of your status as a defendant and advised to obtain counsel. You are also advised that you have the privilege of withdrawing from the stand as a witness and may act as a witness hereafter only on your own request."

Smyth explained that he had been unsuccessful in trying to obtain counsel and requested that counsel be designated for him.

It was done. Lieutenant Commander James O. Banks, Jr., was so chosen.

On Saturday afternoon the navigator, Lieutenant Arthur J. Barrett, Jr., was called as a witness. In the course of his interrogation he was asked: "Do you have in your navigational files, Commander-in-Chief United States Atlantic Fleet restricted letter H1/(1691) dated July 25, 1941, subject: Faulty Soundings on Hydrographic Office Chart No. 1103?"

This letter,[1] signed by Admiral Ernest J. King, had been released July 25, 1941, directing attention to the serious differences between actual and charted depths in Placentia Bay. A resurvey of Placentia Bay and the approach thereto would be undertaken in the spring of 1942.

Barrett replied, "No, sir, I do not."

"Do you know whether or not you have it in your ship's files?"

"We do not have it in the ship's files," Barrett admitted.

He described the events that had taken place from the time he had come to the bridge at 0315 to the time Commander Kelsey and Commander Webb had been alerted to the fact that they were north of their course.

"Did you at this time advise Commander Webb that a change of course was advisable?" the judge advocate asked.

"No, sir."

[1] See Appendix G.

"Did you at this time advise Commander Kelsey that a change of course was advisable?"

"No, sir."

In short order, Barrett was also named a defendant because ". . . with evidence showing that the ship was probably north of the plotted course and approaching landfall, he did not, over a period of a number of minutes of time, advise the change of course to return to the plotted course, and a knowledge on his part that the ship was in what was on the danger side of the plotted course."

So ended the first day of the inquiry.

In comparison to the grim, unhappy scene aboard the *Prairie* in Argentia, it was a brilliant, sparkling day outside. In St. Lawrence, Ena Farrell and her friends decided it was the perfect day to ski to Lawn Point to get pictures of the shipwreck. They started about midday.

Henry Lambert and a party of American sailors were already easing toward the *Pollux* in a small schooner. The ship's bow was gone; the middle section with the forward holds was still intact but appeared to be barely hitched to the rocks. The stern had broken off but was not completely loose; it would undoubtedly part very soon —at any moment, in fact. She leaned to the right on a 30° angle so that the starboard side of the lower bridge was awash.

A moderate sea was running and occasionally the *Pollux* moved as the waves rolled through her and the muffled clang of a door rolled across the sea toward them, activating their imagination, sending prickles of fear up their spine.

They maneuvered the little schooner through the fuel oil and wreckage in the lee of the ship, secured a line to the railing, and Henry Lambert fearlessly climbed aboard. Before the others could follow, a slightly heavier wave rushed through the *Pollux,* causing her to move on the rocks and the door to bang alarmingly. The wind moaning through her struck a chill into the hearts of the bravest. The young officer in charge of the boarding party changed his mind about boarding and ordered Henry off the ship.

Henry said he was perfectly willing to take his chances and explore below deck, but another wave, another moaning tremor, and the eerie banging of the door were too much. The officer urgently signaled Henry into the schooner. Reluctantly, Henry slid down the line, and with all due haste the schooner was backed away.

It was much later that Ena, Ethel Giovannini, and Julia Skinner reached Lawn Point. The ice had disappeared under a covering of snow since Wednesday night, and it was easy to walk right down to the water's edge where Garnaus, Greenfield, and DeRosa had had to hack their way up with knives. In spite of all the girls had heard, it was difficult for them to believe that so many men had died trying to get ashore. *The ship was so close.*

They did not like the sounds issuing from the *Pollux* any more than the Americans had. Ena snapped several pictures, and with tingling spines, visions of dead sailors and ghostly hands slamming that door, they hurried away from the *Pollux*. The sounds followed them for a long time.

On Sunday a storm spun up from the southwest and once more great seas slammed against the coast. The *Pollux* slipped from the rocks and vanished. There was no one to see her go.

During this same storm, what was left of the *Truxtun* was pushed closer to the strip of shingle beneath the rock wall that had claimed so many of her crew. To this time the bodies of Lieutenant Commander Ralph Hickox and eleven crew members were still aboard.

Meanwhile the U. S. Navy had ordered a lightship with a radio beacon to Argentia, and negotiations were already under way with the French people of St. Pierre and Miquelon to re-establish Gallantry Head light.

34

On this stormy Sunday Ensign Henry B. Quekemeyer was called before the court of inquiry. He outlined his duties as given to him by the officer of the deck.

"Did anyone direct you to fix or attempt to fix the navigational position of the ship while you were on watch?" the judge advocate asked.

"No, sir."

Commander John Kelsey, defendant, asked: "Did you make any effort to plot the fathometer soundings?"

"No, sir."

"Did you make any report concerning the soundings?"

"No, sir, I didn't, other than that they were being taken every fifteen minutes and logged."

"Was the time of crossing the 50-fathom curve noted from the results obtained by fathometer?"

"I didn't make any note of it, sir," he told Commander Kelsey. "However, I can say that the officer of the deck asked the quartermaster if we had crossed the 50-fathom curve, and his answer was 'No.'"

"At what time was this?"

"I cannot say, sir. I don't know."

Quekemeyer could not say if the fathometer soundings indicated that the ship had crossed the 50-fathom curve, nor had he heard anything else during the course of his watch concerning it.

Questioned about bearings 190 and 340, he said, "We had a bearing at 190, distance approximately 3,500 yards, which we could not understand, and at about the same time we got another bearing of 340, distance 6 miles, which we assumed was land."

"What did you assume was bearing 190?" the court asked.

"We assumed that it was the *Pollux*. We thought she had messed up the zigzag plan as she had done during previous watches," Quekemeyer said.

"Did you report the fact that you thought you had land, bearing at 340, to anyone?"

Quekemeyer admitted, "I did not make that report."

"Did *anyone* make that report to the officer of the deck, the captain, the navigator, or the division commander?" the court demanded.

Ensign Quekemeyer was quite sure the report was made to the officer of the deck, but by whom he could not say. "I know the officer of the deck was told by someone because when that bearing came out along with the one at 190 he told me personally to check the radar again." Then he had confirmed to the officer of the deck that there was something out there at 190, he said.

He was questioned about Commander Kelsey's order to check the limiting bearings of 340 in the moments before grounding. "Do you know whether any reply was made to the captain's request for a check on the limiting bearings?"

"No, sir, I don't," Quekemeyer said.

"Did the captain wait in the radar room?"

"No, sir."

"Were those bearings verified?"

"Yes, sir, we checked the bearings."

"Then what did you do?"

"I didn't do anything."

"What was done to convey this information to the captain?" the judge advocate wanted to know.

"The only thing that was done was that Ensign Winslow stepped inside from the bridge into the charthouse and was given the bearings 350 to 020, distance 2,700 yards, and this information was conveyed to the captain."

Quekemeyer testified that he had taken readings on radar previously but had never taken readings of land and therefore could not perfectly identify the 340 bearing as land, even though he had assumed it was land because of the distance—approximately 6 miles when he had first observed it.

"Did you then believe you were that close to land?" asked the court.

"No, sir, I didn't," Quekemeyer replied.

"Then, so far as the information and experience at your command, that reading might have disclosed the presence of an unknown ship?"

"Yes, sir."

Now the defendants began to establish that this important information had not been passed along to them. Lieutenant Smyth asked Quekemeyer: "Did you then report to the officer of the deck, the captain, or the division commander that there was an unidentified object on the bearing 340, distance 12,000 yards?"

"No, sir."

Commander Webb, defendant, asked: "Did you know whether *anyone* reported radar contact bearing 340 to the division commander?"

"No, sir."

Smyth asked: "Did the radar operator report such a bearing to your knowledge?"

"To my knowledge, I don't know," Quekemeyer confessed.

Lieutenant Barrett, defendant, made a statement to the court: "I would like to call the attention of the court to the fact that the night order book stated that the 50-fathom curve should be crossed at 0130. I would also like to call the attention of the court to the fact that the 50-fathom curve was actually crossed sometime between 0008 and 0038, as shown in the book of fathometer readings." He turned to Quekemeyer and asked, "Was the navigator [Barrett] notified that the 50-fathom curve had been crossed sooner than expected?"

"To the best of my knowledge, no, sir."

Barrett made another statement to the court: "I would like to call the attention of the witness to the fact that this has been previously introduced as evidence in the night order book to the fact that a 50-fathom curve should be crossed at 0130. I would also like to call the attention of the witness to the fact as shown in the book of

fathometer readings, the 50-fathom curve was actually crossed sometime between 0008 and 0038." He then asked the young ensign:
"Was the navigator notified that the 50-fathom curve had been
crossed earlier than the expected time?"

"To the best of my knowledge, no, sir."

The court asked about the limiting bearings taken just before
grounding: "What was the heading of the ship when you took the
radar readings 350 to 020?"

Henry replied: "I don't know, sir." He was quite distressed by this
time.

The court told him: "You are privileged to make any further
statement covering anything relative to the subject matter of the inquiry that you think should be a matter of record in connection
therewith, that has not been fully brought out by the previous questioning."

Henry replied: "I would like to say that the officer of the deck,
Mr. Smyth, has always created a favorable impression upon me. In
my naval career he has been the only officer of the deck who has
ever outlined definite duties for me to do. He invariably would give
me a check-off list and see that I performed those duties. I have
never on my cruise since I left the Academy seen him sit down on
watch—that is, in the chair that is provided for him while he was the
officer of the deck. He was always out on the wing of the bridge as
much as possible. I was favorably impressed with the fact that he
could take the wind and cold that is encountered in the North Atlantic. I am afraid that I cannot take the weather always as he. He instructed me to be on the wing of the bridge more. Those kind of
statements have clearly and favorably impressed upon my mind just
what kind of a watch he wanted me to stand. That is all I have to
say."

It may not have impressed the court, but Smyth was surprised and
gratified by the tribute from the young ensign.

It was obvious that Ensign Quekemeyer had followed orders to the
letter but, in his inexperience, had exercised no judgment of his own.

Seaman First Class James McPherson, who had been operating
radar since January, testified that he did not report the crucial radar
bearing 340 because the junior officer of the deck was behind him
and observing.

"Did you report this bearing to anyone?" the judge advocate asked.

"Yes, sir, to the navigator, Lieutenant Barrett," he replied.

"Did you report personally to Lieutenant Barrett?"

"Yes, sir."

"Did you make any comment [to the navigator] on this bearing as to what it may be on?"

"No, sir," McPherson said. He too had exercised no judgment.

Lieutenant (jg) Overton D. Hughlett, as communications officer and OOD, explained the operation of radar to the court, describing the effects of overheating. When radar was in this condition it was difficult to get any pips at all on the screen, he told them. However, the condition of the radar equipment aboard the *Wilkes* at this time was excellent, he told the court.

Commander Walter Webb, defendant, asked: "Is it possible that the ice affected radar?"

"It is possible," said Hughlett.

Other than Smyth's testimony earlier of the erratic bearings of radar during his watch, the court did not probe into the possibility of its unreliability.

To affirm to the court that he had not been delinquent in his duties, Smyth, as a defendant, asked: "Is it customary for the officer of the deck on the *Wilkes* to plot positions of the vessel on the chart *during* the watch while on escort duty?"

"In open waters, no, sir," Hughlett replied. "Upon reading night orders, coming on watch, he does not plot the ship's position but studies the charts."

Smyth had done that.

The salient points emerged as nineteen members of the *Wilkes'* crew connected with the crucial watches told their stories, and there seemed to have been a preponderance of errors, each one in itself insignificant, but cumulatively resulting in disaster.

Lieutenant W. H. Johnsen reconstructed Lieutenant Barrett's navigational data, and for four days the court took apart the course of the *Wilkes,* but the fact that emerged was that course 047 degrees true, which had been laid to offset the indraft of current on the eastern side of Placentia Bay and the northwest set westward of Cape Race, had not made enough allowance for leeway. The *Wilkes* was acted upon by a current of .93 knot from 0623 hours the day before, he stated.

The *Wilkes'* course line as laid off from her 2000 hours estimated position apparently did not allow for any current at all, Johnsen said. If a .5-knot current had been allowed, the *Wilkes* would have passed approximately 5 miles abeam of the rock to the south of Corbin Head.

Commander Webb disagreed. "Did not the course laid down by the navigator of the *Wilkes* head for the middle of the entrance to Placentia Bay?"

"The course by the navigator of the *Wilkes* headed his ship a little east of the center of Placentia Bay," Johnsen conceded.

"Therefore, did not the navigator of the *Wilkes* allow for possible set from any direction?"

"Yes," Johnsen said.

Asked by Commander Webb if he considered the charts for the area to be accurate, Johnsen replied, "No, sir, not in all respects."

"If you have to depend on navigation by soundings alone, can you do so with safety?" Webb asked.

"I do not think that I could navigate with safety using the charted depths alone," Johnsen confessed.

He did not refer to the incorrect star fix that had, on the chart, mistakenly put the *Wilkes* farther to the east than she actually was, but he did conclude that the 2000-hour position of the *Wilkes* as he had worked it out was *5.5 miles westerly* of Lieutenant Barrett's 2000-hour position, and the dead-reckoning tracer position was 2 miles to the northward of that, indicating, Johnsen said, existence of a current.

Commander Webb suggested that a severe earthquake and tidal wave that had rocked Newfoundland in 1929, devastating that very area, might have changed some of the soundings.

This suggestion was not accepted by the court, considering that chart No. 981, which they had been using, had corrections to 1934.

On the fifth day, Tuesday, February 24, the *Wilkes* limped out of Argentia for Boston and repairs at the Navy Yard, leaving behind those members of the crew who were testifying at the inquiry. With mixed emotions they watched their ship, in the hands of another crew, steam away.

Signalman Second Class Carl William Schmidt faced the court this day. The judge advocate, Commander George D. Martin, queried him about any signals sent and received during the 0000–0400 watch. There had been no signals, Schmidt said, only an exchange of calls. Exchange of calls identified a ship and her position and were not recorded in the signal log. To this time, none of the *Pollux* crew had been called and, officially at least, no one was aware of the message sent to the *Wilkes* between 0115 and 0130 hours.

Nolfi corroborated Smyth's testimony that at about 0230 he (Nolfi) had reported to the OOD an 80-fathom crossing instead of the expected 50-fathom crossing at 0138.

On Wednesday, February 25, a week after the three ships had grounded, Washington released the information about the disaster to the newspapers. With the announcement, Franklin Delano Roosevelt sent the following message to the people of St. Lawrence, Newfoundland:

I have just learned of the magnificent and courageous work you rendered and of the sacrifices you made in rescuing and caring for the personnel of the United States ships which grounded on your shore. As Commander-in-Chief and on behalf of the Navy, and as President of the United States, and on behalf of our citizens, I wish to express my most grateful appreciation of your heroic action, which is typical of the history of your proud, seafaring community.

The eight men from Lawn who had saved most of the crew of the *Pollux* had inadvertently been overlooked in President Roosevelt's message. This blunder occurred because the U. S. Navy had been unaware that another community had been involved, as the little band of men had quietly and inconspicuously returned to their homes in Lawn, eight to ten miles from St. Lawrence, as soon as they had dropped the survivors at the mine house.

On this same day the court of inquiry gathered at Barrack No. 7, where the *Pollux/Truxtun* crews, designated the P/T Unit under command of Commander Turney, were still recuperating from various injuries and degrees of frostbite. They still suffered nightmares and woke up screaming and weeping for their lost friends. Ensign Alfred Pollack (*Pollux*), was on crutches. Boatswain's Mate George Coleman (*Pollux*), was very distressed; his body had reacted to exposure by blowing up like a balloon and his weight had shot up from 168 pounds to 190 pounds.

It would take George two years of constant exercising to get back to normal weight.

It was touch and go whether or not Wayne Brewer's feet would turn gangrenous. They did not, but they would always cause him considerable pain. He could not forget Edenfield's rash behavior, and at the first opportunity had sought out his shipmate, who had been so badly knocked about he was barely recognizable. Presently, Brewer asked, "Why did you jump back into the sea, Edenfield?"

Edenfield's eyes stared thoughtfully out of his battered, swollen face. "I don't know," he replied.

Commander Turney had shown great concern for the welfare and suffering of the survivors. It was obvious that he was still anguished over the loss of his men, and he had made frequent appearances at the naval barracks. Grindley was impressed by it; no wonder they all loved the man.

It would also impress the court.

The *Pollux* crew, dressed in hand-me-down clothing, were assembled before the court and informed of the subject matter of the inquiry. The judge advocate read Commander Turney's report of the loss of the *Pollux*. It was a straightforward report, greatly detailed in the heroic actions of his crew, but with no mention of the hours of agony and indecision about changing course before the grounding.

The judge advocate then addressed Commander Turney: "Have you any objection to make in regard to the narrative just read to the court, or anything to lay to the charge of any officer or man with regard to the loss of the United States ship *Pollux?*"

Turney replied: "No, sir."

Judge Advocate Martin addressed the crew. "Have you any objection to make in regard to the narrative just read to the court, or anything to lay to the charge of any officer or man with regard to the loss of the United States ship *Pollux?*"

Lieutenant Grindley was taken aback. What should he do? He had not been asked for a report of the hours before the grounding. Was this the proper time to make a charge that his advice had been disregarded? Considering that they had been under the order of the *Wilkes* was it relevant anyway? Looking at Commander Turney's ravaged face, the haunted eyes, he felt great sympathy for the man and thought, "Not now." Later, when he took the stand, as he no doubt would, then he would tell it as it was. Turney would tell it as it was.

Grindley let the opportunity pass.

The same procedure applied to the *Truxtun* men, also attired in a variety of clothing, when Ensign Maddocks' report was read to the pitiful remnants of the crew.

At this stage of the proceedings it appeared to the court that Commander Hugh W. Turney, Lieutenant (jg) William C. Grindley, USNR, of the *Pollux,* and Ensign William J. Maddocks, USN, and Ensign Frederick A. Loughridge, USNR, of the *Truxtun* had an "interest" in the subject matter of the inquiry. They were accordingly called before the court and advised to that effect, and that they would be allowed to be present during the course of the inquiry, examine witnesses, and introduce new matter pertinent to the inquiry in the same manner as the other defendants, Webb, Kelsey, Barrett, and Smyth.

Retiring to the *Prairie* to continue the inquiry, the court announced that on further consideration of evidence that had been adduced, the court designated Commander Turney and Lieutenant Grindley as defendants. They were advised of their change of status.

Grindley's heart sank. To be named a defendant was a polite way of saying you were as guilty as hell in the eyes of the Navy Department. As a defendant he would not be called to testify; therefore his story would not be told unless he made a point of volunteering as a witness, and he was undecided about that.

There appeared to be a dearth of legal counselors at Base Roger. Commander Turney introduced his supply officer, Lieutenant Paul L. Weintraub, USN, as his counsel, and Lieutenant Grindley introduced Lieutenant (jg) Russell J. Schmidt, USNR, the communications officer of the *Pollux,* as his counsel.

The inquiry continued, and through the rigid formality of specific answers to specific questions the *Wilkes, Pollux, Truxtun* story unfolded. No hearsay evidence was admissible.

From Commander John Gabrielson, Lieutenant Weintraub, and Ensign Robert Grayson came stories of the great heroism of the officers and enlisted men of the *Pollux* and the Newfoundland men. None of the officers questioned had apparently witnessed the dissension between Turney and Grindley. The subject was not raised.

The information about the 0130 message transmitted to the *Wilkes* came from Grayson's testimony when the judge advocate asked him if he had seen the lights of any other ship during his watch.

"I saw the lights of the *Wilkes*," Grayson replied, explaining that they had been sending a signal to the flagship. "The exact wording was, I believe, 'Have changed my base course 10° to the right.' "

"Do you know whether or not the *Wilkes* acknowledged for the signal?" the judge advocate asked.

Grayson replied, "The *Wilkes* dashed for each word."

Here was a statement that was diametrically opposed to that of Signalman Carl Schmidt, who had said there had been only an exchange of calls between the two ships at that time.

"You saw this yourself?" asked the judge advocate.

"I saw this."

"Did the *Wilkes* acknowledge receipt of this message after the end of the transmission?"

"I did not see 'Roger,' " Grayson admitted.

Following this information the court decided that Signalman Second Class Carl W. Schmidt had an "interest" in the subject matter of the inquiry. He was so informed and advised to get counsel. Schmidt requested that counsel be detailed for him. Arrangements were made for Lieutenant Commander Banks to act as counsel for him as well as for Smyth.

Lieutenant (jg) George Bradley, officer of the deck of the *Pollux,* was named an interested party because he had been on duty watch at the time of the grounding. Lieutenant (jg) George Bollinger had not immediately reported the sighting of land, which he had seen silhouetted in the *Wilkes'* searchlight, but had crossed from one side of the flying bridge to the other first. He, too, became an interested party.

Schmidt was recalled and examined by the judge advocate, who told him to state specifically the exact procedure that had taken place from the *Wilkes* in regard to the 0130 message.

Who could say what the Navy veteran's feelings were as he faced his superiors? A good man, tried and true in his duties, one of the best.

He told them in detail about the exchange of calls in stormy weather and low visibility, and the one flash he had seen after he had given the *Pollux* a "King" to go ahead. He had used the small blinker gun, he said.

"Did you keep the signal gun trained in the direction of the *Pollux* after you gave him the 'King'?" asked Commander Martin.

"I do not recall whether or not I did, but I think that I did keep the blinker-gun rays on the shield," he replied.

"Did you operate the key or trigger of the blinker gun after you gave the 'King' to the *Pollux?*" Commander Martin asked.

"No, sir, I did not."

"Is it true then that during the time you were on watch you did not receive any other intelligible message except the exchange of calls from the *Pollux?*"

"Yes, sir, that is true," Schmidt replied.

On the seventeenth day after Signalman Schmidt of the *Wilkes* had finished his testimony, all defendants and interested parties were informed that if they desired to call witnesses from either the *Pollux* or the *Wilkes* they should do so, as such witnesses might not be available at future proceedings due to the demands and exigencies of the war situation. This looked very much as if the court of inquiry was drawing to a close.

On the following day, Monday, March 9, Captain Gail Morgan, president of the court of inquiry, made a statement: "The convening authority, Admiral Bristol, this date, instructed the president of the court of inquiry to complete and terminate the taking of testimony at this day's meeting in view of the exigencies of wartime operational requirements, and the necessity for returning all personnel possible to wartime duties at the earliest possible date, and further, due to the fact that considerable time had already been taken to bring out all facts in the case under inquiry." He addressed the judge advocate: "You will call witnesses and take action to permit termination of taking of evidence by the court and the taking of such evidence by defendants and interested parties."

The court of inquiry was being cut short.

Commander George Martin replied: "The judge advocate would like to have it made a matter of record that no witnesses from the *Truxtun* have yet been called and that it was the intention of the judge advocate to call at least ten enlisted-men witnesses and three officers from the *Truxtun*." However, as instructed, the proceedings would be terminated at the end of the day.

Only Maddocks and Loughridge, as interested parties, gave testimony to the events that led to the loss of the *Truxtun*. Their watches had been routine, they said, and neither officer had any apprehension as to the *Truxtun*'s position. Both had been confident the ship was adhering to her dead-reckoning track and all was well. The navigator, Lieutenant A. L. Newman, had been the senior officer on the bridge and made all decisions.

Two more witnesses were called: Commander George Wheeler Wilson, USN, senior medical officer of the naval operating base, Argentia, testified that the dead sailors had died by drowning and exposure. To this date, March 9, only forty-eight bodies had been interred in Argentia, but every day bodies were being recovered, with burial taking place in a special section of the St. Lawrence Cemetery.

Lieutenant Commander Eugene M. Waldron, also of the staff of the USS *Prairie*, had commanded the destroyer USS *Dupont* in 1941, and having operated in the Placentia Bay area, was called to testify about the currents in the area. He told the court that in these waters he had encountered currents that set him to the westward and to the eastward, but never to the southward.

"To your mind," the judge advocate asked, "does the coast pilot of Newfoundland give you a clear picture of the currents in this area?"

"No, sir," he replied. "I found the currents to be rather unpredictable."

The *Wilkes* had not fired rockets to warn the *Truxtun* or the *Pollux,* which seemed incomprehensible to the court. Waldron was asked: "If, while escorting a convoy, you saw rockets, what would you assume?"

He replied, "That torpedo attack had been made on one or more of the ships in convoy."

"What would you do in such case?"

"I would proceed immediately to that spot if it were in my sector."

The court asked, "Could the escort commander in his discretion use rockets for other purposes than indicating torpedo attack and still comply with any existing general instructions on use of rockets?"

"I would say that orders would have to be laid down prior to the occurrence in order to eliminate any chance of an ambiguous meaning," Lieutenant Commander Waldron said.

This testimony from another destroyer commander appeared to vindicate the action not taken by the *Wilkes* to shoot off rockets when she grounded.

The court asked all defendants and interested parties if they desired to make a statement. Grindley, Bradley, and Bollinger, conferring among themselves, decided against it. If the inquiry was finished, what could they say? Grindley, more or less in a vacuum because no official legal counselor had been assigned to him, unwisely made the decision that now was not the time to make a statement that his advice for a drastic change of course had not been heeded. He knew by the tenor of the court of inquiry that the defendants might all be facing court-martial. His story would have to wait.

All defendants and interested parties said nothing. Then the court asked all defendants for their *written arguments*.

Grindley, as a defendant, was very surprised as Webb, Kelsey, Turney, Barrett, and Smyth unfolded their written arguments. All except Grindley had one to present to the court. What the hell was going on? He had not been advised that he could put together an argument that would tell his side of the story. What should he do? Nothing, he told himself; he had no choice now but to wait for the court-martial.

In his argument, Commander Webb reiterated the factors that he considered had caused the groundings: a current of unheard-of velocity, deficient and inaccurate chart soundings, failure of mechanical navigational aids, bad weather, low visibility, and war conditions and orders that required risks to be taken.

He had, he stressed, given the *Pollux* the usual freedom of action during the night in case she needed to change course.

Radar, he reminded the court, gave no indication of the presence of land closer than the one bearing of 340° true, just before grounding, and that the bearing of 20° true was well to the left of the base course of the *Wilkes* when she struck.

Equally as important was the submarine danger, which strictly limited communications at night. The zigzag plan that had been ordered by higher authority added to the danger and difficulty of navigation, while a time of arrival had been set that required fairly high speed and necessitated entering restricted waters during darkness. He said, "I imply no criticism of either of these orders. Undoubtedly there were sound reasons behind them. I mentioned them only to point out why certain things were done, or not done. Naturally, I did not question my orders."

Commander Turney submitted that the *Pollux* was well organized, efficiently manned, and skillfully navigated. All navigational equipment was in excellent material condition and the charts were corrected up to date. The fathometer soundings gave no indication that the ship was not on her plotted course, he said.

Neither the commanding officer, the navigator, the officer of the deck, or any person aboard had any apprehension or indication that the ship was being carried into dangerous waters. The change of course to the right was made only in line with the commanding officer's policy of adhering as nearly as possible to the middle of safe waters.

He recounted the events that took place and submitted that the *Pollux* grounded as a result of her attempt to escape enemy craft by making a run for safe waters under cover of darkness and poor visibility.

Again Grindley was taken by surprise. His commanding officer had said nothing in his written argument about their disagreements; had not indicated that Grindley had been pleading for a change of course hours before the grounding. *Was* it relevant, then, since the commanding officer had to take the blame anyway? Grindley was no fool, but he knew he was out of his depth. The merchant Navy operated in a pretty straightforward way, but the U. S. Navy with its brilliant, ambitious Annapolis men was something else. As a merchant Navy man caught up in the intricacies of U. S. naval law he decided it was more practical to say nothing at this court of inquiry . . . the right time would come at his own court-martial.

Recapping his statement made earlier, Commander Kelsey disputed the court navigator's assumption that there had been a northerly set from 0623 hours, but he felt that the ship had been subjected to a variable current that was of tremendous force during the period 2000 hours to 0410 hours—"far beyond anything indicated by coast pilots," he said.

Lieutenant Barrett pointed out: "Although information that the ship was not making good the track of 047° as laid down by the navigator was at variance with the information in the captain's night order book, it was not reported to the division commander, the commanding officer, or himself."

Lieutenant Smyth refuted the allegations of the court that he had not thoroughly acquainted himself with the position of the ship with reference to vessels in sight, any land, etc., or that he did not take positive action to plot the position of the ship or determine positively that somone else was doing this during his watch.

He had checked the hourly prospective positions to familiarize himself with the location of the vessel during his watch as required by Navy regulations. All instructions laid down in the night order book had been carried out.

The navigator, he said, was in the charthouse at 0315 and had obtained a DRT at 0325 hours that was north of the track of the vessel. *This fact had not been reported to him as the OOD.*

The JOOD was a newly commissioned ensign and considered unreliable to plot any position of the vessel by soundings, and it would have been unsafe and unsound for him, Smyth, to go into the charthouse and leave the controls unattended in the hands of an inexperienced officer or unqualified personnel. It would have impaired his night vision and his efficiency.

He had not turned over the watch to Ensign Winslow, he said, "not because I suspected the *Wilkes* to be in dangerous waters, but because I was uncertain as to her position on the guide, the *Pollux*. I wanted the *Wilkes* to be on station before turning over the responsibility of the deck to a relatively inexperienced watch officer."

The judge advocate, Commander George D. Martin, read his argument, summarizing the events leading to the grounding of the *Wilkes*. "Accepting the fact that the courses of the *Wilkes* laid down from the last fix obtained at 0623 would have carried the ship clear of land, the fact remains that the *Wilkes* did run aground and therefore did experience a set for which the proper allowance was not made.

"It also appears that no instructions or regulations were issued for the convoy as to ceasing zigzagging during thick weather and at night, which, according to war instructions, should normally be done under such circumstances, the responsibility resting with the senior officer present."

The commanding officer, he felt, having been notified by the navigator that the ship was to the northward of the track, and having received notice of a radar contact landward at 0405, had sufficient warning to demand immediate action.

Having been informed of bearing 340° true, distance eight miles at 0315, the navigator should immediately have been warned of danger to a degree necessitating more immediate positive action than merely trying to more accurately fix the ship's position and eventually calling the captain thirty-five minutes later.

The judge advocate submitted that the cause of the grounding of the ships was the failure to set a safe course under existing circumstances, believed to be errors in judgment more than failure of action.

With great efficiency the court of inquiry was brought to a close.

The *Wilkes'* crew involved with the groundings, and the *P/T* Unit, sailed for Boston. The *P/T* Unit, not fully recovered and extremely nervous after the battering they had received, sailed on the USS *Tarazad*. A storm tossed the ship about, but nothing was going to get the majority of these sailors below decks where they could be trapped if the ship happened to be torpedoed. As the seas fell over the ship they found it difficult to control their fright. In their highly nervous condition they dozed fitfully and still cried out for the friends they had watched die.

Once in Boston and on home ground, they were dispatched to the hospital. Seamans would be there for five months.

Meanwhile the court was making its decisions. These decisions would not be made known to the defendants until the ax was ready to fall.

Theo Etchegary (above) and Mike Turpin, two of the Newfound-landers who spent long hours rescuing men from the sea.

Some of the other Newfoundlanders today: Patrick and Clara Tarrant
(top left), Henry Lambert (top right), Joseph Manning (bottom left),
and Lillian Loder (bottom right).

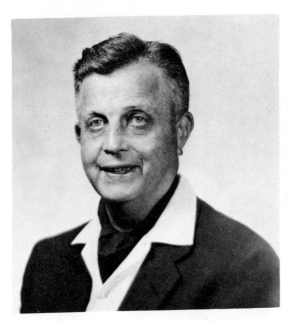

William A. Smyth today. Captain William C. Grindley in 1951.

Laurence A. Weaver, May 1977.

Lawrence J. Calemmo, chief warrant officer, in 1972.

Alfred M. Dupuy as he is today.

Warren A. Greenfield.

At a reunion in New York, May 1977 (from left to right): Walter C. Bulanowski, Ernest Califano, Thomas McCarron, Lawrence Calemmo, and Warren Greenfield. (Courtesy of Warren Greenfield)

James O. Seamans revisited St. Lawrence in 1964. He posed beneath the flag of the *Truxtun*, which was salvaged from the wreck by a Newfoundlander and later framed and hung in the lobby of the St. Lawrence Hospital built by the U. S. Government.

Author Cassie Brown stands in the ravine near the crest of the hill at Lawn Head where survivors of the *Pollux* spent the night. (Derek Brown)

IN MEMORY OF
THE
OFFICERS AND ENLISTED MEN
OF THE U.S. NAVY
WHO LOST THEIR LIVES
IN THE DISASTER OF
— THE —
U.S.S. POLLUX AND U.S.S. TRUXTUN
FEBRUARY 18, 1942

(Courtesy of Cathleen Barnier)

35

Findings of the Court of Inquiry

It was the opinion of the court of inquiry that the cause of the grounding of the USS *Wilkes,* the USS *Pollux,* and the USS *Truxtun* was the failure of the senior officer present, Commander Walter W. Webb, USN, to take prompt and effective action to set a safe course. That in the case of each ship the cause of grounding was the failure of each commanding officer to set a safe course, and the failure of each navigator to establish the position of the ship and advise the captain of safe courses.

The *Wilkes* had navigational facilities superior to the other ships with which to do navigation and should have been able to determine the presence of danger much earlier and more readily than either the *Pollux* or the *Truxtun.*

Negligence was laid at the doors of Lieutenant William A. Smyth and Lieutenant A. J. Barrett, of the *Wilkes,* and Lieutenant (jg) William C. Grindley of the *Pollux.* Grindley because (1) he accepted the navigation of the *Wilkes* to the extent that he did not advise the commanding officer of the *Pollux* of a safe course; (2) having sufficient recordings of soundings available he failed to establish the position of the *Pollux* and the dangers ahead on that ship's base course and to advise the commanding officer thereof.

In brief, the court decided that the recorded fathometer soundings of the *Wilkes* were reasonably accurate and could have been used to establish the most dangerous probable position of the ship, which would have indicated necessary action to have been taken to avoid disaster. "Instead of doing this it appears that the navigator made every effort to make the soundings agree with those of a track as near as possible to the base course," said the court.

The court was convinced that radar bearings taken by the *Wilkes* were reasonably accurate with the exception of bearing 190° true which, it felt, had been read off the relative[1] bearing scale instead of the true bearing scale. "Warnings of the proximity of land were received by radar bearings and distances sufficiently early to have enabled the senior officer present to issue radio orders to change the course of the formation and avoid disaster to every ship," the court said.

After the *Wilkes* had grounded there was still time to prevent disaster to the *Pollux* by immediate warning. Efforts were made to warn the *Pollux* only by searchlight. The *Truxtun* and the *Wilkes* had grounded practically simultaneously.

The surviving officers and personnel of the USS *Truxtun* were of junior rank and ratings and did not occupy positions that permitted them to have pertinent information regarding the navigation and the actions taken thereon during the night of the grounding except in the cases of the officers of the deck from 0000 hours on February 18, 1942, to the time of grounding. Information obtainable from these officers was too little to establish facts comparative to those established in the cases of the *Wilkes* and the *Pollux*.

The court of inquiry also found that for outstanding and commendable work:

1. The civilian personnel of the area near the disaster gave unstintingly of their time, labor, homes, food, and personal effects. They are considered primarily responsible for the saving of practically all the survivors of the USS *Pollux* and, through their care of all the survivors of the USS *Pollux* and the USS *Truxtun*, they minimized further loss from exposure.

2. Lieutenant J. W. Boundy, USN, Lieutenant (jg) George C. Bradley, USNR, and Ensign A. I. Pollack, USNR, risked their lives in efforts to carry lines ashore by swimming.

3. Lieutenant (jg) Russell J. Garnaus, USNR, with the following crew: Garrett Lloyd, Bm1c, USN; Warren A. Greenfield, SM3c, USNR; William A. DeRosa, Bkr3c, USNR; and Joseph L. Calemmo, F1c, USNR, in a motor whaleboat lowered from the USS *Pollux,* made a hazardous

---

[1] Such as "dead ahead," "abeam," "astern," etc., as opposed to an exact bearing; 190° true would have been "astern" on the relative scale.

landing taking a line with them. They secured the first line from the *Pollux* to the rocks. Garnaus, Greenfield, and DeRosa climbed the very steep cliff and started for aid. DeRosa died en route, while Garnaus and Greenfield reached a mining settlement and summoned aid.

4. Alfred M. Dupuy, SK3c, USNR, swam ashore and at great personal risk and disregard for his safety managed to reach the ledge nearest the ship and make it possible to secure a line and start rescue operations. This work was done while Dupuy was barefooted and his clothing was frozen.

5. Isaac H. Strauss, QM3c, USNR, risked his life on two occasions, first by endeavoring to go hand over hand on an untested line secured to a rock by a grapnel hook and on a second occasion by attempting to make a landing by swinging from the end of the boom to the rock.

6. Melvin Bettis, Mldr2c, USN, a passenger for the *Prairie*, swam ashore, made his way to the ledge, and assisted Dupuy make the line for rescue work secure, risking his life in the surf in an attempt to grab the heaving line from the USS *Pollux*.

7. Lieutenant (jg) George C. Bradley, USNR (mentioned in subparagraph 2) with Rex E. Copeland, GM3c, USN, and Bill H. McGinnis, Sea2c, USN, risked their lives in an unsuccessful attempt to paddle a liferaft ashore from the USS *Pollux*.

8. T. E. Johnson, GM1c, USN, risked his life in an unsuccessful attempt to swing to the ledge from a lowered boom in order to secure a line there.[2]

9. W. L. Stanford, SF1c, USN, deserves special commendation for his work on the ledge in securing men in the lines to be hoisted up to safety, remaining on the ledge doing this work until the last man except the commanding officer, USS *Pollux,* had been hoisted from the ledge.

10. Harry M. Egner, BM1c, USN, and James Fex, Sea2c, USN, risked their lives in heavy seas to paddle the first raft ashore from the USS *Truxtun* with a line by means of which most of the survivors of the *Truxtun* were taken ashore.

11. Walter W. Brom, SM1c, USN (deceased), exposed himself to the heavy seas for long periods without regard for his safety or physical comfort in order to keep in communication with the signalman [Parkerson] on the beach.

12. Edward L. Bergeron, A.S.* USN, climbed the cliffs after making

---

[2] The Navy Department in Washington, D.C., has no record of this action in the final analysis, and as only one attempt was made (by Henry Strauss) to swing from the boom, and no story from other survivors corroborates it, the author concludes that the court of inquiry made an error.

* Error. Washington lists Bergeron as Sea2c. The court used A.S.

the beach from the USS *Truxtun* and ran approximately two miles to a mining camp to secure aid for survivors.

13. Ensign H. W. Taylor, USNR (deceased), risked his life in an attempt to save a man in the water.

14. The following persons gave outstanding services in aiding the survivors after they reached the beach, caring for them throughout the night and until removed to places of further safety: Edward B. Petterson, CFC (AA), USN; A. C. Matthews, WT1c, USN; J. G. Berry, CGM, USN; Ensign Edgar DeWitt Brown, USNR; Boatswain M. Pilkington, USN; Pharmacist Haralson (initials unknown); E. A. Thomson, GM3c; H. E. Brooks, QM1c, USN; Lieutenant C. R. Longenecker, MC-V(G), USNR; Elmon R. Pittman, PhM3c, USN; Ray L. Miller, PhM3c, USN; Stanley Barron, PhM3c, USN; James E. Cupero, HA1c, USN; Lieutenant Commander George W. Ashford, USN.

It was recommended that suitable commendation be given to the personnel named; that compensation be given to the civilian personnel of Newfoundland for services and material given during the initial time of the disaster; that a radio navigational aid be installed somewhere near the entrance of Placentia Bay, Newfoundland; that all United States seagoing vessels be equipped with radar equipment and fathometers; and that the Navy kapok life jackets be equipped with crotch straps to prevent them from rising on the body, interfering with the free movement of the arms when the person wearing one strikes, or is floating in, the water.

It was also recommended that appropriate disciplinary action be taken in the case of the defendants Webb, Kelsey, Turney, Barrett, Smyth, and Grindley.

The court having finished with the inquiry on March 19, 1942, passed their findings over to the convening authority, Vice Admiral A. L. Bristol, who appended his own remarks on March 21, 1942:

The evidence indicates that as early as 0023 on February 18, 1942, warning was given, by a sounding which indicated the passage of a fifty-fathom curve, that the course being made good by the *Wilkes* was not in accord with the course intended. From that time on until the ship grounded there was cumulative evidence that the *Wilkes* was being set to the northward of the track laid down on the chart. From 0315 onward, the warnings both from the fathometer and from the radar were so pronounced as to clearly indicate the necessity for immediate corrective action. By 0400 the indications of immediate danger were so clear that instantaneous action to stop all ships in the formation should have been taken.

The acceptance of risks in time of war is not to be confused with relaxation of officerlike qualities of responsibilities, alertness, initiative, judgment, and conscientious attention to duty.

Commander W. W. Webb, the Senior Office Present and the officer in command of the unit, failed to show a proper and continuing sense of responsibility at a time when the ships of his command were approaching dangerous waters. His flagship, the U.S.S. *Wilkes,* was completely equipped with all necessary devices for accurate navigation, including both fathometer and radar, and these devices were operating in a satisfactory manner. Commander Webb failed to take the necessary steps to insure that he was kept fully advised of the existing situations when he was approaching a landfall on a dangerous coast under conditions of darkness, heavy weather, and low visibility. On being apprised of a grave uncertainty in the navigational situation, he failed to act promptly and correctly to avoid disaster.

Commander John D. Kelsey, commanding officer of the USS *Wilkes,* failed to keep himself advised of the navigation of his ship at a time when his ship was approaching a dangerous coast under conditions of bad weather, darkness, and low visibility. When apprised of the uncertainty of the navigational situation, he failed to take immediate and corrective action.

Lieutenant A. J. Barrett, the navigator of the USS *Wilkes,* failed to properly evaluate the information which was at his disposal and further failed to inform promptly his commanding officer that there were serious differences between the actual position of the *Wilkes* and the position as shown by dead reckoning. Lieutenant Barrett displayed a lack of professional knowledge, a lack of proper sense of responsibility, inattention to duty, and negligence.

There is evidence throughout the testimony in the case of the *Wilkes* that the organization and administration of the ship control was seriously at fault. There is evidence of general lack of tautness, instruction, and training, which resulted in poor operational discipline and slack watchkeeping.

The failure of the *Wilkes* to receive the change of course signal initiated by the *Pollux* at 0130 must be considered as seriously affecting the succeeding course of events. There seems little doubt that had this signal been received and reported to proper authority it would have shaken the personnel of the *Wilkes* out of the state of lethargy which apparently existed. The failure of Schmidt, signalman second class, to receive the message also shows laxity and inattention on the part of the bridge personnel. However, there is not sufficient evidence to show culpability on the part of Schmidt.

Lieutenant William A. Smyth failed in several particulars to perform his duties as officer of the deck of the *Wilkes*. The greatest responsibility of the officer of the deck in escort operations in wartime is the handling of his ship and control of the lookout. It is recognized that this of necessity limits his scope in carefully following the navigation of the ship. In spite of this it remains the responsibility of the officer of the deck to advise and report promptly to the captain and to the navigator any discrepancies from the normal or from the unexpected. Lieutenant Smyth received early[3] information in regard to the discrepancy between actual and predicted soundings and failed to report them. He further showed lack of alertness and appreciation of the situation in not bringing quickly to the attention of the commanding officer critical radar information which he had received.[4]

The voluminous testimony of the court navigator, including cross-examination by the defendants, appears to yield further proof of negligent navigational work in the *Wilkes*.

Throughout the navigational testimony as regards the *Wilkes* there is a startling absence of appreciation of the existence and importance of leeway in practical navigation.

The evidence indicates that the situation in the *Pollux* differed in many important factors from that existing in the *Wilkes*. There is a strong impression to be gained from this testimony that the *Pollux* was a well-organized and well-disciplined ship in every department and that the ship control functioned smoothly and effectively throughout the night preceding the grounding.

The loss of the navigational records of the *Pollux* makes it impossible to check the navigation of the ship. The quite proper lack of testimony from the commanding officer and the navigator, after they had been made defendants, makes it impossible to reconstruct the situation as visualized by the commanding officer. Of necessity, the opinion of the reviewing authority approaches more closely conjecture than opinion. That Commander Turney was aware of a situation which required corrective action is evidenced by his change of course at 0130 from 47° true to 57° true. There appears to be two alternatives as the reason back of this change; either that the commanding officer felt he was approaching a dangerous situation or that he was taking action to counteract presumed

---

[3] Incorrect, says Smyth.
[4] Incorrect, says Smyth.

excessive leeway of the *Pollux* in an endeavor to maintain the track intended. In either case, the corrective action was in the right direction and indicates a conscientious endeavor to evaluate the navigational information available and to take steps to insure the safety of his ship. That the *Pollux* grounded is proof that the corrective action was not sufficient. It is noted that both Commander Turney and his navigator were continuously on the bridge or in the charthouse of the *Pollux* throughout the night and that constant endeavor was being made to secure navigation data from the fathometer.

After grounding, during rescue operations, and throughout the remainder of his stay at Argentia, Commander Turney displayed to the highest degree the qualities of leadership, courage, and completely selfless interest in the welfare of his officers and men. The reviewing authority feels the deepest regret that the splendid qualities of this officer had to be brought to his attention through the medium of disaster. It is with the greatest reluctance that the conclusion is reached that Commander Turney failed to interpret available information and to recognize the close proximity of his ship to danger and further failed to take adequate corrective action. There is no evidence of inattention to duty, lack of a sense of responsibility, or carelessness in the performance of duty; there is evidence of a serious error of judgment.

In the case of the navigator of the *Pollux*, Lieutenant (jg) W. C. Grindley, the evidence does not show that he either did or did not advise the commanding officer of the approach of a dangerous situation or of courses to be set other than those actually steered. The evidence does not show negligence on the part of the navigator of the *Pollux*, but in view of the fact of the grounding of the ship, he must share in the responsibility for such grounding and consequent loss of ship.

The convening authority finds no fault with the performance of duty of the officer of the deck of the *Pollux*, nor that of the officer of the deck of the *Truxtun*, and wishes to record his unqualified approval of the general conduct of the officers and men of the *Pollux* and the *Truxtun* and of their performance of duties subsequent to the grounding of their respective ships.

It was recommended that: Commander W. W. Webb be tried by general court-martial on the charge, "Culpable inefficiency in the performance of duty."

Commander John D. Kelsey, USN, be tried by general court-martial on the charge, "Through negligence suffering a vessel of the Navy to be run upon a rock."

Lieutenant A. J. Barrett, USN, be tried by general court-martial on the charge, "Through negligence suffering a vessel of the Navy to be run upon a rock."

Lieutenant W. A. Smyth, USN, be tried by general court-martial on the charge, "Culpable inefficiency in the performance of duty."

Commander Hugh W. Turney, USN, be tried by general court-martial on the charge, "Through negligence suffering a vessel of the Navy to be run upon a rock."

Lieutenant W. C. Grindley, USNR, be tried by general court-martial on the charge, "Through negligence suffering a vessel of the Navy to be run upon a rock."

36

Boston
Spring—1942

There now followed a period when the *P/T* Unit felt they were in limbo. Nothing was happening. Garnaus, Bradley, and Grayson, who were part of the unit designated to testify at the courts-martial, and Grindley, who would be court-martialed, had been quartered in the BOQ at Fargo Barracks, then given ten days' leave to gather another outfit of uniforms and other personal articles and to have a short leave with their families. They had returned to Boston much happier and anxious to get the court-martial trials over with, so they could return to sea and "get the damn war over with."

The huge, barnlike Fargo Barracks were depressing, so they rented an apartment and waited, caught up in endless speculation of what was ahead for the defendants. Their only duty was to report daily to the legal officer, Lieutenant Commander Robert E. Quinn, USNR,[1] 1st Naval District Headquarters. Grindley had told his story to Counselor Quinn, who listened with great interest and advised him that he would have the opportunity to tell it at his own court-martial.

At this time Alfred Dupuy and Henry Strauss received commissions in recognition of their bravery. Dupuy was still in the hospital when he was sworn in as an ensign; Ensign Strauss was invited to move into the apartment with Grindley and his friends. During this period the *Pollux* crew became even more close-knit.

[1] Later governor of Rhode Island; also chief justice, Military Court of Appeals.

Similarly, the *Wilkes'* officers, having been returned to their ship, worked in harmony as they refitted and repaired their ship in the Boston Navy Yard. There was not a word of reproach among Webb, Kelsey, Barrett, and Smyth as they busied themselves getting the *Wilkes* ready to put to sea again. There was a spirit of camaraderie among them.

Nevertheless, Smyth knew, deep down, that he was more afraid of the court-martial than he had ever been fighting the enemy. He had never once experienced a moment of panic when they had sought out the sea wolves so that convoys could safely carry needed supplies across the Atlantic, but the prospect of a court-martial petrified him. Wasn't it a travesty, he thought, to know that they were more apprehensive of what their own people might do to their professional reputations than they were of the foe? His whole career was at stake. God! He was scared.

While the United States Atlantic Fleet Support Force in Argentia had set up the court of inquiry with great efficiency, conversely, the preparation for the general courts-martial dragged.

On leave, in the Bronx, Sam Nicosia kept the promise made to DeRosa on board the *Pollux:* He visited his parents, Mr. and Mrs. Peter DeRosa, and told them in detail the story of their son's heroic actions.

On a happier note, Jack Garnaus and Margaret Huntling were married on March 16. Larry Weaver married Betsy Butler on March 28, and Harry Egner married[2] Dorothy Carney.

On April 6, the *Wilkes* was ordered to Newport, Rhode Island, to escort the cruiser, USS *Augusta*[3] to Casco Bay, Maine. She was headed straight into another disaster.

On April 8, at about 0045 hours, both ships were east of Boston and north of Race Point, heading north on course 000° true, under darkened ship conditions on a zigzag course at a speed of 17½ knots. The *Wilkes* had no lookout on her bow because any muzzle

[2] Date not specified.

[3] The *Augusta* had taken President Franklin D. Roosevelt to Argentia, Newfoundland, in August 1941 for the historic meeting with Prime Minister Winston Churchill of Great Britain and the drafting of the Atlantic Charter.

blast from her guns when trained forward would have killed him, and she had to be prepared to fire on a moment's notice.

Steaming south from Halifax to New York was a three-column convoy of five ships escorted by two British destroyers. The SS *Davila,* an oil tanker owned by Anglo-Saxon Petroleum Co. Ltd. of London, England (British-owned) was port-hand column leader.

The southbound convoy was three miles east of its course and one hour behind schedule. All ships were darkened. The *Davila,* built in 1938, length 483 feet, weighing 12,000 deadweight tons, had a maximum speed of 12½ knots. At the present time she was running at a speed of 9½ knots on a course of 193° true, approaching the *Wilkes* from 013° true. There were ships 400 yards to her starboard and 600 yards astern but no ships on her port hand. At the starboard bridge wing there was one lookout on watch; the mate and an apprentice officer were on the port bridge wing. The *Davila* did not have a lookout posted at the bow although there was no reason why one could not have been there, and it would have been advisable when they were running without lights in a heavily trafficked area. With a distance of 160 feet between the bridge and the bow, a lookout in the bow would have been in a much better position to sight any oncoming ships than the men on the bridge.

The *Wilkes,* running ahead of the *Augusta,* picked up a number of pips, but one, a 30° bearing on her starboard bow at a range of 3,500 yards, was received at about 0052 hours. Commander Kelsey ordered that the bearing at 30° be followed up in case it was a hostile vessel. On the second revolution of the radar antenna 90 seconds later, bearing 30° was at the range of 2,300 yards—*1,200 yards in 90 seconds.* To Kelsey that indicated a moving object on a constant bearing coming toward the *Wilkes* on a collision course— perhaps a destroyer, which could cover such a distance in 90 seconds.

Whether it was friend or foe quickly became of secondary importance when collision appeared imminent.

Commander Kelsey ordered a reduction of speed to 15 knots and a course change to 070° true, to the right, in order to avoid collision and to screen the cruiser *Augusta* from a vessel that was potentially hostile. Fifteen knots gave her sufficient speed to be maneuverable in the event the unknown vessel was the enemy.

This change in course to the right would have been adequate to avoid collision with the *Davila* had the speed and course of that ship corresponded to that indicated by the two radar contacts. They did not. The *Davila* was approaching from a slightly different direction.

The *Wilkes* and the *Davila* sighted each other's loom at about 600 yards. Immediately the *Wilkes* turned on her lights and tried to take evasive action. The mate of the *Davila,* instead of maintaining course and speed, as he should have done according to international rules, since the *Wilkes* was giving way, yelled for an increase in speed and left rudder, and swerved toward the *Wilkes.* Belatedly he ordered the *Davila*'s lights on. The stem of the *Davila* struck the port side of the *Wilkes* between her bridge and stack and penetrated the ship for about 12 feet, cutting open the fire room. The *Davila*'s stem was twisted from starboard to port and damaged for about 20 feet from the bow.

It was touch and go whether the *Wilkes* would stay afloat but her damage-control party again nursed her to Boston.

Lieutenant Barrett had to be cut out of his room.

The *Wilkes*' radar had betrayed her again, and in 1950 a court of inquiry into the collision cleared the vessel of all charges brought against her by the owners of the *Davila.* Ironically the court decided that the SC type of radar on the *Wilkes* was not reliable for navigational purposes—quite different from the decision of the Argentia court of inquiry.

But her crew wondered: Was the *Wilkes* an unlucky ship?

In late May Admiral Ernest J. King, annoyed at the delay in the setting up of the general courts-martial, prodded the Secretary of the Navy, reminding him of the ". . . impairment to the effective exercise of discipline due to delays. . . ."

On May 27, 1942, Acting Secretary of the Navy James Forrestal approved the recommendations of the court of inquiry that Webb, Turney, Barrett, Smyth, and Grindley be brought to trial by general courts-martial.

37

Boston
June 23–July 3, 1942

Commander Walter Webb was brought to trial by general court-martial in Boston, June 23, 1942, on the charge of culpable inefficiency in the performance of duty. Specification[1] (1) ". . . in that he did fail to issue and see effected such timely orders as were necessary to cause each of the said ships of the said naval unit to change to a safe course in due time to avoid disaster . . ." Specification (2) ". . . in that he did fail to issue and see effected such timely orders as were necessary to cause him to be promptly informed of navigational data known and obtained on board the said USS *Wilkes* indicating the proximity of land ahead, and that the said USS *Wilkes* and other said ships of the said naval unit were not making good the course set for safe navigation as it was his duty to do . . ."

The court was comprised of Captain A. Abele, USN (Ret.); Captain William S. Miller, USN (Ret.); Captain Chauncey Shackford, USN (Ret.); Captain Ronan C. Grady, USN (Ret.); Captain Robert H. Grayson, USN; Captain George C. Kriner, USN; Captain Charles J. Wheeler, USN; and Commander James B. Stevens, USN (Ret.), as judge advocate. Captain Jesse J. Burke, U. S. Marine Corps (Ret.), acted as counsel to assist the judge advocate.

Flanked by two counsels, Lieutenant Commander Robert E. Quinn, USNR, and Lieutenant (jg) Sanford T. Abele, Webb pleaded not guilty to the charges.

[1] See Appendix H.

Twelve members of the *Wilkes'* crew, eight of the *Pollux,* and five of the *Truxtun*'s crew would tell their stories of the crucial midwatch.

By this time Radar Bulletin No. 1, "Confidential, Tactical Use of Radar—Official," which stated that ice could diminish the range of radar, had found its way to the *Wilkes,* and then to the general court-martial.

Lieutenant Overton D. Hughlett of the *Wilkes,* again answering specific questions, told the court that he had no special instructions to report the fathometer soundings, radar bearings, land, weather, or unusual navigational data—in fact, no orders to report anything to the unit commander.

Ensign Henry B. Quekemeyer and Quartermaster James McPherson related their stories about the radar pips. Quekemeyer's testimony conflicted slightly with that he had given at the court of inquiry about bearings 340 and 190. This time he seemed sure that he had reported 340 to Lieutenant Smyth, the officer of the deck.

In contradiction to his testimony about the soundings given at the court of inquiry, Seaman First Class Americo Nolfi stated that he had reported the crossing of the 50-fathom curve to Lieutenant Smyth at 0138 when he noticed that the fathometer registered 86 fathoms, and not at 0230, as he had first stated. When the records of the court of inquiry were read to him he seemed confused. He had testified from memory then, he said; now he was testifying from the fathometer logbook. Pointed questioning from Commander Webb, the accused, could not get him to make a clearer statement.

Ensign Robert Grayson of the *Pollux* told about the signal from his ship to the *Wilkes* between 0115 and 0130. He was asked by Commander Webb to make a rough estimate of the distance between the two ships at this time.

"To make a completely rough estimate, I should say that the fact we saw her light would have put her roughly in the neighborhood of possibly 2,000 yards," Grayson said.

Commander Webb picked up the radar logbook of the *Wilkes.* "I show you the entries from 1200 to 0400 on February 18. Will you please read the entry at 0135 referring to the *Pollux?*"

Grayson said, "The entry of 0135 reads: 'Started radar, *Pollux* bearing 318 degrees, 4,700 yards.'"

"Would you say that the *Wilkes* at about that time was 4,700 yards distant from the *Pollux?*"

"It's entirely possible," Grayson replied, "but I don't feel qualified to set a distance."

Commander Webb may have been alerting the court to the fallibility of radar; that it was showing the *Pollux* at 4,700 yards while in actuality the two ships may have been only 2,000 yards apart as Grayson had suggested, or he may have been directing attention to the implausibility of a signal being seen in thick weather at such a distance, or both.

Grayson appeared absolutely convinced that their message to the *Wilkes* at 0130 stating they were changing course 10° to the right had been received. He even thought, but was not sure, that they had been asked to repeat one word, he said.

Signalman First Class Carl Schmidt of the *Wilkes* remembered very little about the exchange of calls between the *Wilkes* and the *Pollux.* "Due to the lapse of time [five months] my memory isn't quite clear," he told the court.

The *Wilkes'* 0623 star sight came under the scrutiny of the court. Plotted by Lieutenant Commander Ernest W. Lomons of the USS *Savannah,* it showed the error where the *Wilkes'* navigator had assumed the star Antares to be west of the meridian, when it was east. This was a 2½-mile error to the southward on a position that was *already indeterminate,* Lomons said.

The error carried through after the course change to 047 true at 2000 hours, with the navigator plotting the dead-reckoning track up the center of Placentia Bay, southeastward of the actual track of the ship.

Normally the error would have been corrected at the crossing of the 100- and 50-fathom lines of the St. Pierre Bank, but the *Wilkes* had approached the Bank in an area where both contour lines were roughly parallel and close together for about 70 miles. Within a 12-mile range the distance between the two lines in many places was roughly 1.5 miles, such as the *Wilkes'* point of crossing. The ship could have spanned the two lines 5 or 6 miles on either side of the crossing and still recorded 1.5 miles.

There was increasing evidence that the ship was to the northward of her assumed track, and the drift increased during the night due to the increasing wind, Lomons said.

On cross-examination Commander Webb asked: "How much of your testimony is based upon information obtained in the court of inquiry records?"

Lomons replied, "It is difficult to separate the record of the court of inquiry from the exhibits, and most of the testimony that I gave is substantiated by both."

Commander Webb demanded that Lomons' testimony be stricken on the technicality that he had used information based on the court of inquiry held in Argentia, which was not in evidence before the court-martial.

It was so done. Commander Philip D. Lohman, navigator of the *Savannah*, replaced Lomons, but in essence corroborated his testimony.

The court asked him: "You have worked out certain positions of the *Wilkes;* therefore, will you present to the court anything you noted or observed in their works that might have caused you to take extra precautions for safe navigation?"

Apparently Lohman could not. "Navigation was off somewhere," he said, "whether it was off from negligence or from accumulation of errors in navigation I have not been able to determine."

Later the judge advocate asked: "From the data and exhibits that you reviewed, does that data show that any allowance was made for current in the course [047° true] laid down by the *Wilkes'* navigator?"

"Not if you wanted to pass approximately into the center of Placentia Bay," Lohman answered.

In a brief appearance Lieutenant Barrett told the court that he had been directed by the captain to inform the division commander that the *Wilkes* was to the north of the course at 0400 hours, approximately ten minutes before the ship grounded.

Hughlett, in Webb's defense, presented Radar Bulletin No. 1 to the court and testified that ice could affect the range of radar. This information had not been known aboard the *Wilkes* at the time of the grounding, he said; therefore they had expected to pick up the Newfoundland coast from at least twenty miles.

In his own defense, Webb had presented a scientist, Lauriston C. Marshall, and an oceanographer, Lieutenant Richard Parmenter, USNR, who was attached to the Antisubmarine Warfare Office.

Marshall attested to the inaccuracies of the SC radar in weather conditions such as the *Wilkes* had experienced.

Parmenter spoke at length of marine currents, the density gradient of the sea, the Ferrelian Force, which causes all currents to bend to the right in the Northern Hemisphere in proportion to the latitude, the propulsion of currents by the Archimedean forces of the sea, and the dangerous character of the Canadian Atlantic coast regarding navigation, which was due to the homogeneous[2] nature of the water.

"Conditions making for maximum danger are found to occur in mid-winter when winter gales render the whole upper 200 to 300 feet of the ocean homogeneous," he told the court; thus the *Wilkes* on the night in question encountered the maximum shoreward set— in this case a set to the west. In Parmenter's opinion a current of 6 knots would not be excessive in that zone.

Then Webb himself stood before the court and with great authority answered the questions asked by the judge advocate, Commander James B. Stevens. His story unfolded as he gave his version of the series of events from 0400 when he was notified that they were north of the track. Asked what methods were used to warn the other ships when land was reported, he told them: "I immediately and personally jumped down to the radio room and instructed the radio operator on watch to broadcast the fact that the *Wilkes* had grounded, so that the other ships would be warned." Then he had tried again to call the *Truxtun* by TBS while they were signaling by searchlight, he said.

"Had you given any special instructions to the captain to take extra precautions for navigation, or ask the captain to keep you informed of navigational data?" the judge advocate asked.

He had not, Webb stated. "Commander Kelsey is a very able officer. I have never considered it necessary to give him specific instructions of that sort." However, Commander Kelsey absolutely understood his desires that reports of any unusual circumstances be made to him, he said.

Commander Kelsey had sent for him at 0400 and, having discovered what the situation was, he had ordered the navigator to work out their position more definitely before changing course and notifying the *Pollux* and the *Truxtun* of the change.

[2] When all parts of water are of equal density.

There was a question about Webb's order to Kelsey to ease over and get in touch with the *Pollux*. "The *Pollux* was in our charge and I naturally wanted to contact her before we changed course definitely," Webb told the court.

He was questioned about all aspects of the voyage, and on Thursday, July 2, 1942, the court was ready to wind up proceedings. Webb asked for, and was granted, permission until the following day to prepare his statement.

In his argument Commander Walter Webb declared that course 047 true was laid down to take care of current and wind effect in either direction. "H.O. 73 states the most we could be set to the left would be at the rate of one knot. It goes on to say that currents are not definite in either direction and great caution has to be exercised," he said, and argued: "Just because the ship went to the left does not mean she was in an unsafe position; she might have gone to the right. Either way might have been safe except for the fact that *the current actually encountered was three, four, or five times greater than in the book*.[3] [*Sailing Directions for Newfoundland*.] For that reason I brought in an expert oceanographer to explain the workings of that current to you. You will not find them in H.O. 73, and there have been no surveys made of those currents in the wintertime at Argentia, but we know from studies made in the last fifteen, twenty, or twenty-five years what currents will do under certain conditions and we know what a current will do in the wintertime."

He continued, "Certainly it is highly significant that two days after the grounding a lightship was ordered up to Argentia with a radio beacon to be there temporarily until a permanent radio beacon could be installed. It is a good deal like locking the barn after the horse is stolen, but it is a precaution which will save other ships going up there in the wintertime." The U. S. Government had negotiated with the Free French at St. Pierre and Miquelon for the re-establishment of the radio beacon at Gallantry Head, he told them. "I do not believe those stations would have been re-established had the department [of the Navy] thought that the grounding of the *Wilkes*, the *Truxtun*, and the *Pollux* was due solely to poor navigation. They recognize the dangerous currents that exist in that area."

Webb objected strongly to the second specification that he had

[3] Italics supplied.

failed to issue orders to be promptly informed of navigation data that indicated proximity of land. The commanding officer and the navigator of the *Wilkes* knew their jobs and made reports to him as were necessary, and kept him informed of all facts that they knew, he said. "I submit that there is nothing, that there were no facts known to the unit commander on the night of February 17, which required him to request, to give specific orders to the commanding officer, the navigator, or the radar operator, or the helmsman, or the signalman, or the quartermaster of the watch, to give him any particular reports."

There was nothing on board the ship that would indicate the set the ship was actually experiencing, he said.

The Sail Cast radar on the *Wilkes* was an obsolete model, he told the court. "Present models have enclosed antennas and are built to operate in bad weather." There was no information on board the *Wilkes* that night that showed that radar was affected by ice or snow. "It seems to me that evidence conclusively shows that the radar did not operate properly," he stated. "If it had been working properly the radar would have shown land over on the left all the way around over to the right."

Commander Webb submitted that the information received aboard the *Wilkes* did not show immediate danger. First because of the radar not operating properly and second because of a set, a current that could be found nowhere in the sailing directions. "The actions of the unit commander I do not believe can be criticized. I think he is entitled to a full acquittal on both specifications of the charge," he said.

The judge advocate did not agree that there was an excessive current. "If the position of the *Wilkes* was to the left of her course at the time her 2000 hours, February 17, position was estimated, as appears to have been the case, judging from the time the second 50 fathoms was crossed, there need not have been any excessive current up to that time. It has not been proved there was such an excessive current of 6 knots, but a set from the 0623 position of a little over a knot." Commander Stevens felt that there was an abundance of navigational data known and obtained on board the *Wilkes* that indicated the proximity of land ahead in ample time to have prevented the grounding. "At 0335, February 18, it was known that the vessel was to the left of the course set for safe navigation, but the accused was not informed of it." He had not been informed of the earlier crossing of the 50-fathom curve even though the navigator had been aware of it shortly after 0300. Nor had he been informed of the unknown object picked up by radar at bearing 340°.

Strangely, the judge advocate considered the testimony about the inaccuracies of radar as irrelevant in the case because the information had not been available to the personnel on board the *Wilkes*. Nor was Radar Bulletin No. 1 relating to the effect of ice on the radar antenna insulator, which Hughlett had presented to the court, considered. That publication had not been available on the *Wilkes* at the time of the grounding either. Why these important factors could not be taken into consideration because they were unknown to the crew members at a time when it could have made the difference between life and death seems strange indeed; however, the court decided that with the extensive use of radar on board nearly every combatant vessel, it was difficult for the prosecution to believe it was of such inaccuracy as to be ignored or disregarded in its indications. The testimony of the expert, therefore, appeared to be inapplicable since the evidence had shown that the information obtained from the radar just prior to the grounding was extremely accurate.

"The operator, whether qualified or not, seemed to have done quite well," the judge advocate said. "He picked up something 8 miles away and followed it down to 6,000 yards on the 340° bearing when he found objects extending from 340° to 020° at 3,000 yards."

The message about the change of course, sent by the *Pollux* to the *Wilkes* at around 0130 hours, the court decided, must have been received in its entirety, since witnesses on the *Pollux* stated they saw a dash from the *Wilkes* after each word sent. If instructions had been in effect to report unusual events to the accused, it was difficult to understand why this was not so reported to him.

The court said that the *Wilkes,* in maintaining course 047° without change until moments before grounding, had made no allowance for leeway or set. "Some power pushed or pulled or forced these ships off their track, and they did ground. Whether it was set from currents or wind or both, the result was just as disastrous."

The judge advocate submitted to the court that both specifications of the charge had been proved against Commander Walter W. Webb.

The court decided that the first specification of the charge of "culpable inefficiency in the performance of duty" was not proved.

The second specification, "in that he did fail to issue and see effected such timely orders as were necessary to cause him to be promptly informed of navigational data known and obtained on board the *Wilkes* indicating proximity of land," was proved.

On July 3, 1942, the court sentenced Webb to lose twenty-five numbers in his grade on the list of commanders. In consideration of the mitigating circumstances shown by the evidence to have existed in connection with the offense, and in view of the great strain under which he had been operating, due to immediate submarine menace, Webb was recommended to the clemency of the reviewing authority, Admiral Ernest J. King.

38

Boston
July 13–August 3, 1942

Commander John D. Kelsey's court-martial began on July 13, 1942. The charge: Through negligence suffering a vessel of the Navy to be stranded. Specification[1] (1) ". . . in that having been informed that the course being made good by the said USS *Wilkes* was to the left of the course set for the safe navigation of the said ship, did, then and there, neglect and fail to exercise proper care and attention in navigating said ship while approaching off the said coast, and to change the course in due time to avoid disaster . . ." Specification (2) ". . . in that he neglected and failed to make allowance for known currents and the wind effect to leeward setting the said ship toward the said coast . . ."

For the first three days the members of the court-martial, having served on Commander Webb's court-martial, were methodically disposed of by Commander Kelsey. The court-martial actually began on Wednesday, July 22, when a new board was convened.

The court was comprised of Captain George N. Barker, USN; Captain Preston B. Haines, USN; Captain John S. Roberts, USN; Captain Wilbur J. Carver, USN (Ret.); Commander Archibald G. Stirling, USN (Ret.); Commander John H. Keefe, USN (Ret.), members; Commander James G. Stevens, USN (Ret.), judge advocate, and his counsel.

Commander Kelsey had two counselors: Lieutenant (jg) Sanford

[1] See Appendix I.

T. Abele, USNR, and Lieutenant Commander Robert E. Quinn, USNR. When the charges were read Kelsey stated that he was not guilty.

There were thirteen witnesses from the *Wilkes* and three from the *Pollux*. Once again the crew members told the judge advocate that no special orders had come down the line that night. This time Ensign Quekemeyer admitted to confusion about the bearings 340 and 190 and made a statement that, as he had originally testified, it was bearing 190 he had reported to the officer of the deck, Lieutenant Smyth.

When asked by the judge advocate what time he had reported the 0138 sounding to Lieutenant Smyth, Quartermaster Nolfi said, "I'm not sure, but I made a statement when my mind was fresher that it was 0230."

Lieutenant Barrett made another brief appearance in the court to establish the fact that at 0350 on the morning of February 18 he had reported to the captain that the *Wilkes* was north of the course.

Quartermaster Third Class George J. Horner of the *Pollux* remained sure that he had received a dash after each word of the message he had signaled to the *Wilkes* around 0130.

"Did you get a Roger for that message?" Commander Kelsey asked.

"No, sir," Horner replied.

Commander Kelsey moved that all of Horner's testimony relating to the sending of the message to the *Wilkes* be stricken from the record on the grounds that the message had not been receipted for.

The court refused.

Ensign Robert Grayson corroborated Horner's story again but, he told the judge advocate, they did not get a receipt for it.

"Were you expecting any further word regarding that signal?"

He was, Grayson said. "I would have expected notice, confirmation, that they were conforming to our course, or orders to come back."

Kelsey asked Grayson: "As you understand communication instruction, if a message has not been receipted for by a Roger, is that message considered received?"

"It is not," Grayson replied.

Q.: "What type of searchlight was used in attempting to send this message to the *Wilkes*?"

A.: "Twelve-inch shutter searchlight on the bridge wing, with a cone to cut it down to a beam of about six inches."

Q.: "And if the direction of that beam is changed a slight degree, is it easy or hard to read?"

A.: "It is harder to read unless bearing directly upon you."

Q.: "Was the *Pollux* zigzagging while this message was being transmitted?"

A.: "She was still zigzagging."

Q.: "Do you know whether the *Wilkes* was zigzagging at the time this message was transmitted?"

A.: "From what I found out since, she was."

Q.: "You didn't know whether the *Wilkes* was making a change of course before, during, or after that message was sent, do you?"

A.: "No, sir."

Undoubtedly Commander Kelsey was directing attention to the fact, as brought out in the court of inquiry, that during the transmitting of the message, the light was most probably not bearing directly upon the *Wilkes,* since the officer of the deck, Lieutenant Smyth, had the impression they were on the starboard quarter of the *Pollux* instead of the bow; therefore the light, which would have been directed forward of the *Pollux*'s bow, had not been bearing directly upon them.

In Commander Kelsey's defense, Lieutenant Hughlett testified to the inaccuracies of radar due to ice, and to the icing of the radio antenna, which had also produced poor results.

On this day Counselor Quinn notified Lieutenant Grindley, navigator of the *Pollux* that he was to be called on the stand the following day to testify in Kelsey's defense. To say that Grindley was surprised was putting it mildly. What could *he* say in Commander Kelsey's defense? He protested that he wasn't prepared and didn't have counsel.

It was more or less to establish the position of the *Wilkes,* Counselor Quinn informed him. "Keep it simple, more or less to a 'Yes' or 'No.' Don't elaborate and don't volunteer any information about yourself and Commander Turney because you might get yourself in too deep, and you don't have any written records."

Grindley listened numbly as the counselor continued: "The proper time for those other details will be when you are called on the stand to testify on your own behalf." He told Grindley to bear in mind that anything he might say under questioning and cross-examination might very well reflect on Commander Turney's hearing. "Keep it simple, don't elaborate," he cautioned again.

Grindley was still disturbed when he told his friends about it that evening. Hank Strauss listened with great skepticism. In the Reserve ranks it was felt that in the Navy all situations were stacked in the favor of the Annapolis men whose careers were the Navy, whereas the Reserve were in only as long as they were forced to be. Once the war was over they would return to civilian life whereas the U.S. naval officer would carry on in the service of his country.

Having seen and heard the dissension between Grindley and Commander Turney and feeling that the navigator had somehow been subtly ignored during the court of inquiry in Argentia, Strauss was very skeptical indeed. "Grindley, you're out of your mind," he said, "this sounds like an Academy against the Reserve stackup, and you're gonna get screwed."

"Yeah, well, I don't have any choice," Grindley said.

Facing the court the following day and not knowing what to expect, he felt totally unprepared. As advised, he answered the questions as briefly as possible and volunteered no information. When he was shown the *Wilkes'* navigation chart and asked to indicate the approximate 2000-hour position of the *Pollux,* he was not invited to draw up a chart but merely to show approximately on the chart where it was in relation to the *Wilkes.* Mentally calculating his own position, Grindley indicated on the chart with a pointer where he thought the *Pollux* to be at that time.

"How far and in what direction is your estimate for the *Pollux*'s 2000 position from that of the *Wilkes'* estimated position?" asked the judge advocate.

Grindley guessed that the *Wilkes'* estimated position was approximately five[2] miles east by south of the *Pollux.*

"How did you obtain this estimated 2000 position?"

Grindley told them about the star fix, sun lines, and radio bearings he had gotten.

Q.: "Did the bearings and navigational fixes obtained by you during February 17, prior to 2000, indicate any set?"

---

[2] According to the *Wilkes'* star fix, which put the ship about five miles southeast of her actual position, the ships were roughly twelve miles apart. Grindley's estimate was correct.

A.: "No."

Q.: "Did it indicate that you were on your base course as laid down by the division commander?"

A.: "Yes, it did."

Q.: "Were you in charge of the navigation of the ship during the night of February 17, February 18?"

A.: "Yes, I was."

Q.: "Did you advise any change of course the night of February 17–18?"

A.: "Yes."

Q.: "And whom did you advise?"

A.: "The commanding officer."

Q.: "What change of course did you advise?"

Oh Jesus! thought Grindley; his heart was thumping against his ribs. He wasn't prepared for this. Should he tell them he had advised a 30° change of course? Had even suggested they turn the ship around and steam back to St. Pierre Bank? Or should he tell them Commander Turney had decided on a 10° change of course? But his instructions had been very clear: Now was not the time; that would come out at his own court-martial.

In the same moment he said, "A 10° change of course from 047 true to 057 true."

"What was the reason for advising such a change of course?" Commander Stevens asked.

Grindley replied, "We had evidently been set off our DR track by current. It was necessary to make this change of course."

Q.: "Was a change of course made?"

A.: "Yes."

Q.: "Did this new course carry the *Pollux* clear of land?"

A.: "We assumed it would."

Q.: "Did the *Pollux* later run aground?"

A.: "Yes."

After that came questions and answers on the details of the navigation of the *Pollux* and the discovery, through soundings, that they had been set five miles to the north and west during the crossing of the St. Pierre Bank. Not knowing about the incorrect star fix, Grindley wondered why his navigational data were necessary at the trial of Commander Kelsey.

That same afternoon Commander Webb was also sworn as a witness for the defense, testifying at length about the navigation of the *Wilkes*. He had personally laid down the course from the 2000-hours position on February 17, he said, and previous to that they were following courses as directed by higher authority. He had more experience than the navigator, Lieutenant Barrett, and worked closely with him. Commander Kelsey and Lieutenant Barrett had concurred in the courses that he had laid down.

Q.: "Was it a usual custom or duty of yours as division commander?"

A.: "It is not the first time I have done it."

Q.: "Will you please explain why it was necessary for you to lay down this track?"

A.: "It wasn't necessary. I was in command of the unit, I felt the responsibility; I worked closely with the navigator. I had more experience than he had."

Q.: "Had any allowance been made during your absence [from the bridge] for set or leeway?"

A.: "Only the twenty-mile allowance that I had made. I made allowance for possible set in any direction by heading up the middle of the entrance of the bay."

There were many questions about Webb's order to Commander Kelsey to "ease over to the left" minutes before the grounding, and Webb honorably admitted: "I am sure that if the accused had been there alone and not under the necessity of carrying out my orders, that he would not have run aground."

The following day the court probed deeper. "You stated yesterday to the effect that in your opinion if you had not been on the bridge, the accused would not have let the *Wilkes* run aground. Did the accused make any recommendation to you regarding the safety of the *Wilkes?*"

"I didn't say that if I had not been on the bridge in the first place," Webb said. "I said if I had not given him orders. None of us had any idea that the base course was heading toward land. He pointed out to me that by coming to the left leg of the zig in order to intercept the *Pollux,* that we would be heading over toward possible danger. I still thought it was well off, but Commander Kelsey being a very prudent officer, as he proved to me in the six months I sailed with him, did point that out to me." Webb added that he believed Kelsey's inclination was to come right.

Q.: "But he did carry out your order?"

A.: "He did."

Q.: "Did the accused persist in such recommendation after he had thus been ordered by you?"

A.: "What do you mean by persist?"

Q.: "In any recommendation he made to you, did he persist in that after he had been ordered to ease over by you?"

A.: "I ordered him to do it once. He pointed out the possibilities of danger. I reiterated my order. There was no further argument. There was no argument."

Q.: "Do you desire it to be understood that you alone are entirely responsible for the grounding of that ship?"

Before the witness could reply, Commander Kelsey rose and objected on the ground that it would incriminate Commander Webb.

"The right of not answering an incriminating question should be exercised by the witness, and not the accused," the judge advocate reprimanded Kelsey.

"I withdraw my objections," Kelsey said, "but I believe the witness should be advised of his rights by the judge advocate."

Webb said, "I exercise my right not to answer this question on the ground that it would incriminate me." The findings of his own trial had not been made public and an incriminating statement might be the basis for another trial, he added.

It was refuted by the judge advocate. "Naval courts and boards are very definite that a trial is finished when the court has arrived at a finding, and in regard to answering this question, the witness gave his opinion in the direct examination freely as to what would have happened if he had not been aboard the ship. He should not be allowed to give that opinion and then hide behind the privilege of self-incrimination when it comes to cross-examination on the reason for that statement."

Nevertheless, on the technical point that his court-martial had not been published, Webb refused to answer the question until the court stated that it considered the witness as not being in jeopardy. At this point the question was asked again: "Do you desire it to be understood that you alone are entirely responsible for the grounding of that ship?"

A.: "Not at all."

Q.: "He [Kelsey] was still responsible for the navigation of the ship?"

A.: "That's right, except insofar as he had to carry out my orders. I was the division commander, senior to him."

Q.: "You did reserve, or take, the right to give orders over protest to the accused?"

A.: "I would not call it a protest. He pointed out certain things which I testified to two or three times here."

Q.: "That certain thing was, land was over that way?"

A.: "Yes, that land was probably in that direction."

Q.: "Wouldn't you consider that a protest?"

A.: "Not necessarily; call it advice."

Q.: "Did you take any other part of the duties of the accused away from him?"

A.: "I didn't take any of the duties away from the accused."

Q.: "Do you think your change of course to close the *Pollux* had anything to do with the grounding?"

"Yes," Webb admitted, "I think if the ship had come hard right at that time, and just let the *Pollux* fare for herself, we would not have run aground, the *Wilkes* would not have run aground."

Lieutenant Commander Parmeter, as he had done in Webb's trial, testified to the possibility of a six-knot current. The judge advocate rejected it.

William E. Holdridge, associate radio engineer, who had supervised the installation of the SC radar in the *Wilkes*, testified for the prosecution that radar had been tested a few days before the ship had left Boston, and it had been in excellent operating condition. Holdridge knew, through technical bulletins only, and from talking to radio electricians on supply ships that had been North during the winter season, that ice diminished the range of radar, he said.

Again, the court refused to consider the evidence that salt, slush, and ice diminished the range of radar and distorted the beams to and from the ship. This information had not been aboard the *Wilkes* and was, therefore, irrelevant, said Commander Stevens, the judge advocate.

The fact that the *Wilkes* had been involved in a collision at sea in April was also irrelevant. It had nothing whatever to do with the *Pollux/Truxtun* disaster and would not receive a mention. Yet, in the light of later findings in 1950, the poor performance of the SC radar was a link in both accidents.

The prosecution did accept Holdridge's statement that radar had been in excellent operating condition when the *Wilkes* had left Boston. Even if the icing of an antenna did affect radar accuracy, the judge advocate said, it had been operating very well up to eight miles that morning. "Even if ice were on an antenna, the pips must demand attention once they appear at all and require all the more attention when they persist, as in the case at hand."

The judge advocate also decided that Commander Webb's testimony about ordering Kelsey to "ease over to the left" indicated bias in favor of the accused. "The division commander testified to the effect that a vague order he had given the accused about 'easing over to the left to get in touch with the *Pollux*' had been instrumental in the grounding of the *Wilkes,* yet he denied having in any way relieved the accused of any of his duties as commanding officer of the *Wilkes,*" the judge advocate said.

Evidence clearly showed that the easing to the left came at the same time as the course change of the zigzag to the left and when the easing over ended, the ship had settled on course 007° true, which course would have been the exact course the ship would normally have taken in zigzagging at about that time, and no evidence was produced to show that the order of Commander Webb to ease over and contact the *Pollux* had been carried out by the accused, said Commander Stevens.

"The accused, therefore, at no time was relieved of any of his duties by the division commander. He had been on the bridge at least ten minutes before the arrival [at 0400] of the division commander, and had at least ten minutes to think over the report of the navigator that the ship had been set to the north of her course, and to take necessary steps to avoid disaster," the judge advocate charged.

The judge advocate declared that evidence showed that Commander Kelsey failed to make allowance for the known currents and wind effect to leeward, setting the ships toward the coast of Newfoundland. A combination of currents and wind caused the ship to be set off the intended track. "Having been informed at 0350 that the *Wilkes* was to the left of her intended track an estimated distance of eleven miles should have caused a reasonably prudent man to have taken prompt action in time to have avoided disaster," he said.

The evidence was conclusive that, in the first specification of the charge against him, the accused at no time between 0350 and the time of grounding issued any order to cause any appreciable change in the course being steered by the *Wilkes* that would carry her clear of the coast.

"If Lieutenant Grindley on the *Pollux* knew that his ship had been set to the left, why did not the accused with almost identical data and proceeding along a course not far distant from the *Pollux,* know that the *Wilkes* had also been set to the left of their base course?" the judge advocate asked.

He submitted that both specifications of the charges had been proven.

In his rebuttal, Commander Kelsey said that he had been informed by the navigator at 0350 that the *Wilkes* was to the left of the base course on a track that would carry her *well clear of land to port.* The division commander, called at 0400, had received the same information, plus information of a radar bearing, 340, distance 8 miles (which he had not received). He *had* been ordered to ease over to the left to contact the *Pollux,* and when he had protested the order was repeated. He had "eased over by following the left leg of the zigzag 007° true, then called for by the [zigzag] plan."

Commander Kelsey refuted the judge advocate's claim that he had done nothing to avoid danger. He had not received any radar report until about 0405, he said, and had ordered a check of the limiting bearings; before this check was received he had ordered the ship to come right to 109. The ship had grounded on a heading of 89° true, but on the information he had received he had carried out his duties to his ship and his superior officer. "The accused [himself] does not contend that by carrying out the order of the division commander to ease over to the *Pollux* the ship was thereby stranded. What change of course he himself would have made at 0400, not knowing the existence of immediate danger, is only a matter of conjecture," he said.

In connection with radar, he reminded the court that the testimony of the prosecution's own witness, Holdridge, had corroborated the evidence that radar failed to function properly under the type of icing conditions experienced on the night of February 17–18.

The lack of navigational fixes due to the atmospheric conditions, the scarcity of charted soundings and inaccuracies on the chart, and the failure of the radar to indicate land in any direction until three or four minutes before grounding were factors that should be considered, he said.

He rejected the statement that he had failed to make allowance for known currents and wind effect. "This course was chosen after a consideration of H.O. 99 and H.O. 93 [*Sailing Directions for Nova Scotia and Newfoundland*], and clearly allowed for maximum currents in any direction plus any wind effect that might be expected," he declared.

The real cause of the grounding, Commander Kelsey continued, was a current far greater than anyone aboard the vessels in the convoy could know or suspect. "The testimony of the navigator of the *Pollux* whose 2000 position was more accurately fixed than that of the *Wilkes*, to the effect that he and his commanding officer could figure on a set no greater than 1.3 knots across the St. Pierre Bank, and whose ship after a 10° change of course to the right was nevertheless set into the shore one-half mile from the *Wilkes*, definitely bears out the theory advanced through Lieutenant Commander Parmenter that density currents and forces not reckoned with in H.O. 73 were the real cause of the disaster."

The lightship which had been so hurriedly dispatched to Argentia after the groundings, argued that the disaster was not caused by the negligence or inefficiency of experienced navigators ". . . but by dangerous, unknown, and unpredictable currents now recognized by high authority to exist," Kelsey said.

The night orders he had written fully covered the navigational situation during the midwatch; there was no evidence that any departure from those night orders had been reported to him prior to 0350. He was, he felt, entitled to a full acquittal.

The judge advocate had the last word: "The fact that the accused was not notified earlier by the navigator that the *Wilkes* was to the left of her course is no defense, since the commanding officer should take appropriate steps to insure that he is promptly informed by his inferiors of danger."

The trial was finished.

The court directed the judge advocate to record the following findings:

"The first specification of the charge proved.

"The second specification of the charge proved.

"And that the accused, John D. Kelsey, commander, U. S. Navy, is of the charge guilty.

"The court sentences him, John D. Kelsey, to lose fifty numbers in his grade [on the list of commanders].

"In consideration of the excellent record of the accused and his demonstrated skill in extricating his stranded ship from a perilous situation, we recommend John D. Kelsey, commander, U. S. Navy, to the clemency of the reviewing authority."

It was August 3, 1942.

39

Star Chamber Proceedings

On August 3, 1942, the commander in chief, United States Fleet, Admiral Ernest J. King, wrote[1] to the Secretary of the Navy, Frank Knox, disapproving the "inadequate" sentence of Commander Webb and recommending radical administrative action, known as Star Chamber proceedings instead of courts-martial, in the cases of Commander Turney, Lieutenant Barrett, Lieutenant Smyth, and Lieutenant (jg) Grindley because the services of the officers and men involved were needed elsewhere. Turney, Barrett, and Smyth would not be given independent command or temporary promotion during the present war, and letters to that effect, with the reasons therefor, were to be attached to their records. Grindley he recommended be ordered to inactive duty, discharged for cause, and not employed again during the war. A letter to that effect with the reasons therefor was to be attached to his record.

As the trial of Commander Kelsey was concluding, Admiral King recommended that it proceed to its conclusion.

This meant that clemency would automatically be denied Commanders Webb and Kelsey as recommended by the courts-martial.

On August 4, Vice Admiral Randall Jacobs, chief of naval personnel, added his endorsement[2] concurring in the recommendations of the commander in chief, United States Fleet.

[1] See Appendix J.
[2] See Appendix K.

On August 4, Lieutenant William A. Smyth was relieved of his duties by official letter[3] and placed under arrest pending trial by general court-martial. His freedom of movement was restricted to the Metropolitan Boston area and Gloucester. With the letter came a certified copy of the charge and specifications,[4] which he hastily perused for the first time: "Culpable inefficiency in the performance of duty."

To be officially under arrest was traumatic,[5] taking precedence over all. Smyth was fiercely proud of his reputation, and the disgrace of arrest was demoralizing and frightening. Was his career finished? Had his life's work gone down the drain? Had it all been for naught? God, he was scared.

For a couple of hours he could think of nothing else, then he reread and fully absorbed the copy of the charge and specifications, and the shock and worry of arrest was replaced by extreme anger, so intense and overpowering that it seemed to consume every fiber of his being.

He read: "Specification (1) In that William A. Smyth, lieutenant, U. S. Navy, while so serving as officer of the deck on board the USS *Wilkes,* said ship making passage from Cape Elizabeth, Maine, to Argentia, Newfoundland, and being on February 18, 1942, under way at a speed of about fifteen knots approaching and off the south coast of Newfoundland during darkness, heavy weather, and low visibility, well knowing that the said ship was expected to cross the fifty-fathom curve at or about 0130 on said date, and having, at or about 0230 on said date, received information showing that the said fifty-fathom curve had been crossed at a time earlier than had been expected, did then and there, fail to promptly report the said crossing of the said fifty-fathom curve to his commanding officer, as it was his, the said Smyth's, duty to do . . ."

"Bull!" Smyth said aloud.

". . . and by reason of which inefficiency the said USS *Wilkes* was at or about 0409 on February 18, 1942, stranded on the south coast of Newfoundland in the vicinity of Lawn Head Point and seriously damaged; the United States then being in a state of war.

---

[3] See Appendix L.
[4] This information given to the author by William A. Smyth.
[5] See Appendix M.

"Specification (2): In that William A. Smyth, lieutenant, U. S. Navy, while so serving as officer of the deck on board the USS *Wilkes,* said ship making passage from Cape Elizabeth, Maine, to Argentia, Newfoundland, and being on February 18, 1942, under way at a speed of about fifteen knots approaching and off the south coast of Newfoundland during darkness, heavy weather, and low visibility, having, at or about 0345 on said date, been informed that a radar bearing of about 340° true on an unknown object . . ."

"Damn lie!" Smyth raged, "there is absolutely no foundation of fact to this charge."

He read on: ". . . had been received on board the said USS *Wilkes,* did then and there, fail to promptly report the receipt of the said radar bearing to his commanding officer, as it was his, the said Smyth's, duty to do, and by reason of which inefficiency the said USS *Wilkes* was at or about 0409 on February 18, 1942, stranded on the south coast of Newfoundland in the vicinity of Lawn Head Point and seriously damaged; the United States then being in a state of war."

It was signed by James Forrestal, Acting Secretary of the Navy.

Smyth was outwardly calm and cool, but his whole body was tingling with a burning, white-hot anger that was manifested in an icy lump somewhere in the center of his being. "Those dirty sons-of-bitches! Sitting on their fat asses in comfortable offices passing judgment on us."

Culpable inefficiency! What did these men, sitting behind fancy desks, enjoying regular hours of work and play, know about the rigors and dangers of crossing the stormy, U-boat-infested North Atlantic? Had they made a single crossing? Were they aware of the general physical exhaustion of all officers concerned? The killing hours and the sheer misery and discomfort of convoy work? Armchair "boys" had no idea what went on at sea in ships; they were still playing war games "by the book," basing opinions and conclusions on their peacetime experience.

Later, when he had calmed down slightly, he said with great intensity: "Piss on 'em! I'll whip them."

On August 5, still angry, he faced the same court members who had tried Commander Webb. His counsel was Lieutenant (jg) Sanford T. Abele, USNR. He began to challenge each member until the court was reduced below the legal quorum of five board members. The court adjourned to wait the appointment of an additional member. Commander James G. Stevens, president, general court-martial, dispatched a message to the Secretary of the Navy requesting adjournment pending appointment of an additional member to the board.

On this same day a dispatch[6] for confidential distribution (marked restricted) was forwarded to Commander Stevens, the judge advocate, from the office of Frank Knox, the Secretary of the Navy: "As to all the charges and specifications in the cases of Commander Hugh W. Turney, USN, Lieutenant Arthur J. Barrett, Jr., USN, Lieutenant William A. Smyth, USN, and Lieutenant (jg) William C. Grindley, USNR, Commander Stevens is authorized and directed to enter *nolle prosequi*."[7] This message was signed by James Forrestal, Secretary of the Navy.

On August 7 the court convened and Smyth requested that Lieutenant Commander Robert E. Quinn, USNR, act as his counsel. Quinn did so.

The judge advocate read a dispatch from the convening authority, authorizing and directing him to enter a *nolle prosequi* as to the charge and both specifications in the case of the accused. However, the court announced that it being below a legal quorum, it would have to wait appointment of an additional member. Smyth was still under arrest.

On August 9, Captain Wilbert Smith, USN (Ret.), was temporarily appointed a member of the general court-martial board. On August 11 the court met, and the record of proceedings of the first and second days of the trial was read and approved. The judge advocate read: "A *nolle prosequi* having been directed by the convening authority and entered as to the first and second specifications of the charge, and to the charge, there is now no charge or specification remaining before this court upon which further proceedings can be had in the case of William A. Smyth, lieutenant, U. S. Navy."

The trials of Commander Turney, Lieutenant Barrett, and Lieutenant (jg) Grindley were also dispatched.

---

[6] See Appendix N.

[7] An entry on the record denoting that the prosecutor or plaintiff will proceed no further in his action or suit, either as a whole or as to some count or as to one or more of several defendants. In a criminal suit *nolle prosequi* can be entered without the defendant's consent until the jury is empaneled, but not afterward.

On August 12, 1942, James Forrestal, Acting Secretary of the Navy, put his seal of approval[8] on the administrative action recommended by Admiral King and concurred in by Vice Admiral Jacobs.

Officially it was over, and there was great rejoicing in the small *Pollux* group still remaining in Boston. Grindley thought he had been exonerated and, therefore, he would receive his promotion to full lieutenant and payment for loss of his clothing and effects, all of which had been held up pending outcome of his court-martial. He did not know that on August 3 Admiral King had recommended that he be discharged from the Navy "for cause."

In a very short time the officers of the *Pollux* were on their way to new assignments; Grindley was dispatched to the frigate *Beaumont* in Jacksonville, Florida, where she was outfitting for South Pacific duty. Orders from the Bureau of Personnel stated that he was to assume duties as first lieutenant.

Then the ax fell. Within a few days Grindley received orders from the Bureau of Personnel detaching him from the *Beaumont* and ordering him to report immediately to the legal officer (Quinn), 1st Naval District, Boston. "What is it all about, sir?" he asked.

Quinn replied, "I'm damned if I know." He didn't see how they could legally reopen the case after declaring *nolle prosequi,* he said, and counseled, "Don't worry about it."

But Grindley went through the tortures of the damned until he decided to go to Washington to get it sorted out. It was here he was notified that he was being placed on the inactive list; he was to proceed to the naval base, Charleston, South Carolina, for medical examination and dismissed from active duty. *A dishonorable discharge!*

Grindley was in a state of shock. What a slap in the face! Here it was wartime, with every available body needed, the country getting its pants kicked off in the Pacific, and he was getting tossed out of the naval service. His life was in ruins. What would his family and friends think? What would his former employer in the merchant Navy think? *What had he done to deserve this?*

A great rage welled up in Grindley. He would not take this lying down. He talked to his congressman, Mendel L. Rivers, who hap-

8 See Appendix O.

pened to be on the House Naval Affairs Committee, who along with other friends in the Congress killed the plans for throwing Grindley out. At the Fargo Barracks in Boston, it filtered down to the ranks that the congressman had really "made waves," stating that they were not going to make *his* constituent the scapegoat; if they tried to crucify Grindley, he would bring the whole sorry mess of the *Pollux/ Truxtun* fiasco to Congress.

With that kind of interest in their direction, the Navy rescinded the order to dismiss Grindley from the service.

He was ordered to the USS *Pontiac,* which was lying in South Boston Naval Shipyard, but he was a marked man. He was given the most menial jobs ordinarily assigned to an ensign and continually embarrassed before all hands at the general-quarters drill, doing the "heel and toe" watches on the quarter deck. It was too much for a chief officer of the merchant Navy. "Why in hell am I doing this?" Grindley asked himself. The U. S. Navy was not his career. Why should he suffer such degradation?

The next morning he had a letter of resignation drawn up.

It was not accepted.

An excerpt from a letter to Dr. Sam Bostic, dated November 26, 1942, reads:

. . . Well, Doc, I certainly found out one thing and that is this—the Navy Dept. doesn't like to have officers go over their head. So I was ordered to sea a couple of days later on the Pontiac the 28th of August to be exact. Since I have been at sea I have discovered by the hard method that I cannot be given an independent command, and then to sort of add insult to injury they are not going to pay my claim for lost clothing, etc. After finding out all this via the long, hard method, I wrote into the Bureau demanding that I be given a court [martial], because as it stood now I was suffering all the losses of a court without the benefit of even having had a hearing. The answer to that one was that my case was a closed book as far as the Navy was concerned, *nolle prosequi* having been declared in my case. I often wonder if the Dept. knows what the meaning of those two words are. Then to top it all off I wrote in a month or so ago asking that under the existing conditions that I be placed on the inactive list. The answer to that one was that due to my long and valued experience that the Dept. didn't think it fit to let me go now with the need of officers. My answer to that one was if I'm so damned experienced why in hell can't I at least have my two stripes—no answer to that one yet, Doc. From what I can gather they had it all planned to pin the whole rap of the three ships on me, and I must say that they have succeeded in their plans, me being the only Reserve that was supposed to have gotten a General [court-martial]. All of the Regular Navy Boys have all been promoted and gotten good jobs in command, etc. Doc, I'm here to say that this thing of being bent over the barrel gets to be pretty tiresome after almost ten months of it. . . .

> Best regards always,
> Bill Grindley

Grindley's resignation was finally approved; however, the Navy had the last word. One of the conditions of his release from the Navy was that he was to return to the merchant vessels; the local draft board had been informed of his release to make certain that is where he should go.

After all he had suffered in the Navy, he was to be controlled by them as a civilian.

The United States Line in New York welcomed Grindley and assigned him as master of the troopship *General Lillington*. Grindley and the *Lillington* made five invasions together: Casablanca, Sicily, Salerno, Anzio, and Rhone Valley, the South of France. Both finished up on VJ Day without a scratch.

There were other vessels after the war, and in 1950 Grindley took the USS *Greeley* to Korea and spent thirty months in a supply shuttle. He was given larger and faster vessels before retiring on January 1, 1970.

The *Pollux* was the only black mark in his career.

Once only did he try to clear his name, but he ran into a brick wall.

In retrospect Captain William C. Grindley speaks of the "rocks and shoals" and "drumhead" type of justice the Navy was dealing out at that time. "There was many a good man nailed to the cross in that era," he says.

40

*Drumhead Justice and
the Green Bowlers*

Lieutenant William A. Smyth, Class of 1934, was one of the men along with Lieutenant (jg) William C. Grindley who was nailed to the cross. Smyth's career was ruined, although he was blissfully unaware of it immediately. Having been subjected to a "Star Chamber proceeding," which deprived him of his right to be heard, he never had the opportunity of a public hearing, although he did try twice in the 1950s. He says: "Admiral King and Acting Secretary of the Navy Forrestal in Washington, D.C., had already adjudged me guilty and taken radical administrative action, known as Star Chamber proceeding, without precedent in the U. S. Navy, and issued a *nolle prosequi* directive to my convened court-martial board as a coverup."

Meanwhile Smyth was not aware of this as he happily returned to duty as a naval aviator, and, after a refresher course, was ordered to *VP-82M* "in whatever port she might be." Ironically, it turned out to be Argentia, Newfoundland, where members of the squadron and station knew all about him. "It was as if some devil in the Navy Department was determined to keep me suffering while my guardian angel was off on a holiday," he recalled.

To his bewilderment, resentment followed Smyth wherever he went. He had not been tried by court-martial, had received no sentence, and was puzzled by the undercurrent of hostility of his fellow men, but he ignored it as best as he could.

It was not until early summer of 1943, after the squadron had been ordered to Boca Chica, Florida, that he was made aware of the true situation. He had been advanced to executive officer despite the loss of precedence, and at a stopover in Quonset Point, Rhode Island, for rest and overhaul, an ALNAV dispatch was received promoting officers within his zone of precedence to the rank of lieutenant commander. Smyth was specifically excepted. His commanding officer received the following message:

> 2 MARCH 1943/OB
> FROM BUPERS X
> ATTENTION INVITED TO PREVIOUS
> DISCIPLINARY ACTION IN CASE OF
> LIEUTENANT WILLIAM A. SMYTH WHICH
> MAKES HIM AN EXCEPTION IN ALNAV
> THREE SEVEN.

In May, Smyth sent a letter to Admiral Randall Jacobs, the chief of Naval Personnel, through official channels, inquiring why he was made an exception inasmuch as he had not received a letter of reprimand, or notification of sentence of general court-martial resulting from the *nolle prosequi* general court-martial in which he was involved. If he was not eligible for temporary promotion because of proposed disciplinary action, he further requested that he be furnished with a copy of disciplinary action preferred against him.

On June 9, 1943, Frank Knox, the Secretary of the Navy, revoked the restriction that Smyth "be not given independent command nor temporary promotion during the present conflict" based on the recommendation of the commander in chief, U. S. Atlantic Fleet, Ernest J. King, and the chief of Naval Personnel, Randall Jacobs.

On the same day Smyth was notified that the President of the United States had appointed him a lieutenant commander in the Navy for temporary services to rank from the eleventh day of May 1943, thereby making him junior to the Class of 1936, which had graduated two years behind him. He was shaken; this amounted to a loss in lineal rank of more than one thousand numbers. His punishment was drastically harsher than that meted out to Commanders Webb and Kelsey, who had been accorded trial by courts-martial!

Resentment and hostility followed Smyth; he was subjected to embarrassment and humiliation as officers he had formerly outranked made a point of harassing him.

While at Boca Chica, Smyth laid what was left of his career on the line by grounding all aircraft after several planes had crashed due to engineering failure. A variety of experts were flown in; Lockheed sent its best engineers and discovered the cause. As Smyth explained it: "The distributor heads were being fabricated from a soybean derivative because of the shortage of rubber and dielectric strength was weak to the point where the distributor would break down, cut off ignition, and thereby render an engine useless. By the application of a Corning compound during routine checks it was discovered the trouble could be averted." But Smyth received no recognition for his positive action.

So it went.

In the San Julian, Cuba, base, he exercised total control of the squadron, but a new over-all commander arrived to take over. It was a classmate of Smyth's who had previously been junior to him in rank. His classmates had been promoted to commanders in September 1943.

There were other assignments: to speed up training of PV crews in Beaufort, South Carolina, and then the training of naval air navigators in Clinton, Oklahoma. He did so with such success that he was promoted to commander in July 1945 and he dared to feel he might continue a successful career in the Navy.

The war ended and because he still was hopeful about his future in the service Smyth remained in the Navy, although he was offered two lucrative positions in civilian life. In Washington a special review board reviewing officer records readjusted his permanent promotion to commander to an earlier date, which reduced the loss of lineal numbers to 417, which made him junior at the tail end of the class of 1935. He was never notified or afforded the opportunity of presenting his case in person or in writing.

Despite recommendations from his commanding officers in 1948 and 1949 that he be immediately promoted to captain, all recommendations were ignored by the top brass. Says Smyth, "I received the run-around from some, but great help from others."

This effort to clear him ended in midair. Docket No. 6323, as prepared by the legal officer, had correlated the facts of his career, and was highly commendable of Smyth. ". . . The fitness reports of Commander Smyth have been outstanding throughout the major portion of his career, and more especially so subsequent to the grounding incident," it stated. But the copy of the docket that was sent to Smyth had the last page severed, so he never did learn what, if anything, was recommended. In any event, he never did receive his fourth stripe.

On October 10, 1947, Smyth was presented with an Air Medal "for meritorious achievement in aerial flight as pilot of a plane in Patrol Squadron 82" and received a letter of commendation from Vice Admiral Marc Andrew Mitscher, deputy chief of Naval Operations (Air), and on October 3, 1950, as a member of Patrol Squadron 82, was authorized to wear a Navy Unit Commendation Bar.

Another effort was made to clear him.[1] Smyth says, "But the devil himself was now in Washington. How had I dared to defy the system! Therefore, by the simple expedient of merely 'passing me over' when the selection boards met, they inflicted final and complete punishment."

From 1952 to 1955 Commander Smyth was under contract to the Argentine Government as senior naval aviation adviser to the Naval War College. A cohort of the Class of 1935 received his fourth stripe and Smyth remained a commander. He says, "The Argentines were confounded and I had a hell of a time holding my head up. It was at this point I finally said, 'The hell with it. I'm going to retire.'

"Upon return to the United States I was assigned, on loan, to the CIA, and the idea intrigued me so I decided to stay on another year or so. It was a happy ending in all respects. But I was about forty years of age and submitted my papers to leave the service. The CIA offered me a GS-15 (equivalent to four stripes) with a promise of early promotion to GS-17 (rear admiral, upper half) in six months. But with the existent pay and retirement situation, and my job offer with General Dynamics, it was more feasible and lucrative to return to civilian life. So I did [in 1956].

"Now usually there is a little ceremony when people retire from the service. All I got was a piece of paper and a 'so long' from some lieutenant at a desk in the Navy Department. This after a total of twenty-six years of devoted attention to duty.

"I remember that, immediately afterward, as we were driving out of Washington, D.C., en route Fort Worth, Texas, I stopped the car,

[1] See Appendix P.

jumped out, stripped off my uniform coat and all insignia from my shirt, repeated a few cuss words, took a deep breath, and got behind the wheel as a great load seemed to lift off my shoulders. At last we were free of the whole stinking mess!

"Therefore, today, as far as I'm concerned, the hell with the Navy! I wouldn't piss on it if it was on fire!"

In October 1977, in a personal interview with me, Commander William A. Smyth had these reflections:

"As war progressed and ships blundered into disastrous situations, sunken ships were 'heroic' and not accused of culpable negligence, etc. In other words, had this happened a little bit later, I question if such detailed and drastic punishment would have materialized—it would have been an 'act of war.'"

One such situation occurred on August 9, 1942, in the South Pacific. Rear Admiral Gunichi Mikawa, commander of the Eighth Japanese Fleet, leading a column of eight ships, sailed boldly into Savo Sound off Guadalcanal, unseen by any of the 16 ships of the Allied Naval Fleet—13 American, 2 Australian, and a British ship —guarding the sound against enemy passage. Through a snowballing series of errors due to indoctrination against breaking radio silence, the inefficiency of SC radar and the short-range voice radio (TBS) due to rain squalls, plus the usual sequence of bad breaks and bad tactics, the Japanese ships sailed unseen into Savo Sound, taking the Allied fleet by surprise. These errors, which cost the U. S. Navy 4 heavy cruisers, with an Australian heavy cruiser and a destroyer severely damaged, and 1,025 lives and 709 wounded, earned Savo Sound the name of "Ironbottom Sound." It was termed the U. S. Navy's worst performance of the war.[2] There were many similarities to the errors that occurred on the *Wilkes* off the coast of Newfoundland six months earlier, but this disaster would not be designated an "act of war."

Smyth continued: "One basic point was overlooked in passing judgment on the *Wilkes* and the *Truxtun:* We maintained station on the *Pollux*. Naturally this does not excuse any single ship from proper navigation or responsibility for individual safety, but it does

[2] Theodore Roscoe, *United States Destroyer Operations in World War II* (Annapolis, Md. United States Naval Institute, 1953).

emphasize the confidence one would have in the *Pollux*'s officers to maintain a proper course and speed while we performed as watch-dogs. . . .

"Unfortunately I have no proof of the fact that the admiral [Bristol] aboard the USS *Prairie* in a private conversation with me said: 'I don't know whether to recommend you for the Navy Cross or a court-martial.' On the other hand, *I* know it.

"Admiral Ernest King's subsequent administrative action or Star Chamber proceedings, and the continuing Watergate-type coverup of this disaster for so many years under the guise of a 'secret' classification by the Navy Department is sadly representative of the type of top leadership existent within our military establishment, both past and present.

"It was expected that subordinates would strictly adhere to conflicting rules, regulations, and orders, but should failure occur, it was the prerogative of the superior—as exemplified by Admiral King—to exercise his will according to his infallible dictatorial judgment, superseding any respect of established lawful procedures.

"The establishment of the Board for Corrections of Naval Records was more fantasy than fact. Despite a personal trip to Washington, D.C., in the early 1950s, and the façade of a court-assigned counsel to allegedly assist me in presenting and pleading my case, I was completely stone-walled.

"It is my continued belief that someone, or a group of subservient officials within the Navy Department, conspired to deny some of us survivors the right to have our day in court and present true facts attendant upon this disaster. Suffice it to state that junior officers were expendable whereas those of more seniority with proper contacts within the department were to be protected.

"Based upon my own personal experience and knowledge of other subordinate officers involved, we were more in awe and frightened by the reactions of our superior armchair officers to our performance of duty and adherence to Navy regulations than we were of the enemy and his threat to life and limb. Contrarily, we sought out the enemy to fight and destroy him.

"It is ironic to presently contemplate that our own people destroyed our careers but not our subsequent spirit and will to win the Battle of the Atlantic and World War II.

"When I was a very young officer I used to hear stories about 'The

Green Bowlers.' It seems that while at the Naval School for Boys (U. S. Naval Academy) there were a chosen few (by whom I know not) who met secretly and were initiated into a mutual admiration society, pledged to help one another rise through the ranks after commissioning until each, or all, wore a broad stripe and bright star on their sleeves. In other words, they would 'control' the Navy. Initiation consisted of drinking a potion from a *green bowl*.

"There was quite a fuss about this so-called 'Society' after World War II and I believe an investigation was launched by the Navy to quell this rampant 'rumor.' As I remember, the final outcome was that the 'Green Bowlers' were a myth.

"Were they? Who conducted the investigation?

"For one, I still wonder. . . ."

Following the disaster Commander John D. Kelsey spent one year as executive officer of a large transport. It was a frustrating and unhappy year for a destroyer man. He requested a transfer to a combat ship and was given command of an assault transport and, after the war, fitting out, commissioning, and command of the new battle cruiser, *Roanoke*. He retired as a rear admiral.

He says: "Of the utmost importance to the *Wilkes* was this message that was alleged to have been transmitted from the *Pollux* to the *Wilkes* and accepted, apparently, by the court as having gotten through. I believe I can say, categorically, that it never got through, it never reached the *Wilkes*. All one has to do is to visualize the conditions that existed on that night; the testimony of the *Pollux* crew is to the effect that they were rolling and wallowing, and it was snowing and blowing, but they stuck to their story that they got a dash after each word, *on one transmission*. This is utterly ridiculous in a situation like that, but from the *Wilkes'* point of view it was pretty damning. I believe the convening authorities accepted that as a fact."

And: "When a ship is stranded, the responsibility is the commanding officer's. There may be extenuating or mitigating circumstances, but the fact remains that it is his ship that is aground and, except in exceedingly rare instances, he still must bear that responsibility. No one else can take it from him."

The *Wilkes* was not an unlucky ship. She continued to serve in the North Atlantic and the West Pacific and, when hostilities ceased, was laid up in Charleston, South Carolina, as of April 1, 1946, out of commission, in reserve, in the Sixteenth Fleet.

When the *Pollux/Truxtun* Unit broke up after the courts-martial, all members were integrated into the Pacific and European conflicts. Calemmo's extrasensory perception saved his life once more. Assigned to the submarine *Shark,* he again felt that disaster was imminent and asked for a transfer to another submarine. The *Shark* departed for patrol and was never heard from again.

Commander Turney was banished[8] to Admiral E. J. King's staff in Washington, D.C., then became active in the amphibious warfare in Europe. He retired in June 1952 with the rank of rear admiral, and died in November 1955 at the age of fifty-six years.

Commander Webb's career did not come to a halt despite the loss of twenty-five numbers, considered heavy enough for a man of his years. The author has no information about his activities in the war operations following his court-martial, but he was promoted to captain and retired from the Navy on January 1, 1947. He died in April 1977 at the age of eighty-two years.

The only information the author has on Lieutenant Arthur J. Barrett is that he remained in the U. S. Navy and retired as a rear admiral. He died in May 1978 at the age of seventy-one.

[8] This information comes from George C. Bradley.

41

Postscript

Two hundred and three American sailors died in the *Pollux/Truxtun* disaster. Of these, ninety were buried with full military honors in the cemetery at St. Lawrence over the next few months. In the first week, forty-eight were buried in Argentia, among them: Phillip Jewett, Glen Wiltrout, Frank Hak, Peter Manger, John Schuster, William DeRosa, Alexander Harris, and James Foster from the *Pollux*. The recovery of bodies continued for months, but an indeterminate number were never recovered. After the war, the bodies were exhumed and returned to the United States.

Stormy seas kept Navy divers from searching the wreckage of the *Truxtun* until the first week in March. The body of Lieutenant Commander Ralph Hickox was identified by his class ring. Various limbs and other parts of bodies were found in the fuel oil. Most were unidentifiable and it was recommended by Lieutenant H. Von A. Burkart, who had been in charge of salvage operations, that hereafter identification tags be obtained for all service personnel.

The *Truxtun*'s flag had been salvaged from the wreck by Newfoundlander Albert Beck two days after the shipwreck, and passed to the authorities.

The U. S. Navy tried to dispose of the gelatinous mass of fuel oil in Chambers Cove by setting fire to it with the aid of gasoline. Because it was so thoroughly saturated with salt water it burned for twenty-four hours with little or no impact, except to send stinking black smoke skyward. Over the following months it was gradually carried away by the tides.

Several weeks after the disaster a body washed ashore at High Beach, four or five miles west of Lamaline, which is forty to fifty miles west of Lawn Head. A bracelet identified the body as Perique Gomez of the *Pollux*. The Reverend Sydney Bradbrook of Lamaline notified Argentia and was advised to bury the young man in the Anglican cemetery there. Naval authorities gave the minister the address of Gomez's parents in New Orleans so they could receive details of the funeral. The grateful mother sent money to buy a cut-glass wine cruet to be used at communion services, in memory of her son. It is still in use.

Many inquiries came to the people of St. Lawrence from parents of the victims. "Is there any trace of a young twenty-year-old man named Mario Izzo, member of the crew of the USS *Pollux?*" one such letter pleaded. His mother had had a dream that he was alive, a victim of amnesia; she enclosed snapshots of her son to be passed around.

The U.S. naval authorities, having discovered that Ena Farrell had taken snapshots of the wrecked ships and other activities of the disaster, decided that for security reasons they must persuade her to give her film to them. Lieutenant Commander W. R. McCaleb presented himself at her door and explained why she should comply with their request.

Ena refused point-blank. She knew she would never see her film again if she let the Navy have it. McCaleb tried several times to persuade her to pass over the pictures, without success.

Later, through the editor of the St. John's [Newfoundland] *Evening Telegram,* which was an affiliate of the Associated Press, her pictures, which had been taken with a five-dollar camera, appeared in the major newspapers in the United States and Canada.

Vice Admiral A. L. Bristol, the convening authority of the court of inquiry in Argentia, died of a heart attack aboard the flagship *Prairie* on April 20, 1942.

In gratitude to the rescuers, Richard D. Seamans, father of Jim Seamans, prevailed upon his congressman George J. Bates[1] of

---

[1] Bates was a congressman from 1936 to 1948.

Salem, Massachusetts, to put a bill through the U. S. Congress to provide money for a hospital in St. Lawrence.

Lieutenant George W. Bollinger survived the disaster in 1942 but it would claim him eventually.[2] Plagued by a kidney infection contracted immediately after the crawl along the clifftops, it turned to Bright's disease. He retired from the Navy with the rank of lieutenant commander in late 1945. He died April 21, 1954.

Two months later, on June 6, the United States Government presented the people of St. Lawrence and Lawn with a 400,000-dollar fully equipped hospital. The *Truxtun's* flag was flying over the hospital as the United States ambassador to Canada, R. Douglas Stuart, passed the key of the hospital to Newfoundland Premier Joseph R. Smallwood[3] "as a token of gratitude and respect the people of the United States feel for the people of Newfoundland." The hospital plaque read:

Presented by the President of the United States to the people of St. Lawrence and Lawn, Newfoundland, on behalf of the people of the United States in gratitude:

For the dauntless valor displayed by the people of St. Lawrence on February 18, 1942, when during a snowstorm two ships of the United States Navy, the USS *Truxtun* and the USS *Pollux*, were wrecked on the barren and rocky coast of Newfoundland, the intrepid and selfless residents of this community at great risk to themselves as in the face of cold and high winds undertook rescue operations and gave aid and comfort to the survivors of the two ships.

The people of the United States of America in presenting this hospital, desire to express their gratitude for the fortitude and generosity displayed by the heroic people of Newfoundland on that night. It is hoped that the hospital will serve as a living memorial to the 203 officers and men of the United States Navy who lost their lives in the disaster and as a vital reminder of the inherent courage of mankind.

After the dedication ceremony the *Truxtun* flag was hauled down and placed on a wall, behind glass, in the lobby of the hospital.

The sailors who had been cared for by the women of St. Lawrence kept in touch with their benefactors. Each Christmas brought an in-

2 Told to the author by Bollinger's sister, Mrs. Harry Hummel.
3 Newfoundland became the tenth province of Canada on April 1, 1949.

pouring of letters and cards from all parts of the world. Over the years the letters have dwindled, but a handful still keep in touch.

In the summer of 1964 James O. Seamans returned to the scene of the disaster with his wife and daughter to visit with Mrs. Lillian Loder, who had tended him so lovingly. He came to sit beneath the flag and to visit Chambers Cove and what was left of the *Truxtun*. Today only bits and pieces of that wreckage are scattered around the cove.

In St. Lawrence the mines have closed. Most of the brave miners who participated in the rescue of the American sailors died in early middle age of miners' disease; only a handful still live. Gradually men are returning to the sea for their livelihood.

The *Pollux* still sits on the ocean bottom off from the Big Head, the target of the occasional skin diver; but not too many brave the cold sea and strong current. Bits of wreckage still strew the cove where Calemmo, Lloyd, and the others were trapped. It is as isolated as it was in 1942.

Chambers Cove is still as forbiddingly beautiful. Stark Pinnacle Head broods darkly over the sea, visible for miles to the fishermen. The youth of St. Lawrence have a special interest in it; for years they could find souvenirs of the *Truxtun* and her crew, stuck to the rock face in fuel oil. To this day, a residue of the *Truxtun*'s fuel oil coats the palisades of Chambers Cove. It is particularly noticeable on the pink cliff.

Appendixes

Appendix A

The Men Who Received Medals

USS *Pollux*
Officers

Lieutenant J. W. Boundy,[1] Navy Commendation Medal
Lieutenant (jg) George C. Bradley, Navy Commendation Medal
Lieutenant (jg) Russell J. Garnaus, Navy and Marine Corps Medal
Ensign Alfred I. Pollack, Navy Commendation Medal

Enlisted men

Moulder Second Class Melvin Bettis,[1] Navy Commendation Medal
Fireman First Class Joseph Lawrence Calemmo, Navy Commendation Medal
Gunner's Mate Third Class Rex E. Copeland, Navy and Marine Corps Medal (post.)
Baker Third Class William A. DeRosa, Navy and Marine Corps Medal (post.)
Storekeeper Third Class Alfred M. Dupuy, Navy and Marine Corps Medal
Signalman Third Class Warren A. Greenfield, Navy Commendation Medal
Boatswain's Mate First Class Garrett Lloyd, Navy Commendation Medal
Seaman Second Class Bill M. McGinnis, Navy and Marine Corps Medal (post.)
Quartermaster Third Class Isaac H. Strauss, Navy Commendation Medal

[1] Passenger for the USS *Prairie.*

USS *Truxtun*
Officers

Ensign H. W. Taylor, Navy and Marine Corps Medal (post.)

Enlisted men

Seaman Second Class Edward L. Bergeron, Navy Commendation Medal
Signalman First Class Walter W. Brom, Navy and Marine Corps Medal (post.)
Boatswain's Mate First Class Harry M. Egner, Navy Commendation Medal
Seaman Second Class James Fex, Navy Commendation Medal
Chief Fire Controlman (AA) Edward B. Petterson, Navy Commendation Medal

Appendix B

The 140 Survivors
of the USS *Pollux*

Officers

Althouse, Jack M., Ensign (passenger)
Bollinger, George W., Lieutenant (jg)
Bostic, Sam C., Lieutenant Commander
Boundy, James W., Lieutenant (passenger)
Bradley, George C., Lieutenant (jg)
Brown, Edgar DeWitt, Ensign
Dougherty, Philip K., Lieutenant (jg)
Gabrielson, John E., Lieutenant Commander
Garnaus, Jack R., Lieutenant (jg)
Grayson, Robert H., Ensign
Grindley, William C., Lieutenant (jg)
Pollack, Alfred I., Ensign
Schmidt, Russell J., Lieutenant (jg)
Stroik, Edward A., Lieutenant
Turney, Hugh W., Commander
Verell, Edward D., Pay Clerk
Weintraub, Paul L., Lieutenant
Whitney, Robert B., Ensign (passenger)
Wrensh, Donald B., Ensign (passenger)

Enlisted personnel

Adams, Pleasant A., SC2c
Appel, Arthur W., Sea1c
Ashbridge, Robert C., CMM

Barnes, Walton D., AS
Barry, Robert J., SC3c
Baumgarth, John G., Sea1c
Berry, Jabin G., CGM
Bettis, Melvin, Mldr2c (passenger)
Bjerre, Walter, F1c
Bomar, Bernard B., AS
Bowker, George, Sea2c
Bowser, Herbert T., Sea2c
Brehm, Fred C., SK3c
Brewer, Wayne H., AS
Brooks, Harold E., QM1c
Brown, Ralph, CSM
Buck, Frank T., SK3c
Bulanowski, Walter Charles, MM1c
Cadugan, Roswell D., F2c
Cady, Donald W., RM3c
Calemmo, Lawrence J., F1c
Califano, Ernest L., F2c
Callahan, Thomas P., EM1c
Carden, Jack, EM3c
Carey, John H., AS
Charbonneau, William R., RM3c
Cheetham, Kenneth, RM3c
Clark, Homar L., F1c
Cline, Carl B., F3c
Coleman, George L., BM2c
Collins, Robert M., Sea1c
Conine, Robert G., CQM
Cowan, David J.,[2] RM3c
Cox, John, Sea2c
Cox, Oscar Kemp, RM1c
Crump, Jack Mayo, MM2c
Davis, Harry Edward, SK2c
Davis, Robert Lee, AS
Davis, Warren H., AS
Dawson, Leon, Matt1c
Dodson, Charles F., SK2c
Drag, Henry W., F2c

[2] The author has lists from the court of inquiry and from the Navy Department. The Navy Department list says: T. J. Cowen.

Duncan, Lawrence B., AS
Dunlap, John Arthur, SC3c
Dupuy, Alfred M., SK3c
Eaves, Harold W., F1c
Edenfield, James R., AS
Eitelbach, William J., Jr.,[3] F1c
Elliott, George Andrew, Sea1c
Enfinger, James C., Sea2c
Evans, James Vance, AS
Falvey, Cornelius J., CEM F4c FR
Gieryn, Eugene S., Sea2c
Glazer, Barnett, AS
Gossum, Rupert E., CSK
Greene, Herbert J.,[4] Sea1c
Greenfield, Warren A., SM2c
Hall, George C., SK3c
Haney, William A., F3c
Hanson, E. L.,[5] SK1c
Heldt, William C., Sea1c
Hentosh, Michael, F2c
Herlong, Robert A., Jr.,[6] Sea2c
Hoffman, Frank G., Sea2c
Horner, George J., Sea1c
Hughes, Leon H., Jr., SK2c
Hukel, Thomas S., Sea2c
Jackson, Everett L., AS
Jalanivich, David W., AS
Janocha, Joseph J., BM2c
Johnson, George W., Sea1c
Johnson, Kenneth C., F3c
Jordan, Burt C., AS
Keene, Elmer W., MM2c
Kelley, Olin John, CM3c (passenger)
Keppel, Joseph F., AS
Knighten, Leon O.,[7] AS
Lamb, Albert Ross, F2c

[3] Or Eitelback, William J., Jr.
[4] Or Greene, Hubert J.
[5] Or Hanson, H. N.
[6] Or Hurlong, Robert A., Jr.
[7] Or Knighton, Leon O.

Lecours, Joseph Edward[8] CSK(AA)
Lee, Thomas Edward, RM3c
Lewis, Howard Thomas, AS
Lloyd, Garrett, BM1c
Malone, Arthur Peter, Sea1c
Marlow, Charles Ray, SK3c
Matthews, Arthur C., WT1c
McCarron, Thomas James, Sea1c
McCormick, Daniel Edward, CWT(FR)
McFarland, John L., Jr., EM2c
Miller, Lloyd Wayne, PhM1c (passenger)
Miller, Robert Leonard, Sea2c
Mongeau, Norman Theodore, SK1c
Nicosia, Samuel L., SK3c
O'Connor, Robert G.,[9] Cphm F4c
Parker, Ralph W., CRM
Paulsen, Arthur May, CCStd(FR)
Pfeifer, Ernest Henry,[10] F1c
Phillips, Walter C., CFC(FR)
Pond, Stewart Montell, Sea1c
Popolizio, Vincent J., F2c
Pulver, Paul Enoch, SK1c
Quinn, Joseph Grover, Sea2c
Reich, John Joseph, WT2c
Retzlaff, William F., SK2c
Roberts, Milton H., Y3c (passenger)
Ross, James Macbeth, F2c
Shaner, Jesse Allison, F1c
Sipperley, Edward F., F1c
Smith, Irving, CMM
Speece, Harold Ray, MM1c
Stanford, William L., SF1c
Strauss, Isaac Henry, QM3c
Tabeling, Raymond G., MM2c
Taylor, John Caldwell, PhM3c
Tebbach, William J.,[11] —
Thomson, Edward Allan, GM3c

[8] Or Lecours, E. A.
[9] Or O'Connore, Robert G.
[10] Or Pfiefer, E. H.
[11] Tebbach's name was not on the court of inquiry list; therefore his rating is not listed.

Trojack, George, SK2c
Turner, Thomas Requa, QM3c
Wasco, Walter W., CPhM (passenger)
Weaver, Laurence A., Jr., SK2c
Wood, William, GM3c
Woody, Troy Lee, OS2c

Appendix C

The 93 Men Who Lost Their Lives on the USS *Pollux*[12]

Officer

Clarke, Francis Xavier, Ensign

Enlisted Personnel

Atkins, Golden, AS
Bean, Leslie Elmer, AS
Brown, Thomas Hayward, AS
Brunson, Theodore Raymond (no rating on list)
Buckwell, Crowell Harding, AS
Budka, William, WT2c
Butler, David Eugene, AS
Cannon, Clyde Cecil, Sea2c
Carrington, Carl Ulysses, Matt2c
Christianson, Harris Curtis (passenger)
Chrysanthem, George, Sea1c
Cochrane, Donald Ivan, SK3c
Conley, Harold Francis, Jr. (passenger)
Cool, Orland Robert, Sea1c

[12] The official list from the Navy Department did not contain the ratings of the victims. Ratings are supplied from Dr. Bostic's personal files.

Copeland, Rex Edmund, GM3c
Cruza, Joseph, Jr. (passenger)
Culpan, Raymond, Bkr1c
DeRosa, William Anthony, Bkr3c
Ducre, Bernard Herman, Matt3c
Dunn, James Earl, BM1c
Edwards, Floyd Lee, Sea1c
Edwards, James David, SK3c
Edwards, Winson A., EM2c
Farber, Richard Paul, Sea2c
Flechsenhaar, Howard, SK3c
Foster, James Henderson, Matt3c
Gates, Nelson Edward, SK3c
Gavin, Thomas V., Jr., AS
Genetti, Frederick Alfred, Sea2c
Giles, O. H., Jr., AS
Gipson, Feroll Myron, BM2c
Gomez, Perique, Jr., MM1c
Gorman,[13] William Francis, MM1c
Greer, James O., AS
Hak, Frank Joseph, SK3c
Hardy, Arthur H., AS
Harris, Tommie (Alexander A.), Matt2c
Henderson, George Warren, AS
Hill, James Thomas, Sea1c
Hixon, James Henry, AS
Isbell, Robert Lefette, AS
Izzo, Mario Fred, F1c
Jabkowsky, Edward Vincent, CBM
Jewett, Phillip Loren, Mmsth2c
Johnson, Lee Edward, GM1c
Johnson, Thomas Erwin, Jr., GM1c
Kavenaugh, L. Wm. (passenger)
Kemp, William Bedell Mmsth1c
Killelea, Charles F., SF3c
Kirkham, Fred, EM1c
Landrey,[14] Andre J., AS
Lanning, Ronald Ross, Phm1c
Lentsch, William J., Bkmr2c
Lindup, Joseph J., AS

[13] Or Groman.
[14] Or Laundrey.

Manger, Peter, Sea1c
Marks, George A., BM1c
Martenas, Bruce A., MM2c
Mayo, Milburn Wm., Sea1c
McGinnis, Bill M., Sea2c
McKay, Chester R., BM2c
Merkl, John Wm., Jr., SK3c
Meyer, Theodore H., SK2c
Meyers, Joseph, Sea2c
Nanck, Edward, F2c
Neville, Joseph P., WT1c
Newman, Charles P., (passenger)
Phillips, John J., WT1c
Popp, Walter E., MM1c
Pritchard,[15] Charles L., (passenger)
Protz, Christian Fred, Jr., F2c
Ricaf, Rente Jacinto, OC1c
Riordan, James J., Y2c
Rosenblatt, Murray, Sea1c
Runyan, Joseph B., SK3c
Sanford, George E., Matt2c
Schultz, Clarence E., Y2c
Schuster, John Charles, Jr., GM3c
Simcox, John D., Sea1c
Smithers,[16] Donald A., SK3c
Spencer, William Lee, Matt1c
Stewart, William P., Sea2c
Sweeney, Francis J., F1c
Tholen, Edward H., Sea1c
Tortorici, Acursio (Gus), Sea1c
Tredeau, Alphonse (passenger)
Umali, Donato, OS1c
Ward, William J., Y2c
Webb, Rupert C., SK3c
White, William A., WT2c
Wiltrout, Glen E., BM2c
Yackee,[17] Raymond Francis, CM2c
Zoller, Russell C., Y3c

[15] Or Prichard
[16] Or Smithies
[17] Or Wackee

Appendix D

The 46 Survivors of the USS *Truxtun*

Officers

Loughridge, Frederick Ardel, Ensign D-V(G), USNR
Maddocks, William John, Ensign, USN
Seamans, James Otis, Ensign, USN

Enlisted Men

Battipaglia, John, Sea1c USN
Bergeron, Edward Louis, Sea2c, USN
Brollini, John Alfred, Sea2c, USN
Brown, Roscoe James, Sea1c, USN
Buie, Edison Pete, F1c, USN
Chadwick, Curne William, SM3, USNR
Dailey, Oliver Bernard, Sea1c, USN
Egner, Harry McKinley, BM1c, USN
Fex, James, Sea2c, USN
Fitzgerald, Donald Francis, Sea2c, USNR
Gaddy, George Washington, CCstd, USN
Gustafson, William Theodore, GM2c, USN
Hopper, Harry P., Jr., Sea1c, USN
Houff, Albert C., Jr., Sea1c, USN
Hulson, John Dallas, Sea1c, USN
Hyde, "J." "D.", Sea2c, USN
Kendzierski, Stanislaus J., SC3c, USN
Ketchie, Marvin E., Sea2c, USN

Leggett, Lovira Wright, RM3c, USN
Lewis, Edward Thomas, Sea2c, USN
McInerney, Edward A., F2c, USN
McLaughlin, William Allen, F3c, USN
Medich, Mike, SK3c, USN
Moak, James Alvin, F1c, USN
Mowell, D. D., F1c, USN
Moxley, Claude Edward, Sea2c, USN
Perrault, Arthur C., AS, USN
Perry, Edward Albert, AS, USNR
Peszko, Henry, AS, USN
Petterson, Edward Bannon, CFC, USN
Phillips, Lanier W., MAtt3c, USN
Plummer, Eugene Keith, F3c, USN
Robinson, Earl Sanderson, Sea1c, USN
Romaine, Charles T., Sea2c, USN
Shelley, William Francis, SF1c, USN
Shields, John Arthur, FC3c, USN
Shuttleworth, Herbert Raymond, F3c, USNR
Spillette, Richard Garth, WT2c, USN
Sujka, Thadeus, Sea2c, USN
Thornton, George, Sea2c, USN
Vendolla, Joseph Edward, CM3c, USN
Weakley, Wayne Marion, MM2c, USN
Young, Charles Earl, Cox, USN

Appendix E

The 110 Men Who Lost Their Lives on the USS *Truxtun*

Officers

Anderson, Elmer Dean, Lieutenant
Danforth, James Walker, Lieutenant (jg)
Gillie, James Ross, Lieutenant (jg)
Hickox, Ralph, Lieutenant Commander
Newman, Arthur Lester, Lieutenant
Potter, C. K., Ensign
Reiter, Charles, Lieutenant (jg) (MC)
Taylor, Howard W., Ensign

Enlisted personnel[18]

Aycock, William H.
Blaylock, Fred Powell
Borus, Felix Ed.
Boyce, Milton L.
Bramlett, Adrean
Britt, Prentiss Gaston
Brockway, Marvin S.

[18] This is the official list from the Navy Department and does not contain the ratings of the victims.

Brom, Walter William
Brooks, Robert William
Brothers, Walter E., Jr.
Buck, Joseph Almerian, Jr.
Buncker, Marshall A.
Butterworth, William E.
Carpenter, James L.
Cassey, Robert Lee
Cato, James Henry
Cato, Leo Franklen
Compton, Lewis De Liessiline
Coon, Ernest Lyle
Coteren, Marshel Foch
Creach, Edsel David
Crisafulli, Charles Carman
Crockett, Marshall Gordon
Croom, James Leo
Dasus, Marvin Alvin
Dayo, Tomas
Devore, George R.
Doucette, Joseph F., Jr.
Dusak, Andrew M.
Estabrook, Lewis E.
Fidler, Charles W.
Fisher, Ernest G.
French, Harold E., Jr.
Gadbois, Oscar
Gambrill, Raymond Alfred
Garrison, James A.
Goff, William L.
Gregg, Russell E.
Hall, Norman F.
Harris, William Otis
Healey, Lawrence V.
Heffelbower, Charles R.
Horvath, Edward J.
Houston, Earl N.
Johnson, Alan H.
Jones, Sloan J.
Kane, Frederick William
Kowal, Chester J.
Krenfle, William R.

Landry, Kenneth E.
Lane, Elmer V.
Langston, Henry G.
LeRouge, Merlin F.
Lisi, Charles
Loehnberg, Lewis M.
Lovell, George Robert
Maddox, Thomas Emmett
Maeger, Sherrill Galt
Mahan, John James
Matthews, Lewis Raymond
McNeely, Herman M.
McPeek, Norman John
Meadows, Alvin Lee
Milan, L. B.
Miles, Samuel Willard
Moore, Tommy Howard
Morgan, Thomas Gale
Mulkerrin, Michael J.
Noah, Howard J.
O'Neal, Morris Allen
Ostrowski, Joseph
Parkerson, Clifford H.
Pease, Harry Norman
Pelletine, Paul Romeo
Perrier, Leo Paul
Pharmer, Paul Daniel
Polak, Henry Joseph
Potts, John Pershing
Ray, Patrick Henry
Richters, Joseph William
Rooker, Stanley Irvin
Ross, Norman Carl
Rude, Julius
Ryckeghem, Maurice J.
Samborek, Edward Joseph
Scott, Richard Elsworth
Sedgwick, John S.
Sharp, Wade Elmer
Smith, Frank William
Sommer, Verlin Bernard
St. John, Lewis H.

Steller, Alfred William, Jr.
Sypeck, Simon Joseph
Tarwater, Vincent Francis
Thursby, Wallace F.
Tinney, Roland Harold
Troutner, Milburn Emmerson
Turner, Billy Gene
Tyloch, Stanley Joseph
Vrabel, Joseph
Weidlich, Paul Clement
Wright, Robert Allen

Appendix F

Officers and Crew of the USS *Wilkes*[19]

Officers

Barrett, Arthur J., Lieutenant, USN
Hughlett, Overton D., Lieutenant (jg), USN
Kelsey, J. D., Commander, USN
Quekemeyer, Henry B., Ensign, USN
Smyth, William A., Lieutenant, USN
Webb, W. W., Commander, USN
Whiting, J. R., Ensign, USNR
Winslow, Warren, Ensign, USNR
Wolsieffer, F., Lieutenant, USN

Enlisted personnel

Armstrong, Ruppert F., RM1c
Betz, Joseph O., MM2c
Brantman, Harold, Sea2c
Buskirk, Victor F., Sea2c
Cadle, David D., Sea2c
Champagne, William A., Sea2c
Chamsky, John A., AS

---

[19] The author requested a list of the *Wilkes* crew from the Bureau of Naval Personnel, Department of the Navy. The Department was unable to find a complete list for that particular trip, or a good-quality film of the names they did find. The author apologizes for any incorrect spelling of the names of the enlisted men named above.

Chester, Barry V., AS
Chomka, Michael, Sea2c
Connolly*
Cravens, Carl A., OS3c
Davies, Wilbur C., F3c
Fitzgerald, H. C., Jr., FM2c
Fullerton, Kenneth W., Sea2c
Fusco, F. W., AS
Gabriel, Gustav E., Sea3c
Giese, Carl, MM2c
Glasgow, L. N., AS
Healy, John A., F3c
Hon, Alvin M., MM2c
Hopkins, W. C., Y3c
Hovey, Richard E., F3c
Hunter, Ted, CGM
Kelley, Lawrence E., F2c
King, John H., Jr., Sea2c
Koegler, George H., CRM
Korpeter, Michael, GM3c
Kuenstler, John E., Sea2c
Leathe, Ronald W., Sea2c
Leone, George, TM3c
Lewis, F. R., TM2c
MacLeod, Irving R., GM3c
Manalany, Michael, AS
Matthews, John C., SM3c
McPherson, Henry Y., Sea2c
McPherson, James R., Sea1c
McReis, Robert E., AS
Meier, Robert A., Sea2c
Molle, Anthony F., F3c
Monck, Clarence C., GM3c
Moroz, Frank A., AS
Morrell, Kenneth S., AS
Murphy, Joseph J., AS
Nicholas, John J., AS
Nokrish, Robert C., AS
Noland, Robert F., QM3c
Nolfi, Americo, Sea1c

* The Christian name and rank of Connolly was not established either
through the court of inquiry, the courts-martial, or the list from Washington,
D.C.

Norrell, K. S., AS
Norton, Clarence E., AS
Norton, Philip W., AS
Notariak, Joseph L., AS
O'Connell, Edward J., AS
Odabashian, John, AS
O'Grady, John T., AS
O'Leary, Francis E., AS
O'Neill, Robert, AS
O'Neill, William J., AS
Oneto, Fiore A., AS
Oppedisano, C., AS
Orr, Lynn W., AS
Ostrowski, Robert, Sea1c
Pal, Eugene, AS
Palorak, Edward B., AS
Pearce, Irvin T., AS
Petanelli, Louis, AS
Pettik, John, Jr., AS
Pierce, Kenneth M., AS
Pisani, Joseph A., AS
Piti, George A., F3c
Ponti, Robert, F3c
Pretty, James E., AS
Purcell, Pierce W., AS
Putaansuu, Thorwald W., AS
Quarn, John Frederick, AS
Quintal, John, Jr., Sea2c
Rasick, Michael J., AS
Reges, Larry Gray, AS
Reilly, Charles E., AS
Reisinger, Robert S., AS
Revay, Joseph E., AS
Reynolds, Everett, FC2c
Richardson, William F., AS
Robertson, John J., AS
Robillard, Andrew J., AS
Rollison, Harold E., AS
Romoska, Joseph J., AS
Rowe, Warren L., AS
Roy, Russel, AS
Sabados, Frank J., AS

Saccretti, Cosmo, AS
Saccucci, Frederick J., AS
Schmidt, Carl W., Jr., SM2c
Shannon, K. H., GM2c
Sienkiewicz, Richard E., F3c
Slocum, Paul W., SK1c
Smith, Edrick A., F2c
Stanley, H. S., Sea1c
Stark, Edward H., Sea2c
Symonds, John W., F3c
Thurman†
Vacanti, Joseph C., Sea2c
Vallone, Carl, F3c
Warren, Andrew, F3c
Whitman, Ellery A., Sea1c
Wojton, Stanislaus L., GM3c

† The Christian name and rank of Thurman was not included in the court of inquiry, the courts-martial, or the official list from Washington, D.C.

Appendix G

Letter re Soundings on H.O. Chart No. 163

UNITED STATES ATLANTIC FLEET
USS *Augusta*, Flagship

Care Postmaster, New York, N.Y.
July 25, 1941

From: Commander-in-Chief, United States Atlantic Fleet
To: ATLANTIC FLEET

Subject: Faulty Soundings on H.O. Chart No. 1103.

References: (a) H.O. Chart 981 (6th edition, March 1934).
(b) H.O. Chart 1103 (edition of March 18, 1926).

1. The USS *Nashville* while approaching Placentia Bay from the southwest, found the soundings on references (a) and (b) sparse but good, particularly in the region of St. Pierre Bank and the approach to Placentia Bay (south of lat. 46°—40′N). This was proved by the ability of the ship to establish her position within one mile in a fog, solely through fathometer soundings, and to thereby correct an error of seven miles in the dead-reckoning position. Later, while proceeding up Placentia Bay to Argentia, in clear weather, serious differences between actual and charted depths were discovered.

2. A resurvey of Placentia Bay and the approaches thereto can not be undertaken until the spring of 1942. In view of the potential importance of this region and of the prevalence of fogs there, all vessels of this Fleet when operating in Newfoundland waters shall conduct sonic surveys as opportunity and circumstances permit.

3. All data obtained on such sonic surveys shall be reported to the Hydrographic Office in accordance with standard instructions (N.H.O. Form No. 23).

/s/ E. J. KING

DISTRIBUTION:
List 1, Case 2, A1 (less AF, AG, AH)
List 1, Case 2, AF-O, AG-O, AH-O

/s/ G. L. RUSSELL
    Flag Secretary.

Appendix H

Charge and Specifications in the Court-Martial of Commander Walter W. Webb

Navy Department
Washington

May 30, 1942

To: Commander James G. Stevens, U. S. Navy Ret.,
Judge Advocate, General Court-Martial,
U. S. Navy Yard, Boston, Massachusetts, convened by Navy
Department precept dated May 20, 1942.
Subject: Charge and specifications in case of Commander
Walter W. Webb, U. S. Navy.

1. The above-named officer will be tried before the general
court-martial of which you are judge advocate, upon the following charge
and specifications. You will notify the president of the court accordingly,
inform the accused of the date set for his trial, and summon all witnesses,
both for the prosecution and the defense.

CHARGE
CULPABLE INEFFICIENCY IN THE PERFORMANCE OF DUTY
SPECIFICATION 1

In that Walter W. Webb, commander, U. S. Navy, while so serving on board the USS *Wilkes* as commander of Destroyer Division 26 and in command of a naval unit composed of the said USS *Wilkes,* the USS *Truxtun,* and the USS *Pollux,* said ships making passage in company with each other from Cape Elizabeth, Maine, to Argentia, Newfoundland, and being on February 18, 1942, under way at a speed of about fifteen knots approaching and off the south coast of Newfoundland during darkness, heavy weather, and low visibility, and the said Webb, having, at or about 4:00 A.M., on said date, been informed that the course being made good by the said USS *Wilkes* was to the left of the course set for the safe navigation of the said ship and other said ships of the said naval unit, did, then and there, fail to issue and see effected such timely orders as were necessary to cause each of the said ships of the said naval unit to change to a safe course in due time to avoid disaster, as it was his, the said Webb's, duty to do, and by reason of which inefficiency the said USS *Wilkes,* USS *Truxtun,* and USS *Pollux* were stranded, said stranding occurring in the vicinity of Lawn Head Point, Newfoundland, between the hours of about 4:09 A.M. and about 4:19 A.M., February 18, 1942, and as the result of said stranding the said USS *Wilkes* was seriously damaged and the said USS *Truxtun* and USS *Pollux* were lost with the loss of about two hundred and three lives of naval personnel aboard the said USS *Truxtun* and USS *Pollux;* the United States then being in a state of war.

SPECIFICATION 2

In that Walter W. Webb, commander, U. S. Navy, while so serving on board the USS *Wilkes* as commander of Destroyer Division 26 and in command of a naval unit composed of the said USS *Wilkes,* the USS *Truxtun,* and the USS *Pollux,* said ships making passage in company with each other from Cape Elizabeth, Maine, to Argentia, Newfoundland, and being on February 18, 1942, under way at a speed of about fifteen knots approaching and off the south coast of Newfoundland during darkness, heavy weather, and low visibility, did fail to issue and see effected such timely orders as were necessary to cause him, the said Webb, to be promptly informed of navigational data known and obtained on board the said USS *Wilkes* indicating the proximity of land ahead and that the said USS *Wilkes* and other said ships of the said naval unit were not making good the course set for safe navigation, as it was his, the said

Webb's duty to do, the said data being necessary for the safe navigation of the said ships under his, the said Webb's, command, and by reason of which inefficiency the said USS *Wilkes,* USS *Truxtun,* and USS *Pollux* were stranded, said stranding occurring in the vicinity of Lawn Head Point, Newfoundland, between the hours of about 4:09 A.M. and about 4:19 A.M., on said date, and as the result of said stranding the said USS *Wilkes* was seriously damaged and the said USS *Truxtun* and USS *Pollux* were lost with the loss of about two hundred and three lives of naval personnel aboard the said USS *Truxtun* and USS *Pollux;* the United States than being in a state of war.

JAMES FORRESTAL
Acting Secretary of the Navy

Appendix I

Charge and Specifications in the Court-Martial of Commander John D. Kelsey

NAVY DEPARTMENT

WASHINGTON

May 30, 1942

To: Commander James G. Stevens, U. S. Navy Ret.,
Judge Advocate, General Court-Martial,
U. S. Navy Yard, Boston, Massachusetts, convened by Navy
Department precept dated May 20, 1942.

Subject: Charge and specifications in case of Commander John
D. Kelsey, U. S. Navy.

1. The above-named officer will be tried before the general
court-martial of which you are judge advocate, upon the following charge
and specifications. You will notify the president of the court accordingly,
inform the accused of the date set for his trial, and summon all
witnesses, both for the prosecution and the defense.

CHARGE
THROUGH NEGLIGENCE SUFFERING A VESSEL OF THE NAVY
TO BE STRANDED
SPECIFICATION 1

In that John D. Kelsey, commander, U. S. Navy while so serving in
command of the USS *Wilkes,* said ship making passage from Cape
Elizabeth, Maine, to Argentia, Newfoundland, and being on February 18,
1942, under way at a speed of about fifteen knots approaching and off
the south coast of Newfoundland during darkness, heavy weather, and
low visibility, and the said Kelsey, having, at or about 3:50 A.M., on said
date, been informed that the course being made good by the said USS
Wilkes was to the left of the course set for the safe navigation of the said
ship, did, then and there, neglect and fail to exercise proper care and
attention in navigating the said ship while approaching and off the said
coast, in that he neglected and failed to direct a course to be steered by
the said ship that would carry the said ship clear of the aforesaid coast,
and to change the course in due time to avoid disaster; and he, the said
Kelsey, through said negligence, did suffer the said USS *Wilkes* to be
stranded on the south coast of Newfoundland in the vicinity of Lawn
Head Point at or about 4:09 A.M., on the day aforesaid, in consequence
of which the said USS *Wilkes* was seriously damaged; the United States
then being in a state of war.

SPECIFICATION 2

In that John D. Kelsey, commander, U. S. Navy, while so serving in
command of the USS *Wilkes,* said ship making passage from Cape
Elizabeth, Maine, to Argentia, Newfoundland, and being on February 18,
1942, under way at a speed of about fifteen knots approaching and off
the south coast of Newfoundland during darkness, heavy weather, and
low visibility, did, nevertheless, neglect and fail to exercise proper care
and attention in navigating said ship while approaching and off the said
coast, in that he neglected and failed to make allowances for known
currents and the wind effect to leeward setting the said ship toward the
said coast, and he, the said Kelsey, through said negligence, did suffer the
said USS *Wilkes,* at or about 4:09 A.M., on the day aforesaid to be
stranded on the south coast of Newfoundland in the vicinity of Lawn
Head Point, in consequence of which the said USS *Wilkes* was seriously
damaged; the United States then being in a state of war.

JAMES FORRESTAL
Acting Secretary of the Navy

Appendix J

Letter Authorizing Radical Administrative Action Instead of Court-Martial

UNITED STATES FLEET
Headquarters of the Commander in Chief
Navy Department, Washington, D.C.

Aug 3 1942

Second Endorsement
J.A.G. 1tr 00–Webb, Walter W.
A17–20 (420525) A (7–16–42) of
July 24, 1942.

From: Commander in Chief, United States Fleet
  To: The Secretary of the Navy

Via: The Chief of Naval Personnel

Subj: General Court Martial in the case of Commander Walter W.
  Webb, U. S. Navy, convened June 23, 1942, at the Navy Yard,
  Boston, Massachusetts, by order of the Secretary of the Navy.

1. Forwarded.

2. The sentence in this case is considered inadequate but in order that Commander Webb may not escape punishment, approval of the proceedings, findings, and sentence is recommended.

3. The Commander in Chief believes that the other officers who have been recommended for trial by General Court-Martial as a result of this disaster are deserving of such trial. Under present circumstances, however, the services of the officers and men involved are needed elsewhere, and radical administrative action short of court-martial proceedings will permit the best over-all war effort. It is therefore recommended that:

(a) Commander Hugh W. Turney and Lieutenants Arthur J. Barrett, Jr., and William A. Smyth be not given independent command nor temporary promotion during the present war, and that letters to that effect, with the reasons therefor, be attached to their records.

(b) Lieutenant (junior grade) William C. Grindley, Jr., USNR, be ordered to inactive duty and then discharged for cause and not employed again during this war; and that a letter to that effect, with the reasons therefor, be attached to his record.

4. In view of the fact that the trial of Commander John D. Kelsey, USN, is nearly completed, it is recommended that it proceed to its conclusion.

E. J. KING

Appendix K

Letter of Endorsement After Commander Walter Webb's Court-Martial

Aug 4 1942

Third Endorsement

From: The Chief of Naval Personnel.
To: The Secretary of the Navy.

Subject: General court-martial in the case of Commander Walter W. Webb, U. S. Navy, convened June 23, 1942, at the Navy Yard, Boston, Massachusetts, by Order of the Secretary of the Navy.

1. Forwarded, recommending approval of the proceedings, findings, and sentence of the general court martial in the attached case of Commander Walter W. Webb, U. S. Navy.

2. The Chief of Naval Personnel concurs in the recommendations of the Commander in Chief, United States Fleet, as stated in paragraphs 3 and 4 of the second endorsement.

RANDALL JACOBS
The Chief of Naval Personnel

Appendix L

Letter Placing Lieutenant William A. Smyth Under Arrest Pending Trial

HEADQUARTERS
FIRST NAVAL DISTRICT
North Station Office Building
150 Causeway Street, Boston, Mass.

August 4, 1942

From: The Commandant, First Naval District
To: Lieutenant William A. Smyth, U. S. Navy
      Headquarters, First Naval District

Subj: Arrest

Ref: (a) Letter SecNav to Comone, JAG:B:TTS:lh 00/A17–20
         (420530) B, May 30, 1942

1. You are hereby relieved of your present duties and are placed under arrest pending your trial by General Court-Martial.

2. The limits of your arrest will be the Metropolitan Boston Area and Gloucester.

3. In compliance with reference (a) you will report to Captain Clarence A. Aberle, U. S. Navy (Ret.), at the time and place designated for trial.

4. A certified copy of the charge and specifications is enclosed.

WILSON BROWN
Rear Admiral, U. S. Navy
Commandant, First Naval District

1st Endorsement.
Navy Yard, Boston, Massachusetts,
August 11, 1942.

1. Reported this date.

Clarence A. Abele
Captain, U. S. Navy, Ret.,
President, General Court-Martial

Appendix M

Charge and Specifications in the Court-Martial of Lieutenant Smyth

NAVY DEPARTMENT
WASHINGTON

May 30, 1942

To: Commander James G. Stevens, U. S. Navy (Ret.), Judge Advocate, General Court-Martial, U. S. Navy Yard, Boston, Massachusetts, convened by Navy Department precept dated May 20, 1942.

Subject: Charge and specification in case of Lieutenant William A. Smyth, U. S. Navy.

1. The above-named officer will be tried before the general court-martial of which you are judge advocate, upon the following charge and specifications. You will notify the president of the court accordingly, inform the accused of the date set for his trial, and summon all witnesses, both for the prosecution and the defense.

CHARGE
CULPABLE INEFFICIENCY IN THE PERFORMANCE OF DUTY
SPECIFICATION 1

In that William A. Smyth, lieutenant, U. S. Navy, while so serving as officer of the deck on board the USS *Wilkes,* said ship making passage from Cape Elizabeth, Maine, to Argentia, Newfoundland, and being on February 18, 1942, under way at a speed of about fifteen knots approaching and off the south coast of Newfoundland during darkness, heavy weather, and low visibility, well knowing that the said ship was expected to cross the fifty-fathom curve at or about 1:30 A.M., on said date, and having, at or about 2:30 A.M., on said date, received information showing that the said fifty-fathom curve had been crossed at a time earlier than had been expected, did then and there, fail to promptly report the said crossing of the said fifty-fathom curve to his commanding officer, as it was his, the said Smyth's, duty to do, and by reason of which inefficiency the said USS *Wilkes* was at or about 4:09 A.M., on February 18, 1942, stranded on the south coast of Newfoundland in the vicinity of Lawn Head Point and seriously damaged; the United States then being in a state of war.

SPECIFICATION 2

In that William A. Smyth, lieutenant, U. S. Navy, while so serving as officer of the deck on board the USS *Wilkes,* said ship making passage from Cape Elizabeth, Maine, to Argentia, Newfoundland, and being on February 18, 1942, under way at a speed of about fifteen knots approaching and off the south coast of Newfoundland during darkness, heavy weather, and low visibility, having, at or about 3:45 A.M., on said date, been informed that a radar bearing of about 340° true on an unknown object had been received on board the said USS *Wilkes,* did then and there, fail to promptly report the receipt of the said radar bearing to his commanding officer, as it was his, the said Smyth's, duty to do, and by reason of which inefficiency the said USS *Wilkes* was at or about 4:09 A.M., on February 18, 1942, stranded on the south coast of Newfoundland in the vicinity of Lawn Head Point and seriously damaged; the United States then being in a state of war.

/s/ JAMES FORRESTAL
Acting Secretary of the Navy

Appendix N

Dispatch Authorizing Nolle Prosequi

August 5, 1942.

Restricted Confidential Distribution
051537 (P)

From: Secretary of the Navy
  To: Commandant, First Naval District

 Subj: Officer Personnel, cases of,

1. This dispatch is for the action of Commander James George Stevens, USN (Ret.), judge advocate, GCM.

2. As to all the charges and specifications in the cases of Commander Hugh W. Turney, USN, Lt. Arthur J. Barrett, Jr., USN, Lt. William A. Smyth, USN, and Lt. (jg) William C. Grindley, Jr., USNR, Commander Stevens is authorized and directed to enter *Nolle Prosequi.*

3. All papers are to be returned to the Secretary of the Navy, office of the judge advocate general.

4. This message was signed by James Forrestal, Acting Secretary of the Navy.

Distribution:
Comdt.
C/S
Commander Stevens
Duty Officer

Appendix O

James Forrestal's Approval of Radical Administrative Action

DEPARTMENT OF THE NAVY
WASHINGTON, D.C.

August 12, 1942.

Fourth Endorsement
J.A.G. 1tr 00–Webb, Walter W.
A17–20(420525)A (7–16–42)
of July 24, 1942

Subject: Administrative action in the cases of Commander Hugh W. Turney, Lieutenants Arthur J. Barrett, Jr., and William A. Smyth, U. S. Navy, and Lieutenant (junior grade) William C. Grindley, Jr., U. S. Naval Reserve—in lieu of trial by general Court-Martial.

1. The administrative action recommended by the Commander in Chief, United States Fleet, in the cases of the subject-named officers, concurred in by the Chief of Naval Personnel, is hereby approved and

directed. A *nolle prosequi* has been authorized and directed to be entered
to the charges and specifications on which they were ordered to be tried
by general court-martial.

JAMES FORRESTAL
Acting Secretary of the Navy

Copy to:
  Cominch
  BuPers

Appendix P

Letter Advising Lieutenant Smyth of Action Taken to Clear Him

THE GENERAL COURT-MARTIAL
POTOMAC RIVER NAVAL COMMAND
RECEIVING STATION
WASHINGTON 25, D.C.

October 15, 1951

Commander W. A. Smyth, USN
Naval Reserve Officers' Training Corps
Purdue University
Lafayette, Indiana

My dear Commander:

The complete file in your case has been turned over to me, as Commander Cheasty is in Bethesda Hospital with a heart condition and will undoubtedly remain there for some time.

I talked with a civilian, Bertram Williams, the board member on your case, last Friday. I turned over to him the five exhibits that you forwarded to Commander Cheasty. This is all the information they need. He will write a brief on the case and set a date for a hearing. I will have the citations covering the limits of Admiral King's authority to take the action that he did in your case. As a matter of fact, of course, there are no citations because he did not have, nor does anyone have, the authority to take the action that was taken in your case.

I also advised the board that you desired to appear in person. In my opinion this is very important. Of course I am probably biased in your favor but I do have hopes that the injustice that you suffered in this case will be corrected.

I notice where the "j.g." Grindley was discharged from the service. Do you know his address? If so, you should write to him and have him file a petition also.

Sincerely yours,

SAMUEL S. PLATT,
Lieutenant Commander, USNR,
Legal Office, PRNC Headquarters,
Naval Gun Factory, Washington 25, D.C.